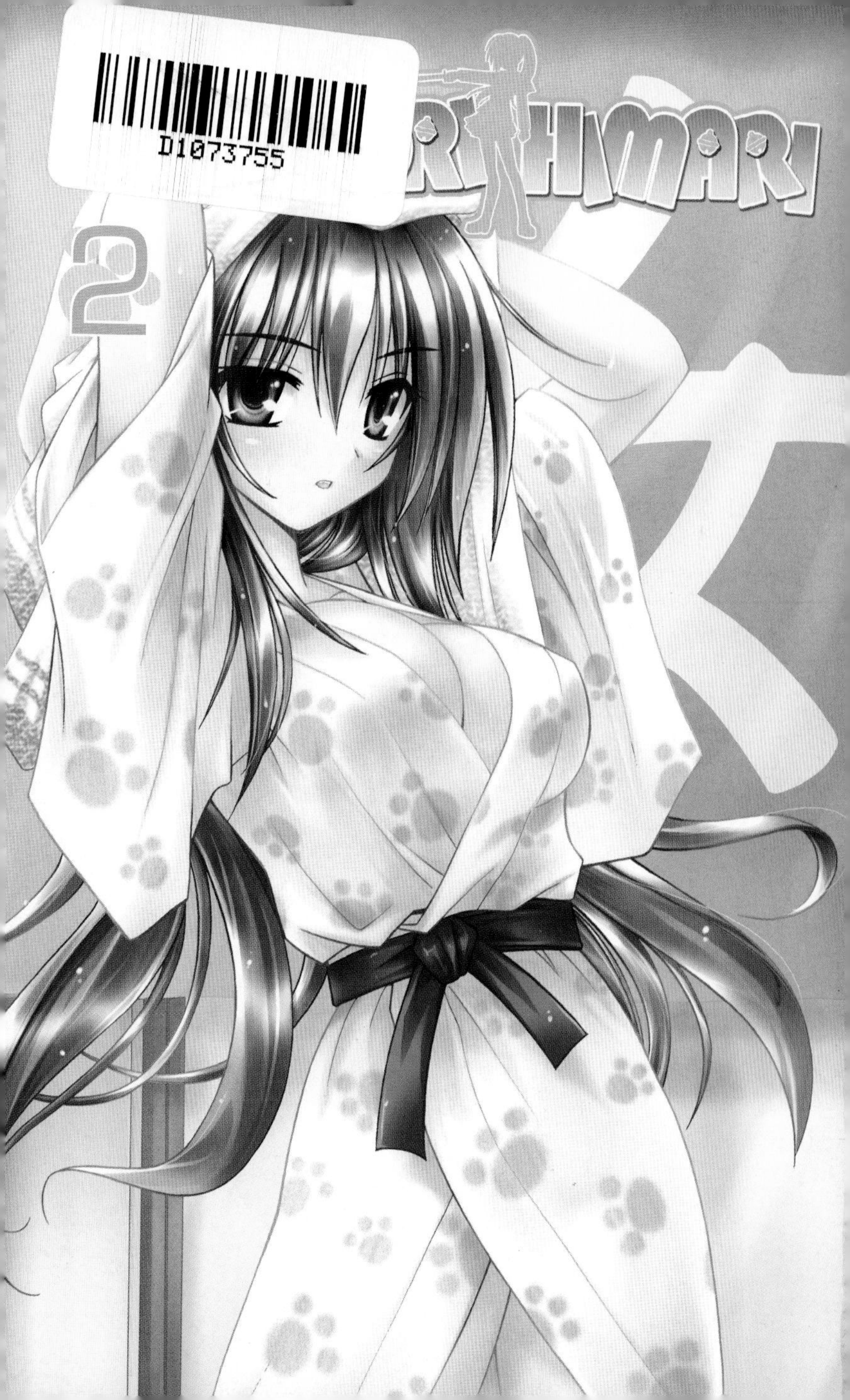
HIMARI
2

CONTENTS

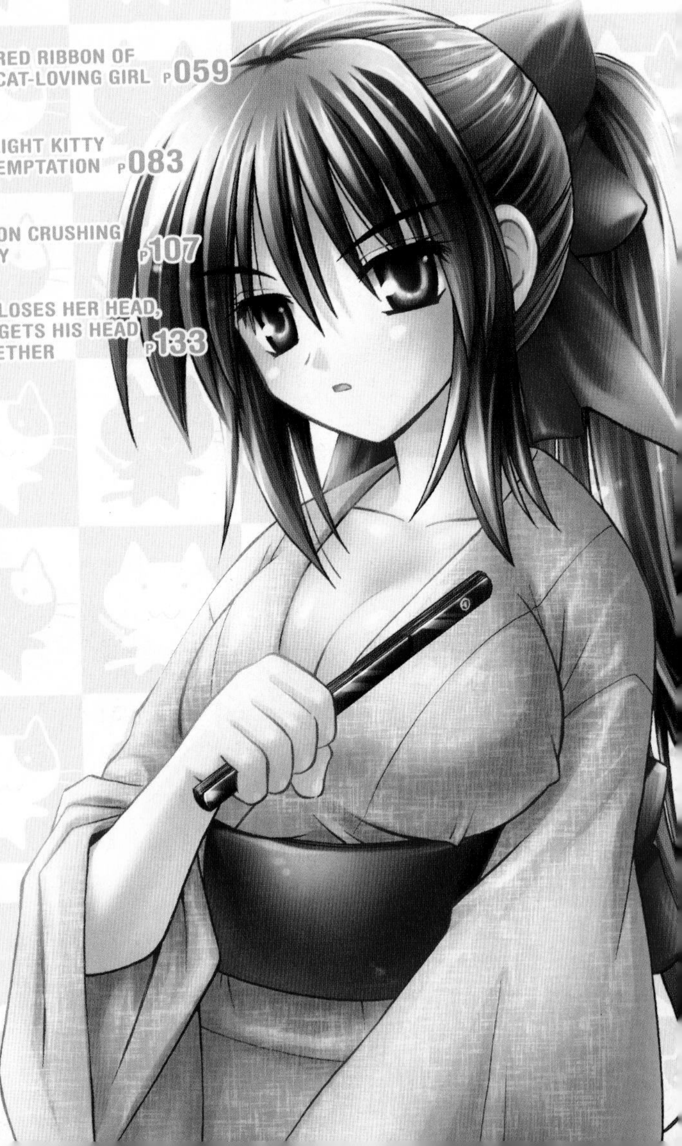

MENAGERIE 7: CONFUSED FOREST CAT

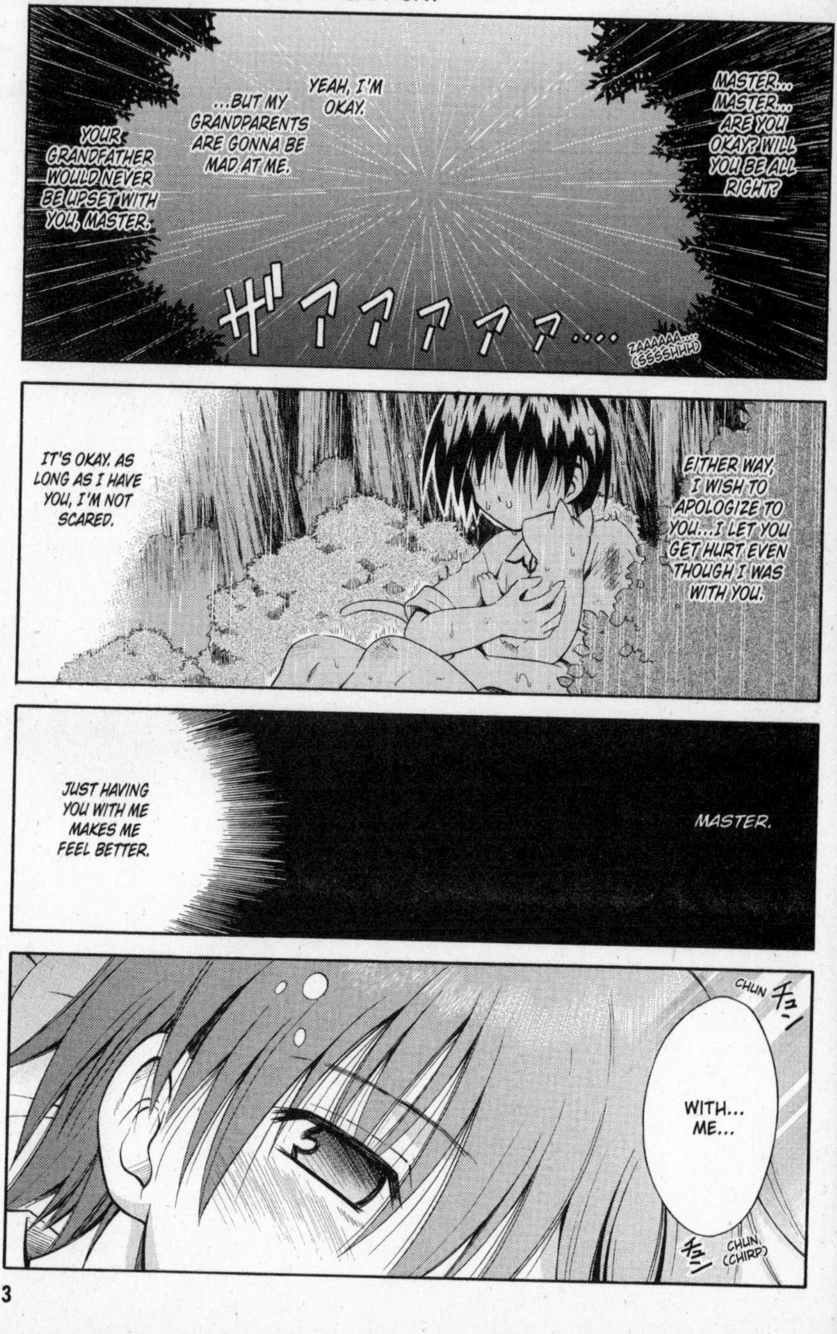
MASTER... MASTER... ARE YOU OKAY? WILL YOU BE ALL RIGHT?
YEAH, I'M OKAY.
...BUT MY GRANDPARENTS ARE GONNA BE MAD AT ME.
YOUR GRANDFATHER WOULD NEVER BE UPSET WITH YOU, MASTER.
ザァァァァァ....
ZAAAAAA.... (SSSSHHHH)
EITHER WAY, I WISH TO APOLOGIZE TO YOU...I LET YOU GET HURT EVEN THOUGH I WAS WITH YOU.
IT'S OKAY. AS LONG AS I HAVE YOU, I'M NOT SCARED.
MASTER.
JUST HAVING YOU WITH ME MAKES ME FEEL BETTER.
チュン
CHUN
WITH... ME...
チュン
CHUN (CHIRP)

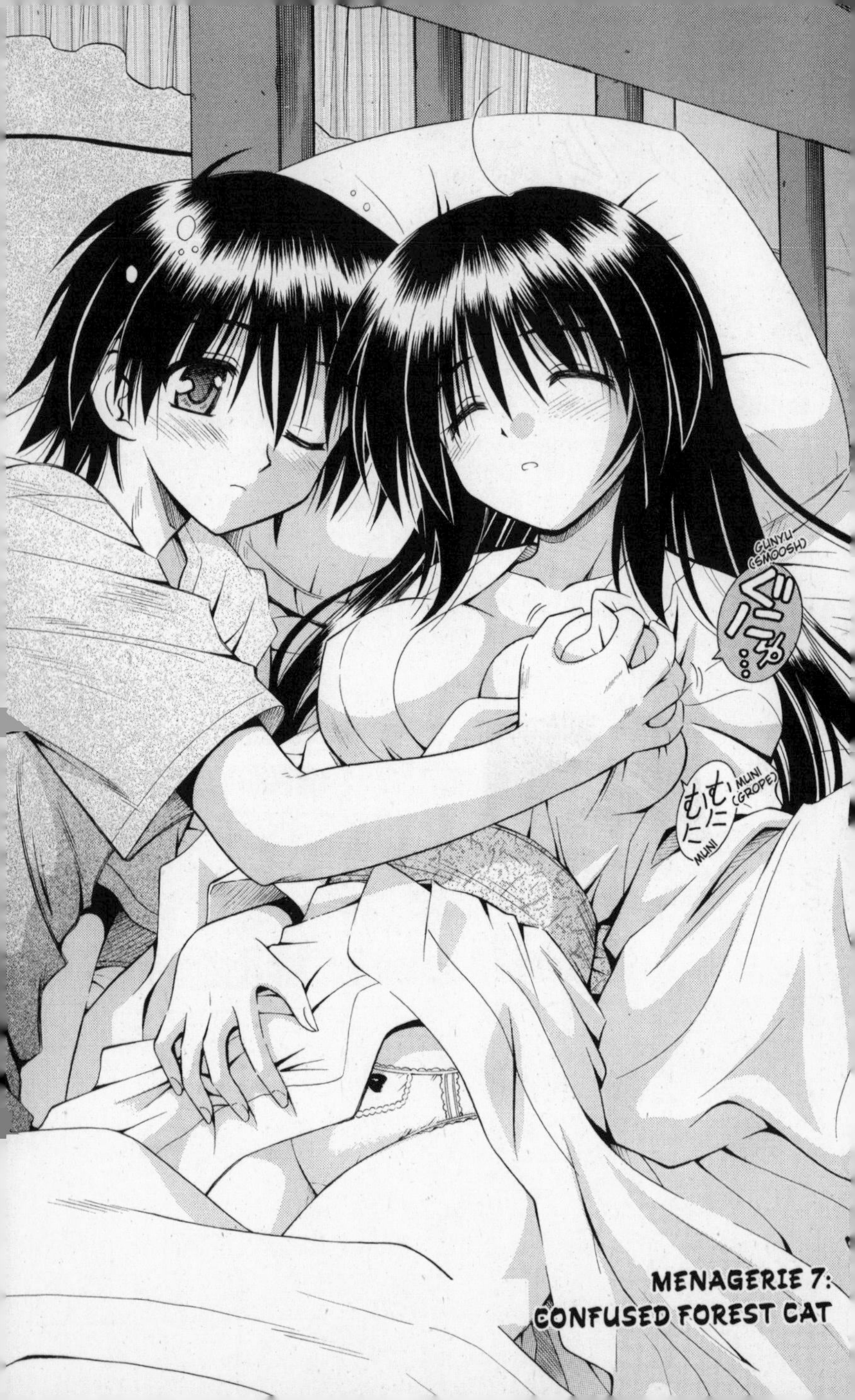
ぐにゅ…
GUNYU (SMOOSH)
むにむに
MUNI (GROPE) MUNI

MENAGERIE 7: CONFUSED FOREST CAT

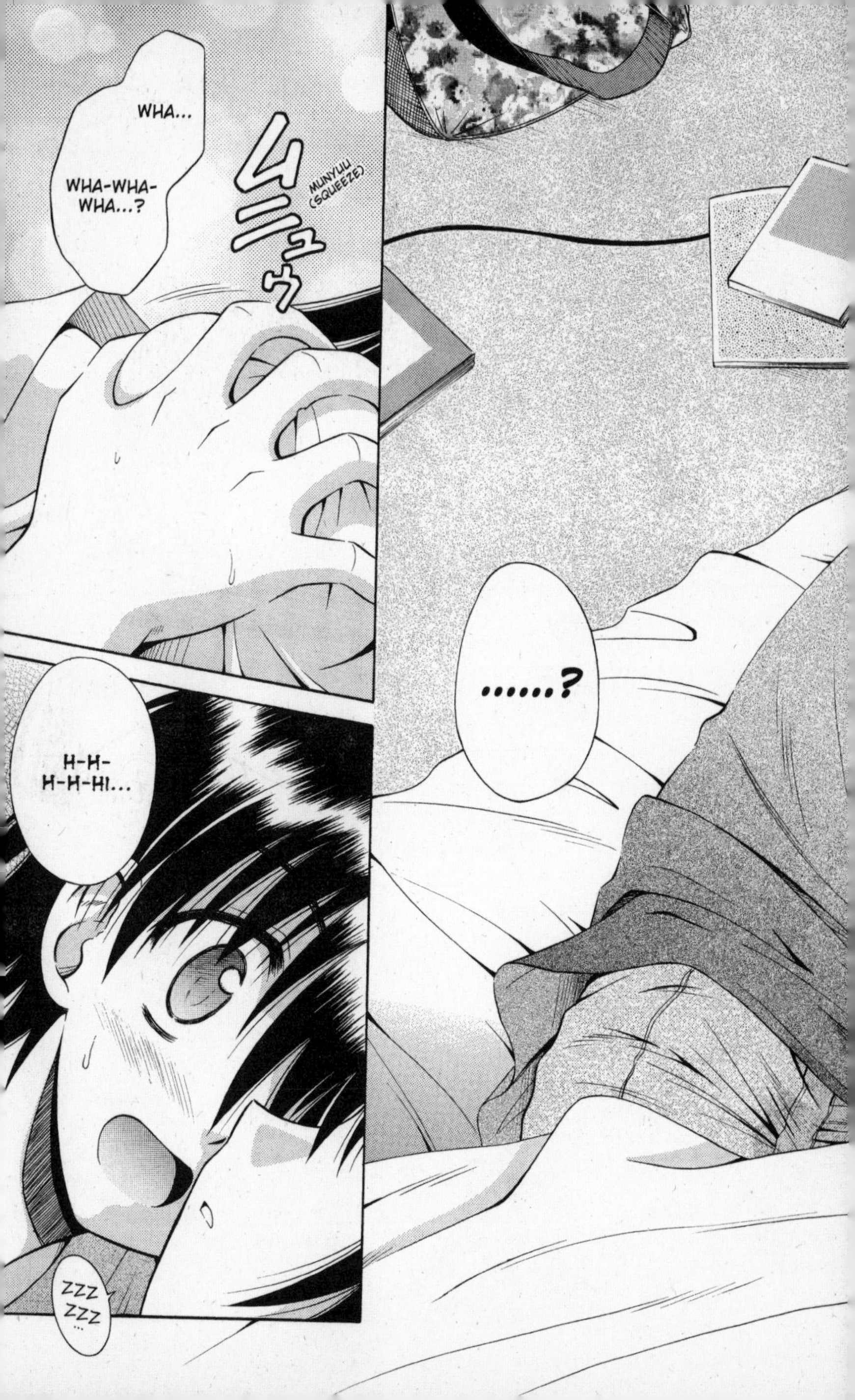
......?
WHA...
WHA-WHA-WHA...?
MUNYUU (SQUEEZE)
H-H-H-H-HI...
ZZZ ZZZ ...

NN...

C-CALM DOWN. IF I... C-CAUSE A RACKET NOW...

...HIMARI WILL WAKE UP AND CATCH ME...

UH.... NN.... PUNI PUNI PUNI (PINCH) PUNI

BUT HER SLEEPING FACE IS SO CUTE. AND HER BREASTS ARE SO SOFT. I'VE WANTED TO FEEL THEM FOR SO LONG.

I JUST CAN'T SEEM TO MOVE MY RIGHT HAND.

UWAH, WHAT AM I THINKING?

I OUGHTA JUST TAKE MY HAND AWAY AND GET OUT OF BED.

EASY PEASY.

...DO YOU ENJOY GIRLS' BREASTS, YOUNG LORD?

ZZZ...

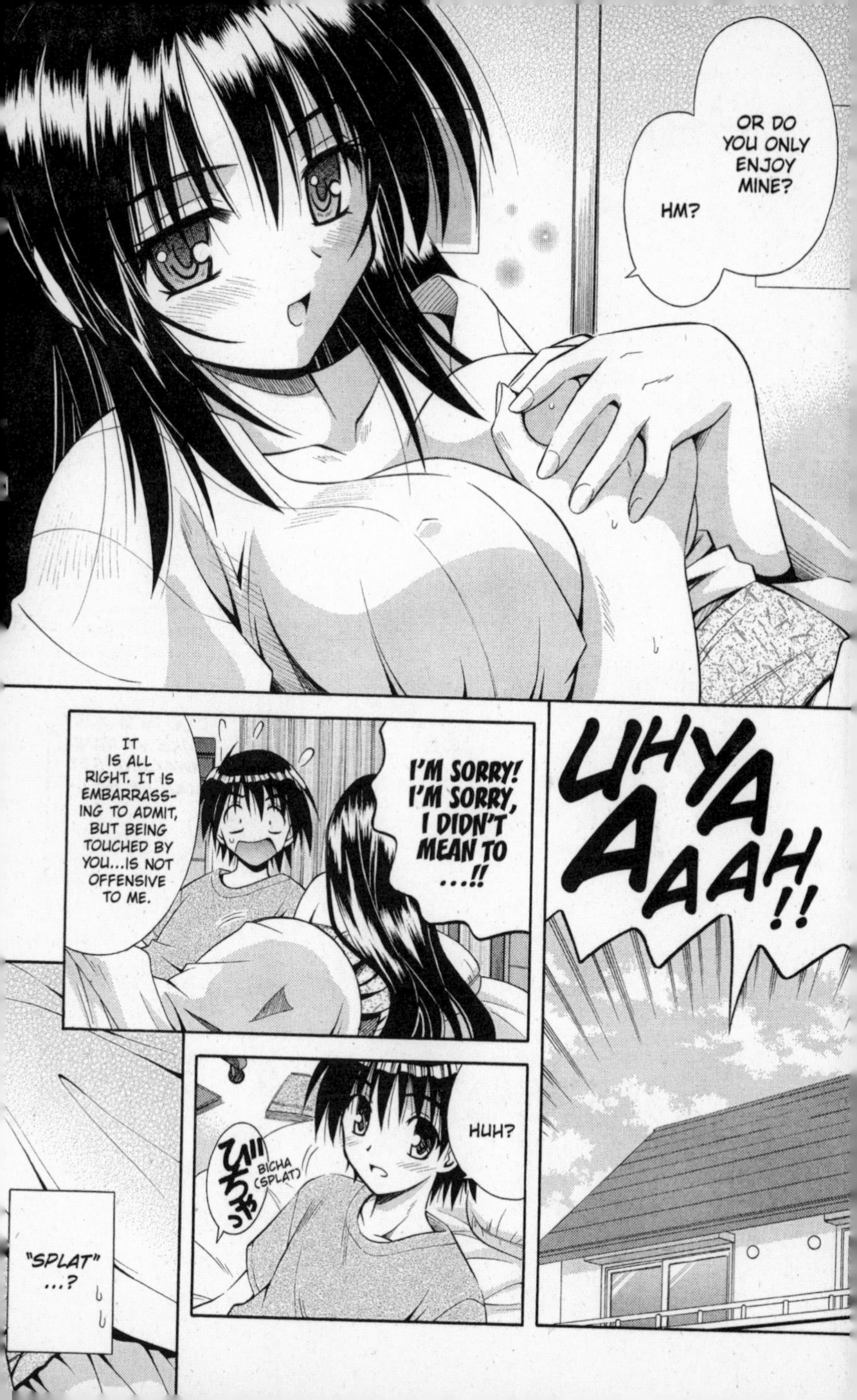
OR DO YOU ONLY ENJOY MINE?
HM?
UHYAAAAH!!
I'M SORRY! I'M SORRY, I DIDN'T MEAN TO ...!!
IT IS ALL RIGHT. IT IS EMBARRASSING TO ADMIT, BUT BEING TOUCHED BY YOU...IS NOT OFFENSIVE TO ME.
HUH?
びちゃっ
BICHA (SPLAT)
"SPLAT" ...?

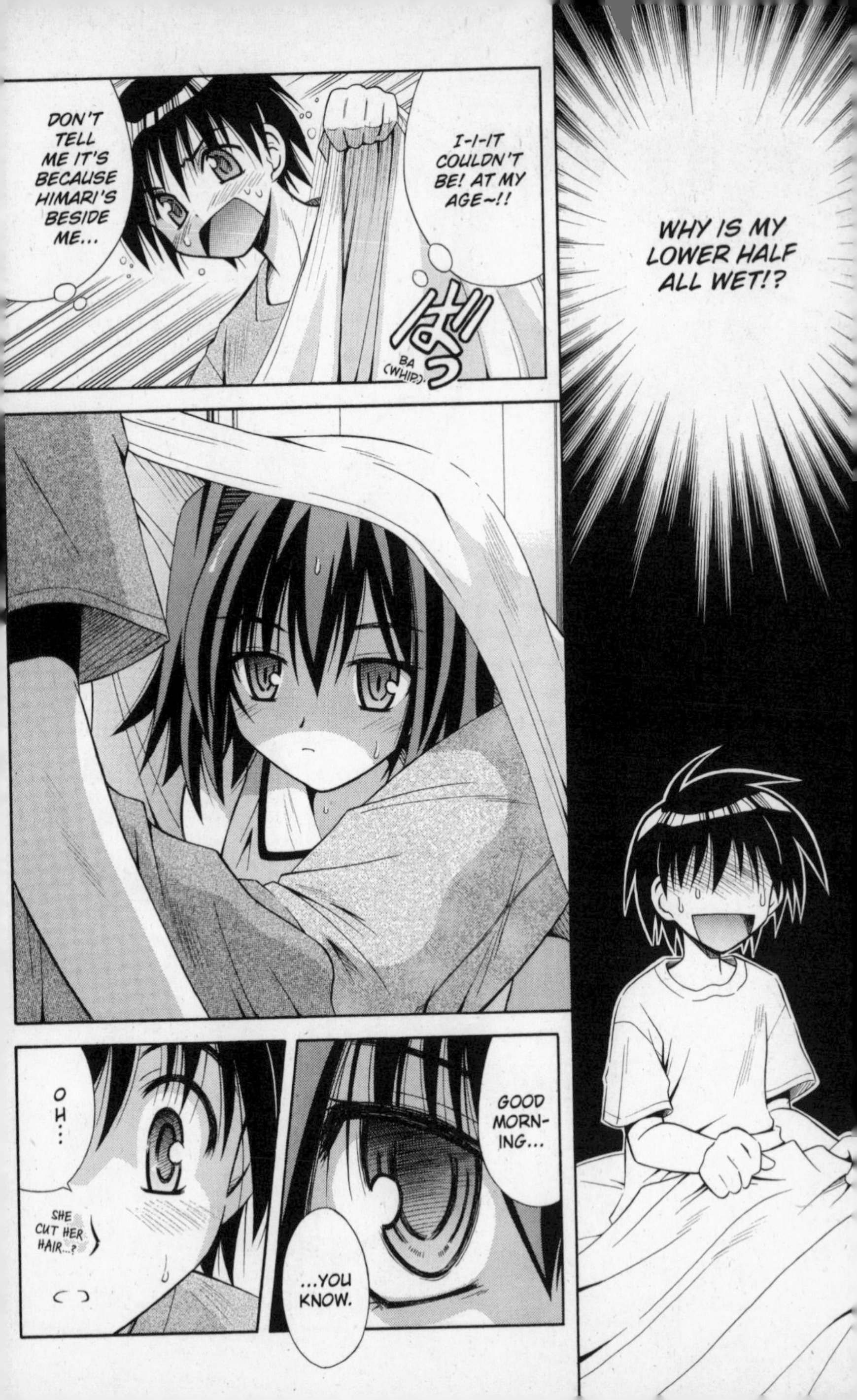
WHY IS MY LOWER HALF ALL WET!?
I-I-IT COULDN'T BE! AT MY AGE~!!
DON'T TELL ME IT'S BECAUSE HIMARI'S BESIDE ME...
ぱっ
BA (WHIP)
GOOD MORNING...
...YOU KNOW.
OH...
SHE CUT HER HAIR...?

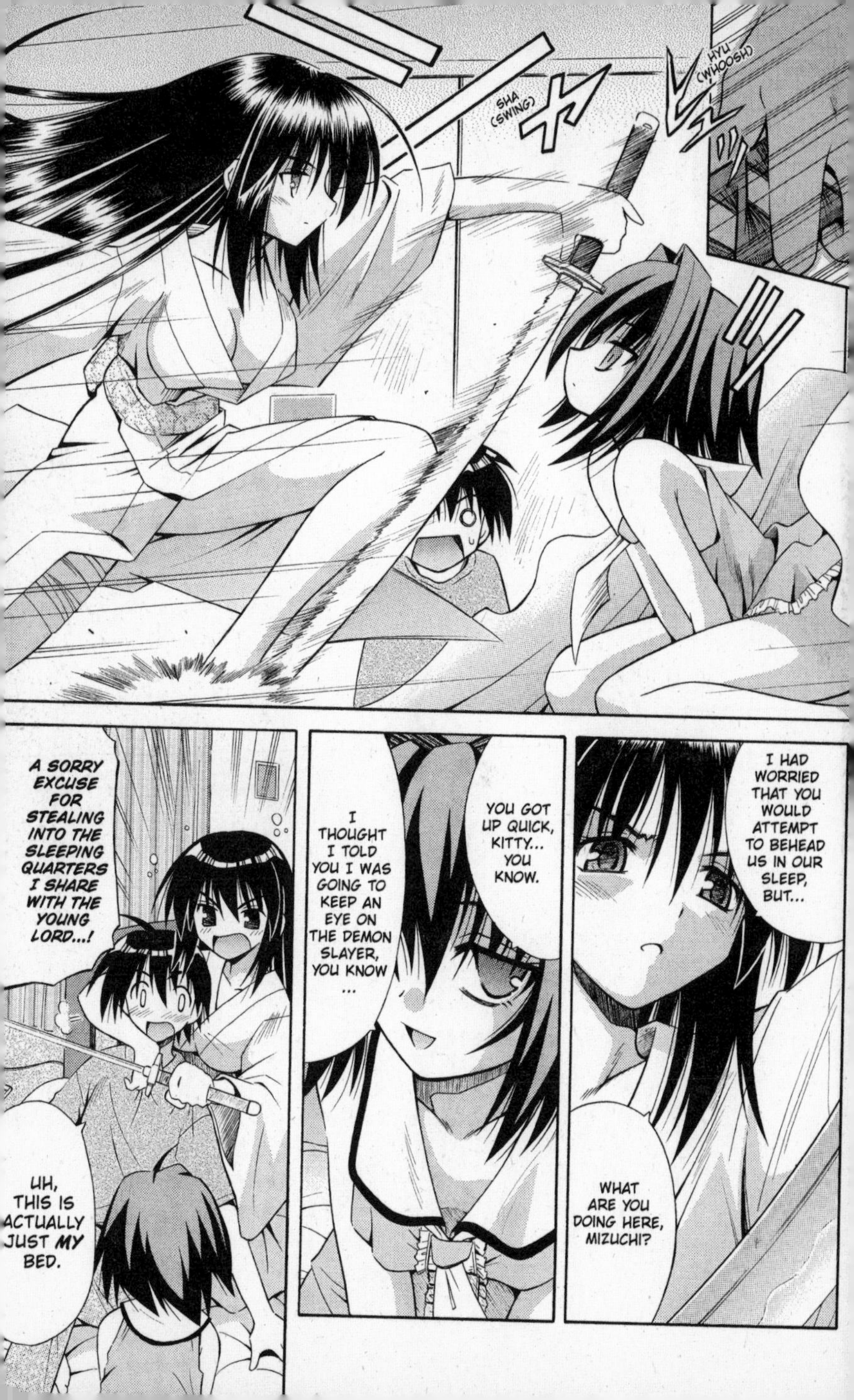
HYU (WHOOSH)
SHA (SWING)
I HAD WORRIED THAT YOU WOULD ATTEMPT TO BEHEAD US IN OUR SLEEP, BUT...
WHAT ARE YOU DOING HERE, MIZUCHI?
YOU GOT UP QUICK, KITTY... YOU KNOW.
I THOUGHT I TOLD YOU I WAS GOING TO KEEP AN EYE ON THE DEMON SLAYER, YOU KNOW...
A SORRY EXCUSE FOR STEALING INTO THE SLEEPING QUARTERS I SHARE WITH THE YOUNG LORD...!
UH, THIS IS ACTUALLY JUST *MY* BED.

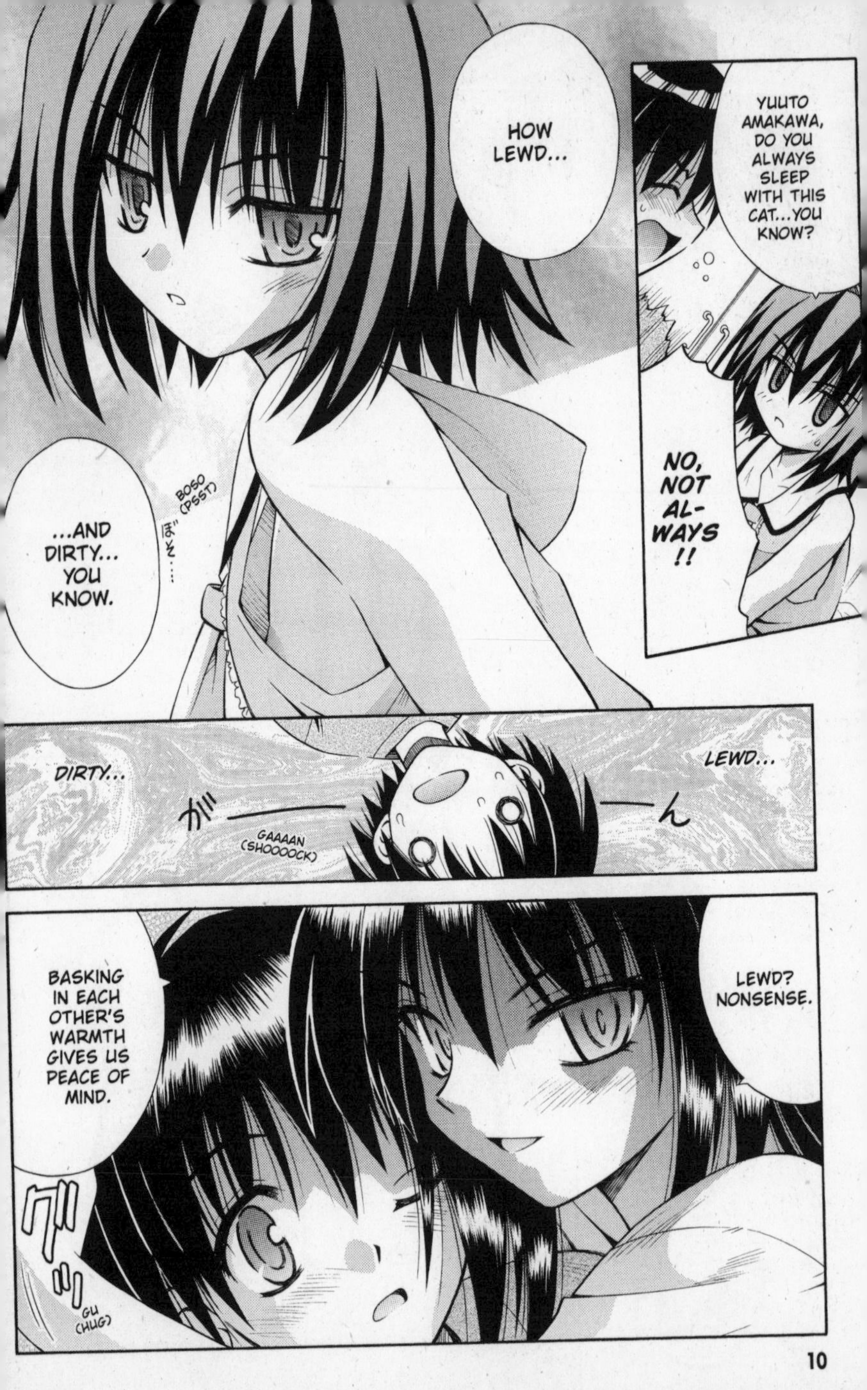
YUUTO AMAKAWA, DO YOU ALWAYS SLEEP WITH THIS CAT...YOU KNOW?
NO, NOT AL-WAYS!!
HOW LEWD...
BOSO (PSST)
ぼそ…
...AND DIRTY... YOU KNOW.
LEWD...
がーーん
GAAAAN (SHOOOOCK)
DIRTY...
LEWD? NONSENSE.
BASKING IN EACH OTHER'S WARMTH GIVES US PEACE OF MIND.
GU (HUG)

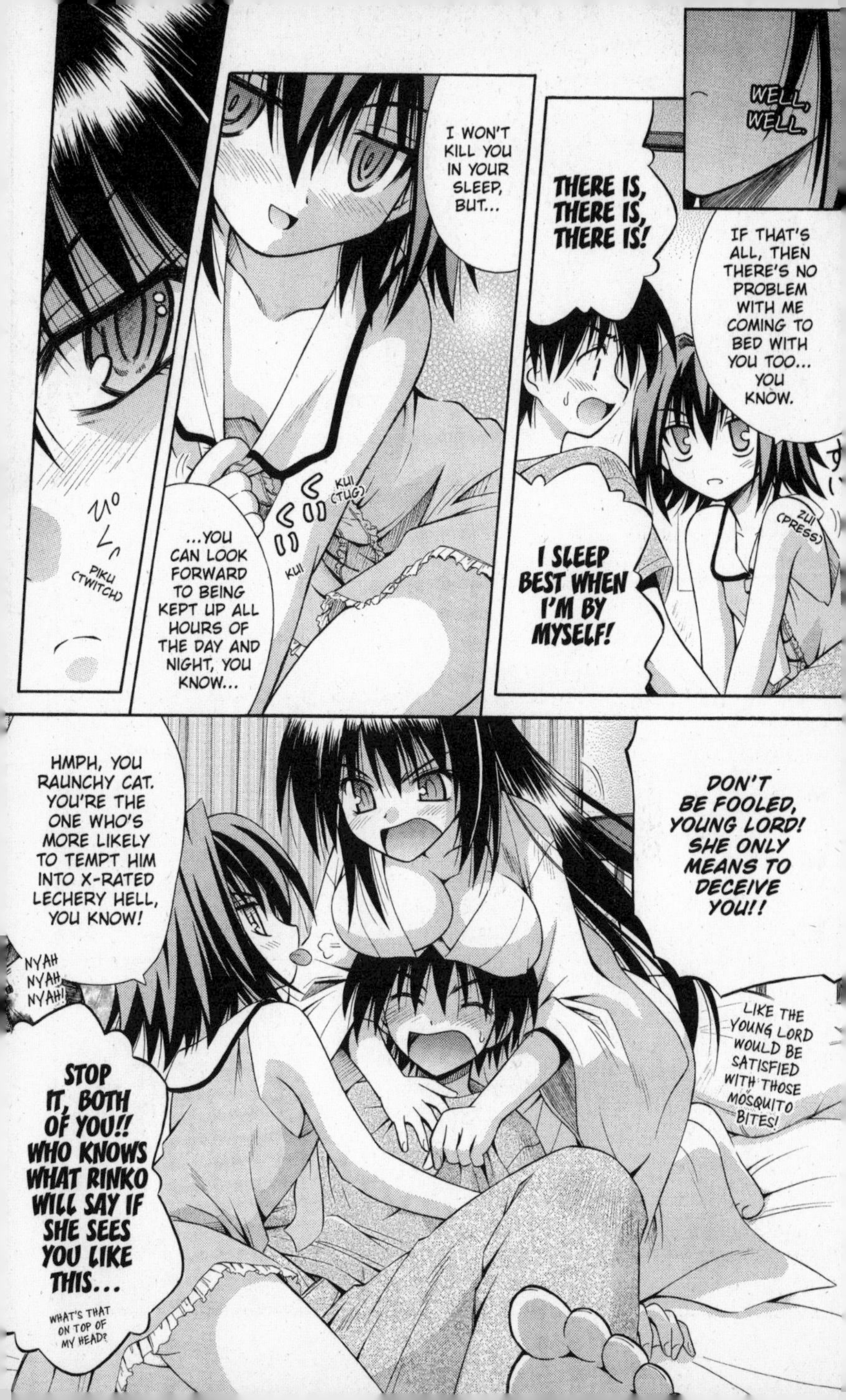
WELL, WELL.
IF THAT'S ALL, THEN THERE'S NO PROBLEM WITH ME COMING TO BED WITH YOU TOO... YOU KNOW.
ZUI (PRESS)
THERE IS, THERE IS, THERE IS!
I SLEEP BEST WHEN I'M BY MYSELF!
I WON'T KILL YOU IN YOUR SLEEP, BUT...
KUI (TUG)
KUI
...YOU CAN LOOK FORWARD TO BEING KEPT UP ALL HOURS OF THE DAY AND NIGHT, YOU KNOW...
PIKU (TWITCH)
DON'T BE FOOLED, YOUNG LORD! SHE ONLY MEANS TO DECEIVE YOU!!
LIKE THE YOUNG LORD WOULD BE SATISFIED WITH THOSE MOSQUITO BITES!
HMPH, YOU RAUNCHY CAT. YOU'RE THE ONE WHO'S MORE LIKELY TO TEMPT HIM INTO X-RATED LECHERY HELL, YOU KNOW!
NYAH NYAH NYAH!
STOP IT, BOTH OF YOU!! WHO KNOWS WHAT RINKO WILL SAY IF SHE SEES YOU LIKE THIS...
WHAT'S THAT ON TOP OF MY HEAD?

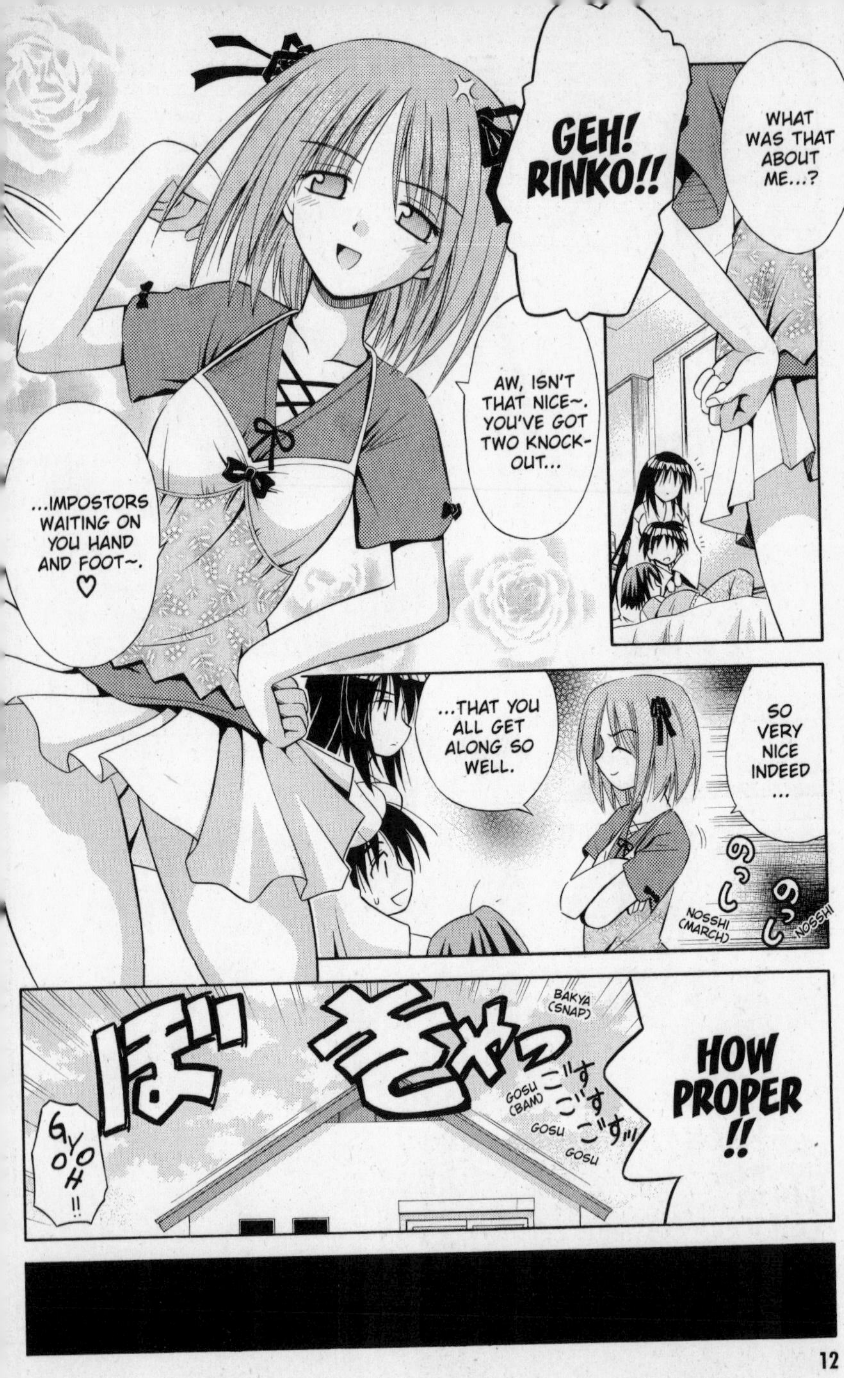
WHAT WAS THAT ABOUT ME...?
GEH! RINKO!!
AW, ISN'T THAT NICE~. YOU'VE GOT TWO KNOCK-OUT...
...IMPOSTORS WAITING ON YOU HAND AND FOOT~. ♡
SO VERY NICE INDEED...
のっし NOSSHI
のっし NOSSHI (MARCH)
...THAT YOU ALL GET ALONG SO WELL.
HOW PROPER!!
ごすごすごすッ GOSU (BAM) GOSU GOSU
ばきゃっ BAKYA (SNAP)
GYOOH!!

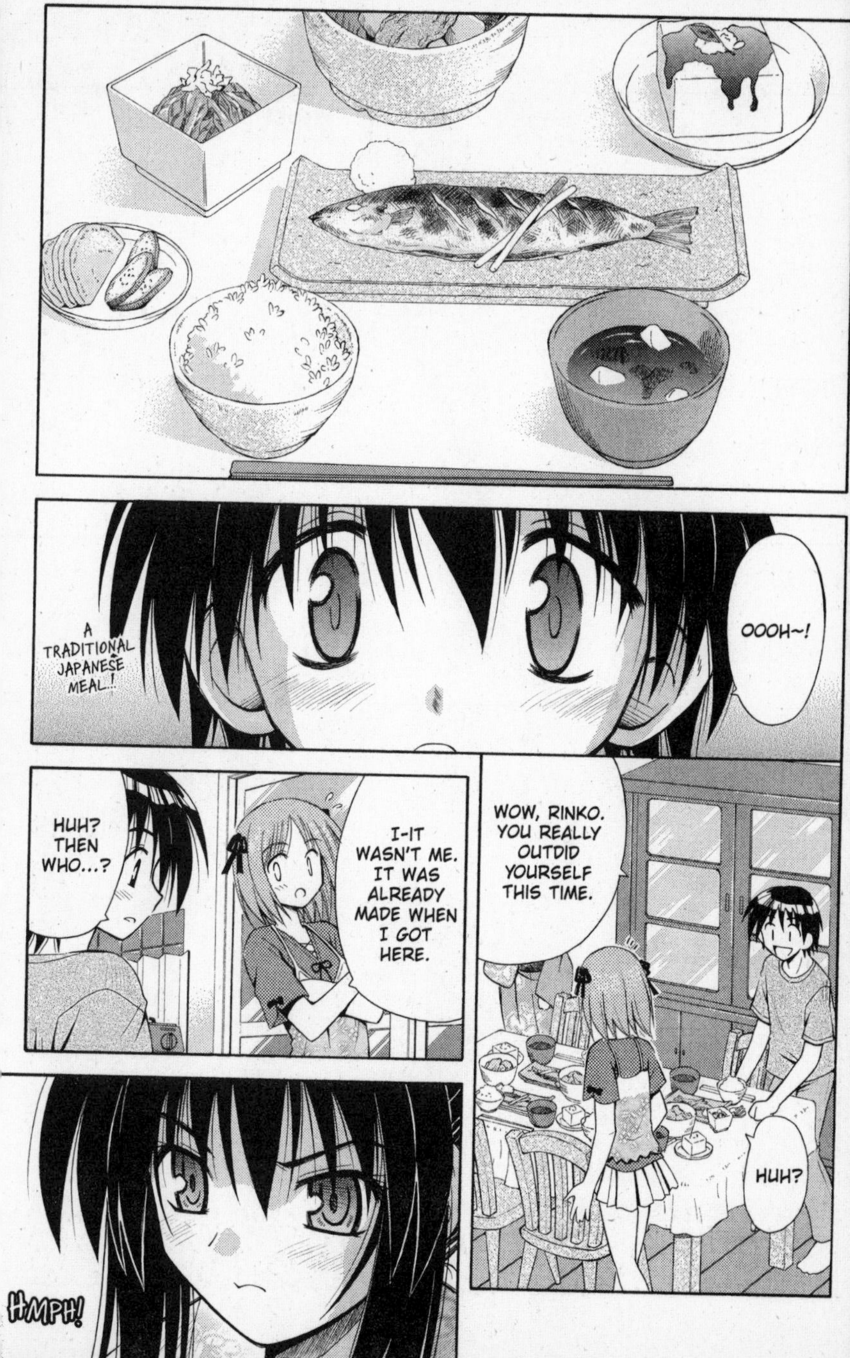
OOOH~!
A TRADITIONAL JAPANESE MEAL...!
WOW, RINKO. YOU REALLY OUTDID YOURSELF THIS TIME.
HUH?
I-IT WASN'T ME. IT WAS ALREADY MADE WHEN I GOT HERE.
HUH? THEN WHO...?
HMPH!

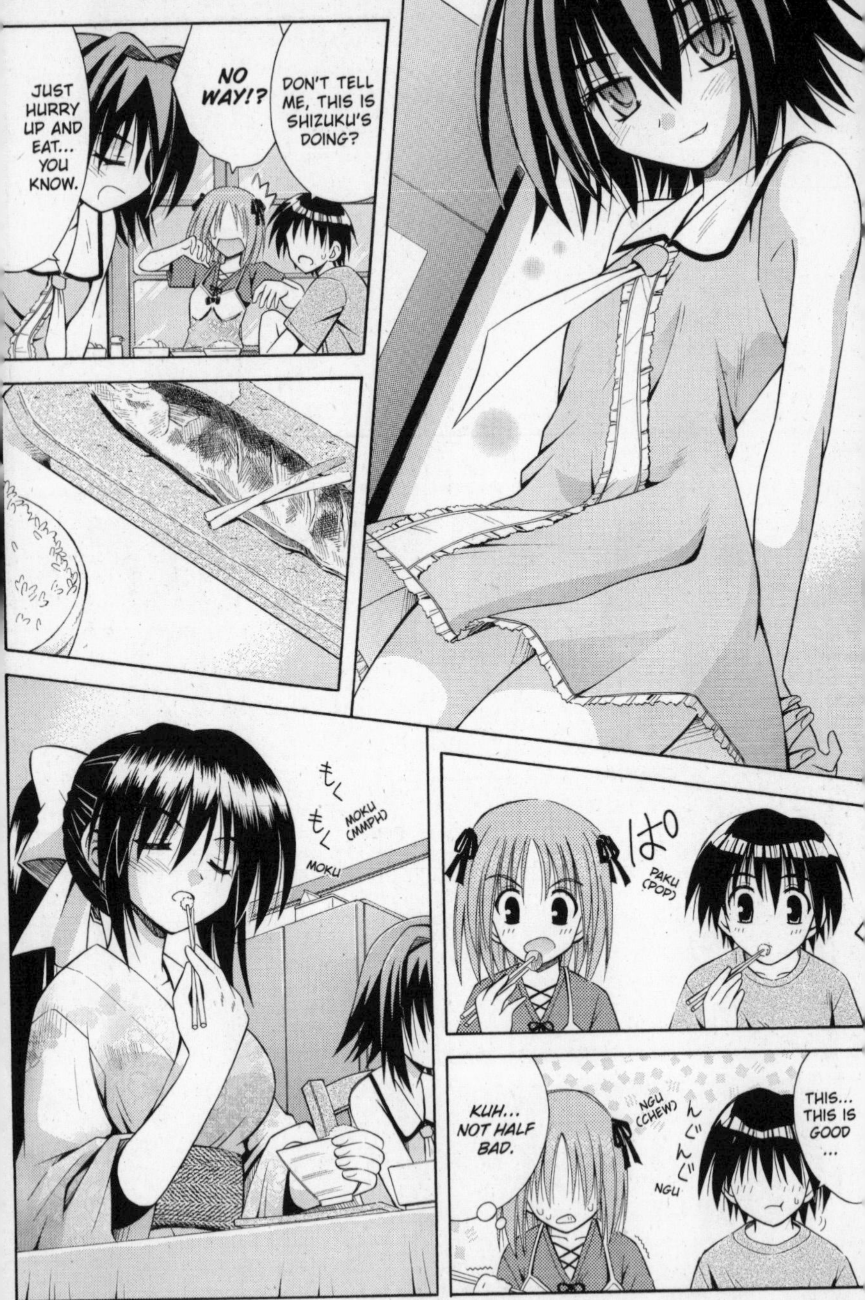
DON'T TELL ME, THIS IS SHIZUKU'S DOING?
NO WAY!?
JUST HURRY UP AND EAT... YOU KNOW.
ぱく
PAKU (POP)
THIS... THIS IS GOOD ...
んぐんぐ
NGU (CHEW)
NGU
KUH... NOT HALF BAD.
もく もく
MOKU (MMPH)
MOKU

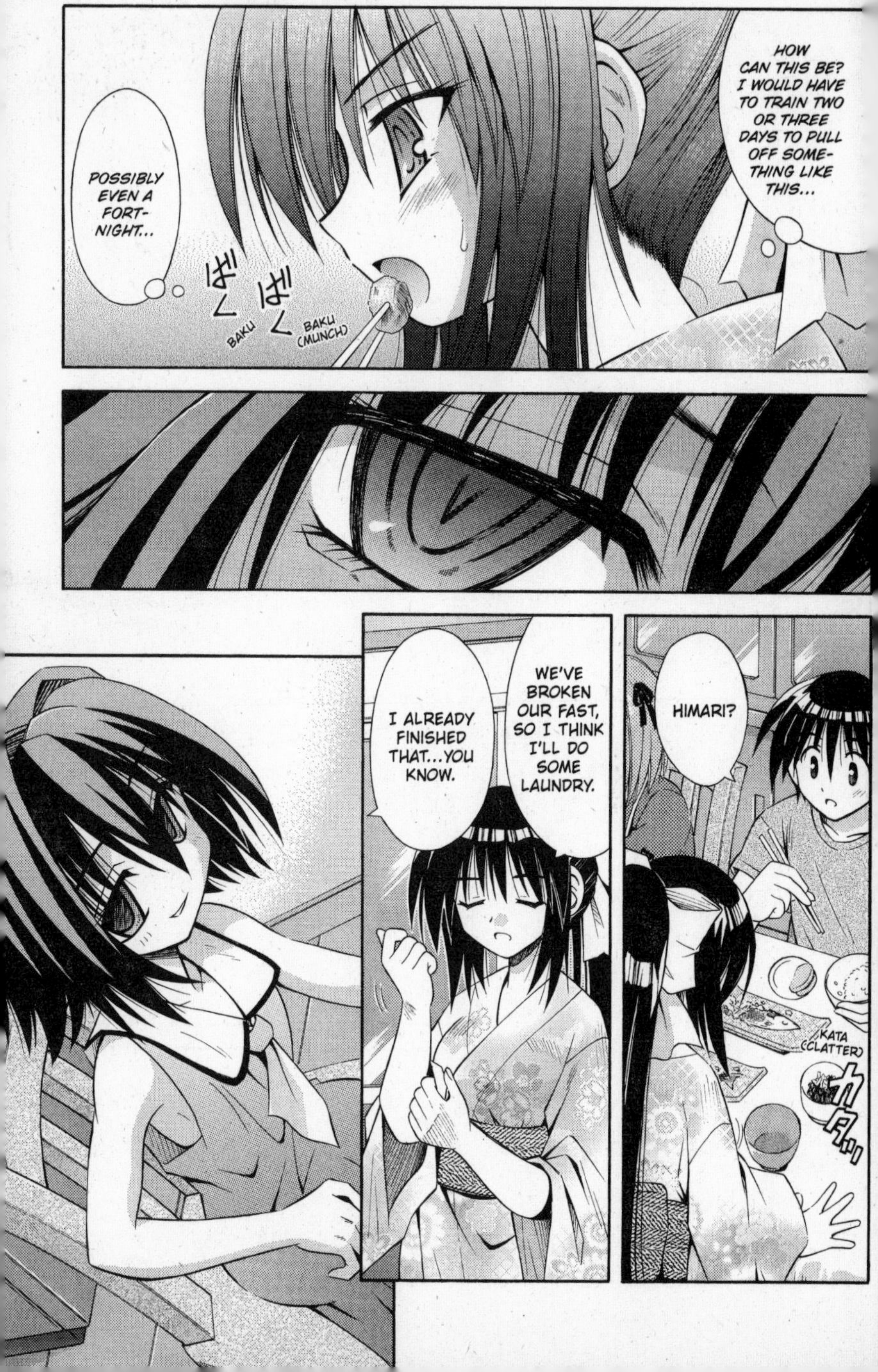
HOW CAN THIS BE? I WOULD HAVE TO TRAIN TWO OR THREE DAYS TO PULL OFF SOME-THING LIKE THIS...
POSSIBLY EVEN A FORT-NIGHT...
BAKU (MUNCH)
BAKU
HIMARI?
KATA (CLATTER)
WE'VE BROKEN OUR FAST, SO I THINK I'LL DO SOME LAUNDRY.
I ALREADY FINISHED THAT...YOU KNOW.

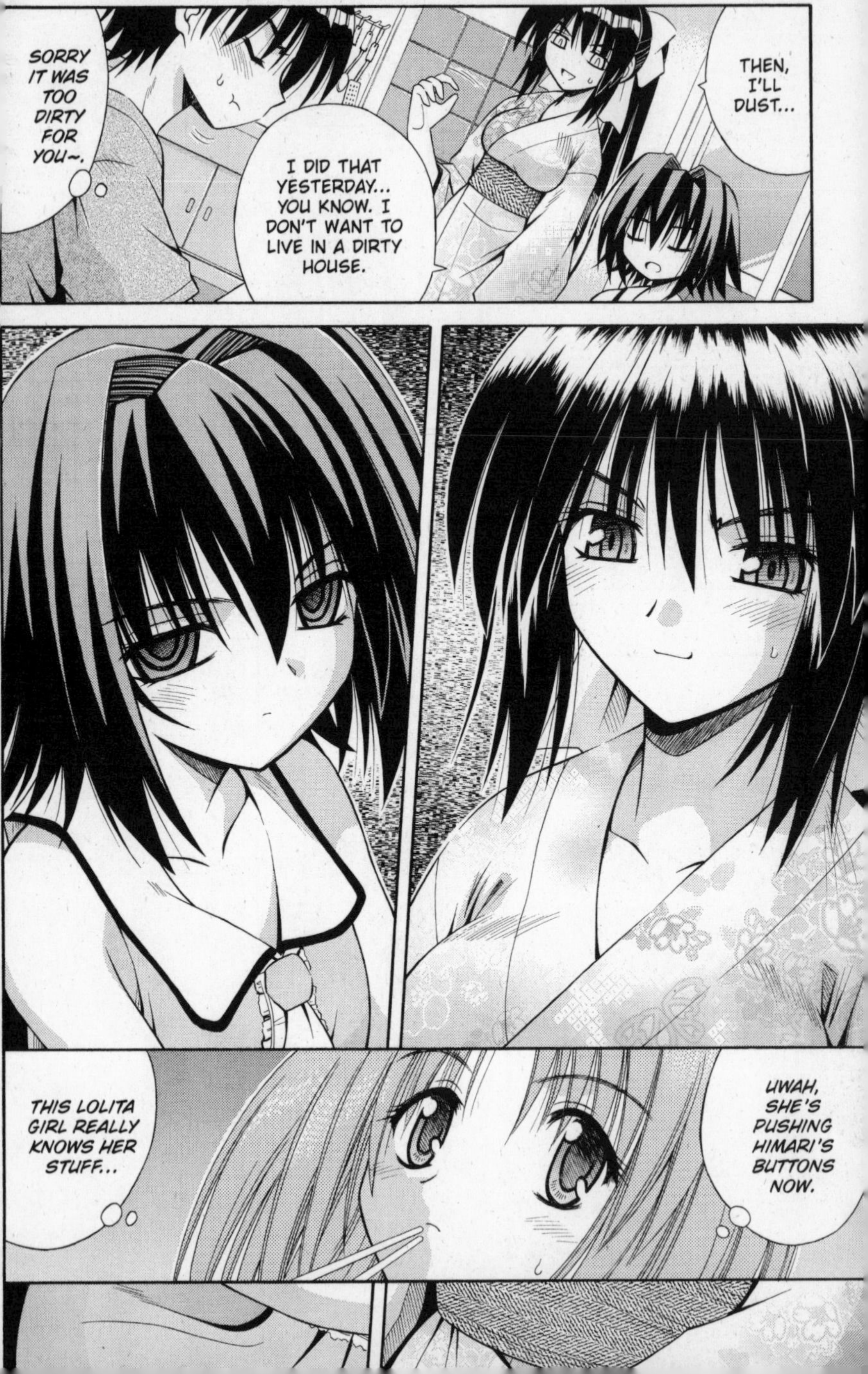
THEN, I'LL DUST...
I DID THAT YESTERDAY... YOU KNOW. I DON'T WANT TO LIVE IN A DIRTY HOUSE.
SORRY IT WAS TOO DIRTY FOR YOU~.
UWAH, SHE'S PUSHING HIMARI'S BUTTONS NOW.
THIS LOLITA GIRL REALLY KNOWS HER STUFF...

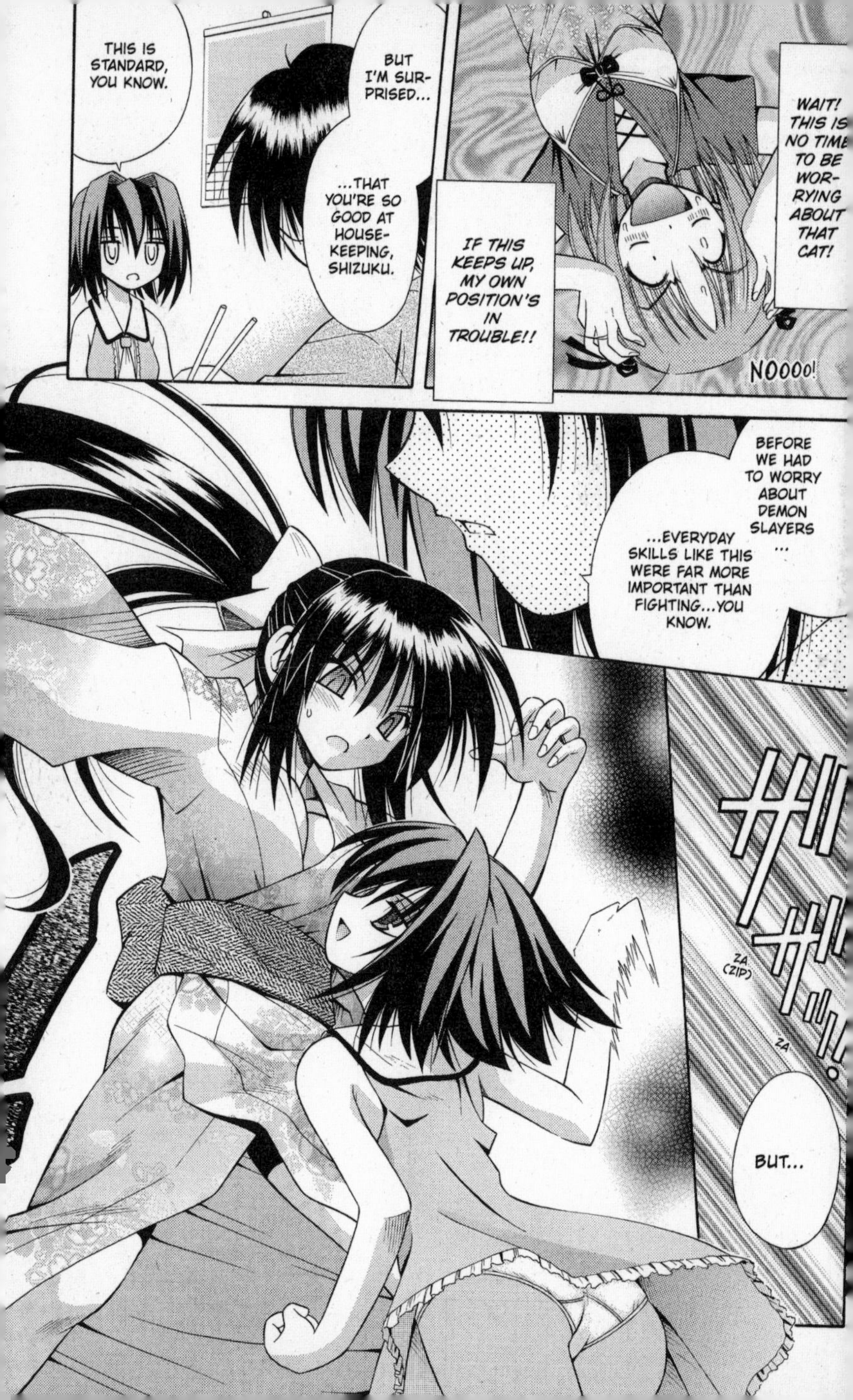
WAIT! THIS IS NO TIME TO BE WOR-RYING ABOUT THAT CAT!
NOOOO!
IF THIS KEEPS UP, MY OWN POSITION'S IN TROUBLE!!
BUT I'M SUR-PRISED...
...THAT YOU'RE SO GOOD AT HOUSE-KEEPING, SHIZUKU.
THIS IS STANDARD, YOU KNOW.
BEFORE WE HAD TO WORRY ABOUT DEMON SLAYERS...
...EVERYDAY SKILLS LIKE THIS WERE FAR MORE IMPORTANT THAN FIGHTING...YOU KNOW.
ZA (ZIP)
ZA
BUT...

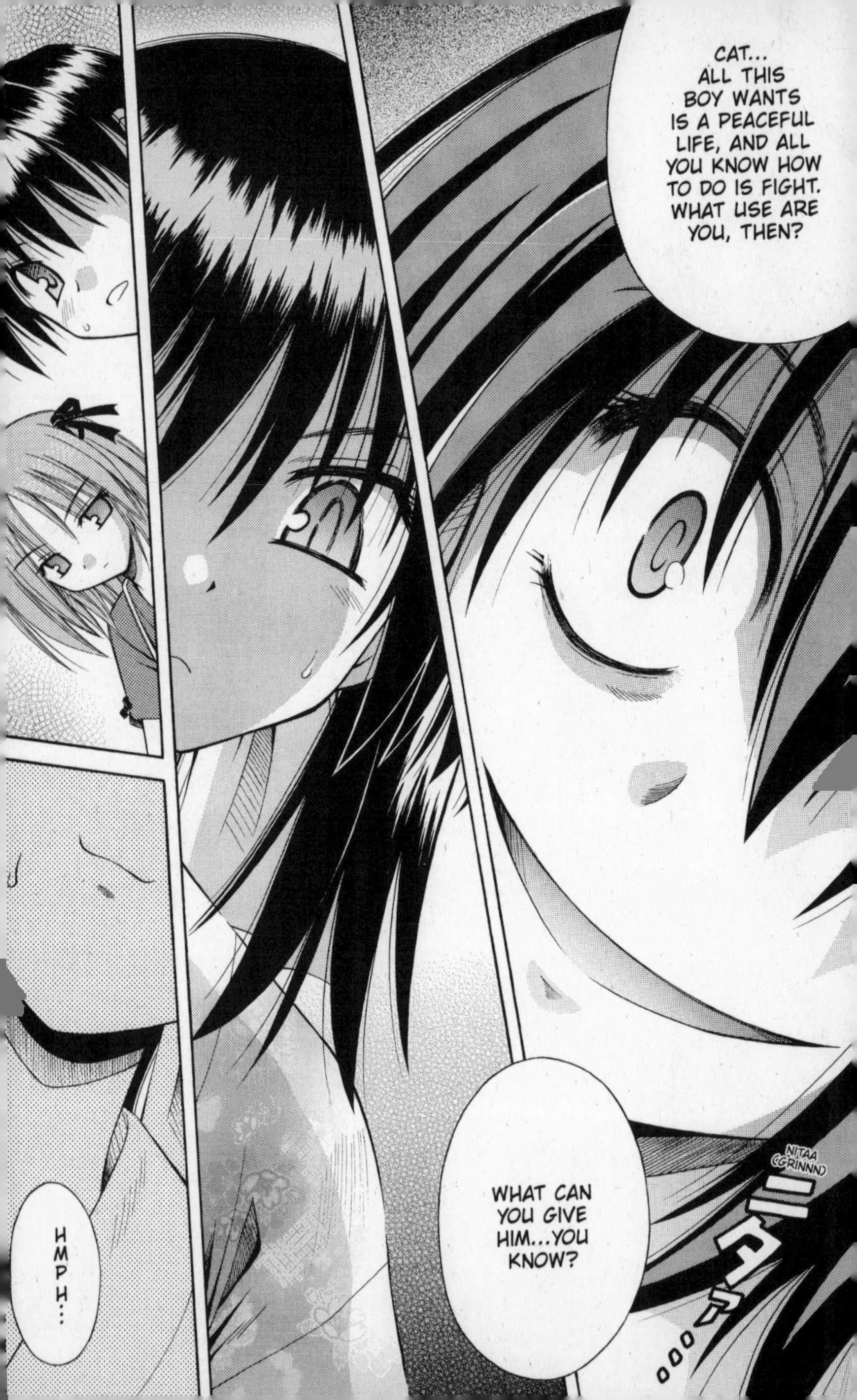
CAT... ALL THIS BOY WANTS IS A PEACEFUL LIFE, AND ALL YOU KNOW HOW TO DO IS FIGHT. WHAT USE ARE YOU, THEN?
WHAT CAN YOU GIVE HIM...YOU KNOW?
NITAA (GRINNN)
HMPH...

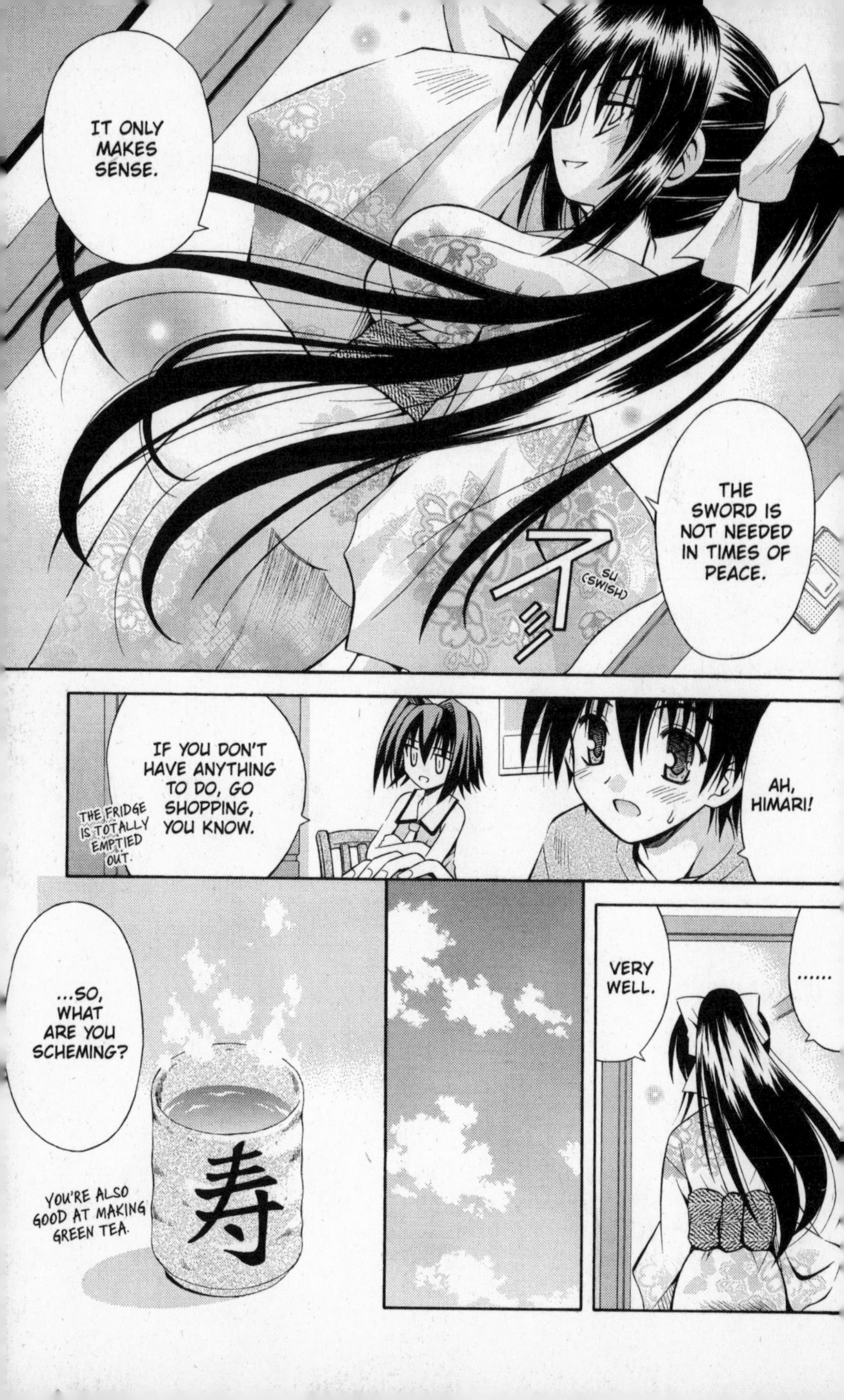
THE SWORD IS NOT NEEDED IN TIMES OF PEACE.
SU (SWISH)
IT ONLY MAKES SENSE.
AH, HIMARI!
IF YOU DON'T HAVE ANYTHING TO DO, GO SHOPPING, YOU KNOW.
THE FRIDGE IS TOTALLY EMPTIED OUT.
......
VERY WELL.
...SO, WHAT ARE YOU SCHEMING?
寿
YOU'RE ALSO GOOD AT MAKING GREEN TEA.

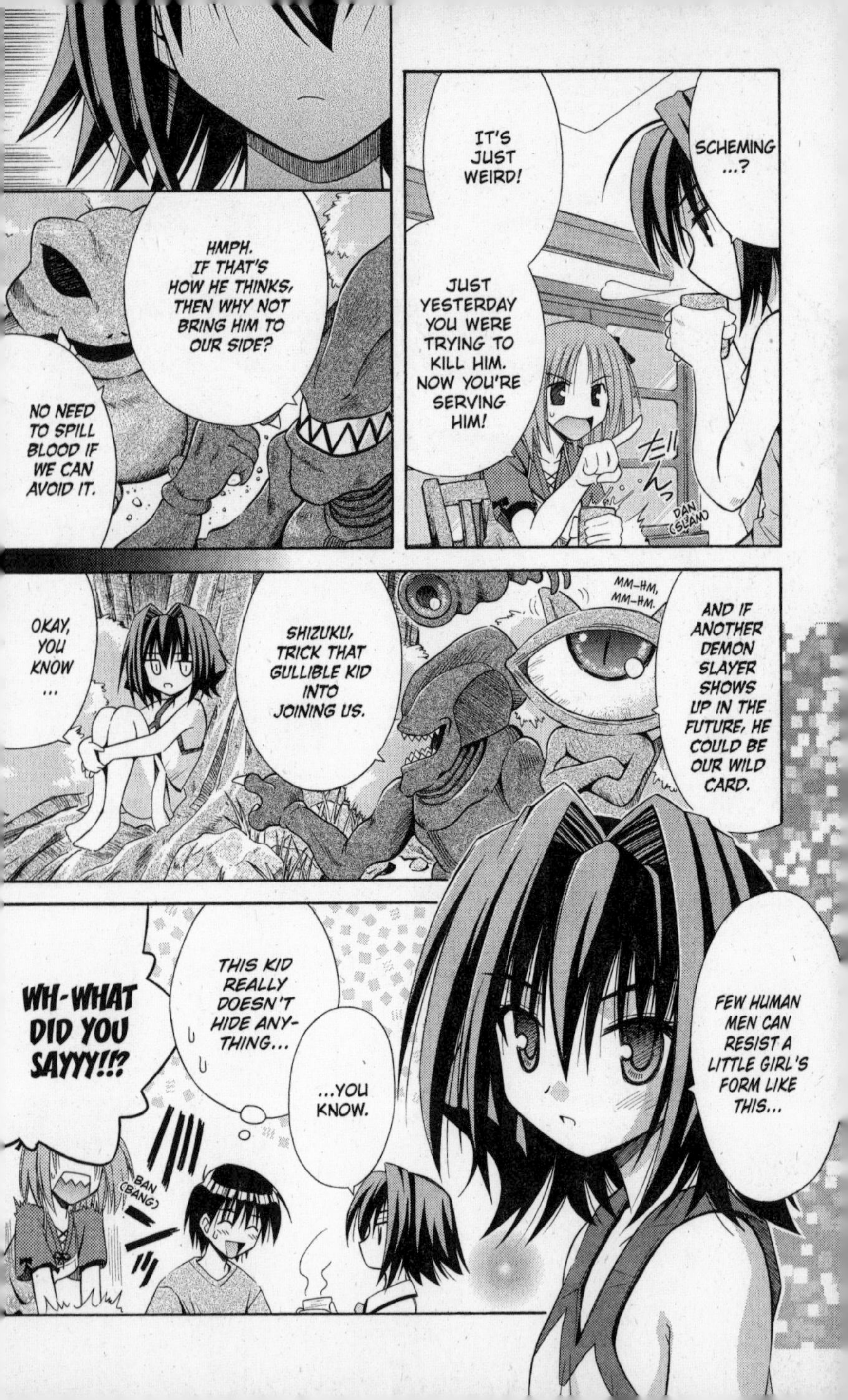
SCHEMING ...?
IT'S JUST WEIRD!
JUST YESTERDAY YOU WERE TRYING TO KILL HIM. NOW YOU'RE SERVING HIM!
だんっ
DAN (SLAM)
HMPH. IF THAT'S HOW HE THINKS, THEN WHY NOT BRING HIM TO OUR SIDE?
NO NEED TO SPILL BLOOD IF WE CAN AVOID IT.
AND IF ANOTHER DEMON SLAYER SHOWS UP IN THE FUTURE, HE COULD BE OUR WILD CARD.
MM-HM, MM-HM.
SHIZUKU, TRICK THAT GULLIBLE KID INTO JOINING US.
OKAY, YOU KNOW ...
FEW HUMAN MEN CAN RESIST A LITTLE GIRL'S FORM LIKE THIS...
...YOU KNOW.
THIS KID REALLY DOESN'T HIDE ANY-THING...
WH-WHAT DID YOU SAYYY!!?
BAN (BANG)

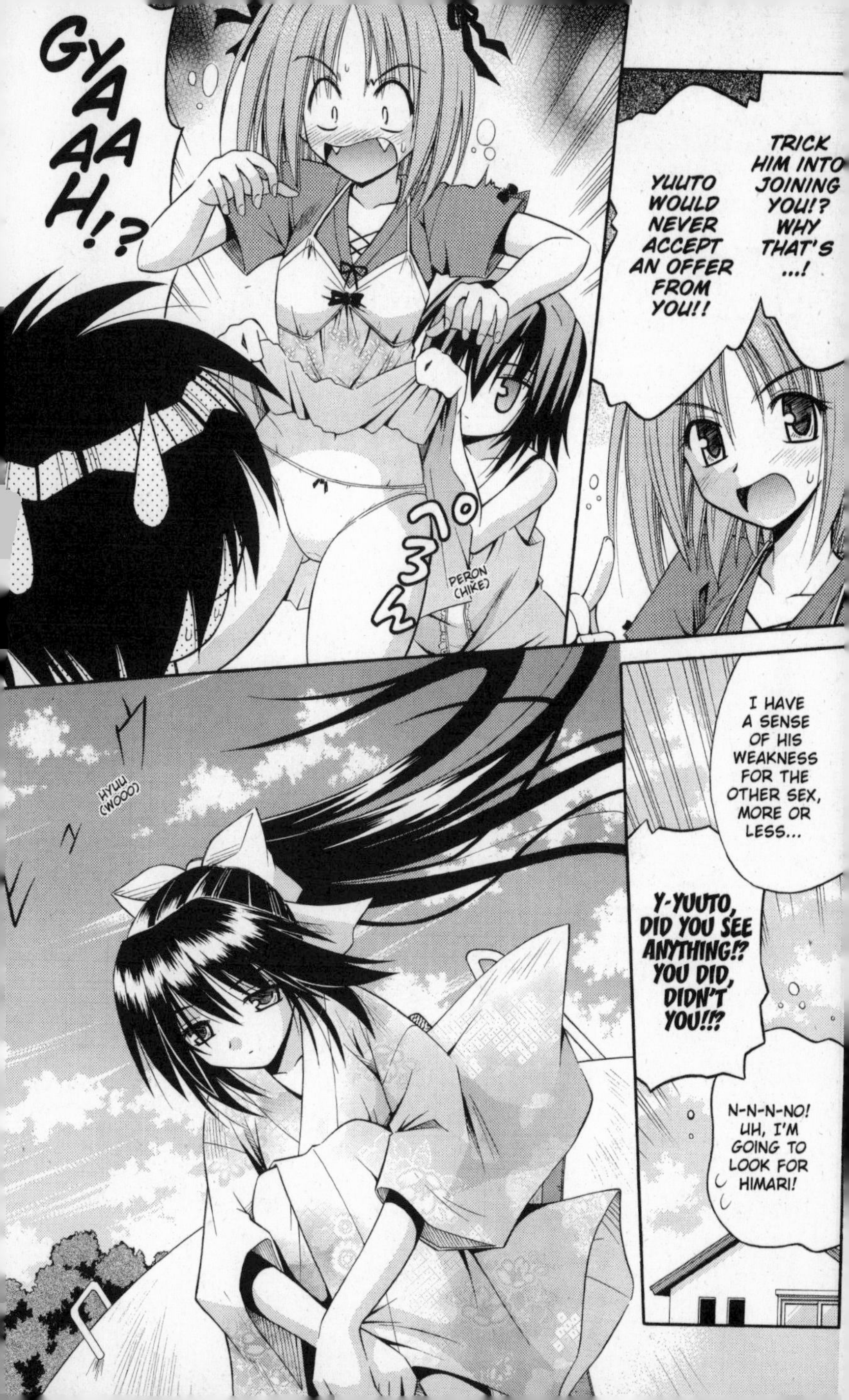
TRICK HIM INTO JOINING YOU!? WHY THAT'S ...!
YUUTO WOULD NEVER ACCEPT AN OFFER FROM YOU!!
GYAAAH!?
PERON (HIKE)
I HAVE A SENSE OF HIS WEAKNESS FOR THE OTHER SEX, MORE OR LESS...
Y-YUUTO, DID YOU SEE ANYTHING!? YOU DID, DIDN'T YOU!!?
N-N-N-NO! UH, I'M GOING TO LOOK FOR HIMARI!
HYUU (WOOO)

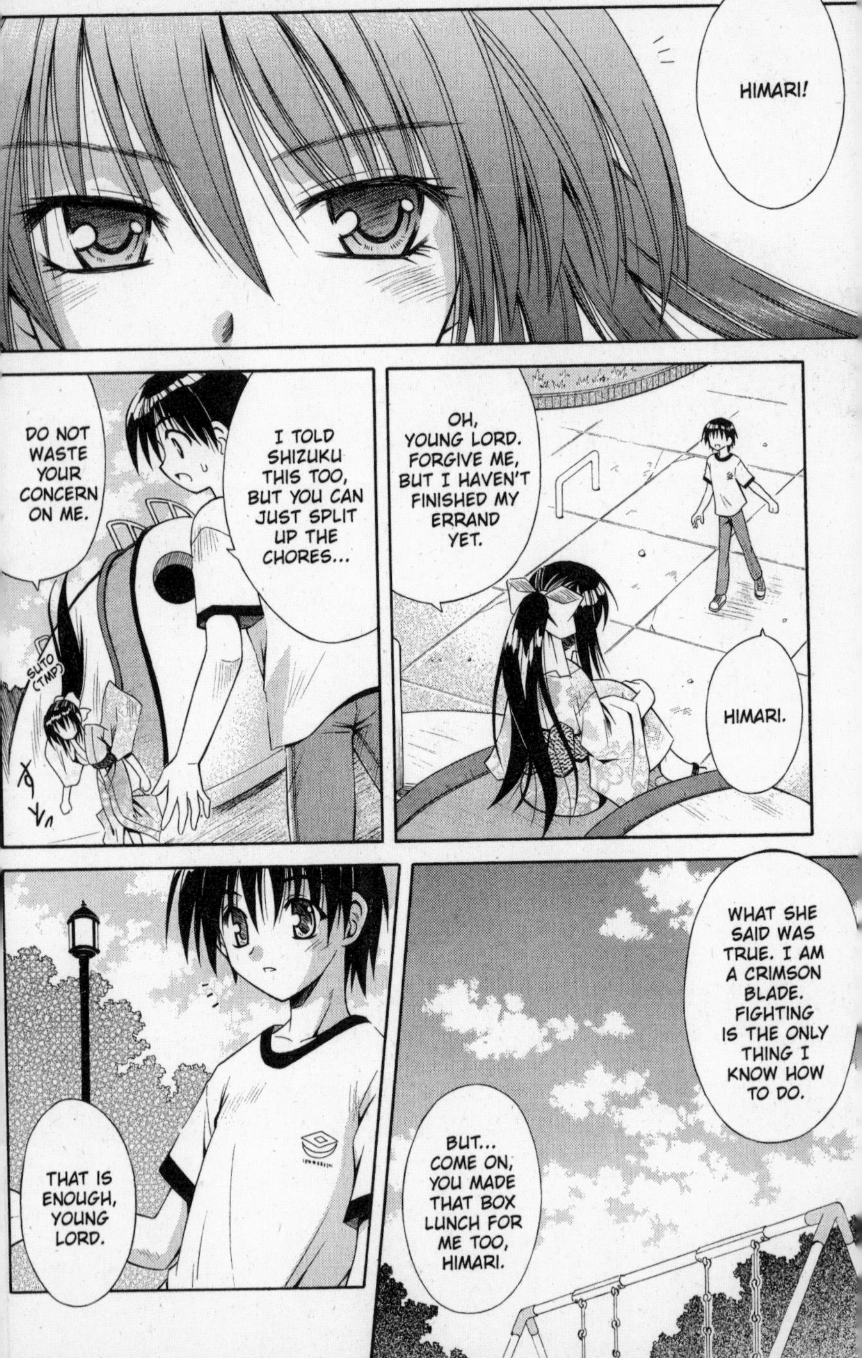
HIMARI!
OH, YOUNG LORD. FORGIVE ME, BUT I HAVEN'T FINISHED MY ERRAND YET.
HIMARI.
I TOLD SHIZUKU THIS TOO, BUT YOU CAN JUST SPLIT UP THE CHORES...
DO NOT WASTE YOUR CONCERN ON ME.
SUTO (TMP)
WHAT SHE SAID WAS TRUE. I AM A CRIMSON BLADE. FIGHTING IS THE ONLY THING I KNOW HOW TO DO.
BUT... COME ON, YOU MADE THAT BOX LUNCH FOR ME TOO, HIMARI.
THAT IS ENOUGH, YOUNG LORD.

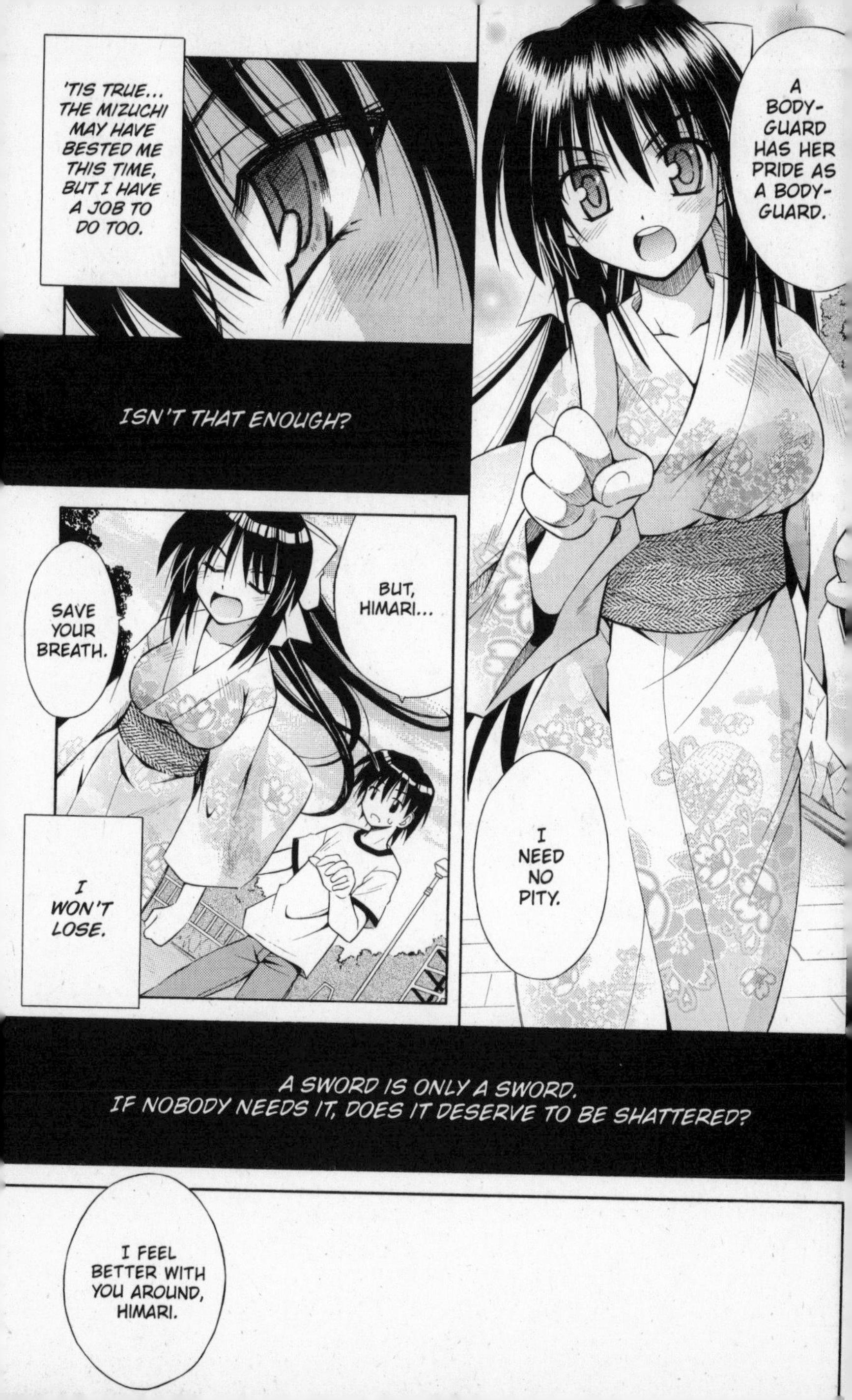

A BODY-GUARD HAS HER PRIDE AS A BODY-GUARD.
I NEED NO PITY.
'TIS TRUE... THE MIZUCHI MAY HAVE BESTED ME THIS TIME, BUT I HAVE A JOB TO DO TOO.
ISN'T THAT ENOUGH?
BUT, HIMARI...
SAVE YOUR BREATH.
I WON'T LOSE.
A SWORD IS ONLY A SWORD.
IF NOBODY NEEDS IT, DOES IT DESERVE TO BE SHATTERED?
I FEEL BETTER WITH YOU AROUND, HIMARI.

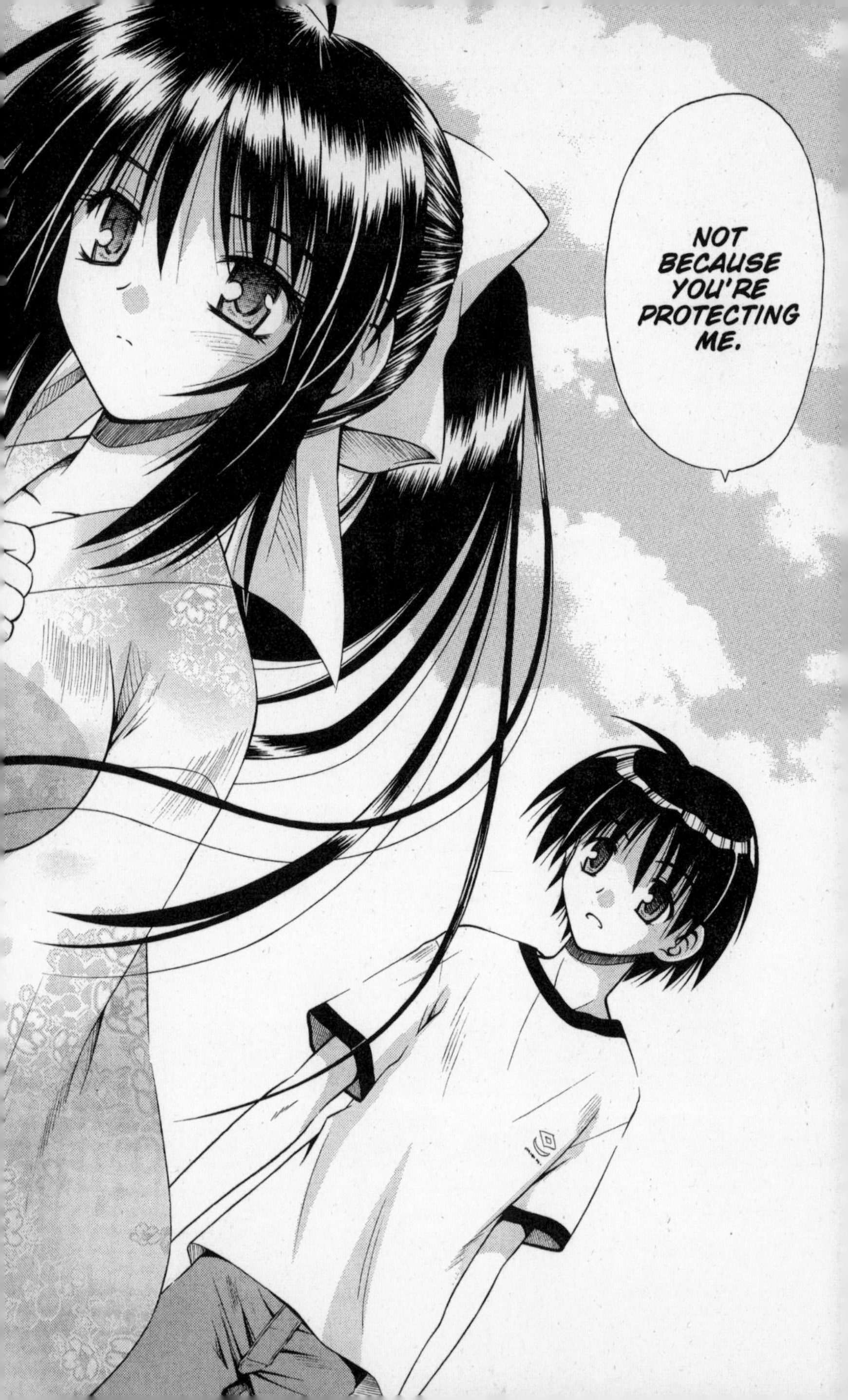
NOT BECAUSE YOU'RE PROTECTING ME.

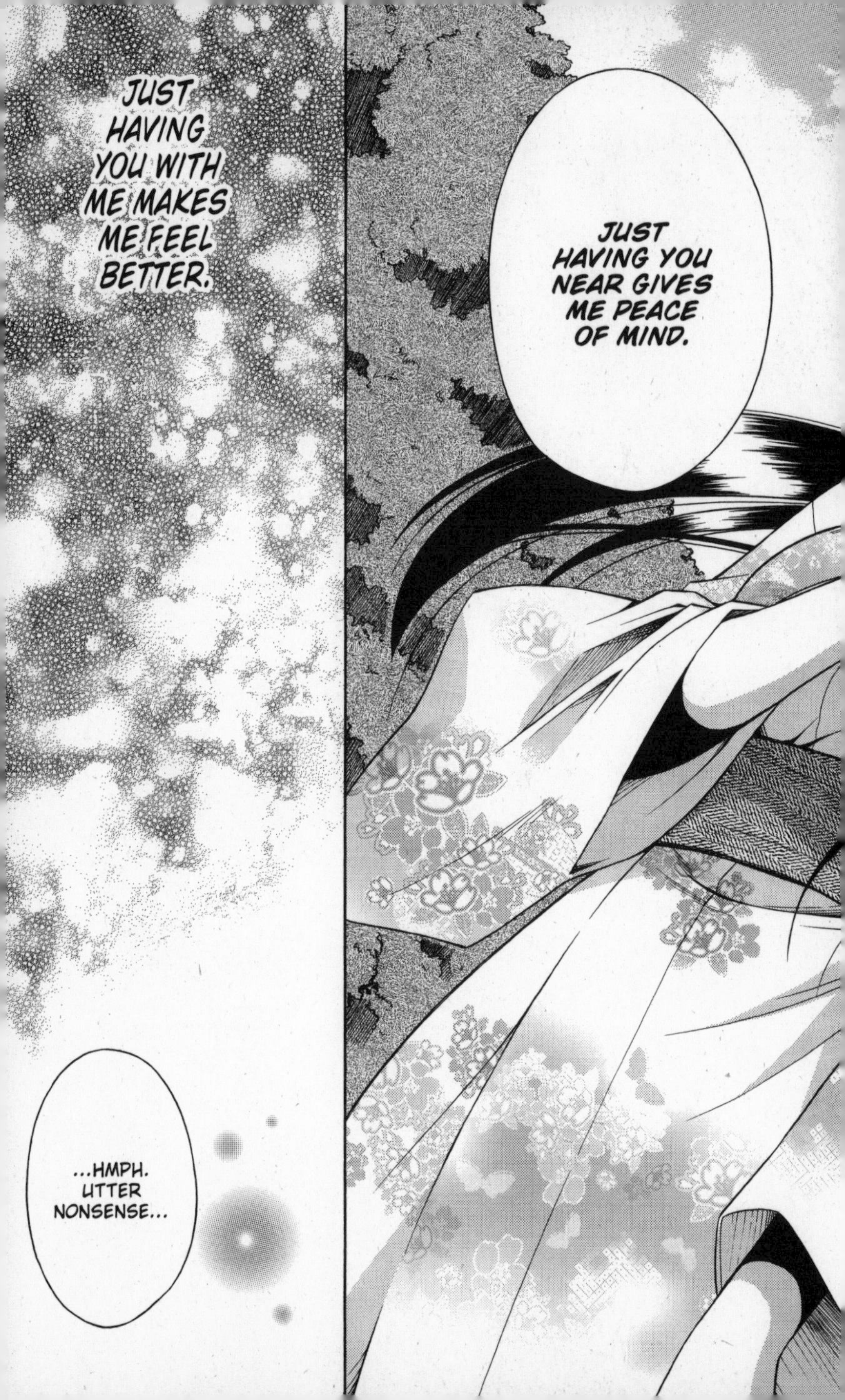
JUST HAVING YOU NEAR GIVES ME PEACE OF MIND.
JUST HAVING YOU WITH ME MAKES ME FEEL BETTER.
...HMPH. UTTER NONSENSE...

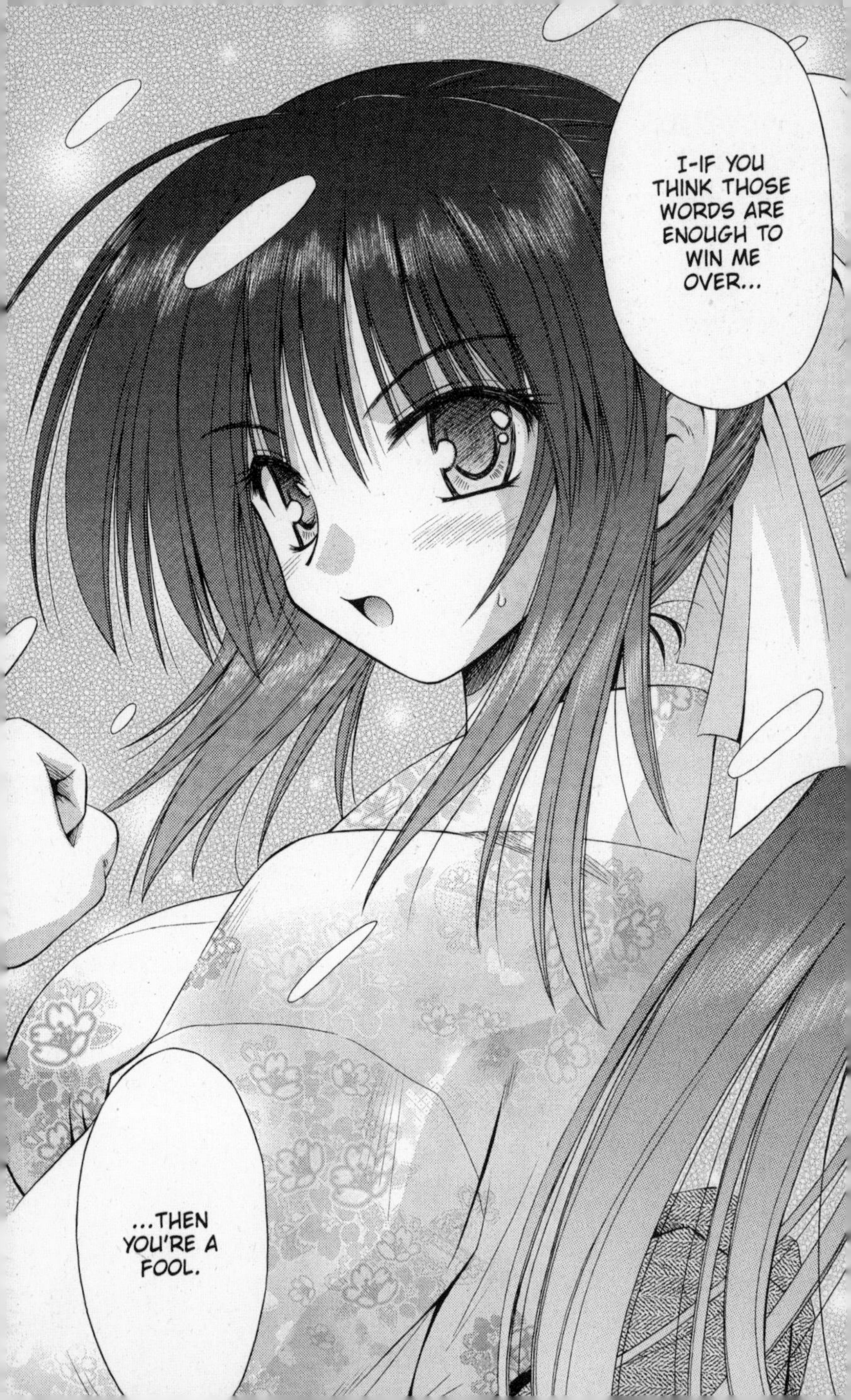
I-IF YOU THINK THOSE WORDS ARE ENOUGH TO WIN ME OVER...
...THEN YOU'RE A FOOL.

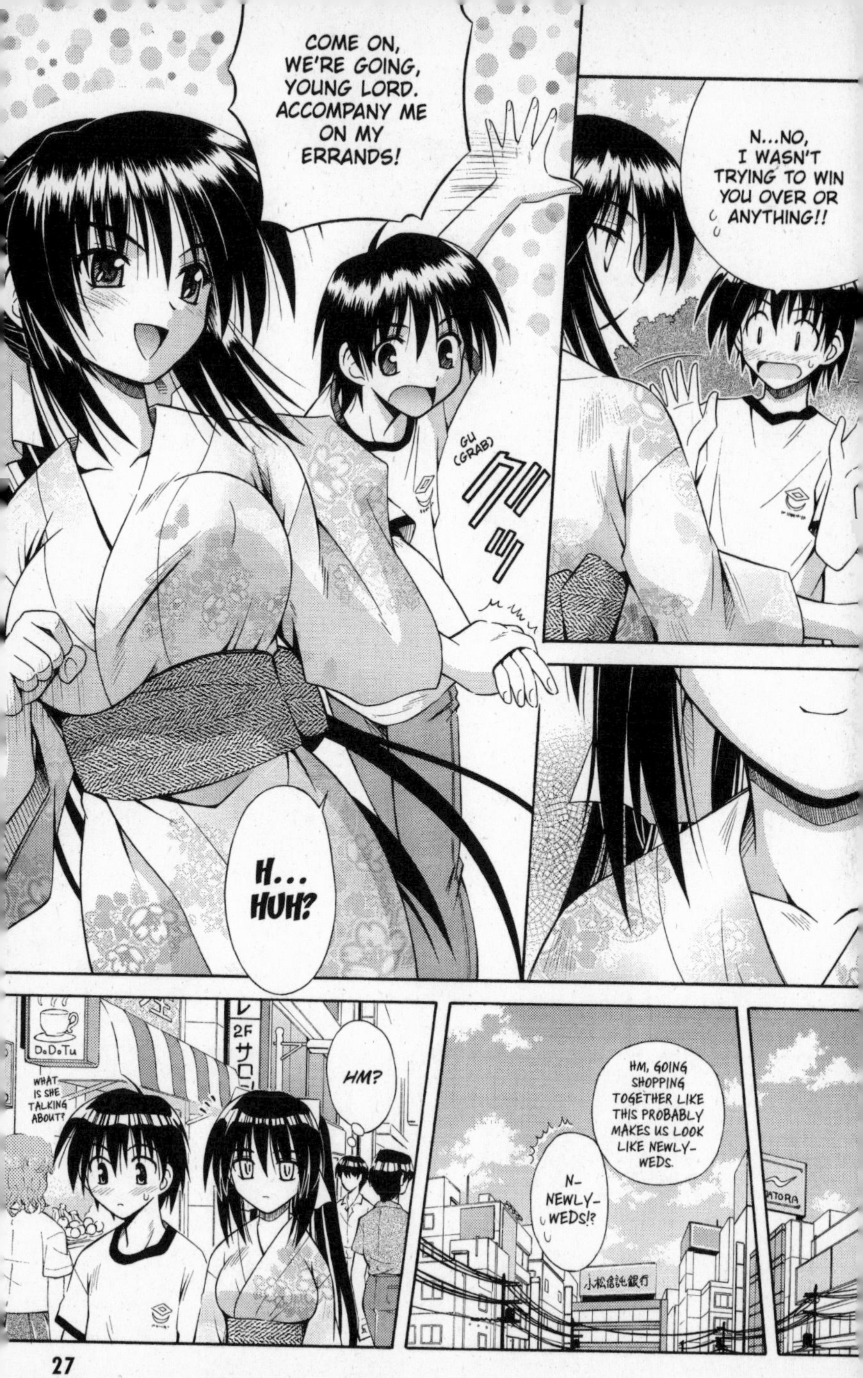
N...NO, I WASN'T TRYING TO WIN YOU OVER OR ANYTHING!!
COME ON, WE'RE GOING, YOUNG LORD. ACCOMPANY ME ON MY ERRANDS!
GU (GRAB)
H... HUH?
HM, GOING SHOPPING TOGETHER LIKE THIS PROBABLY MAKES US LOOK LIKE NEWLY-WEDS.
N-NEWLY-WEDS!?
HM?
WHAT IS SHE TALKING ABOUT?

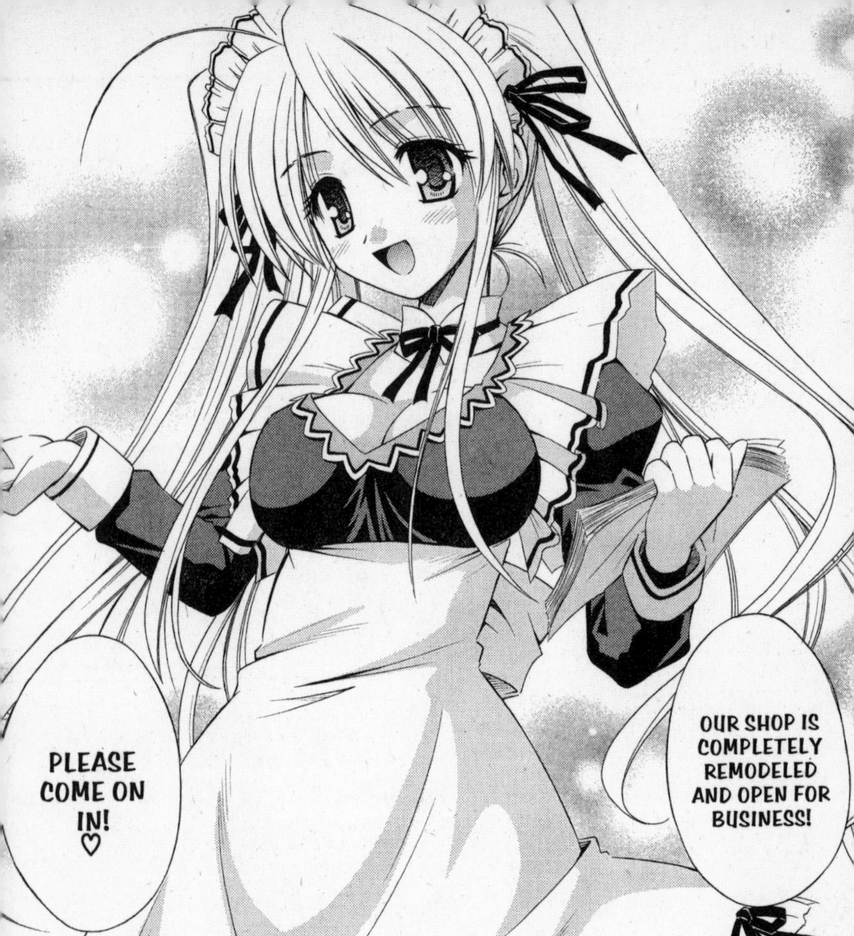
OUR SHOP IS COMPLETELY REMODELED AND OPEN FOR BUSINESS!
PLEASE COME ON IN! ♡

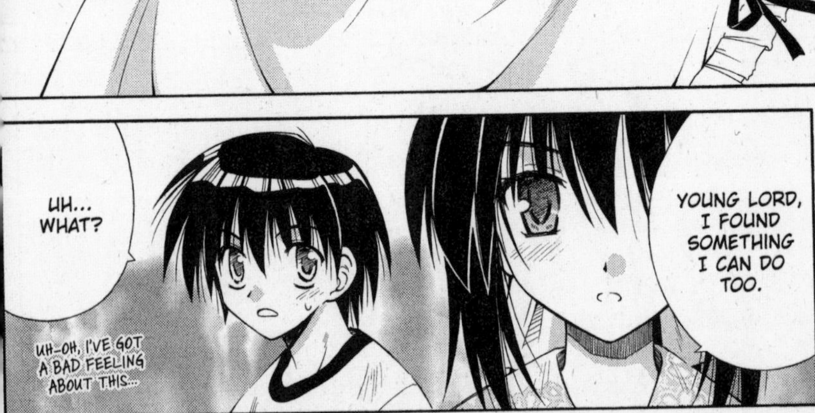
YOUNG LORD, I FOUND SOMETHING I CAN DO TOO.
UH... WHAT?
UH-OH, I'VE GOT A BAD FEELING ABOUT THIS...

MENAGERIE 8: MAID IN KITTY

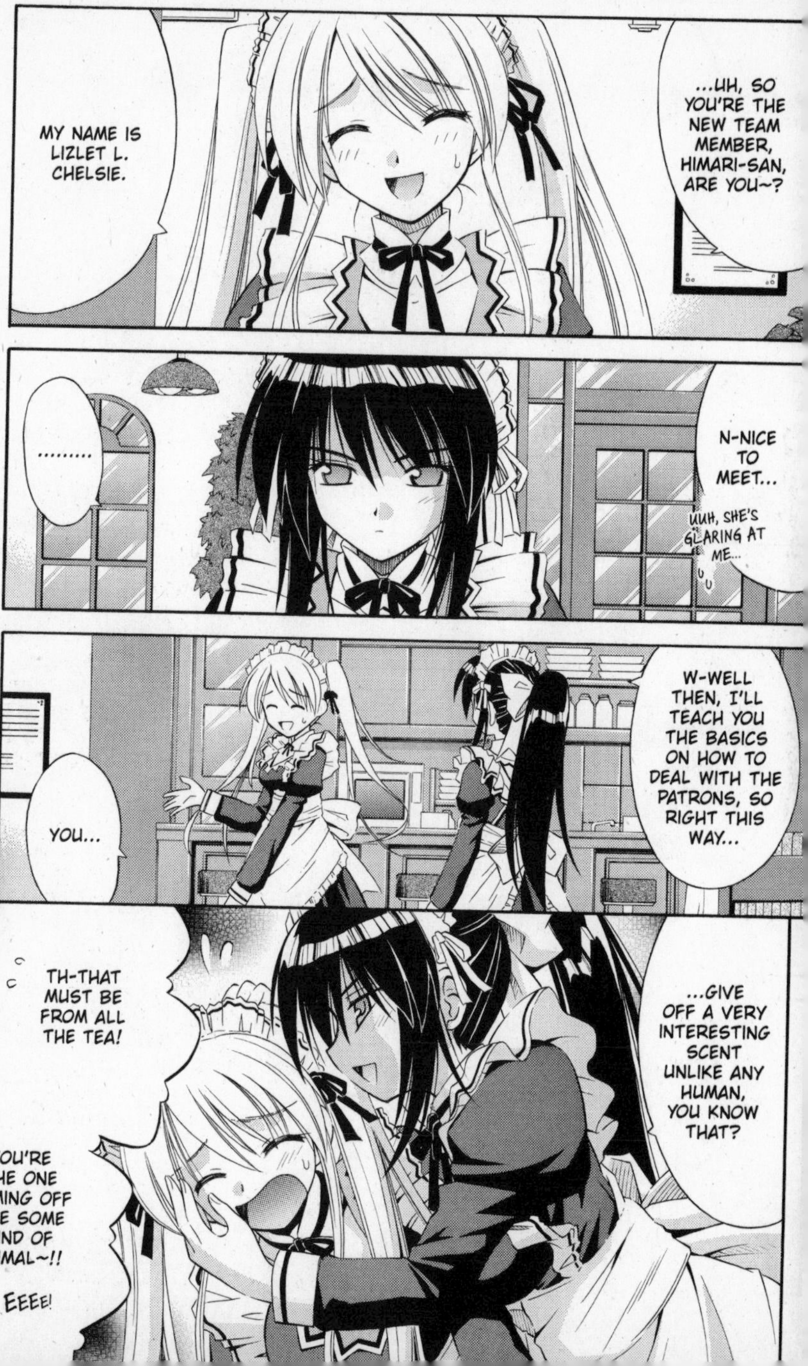
...UH, SO YOU'RE THE NEW TEAM MEMBER, HIMARI-SAN, ARE YOU~?
MY NAME IS LIZLET L. CHELSIE.
N-NICE TO MEET...
UUH, SHE'S GLARING AT ME...
....
W-WELL THEN, I'LL TEACH YOU THE BASICS ON HOW TO DEAL WITH THE PATRONS, SO RIGHT THIS WAY...
YOU...
...GIVE OFF A VERY INTERESTING SCENT UNLIKE ANY HUMAN, YOU KNOW THAT?
TH-THAT MUST BE FROM ALL THE TEA!
YOU'RE THE ONE COMING OFF LIKE SOME KIND OF ANIMAL~!!
EEEE!

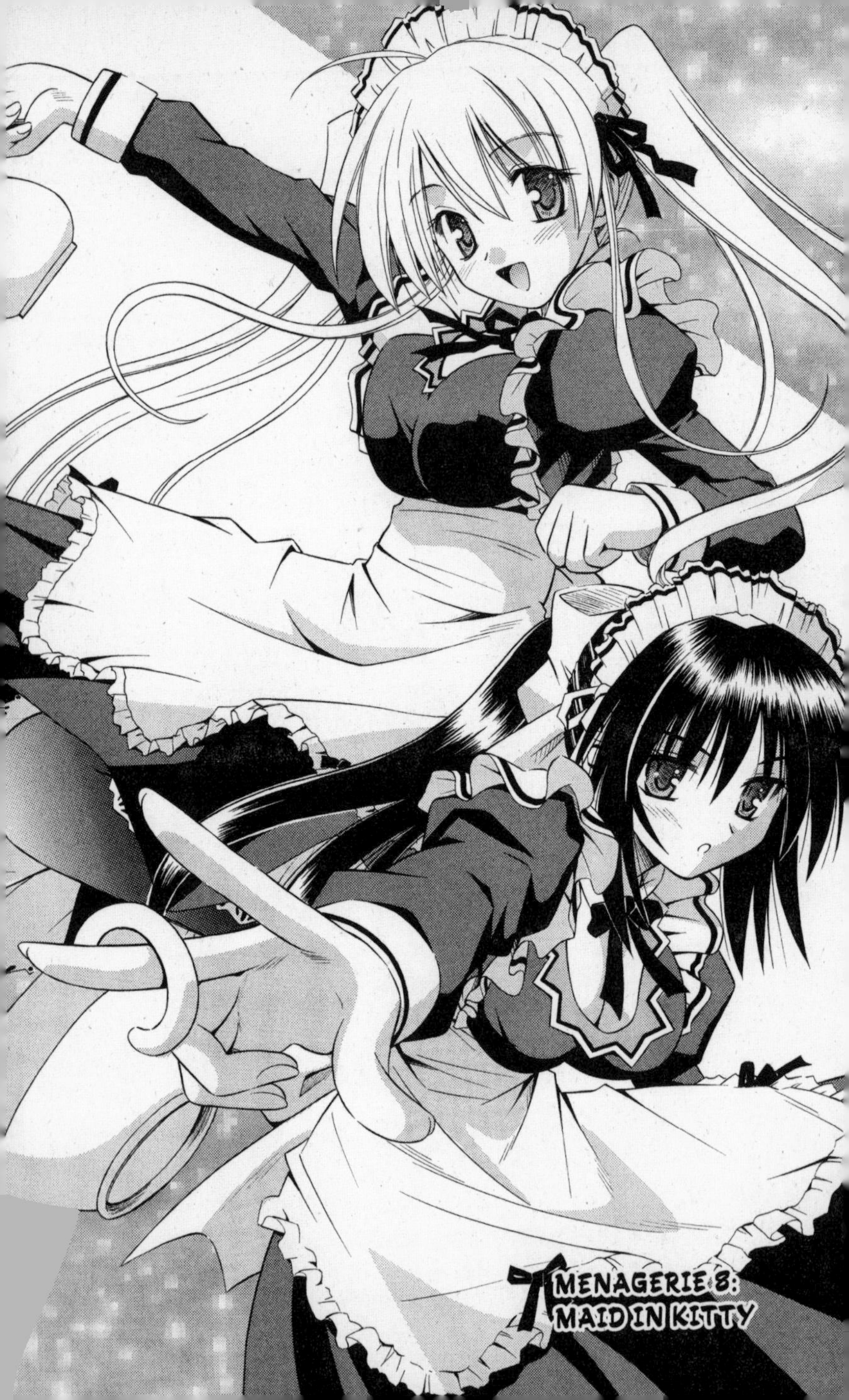
MENAGERIE 8:
MAID IN KITTY

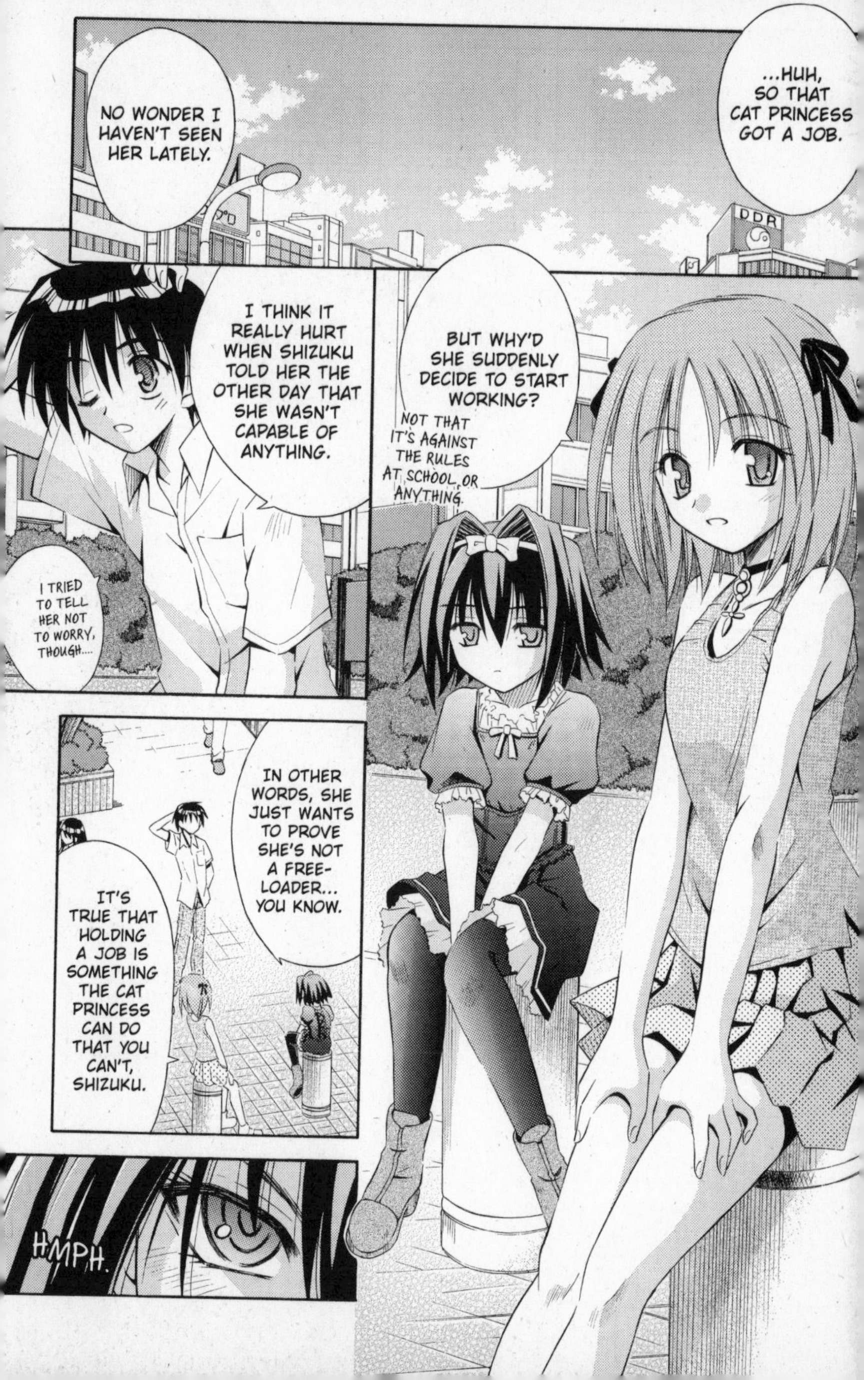
...HUH, SO THAT CAT PRINCESS GOT A JOB.
NO WONDER I HAVEN'T SEEN HER LATELY.
BUT WHY'D SHE SUDDENLY DECIDE TO START WORKING?
NOT THAT IT'S AGAINST THE RULES AT SCHOOL OR ANYTHING.
I THINK IT REALLY HURT WHEN SHIZUKU TOLD HER THE OTHER DAY THAT SHE WASN'T CAPABLE OF ANYTHING.
I TRIED TO TELL HER NOT TO WORRY, THOUGH....
IN OTHER WORDS, SHE JUST WANTS TO PROVE SHE'S NOT A FREE-LOADER... YOU KNOW.
IT'S TRUE THAT HOLDING A JOB IS SOMETHING THE CAT PRINCESS CAN DO THAT YOU CAN'T, SHIZUKU.
HMPH.

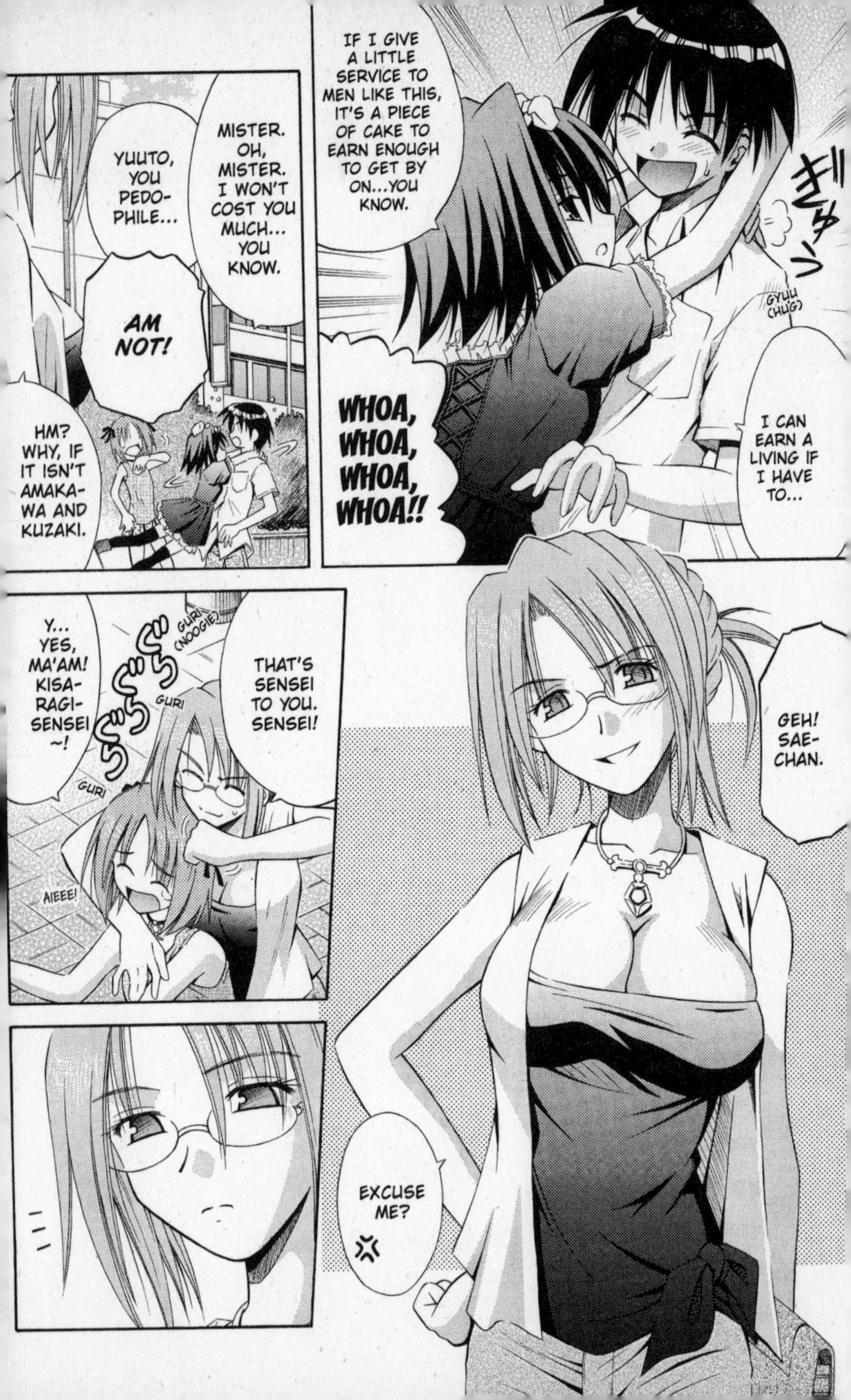
IF I GIVE A LITTLE SERVICE TO MEN LIKE THIS, IT'S A PIECE OF CAKE TO EARN ENOUGH TO GET BY ON...YOU KNOW.
GYUU (HUG)
I CAN EARN A LIVING IF I HAVE TO...
WHOA, WHOA, WHOA, WHOA!!
MISTER. OH, MISTER. I WON'T COST YOU MUCH... YOU KNOW.
YUUTO, YOU PEDO-PHILE...
AM NOT!
HM? WHY, IF IT ISN'T AMAKAWA AND KUZAKI.
GEH! SAE-CHAN.
EXCUSE ME?
THAT'S SENSEI TO YOU. SENSEI!
GURI (NOOGIE)
GURI
GURI
Y... YES, MA'AM! KISARAGI-SENSEI ~!
AIEEE!

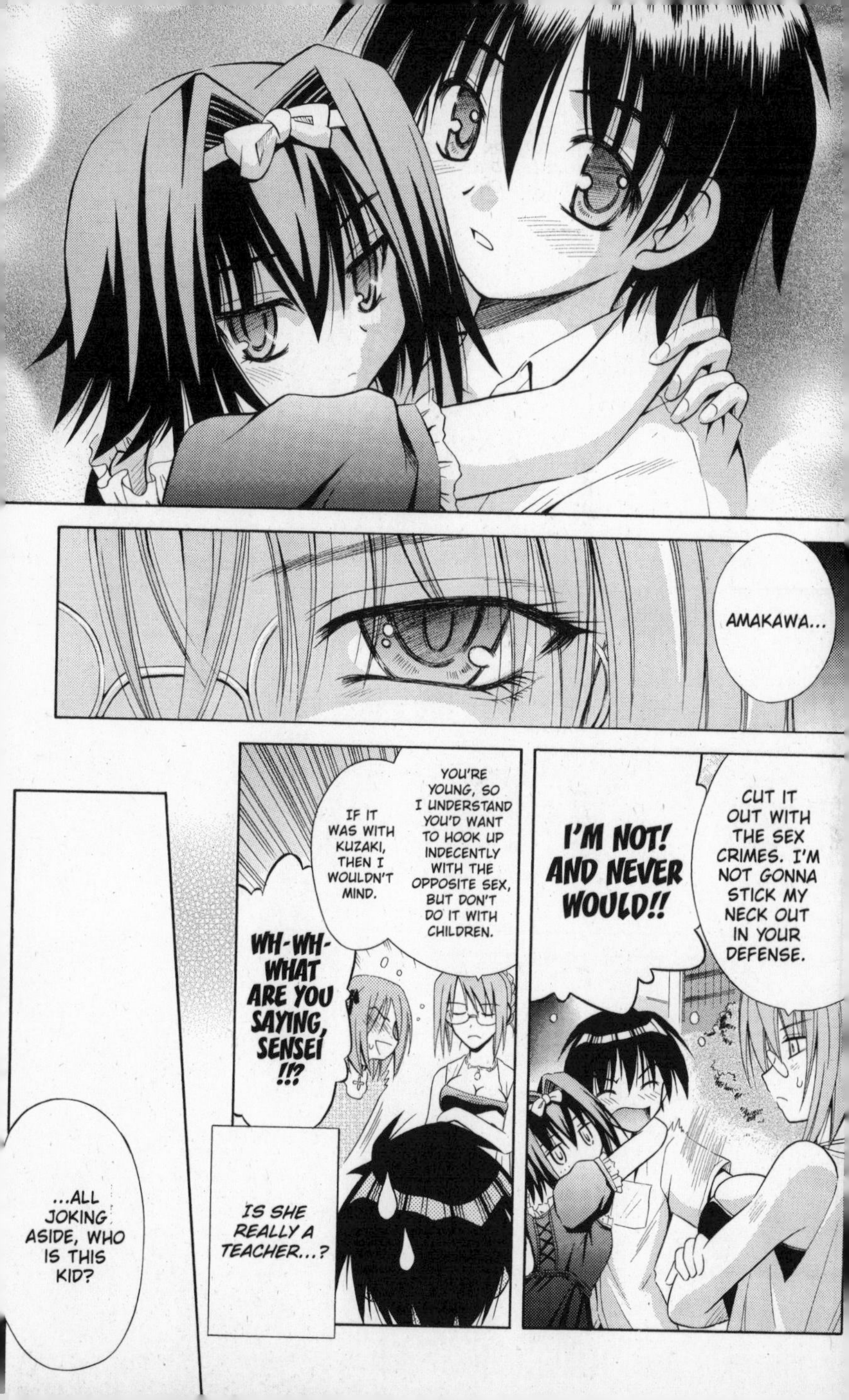
AMAKAWA...
CUT IT OUT WITH THE SEX CRIMES. I'M NOT GONNA STICK MY NECK OUT IN YOUR DEFENSE.
I'M NOT! AND NEVER WOULD!!
YOU'RE YOUNG, SO I UNDERSTAND YOU'D WANT TO HOOK UP INDECENTLY WITH THE OPPOSITE SEX, BUT DON'T DO IT WITH CHILDREN.
IF IT WAS WITH KUZAKI, THEN I WOULDN'T MIND.
WH-WH-WHAT ARE YOU SAYING, SENSEI !!?
IS SHE REALLY A TEACHER...?
...ALL JOKING ASIDE, WHO IS THIS KID?

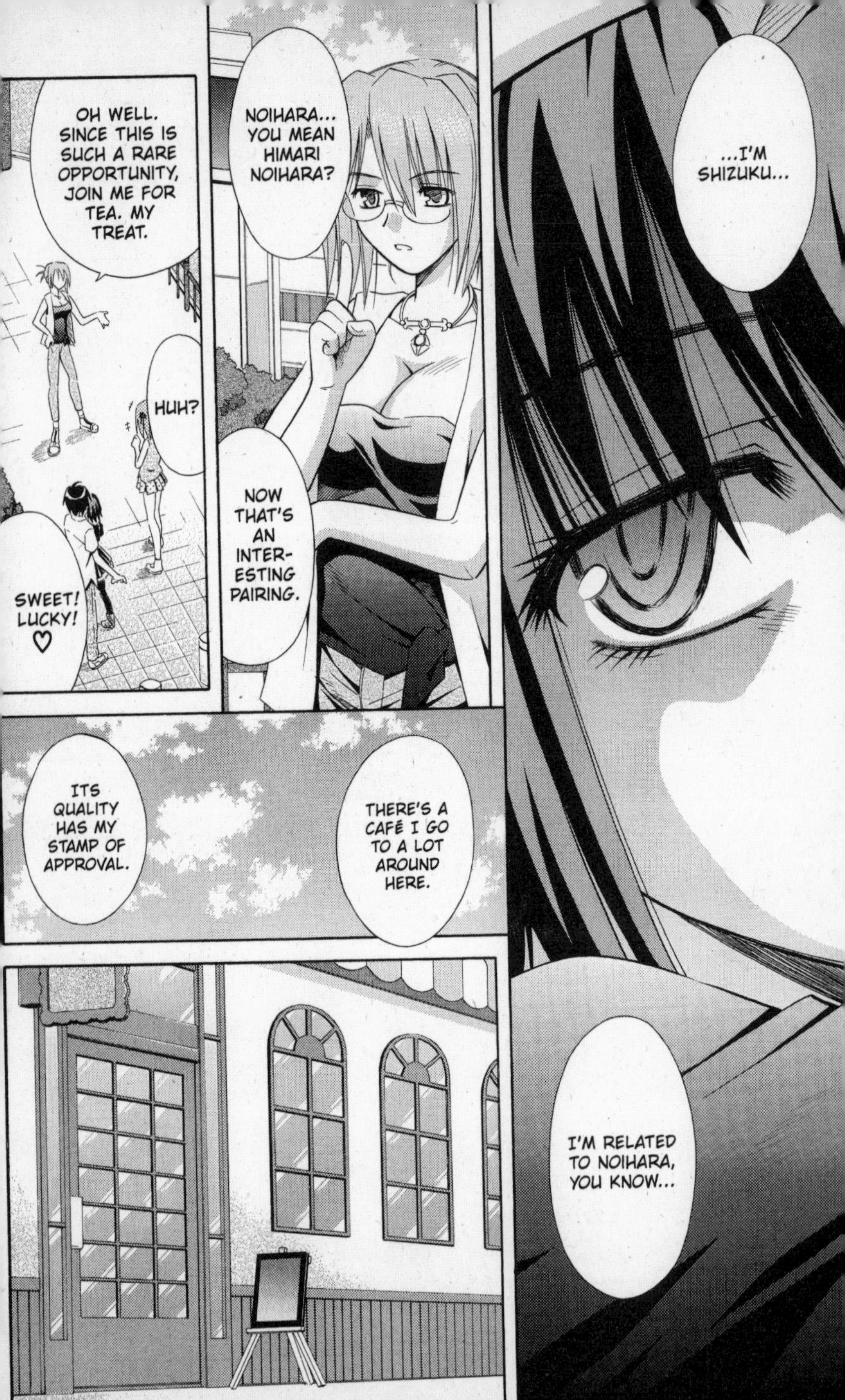
...I'M SHIZUKU...
I'M RELATED TO NOIHARA, YOU KNOW...
NOIHARA... YOU MEAN HIMARI NOIHARA?
NOW THAT'S AN INTERESTING PAIRING.
OH WELL. SINCE THIS IS SUCH A RARE OPPORTUNITY, JOIN ME FOR TEA. MY TREAT.
HUH?
SWEET! LUCKY! ♡
THERE'S A CAFÉ I GO TO A LOT AROUND HERE.
ITS QUALITY HAS MY STAMP OF APPROVAL.

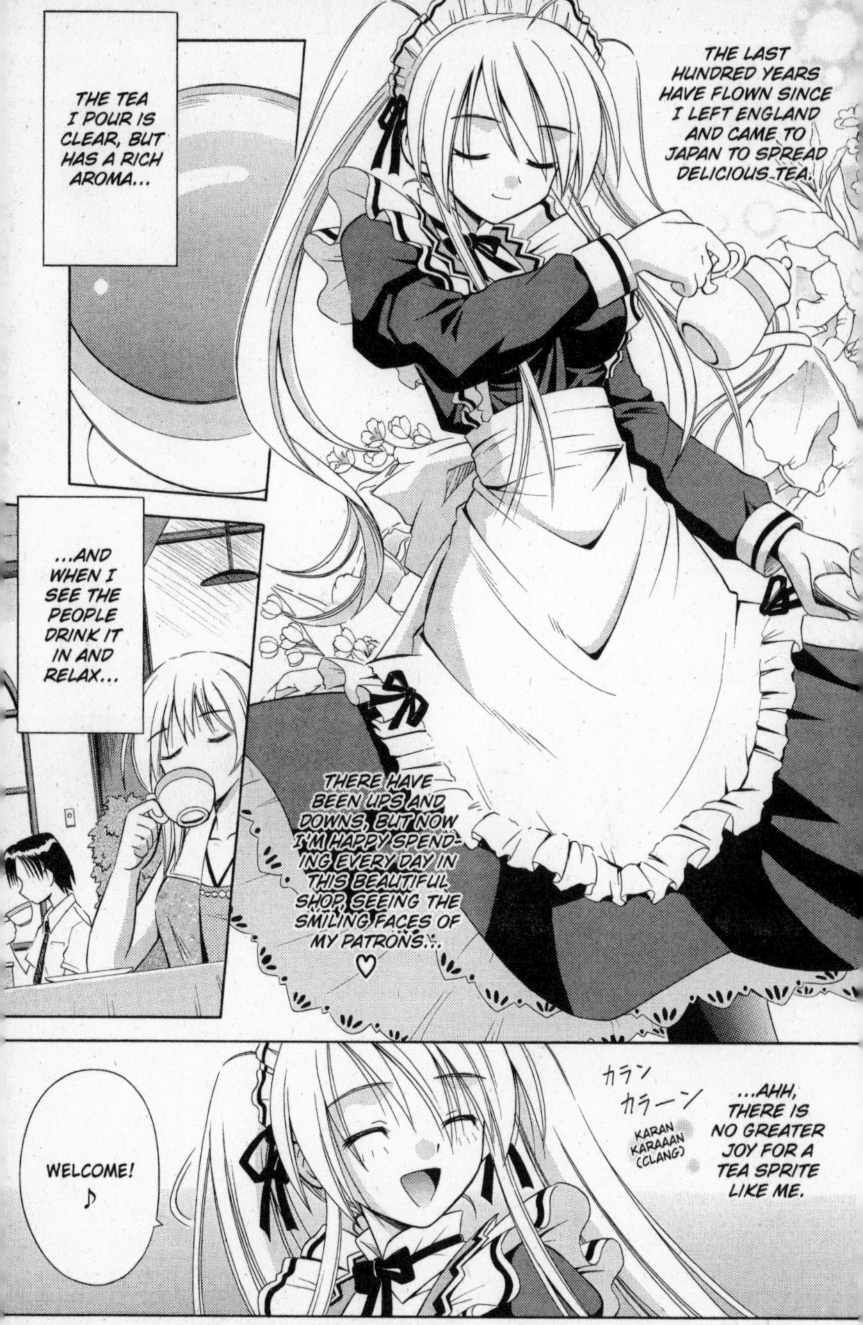
THE LAST HUNDRED YEARS HAVE FLOWN SINCE I LEFT ENGLAND AND CAME TO JAPAN TO SPREAD DELICIOUS TEA.
THERE HAVE BEEN UPS AND DOWNS, BUT NOW I'M HAPPY SPENDING EVERY DAY IN THIS BEAUTIFUL SHOP, SEEING THE SMILING FACES OF MY PATRONS... ♡
THE TEA I POUR IS CLEAR, BUT HAS A RICH AROMA...
...AND WHEN I SEE THE PEOPLE DRINK IT IN AND RELAX...
カラン カラーン
KARAN KARAAAN (CLANG)
...AHH, THERE IS NO GREATER JOY FOR A TEA SPRITE LIKE ME.
WELCOME! ♪

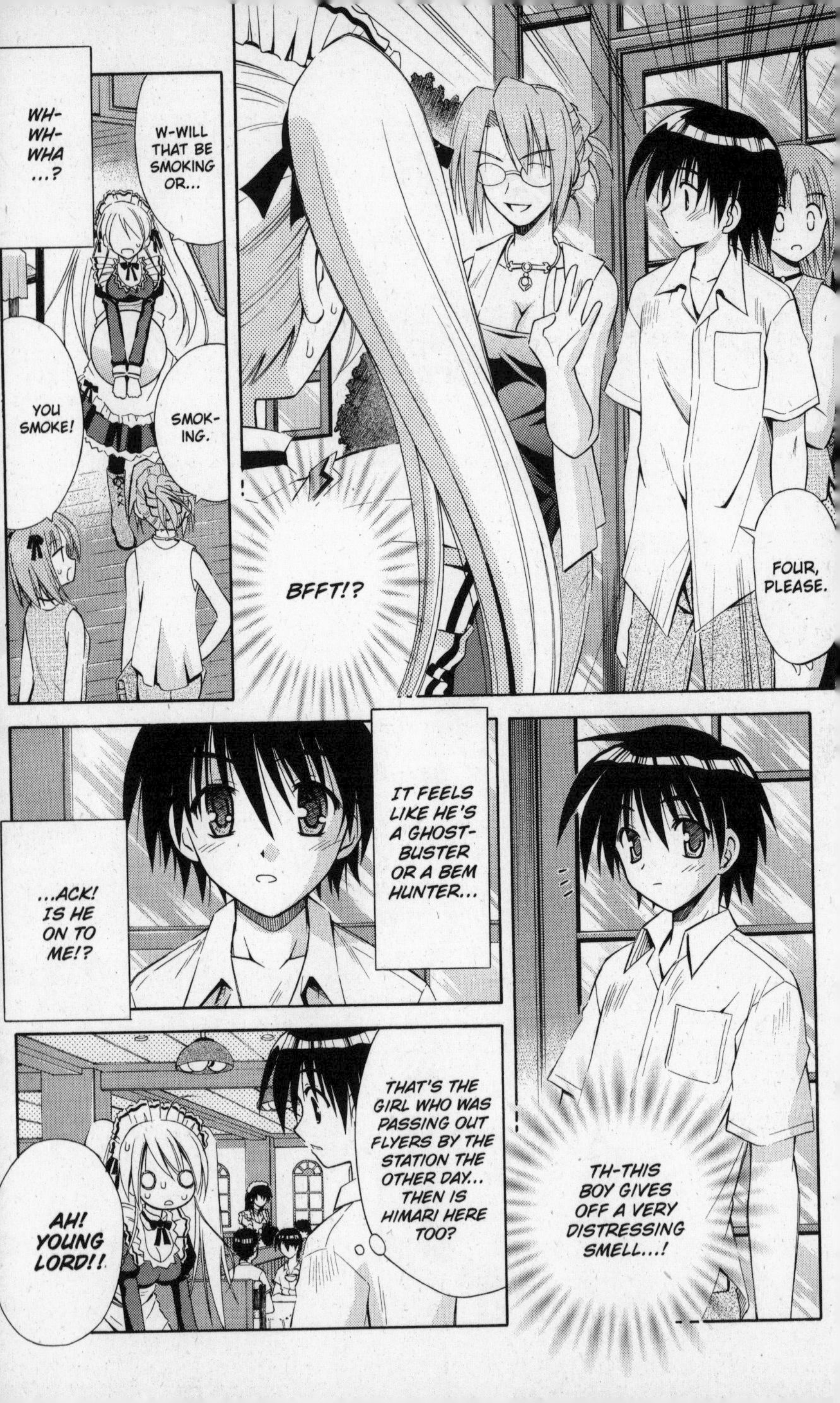
FOUR, PLEASE.
BFFT!?
W-WILL THAT BE SMOKING OR...
WH-WH-WHA ...?
SMOK-ING.
YOU SMOKE!
TH-THIS BOY GIVES OFF A VERY DISTRESSING SMELL...!
IT FEELS LIKE HE'S A GHOST-BUSTER OR A BEM HUNTER...
...ACK! IS HE ON TO ME!?
THAT'S THE GIRL WHO WAS PASSING OUT FLYERS BY THE STATION THE OTHER DAY... THEN IS HIMARI HERE TOO?
AH! YOUNG LORD!!

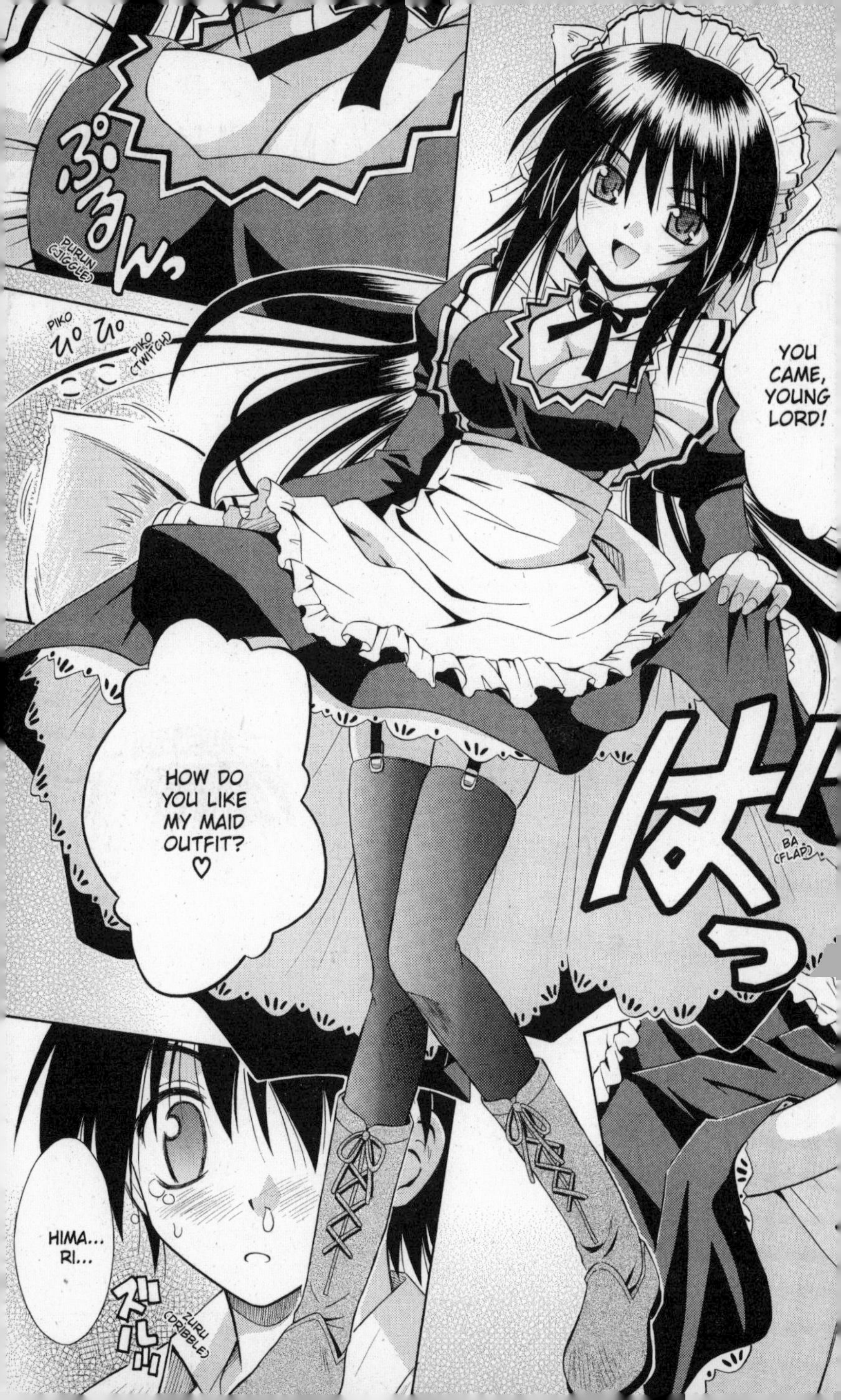
YOU CAME, YOUNG LORD!
HOW DO YOU LIKE MY MAID OUTFIT? ♡
BA (FLAP)
PURUN (JIGGLE)
PIKO PIKO (TWITCH)
HIMA... RI...
ZURU (DRIBBLE)

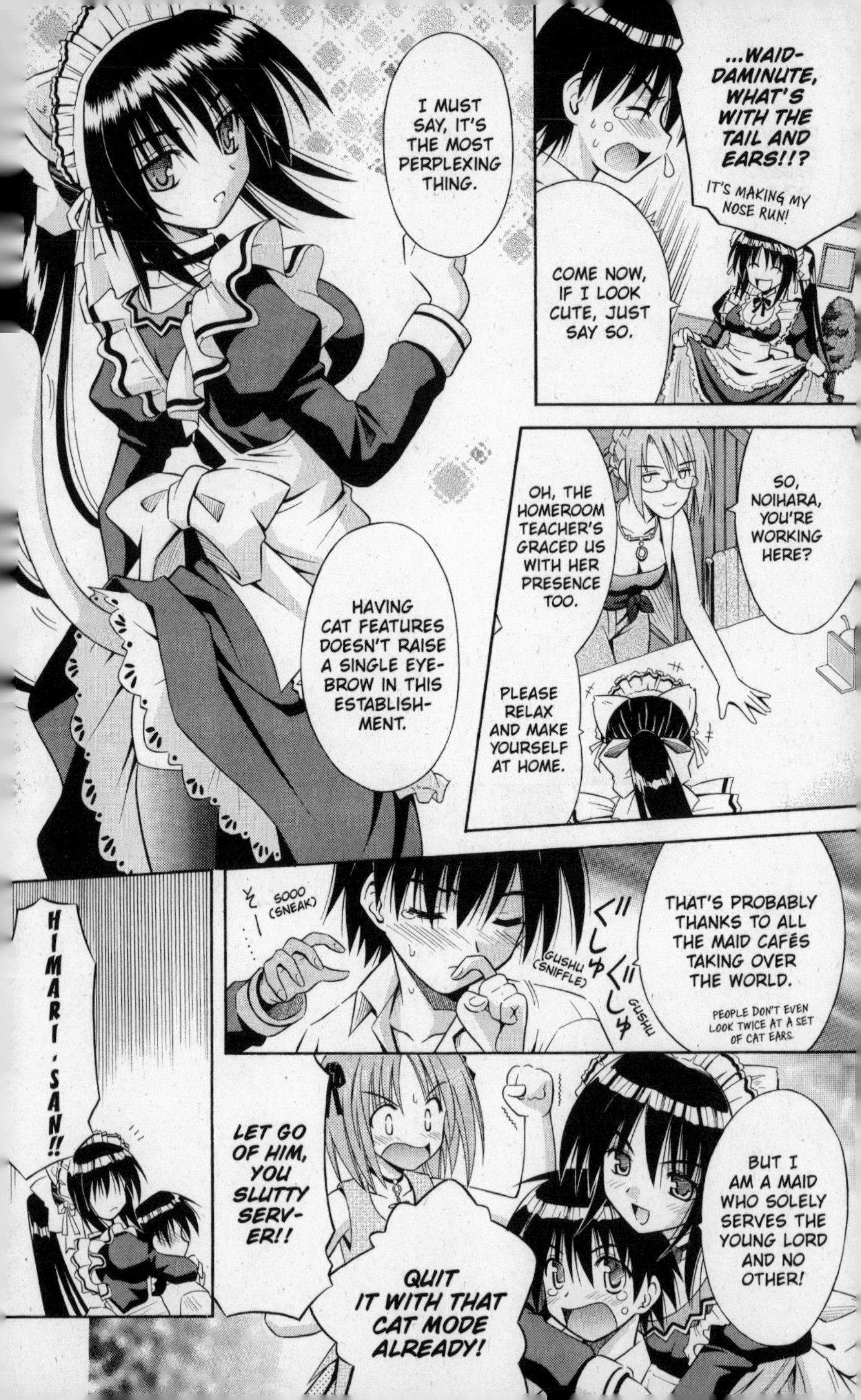
...WAID-DAMINUTE, WHAT'S WITH THE TAIL AND EARS!!?
IT'S MAKING MY NOSE RUN!
COME NOW, IF I LOOK CUTE, JUST SAY SO.
SO, NOIHARA, YOU'RE WORKING HERE?
OH, THE HOMEROOM TEACHER'S GRACED US WITH HER PRESENCE TOO.
PLEASE RELAX AND MAKE YOURSELF AT HOME.
I MUST SAY, IT'S THE MOST PERPLEXING THING.
HAVING CAT FEATURES DOESN'T RAISE A SINGLE EYE-BROW IN THIS ESTABLISH-MENT.
THAT'S PROBABLY THANKS TO ALL THE MAID CAFÉS TAKING OVER THE WORLD.
PEOPLE DON'T EVEN LOOK TWICE AT A SET OF CAT EARS.
GUSHU
GUSHU (SNIFFLE)
SOOO (SNEAK)
BUT I AM A MAID WHO SOLELY SERVES THE YOUNG LORD AND NO OTHER!
LET GO OF HIM, YOU SLUTTY SERV-ER!!
QUIT IT WITH THAT CAT MODE ALREADY!
HIMARI-SAN!!

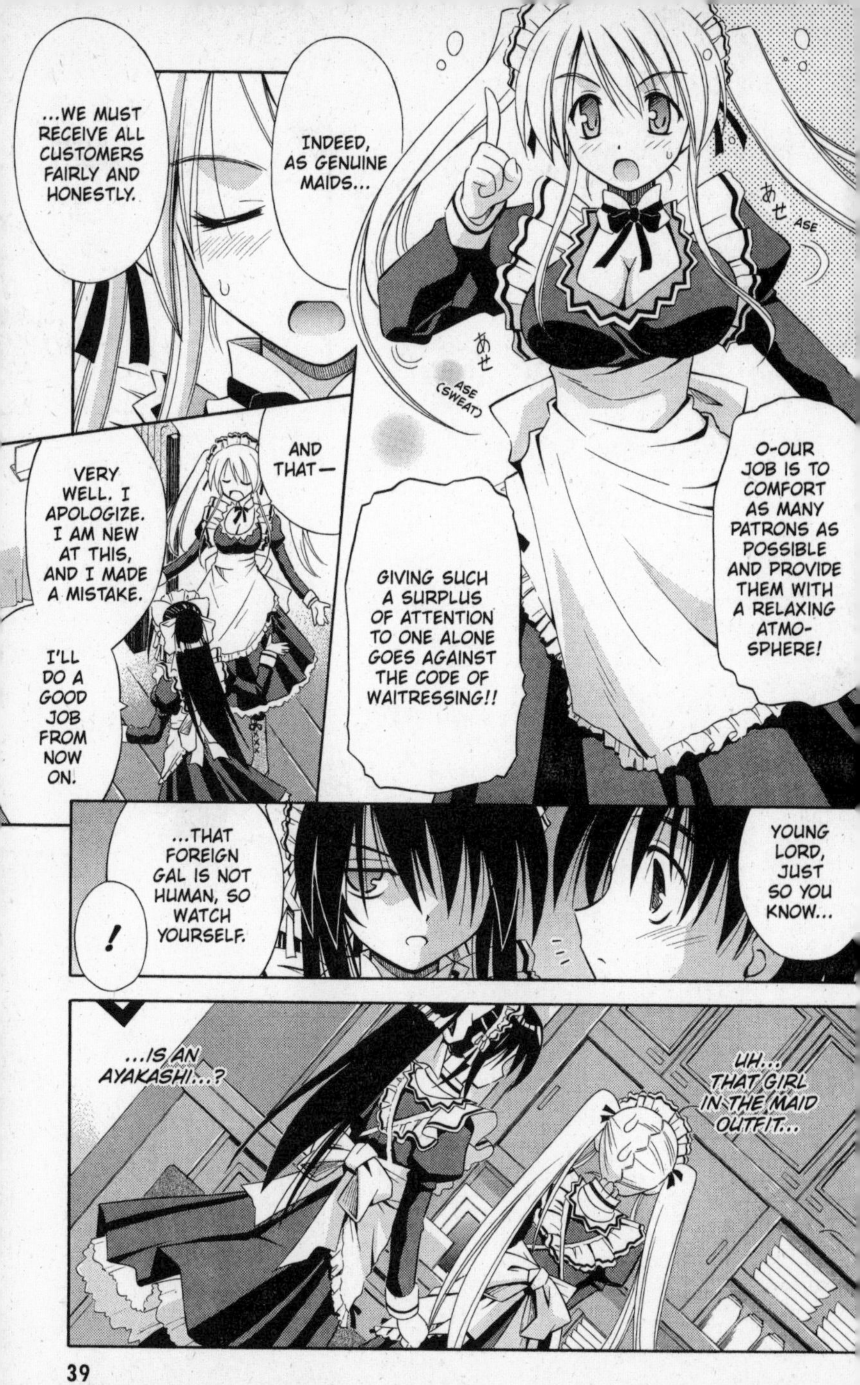
INDEED, AS GENUINE MAIDS...
...WE MUST RECEIVE ALL CUSTOMERS FAIRLY AND HONESTLY.
あせ ASE
あせ ASE (SWEAT)
AND THAT—
GIVING SUCH A SURPLUS OF ATTENTION TO ONE ALONE GOES AGAINST THE CODE OF WAITRESSING!!
O-OUR JOB IS TO COMFORT AS MANY PATRONS AS POSSIBLE AND PROVIDE THEM WITH A RELAXING ATMO-SPHERE!
VERY WELL. I APOLOGIZE. I AM NEW AT THIS, AND I MADE A MISTAKE.
I'LL DO A GOOD JOB FROM NOW ON.
YOUNG LORD, JUST SO YOU KNOW...
...THAT FOREIGN GAL IS NOT HUMAN, SO WATCH YOURSELF.
!
UH... THAT GIRL IN THE MAID OUTFIT...
...IS AN AYAKASHI...?

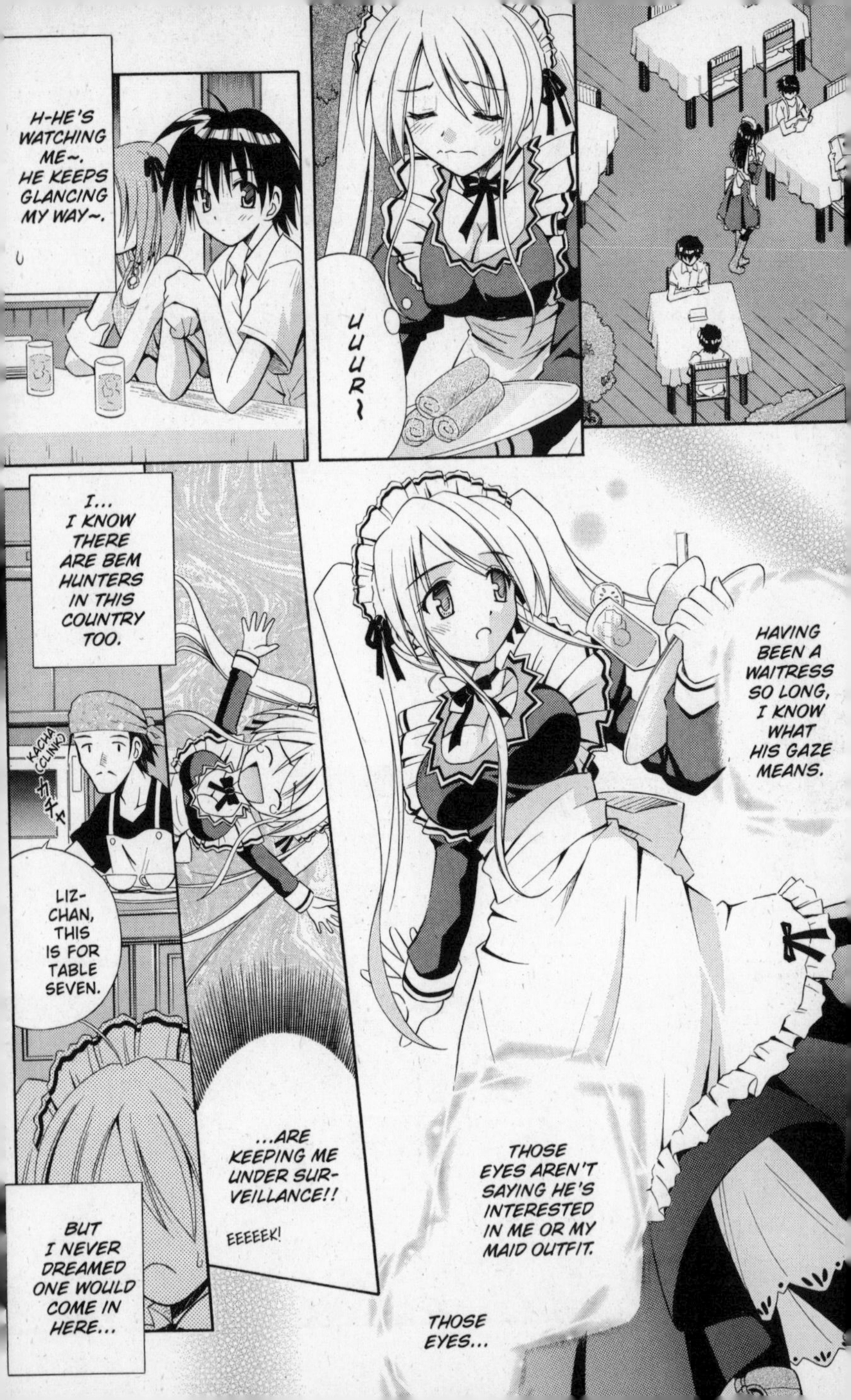
UUURI~
H-HE'S WATCHING ME~. HE KEEPS GLANCING MY WAY~.
HAVING BEEN A WAITRESS SO LONG, I KNOW WHAT HIS GAZE MEANS.
THOSE EYES AREN'T SAYING HE'S INTERESTED IN ME OR MY MAID OUTFIT.
THOSE EYES...
I... I KNOW THERE ARE BEM HUNTERS IN THIS COUNTRY TOO.
KACHA (CLINK)
LIZ-CHAN, THIS IS FOR TABLE SEVEN.
...ARE KEEPING ME UNDER SUR-VEILLANCE!!
EEEEEK!
BUT I NEVER DREAMED ONE WOULD COME IN HERE...

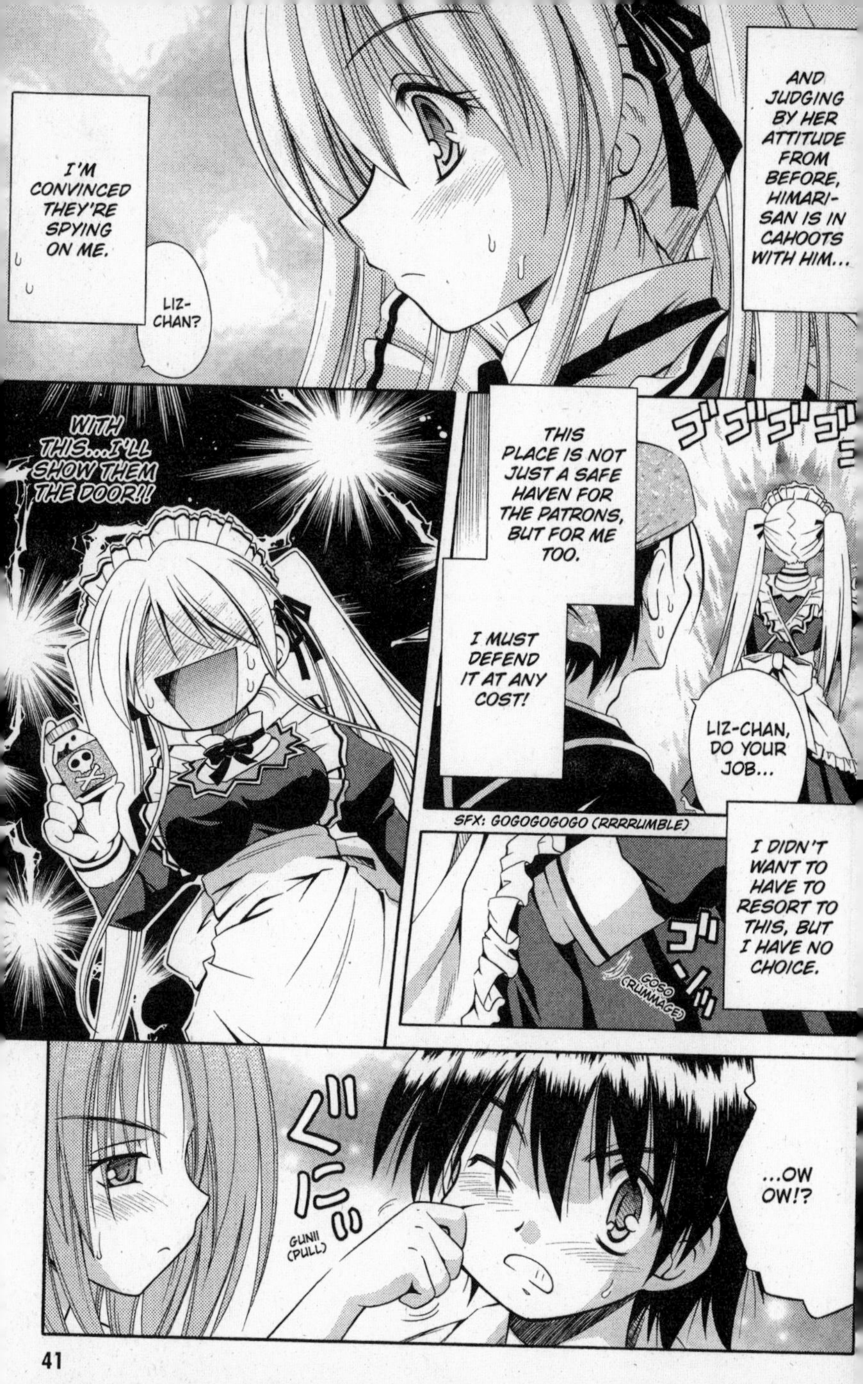
AND JUDGING BY HER ATTITUDE FROM BEFORE, HIMARI-SAN IS IN CAHOOTS WITH HIM...
I'M CONVINCED THEY'RE SPYING ON ME.
LIZ-CHAN?
THIS PLACE IS NOT JUST A SAFE HAVEN FOR THE PATRONS, BUT FOR ME TOO.
I MUST DEFEND IT AT ANY COST!
LIZ-CHAN, DO YOUR JOB...
SFX: GOGOGOGOGO (RRRRUMBLE)
I DIDN'T WANT TO HAVE TO RESORT TO THIS, BUT I HAVE NO CHOICE.
GOSO (RUMMAGE)
WITH THIS...I'LL SHOW THEM THE DOOR!!
...OW OW!?
GUNII (PULL)

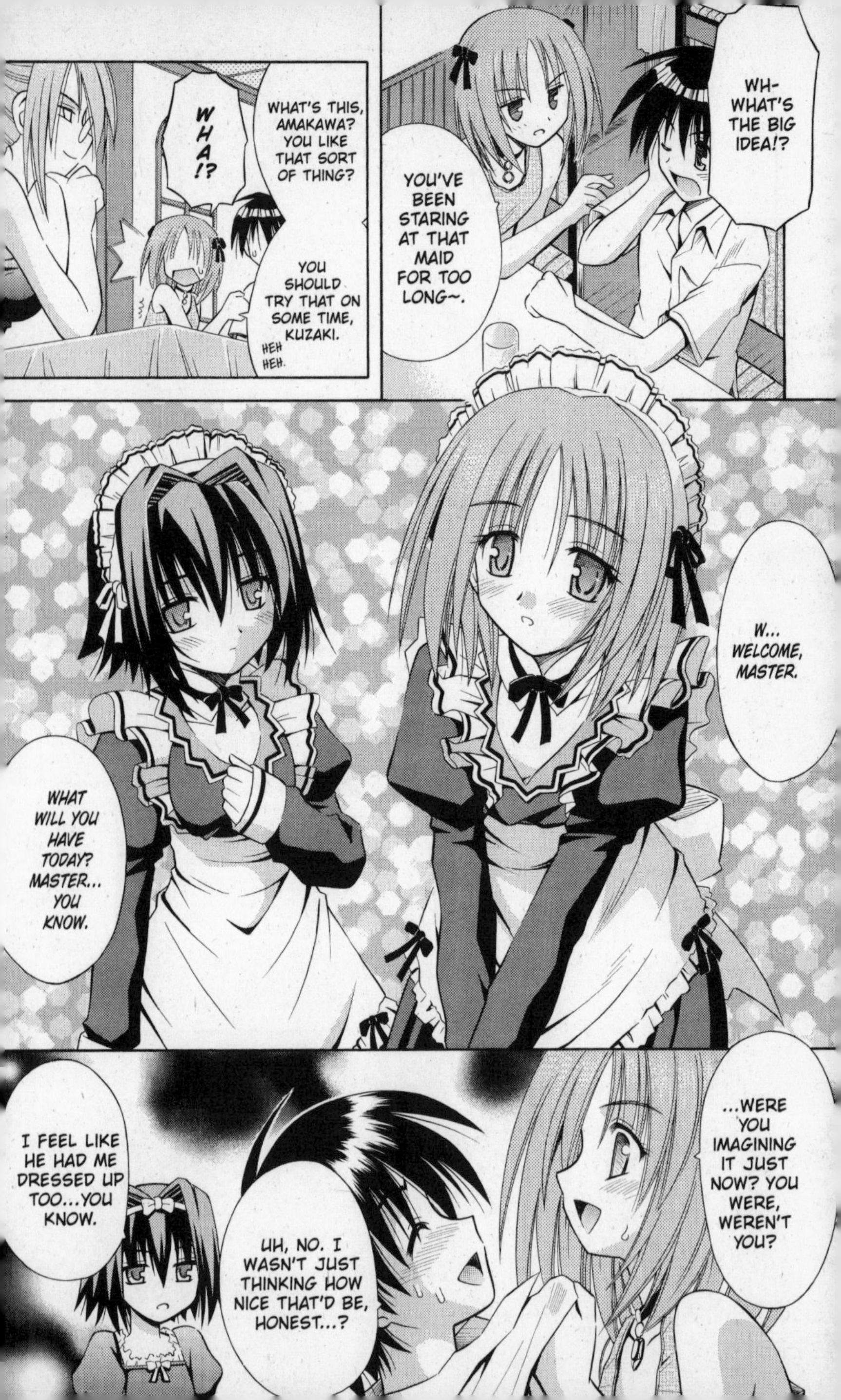

WH-WHAT'S THE BIG IDEA!?
YOU'VE BEEN STARING AT THAT MAID FOR TOO LONG~.
WHAT'S THIS, AMAKAWA? YOU LIKE THAT SORT OF THING?
WHA!?
YOU SHOULD TRY THAT ON SOME TIME, KUZAKI.
HEH HEH.
W... WELCOME, MASTER.
WHAT WILL YOU HAVE TODAY? MASTER... YOU KNOW.
...WERE YOU IMAGINING IT JUST NOW? YOU WERE, WEREN'T YOU?
UH, NO. I WASN'T JUST THINKING HOW NICE THAT'D BE, HONEST...?
I FEEL LIKE HE HAD ME DRESSED UP TOO...YOU KNOW.

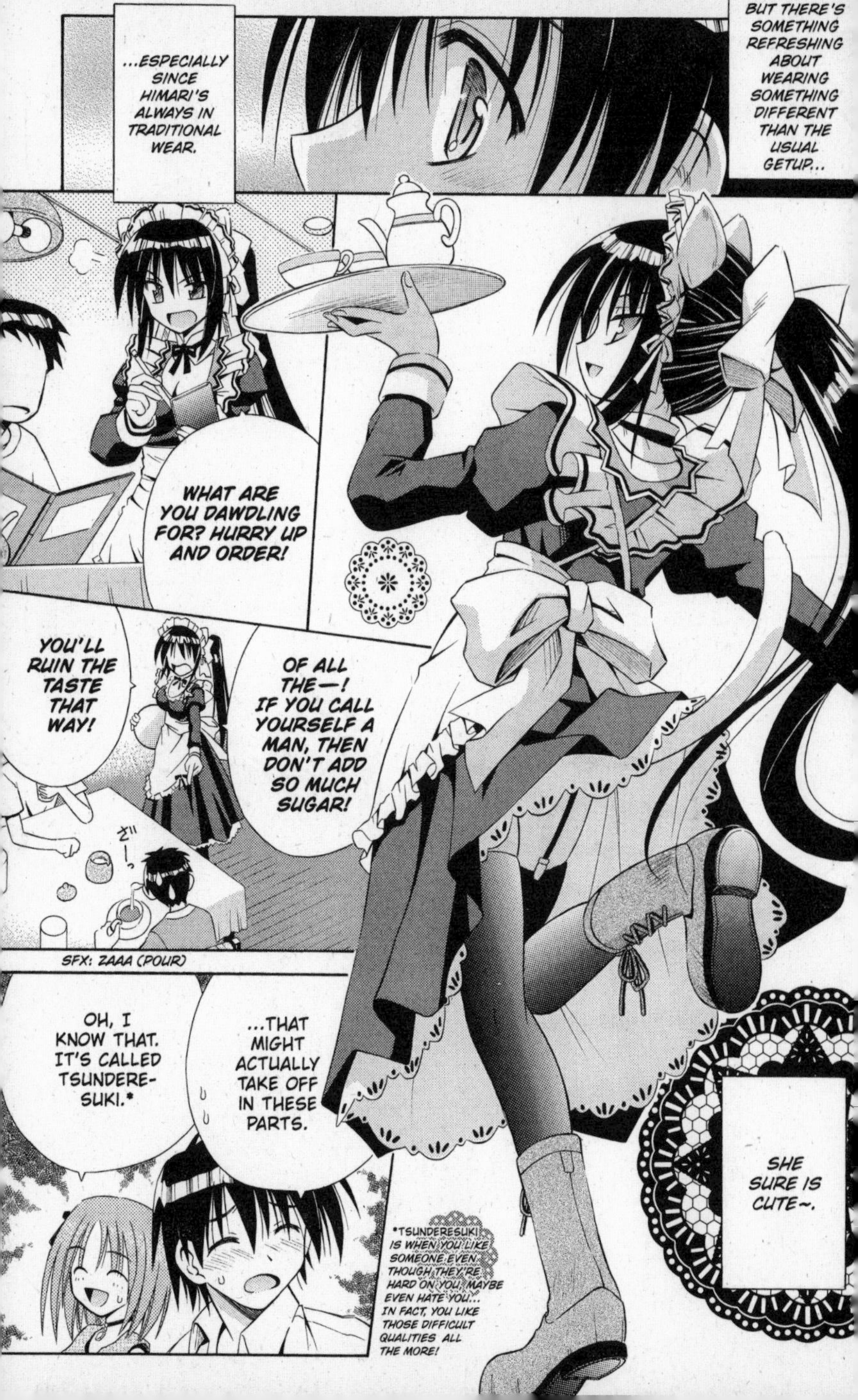
BUT THERE'S SOMETHING REFRESHING ABOUT WEARING SOMETHING DIFFERENT THAN THE USUAL GETUP...
...ESPECIALLY SINCE HIMARI'S ALWAYS IN TRADITIONAL WEAR.
SHE SURE IS CUTE~.
WHAT ARE YOU DAWDLING FOR? HURRY UP AND ORDER!
OF ALL THE—! IF YOU CALL YOURSELF A MAN, THEN DON'T ADD SO MUCH SUGAR!
YOU'LL RUIN THE TASTE THAT WAY!
SFX: ZAAA (POUR)
...THAT MIGHT ACTUALLY TAKE OFF IN THESE PARTS.
OH, I KNOW THAT. IT'S CALLED TSUNDERE-SUKI.*
*TSUNDERESUKI IS WHEN YOU LIKE SOMEONE EVEN THOUGH THEY'RE HARD ON YOU, MAYBE EVEN HATE YOU... IN FACT, YOU LIKE THOSE DIFFICULT QUALITIES ALL THE MORE!

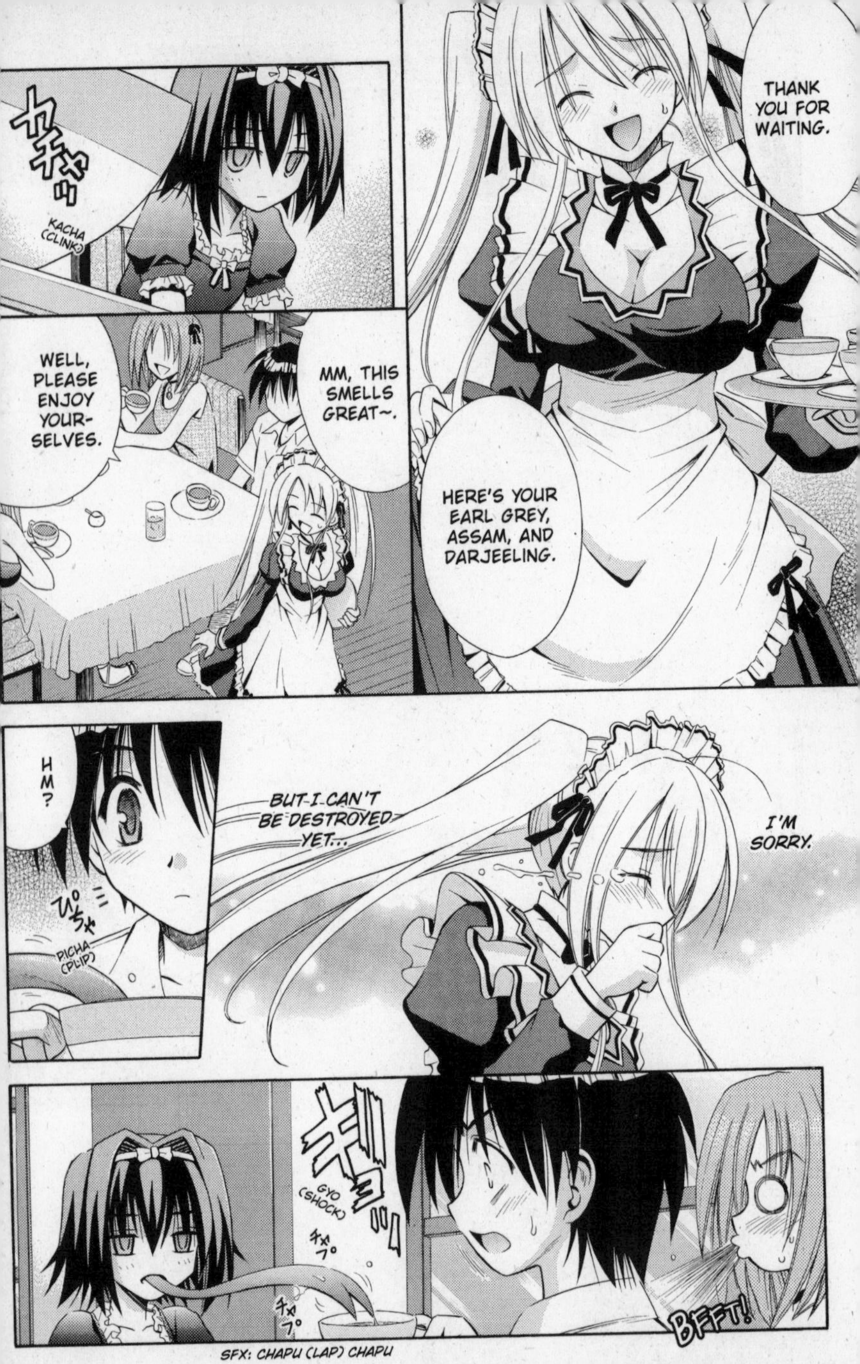
THANK YOU FOR WAITING.
HERE'S YOUR EARL GREY, ASSAM, AND DARJEELING.
KACHA (CLINK)
MM, THIS SMELLS GREAT~.
WELL, PLEASE ENJOY YOURSELVES.
I'M SORRY.
BUT I CAN'T BE DESTROYED YET...
HM?
PICHA (PLIP)
BFFT!
GYO (SHOCK)
SFX: CHAPU (LAP) CHAPU

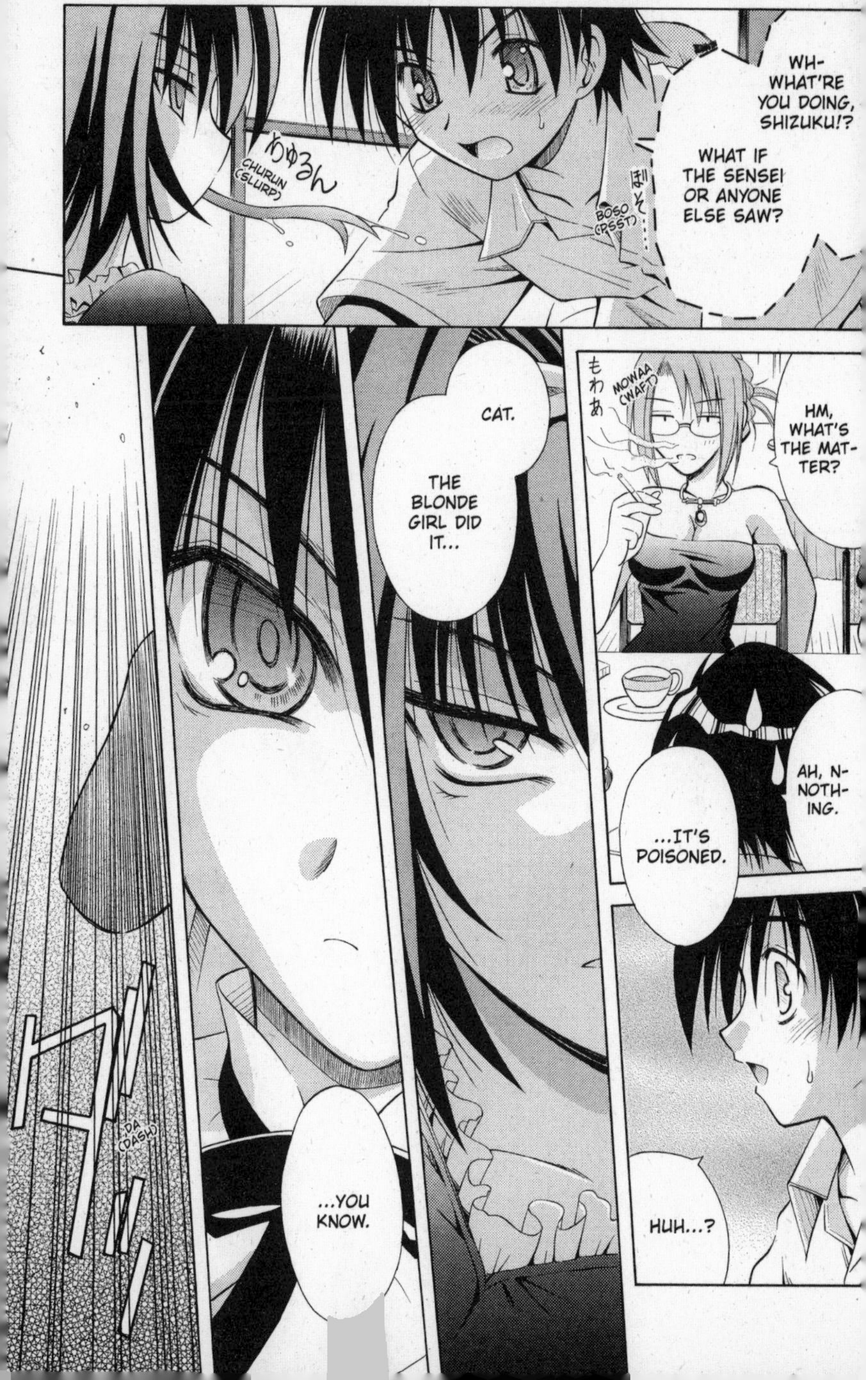

WH- WHAT'RE YOU DOING, SHIZUKU!?
WHAT IF THE SENSEI OR ANYONE ELSE SAW?
ぼそ…
BOSO (PSST)
ちゅるん
CHURUN (SLURP)
HM, WHAT'S THE MAT-TER?
もわあ
MOWAA (WAFT)
AH, N-NOTHING.
...IT'S POISONED.
HUH...?
CAT.
THE BLONDE GIRL DID IT...
...YOU KNOW.
ダッ
DA (DASH)

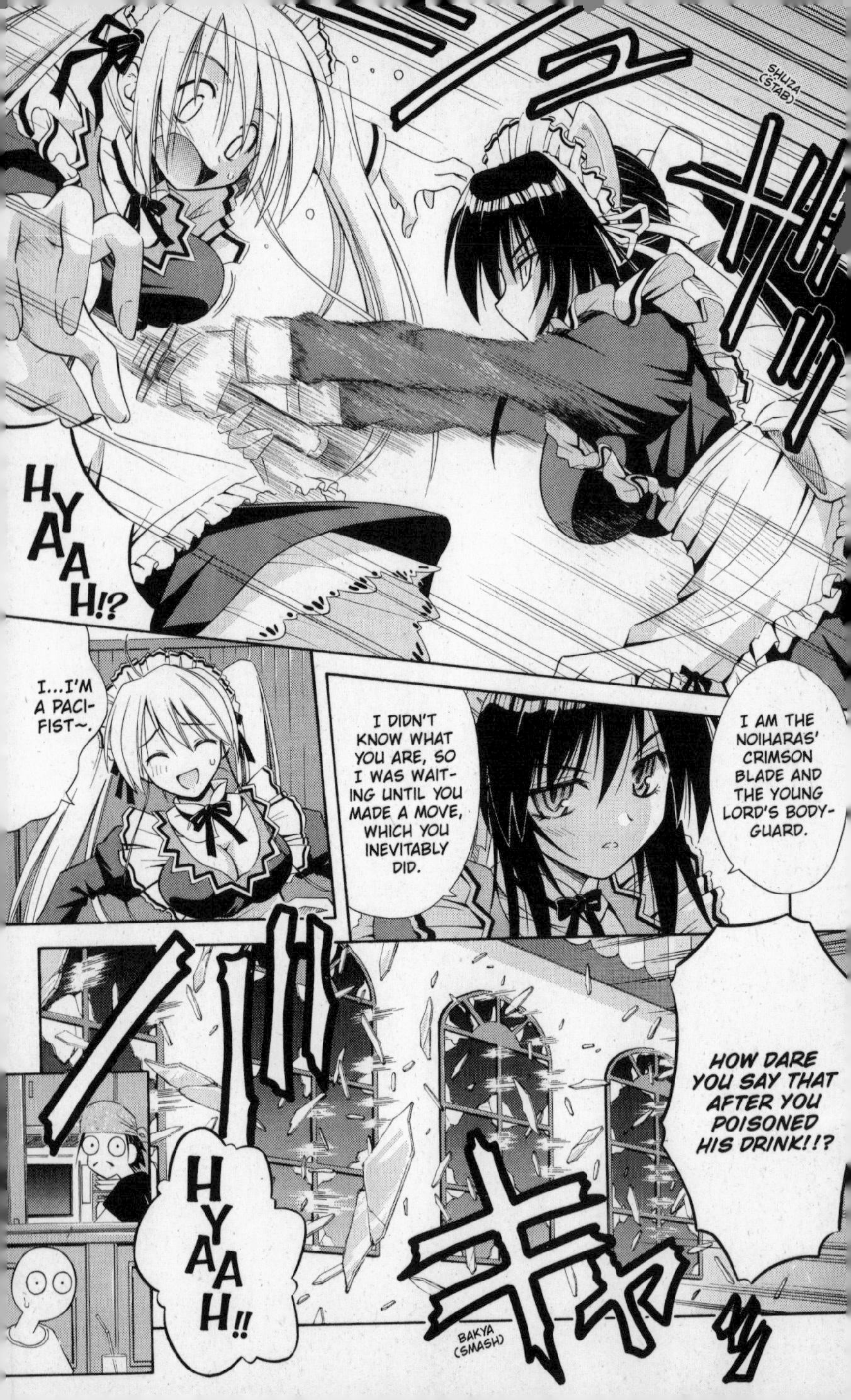
SHUZA (STAB)
HYAAH!?
I AM THE NOIHARAS' CRIMSON BLADE AND THE YOUNG LORD'S BODY-GUARD.
I DIDN'T KNOW WHAT YOU ARE, SO I WAS WAIT-ING UNTIL YOU MADE A MOVE, WHICH YOU INEVITABLY DID.
I...I'M A PACI-FIST~.
HOW DARE YOU SAY THAT AFTER YOU POISONED HIS DRINK!!?
BAKYA (SMASH)
HYAAH!!

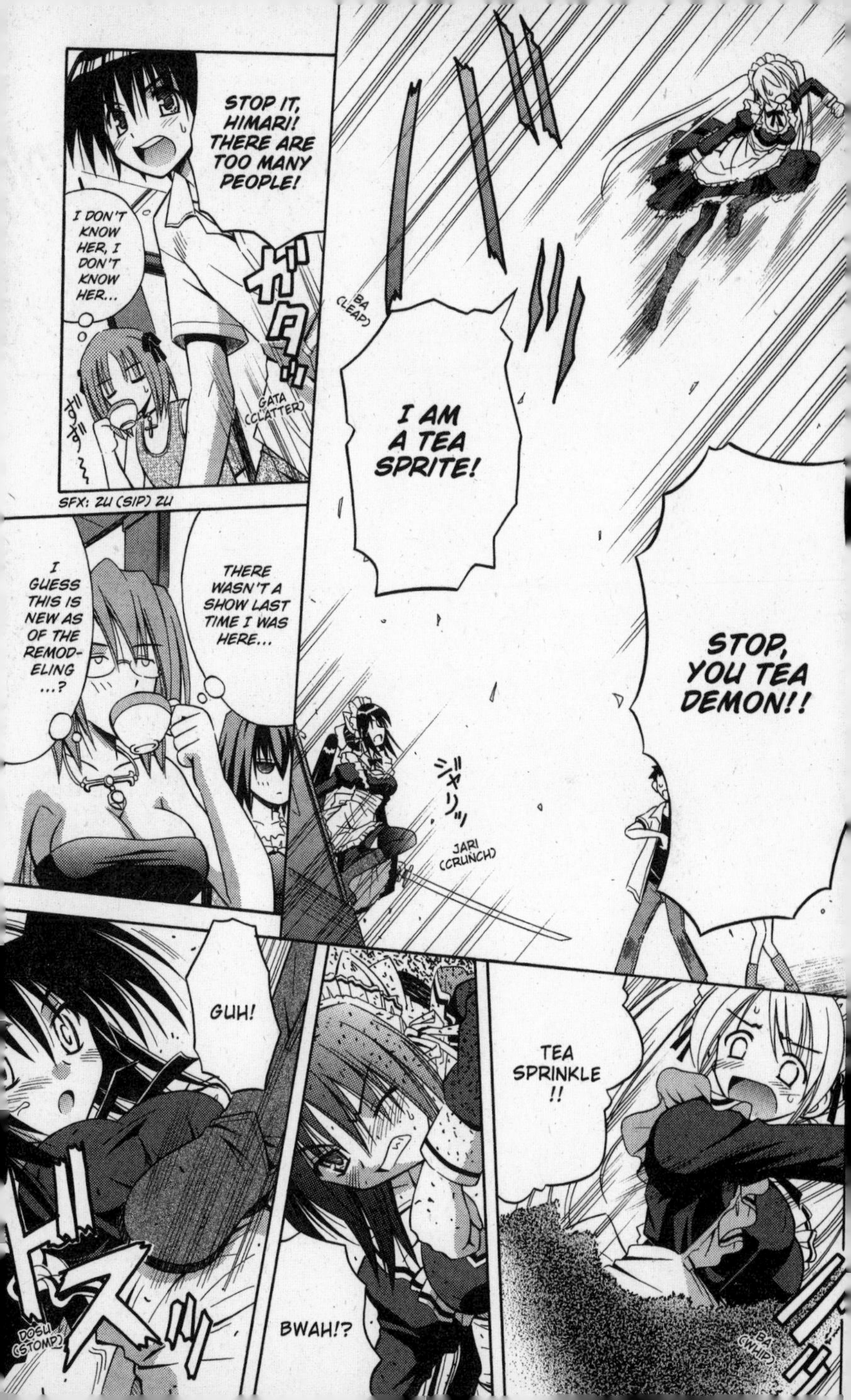
BA (LEAP)
I AM A TEA SPRITE!
STOP, YOU TEA DEMON!!
JARI (CRUNCH)
STOP IT, HIMARI! THERE ARE TOO MANY PEOPLE!
I DON'T KNOW HER, I DON'T KNOW HER...
GATA (CLATTER)
SFX: ZU (SIP) ZU
THERE WASN'T A SHOW LAST TIME I WAS HERE...
I GUESS THIS IS NEW AS OF THE REMODEL-ELING ...?
TEA SPRINKLE !!
BA (WHIP)
BWAH!?
GUH!
DOSU (STOMP)

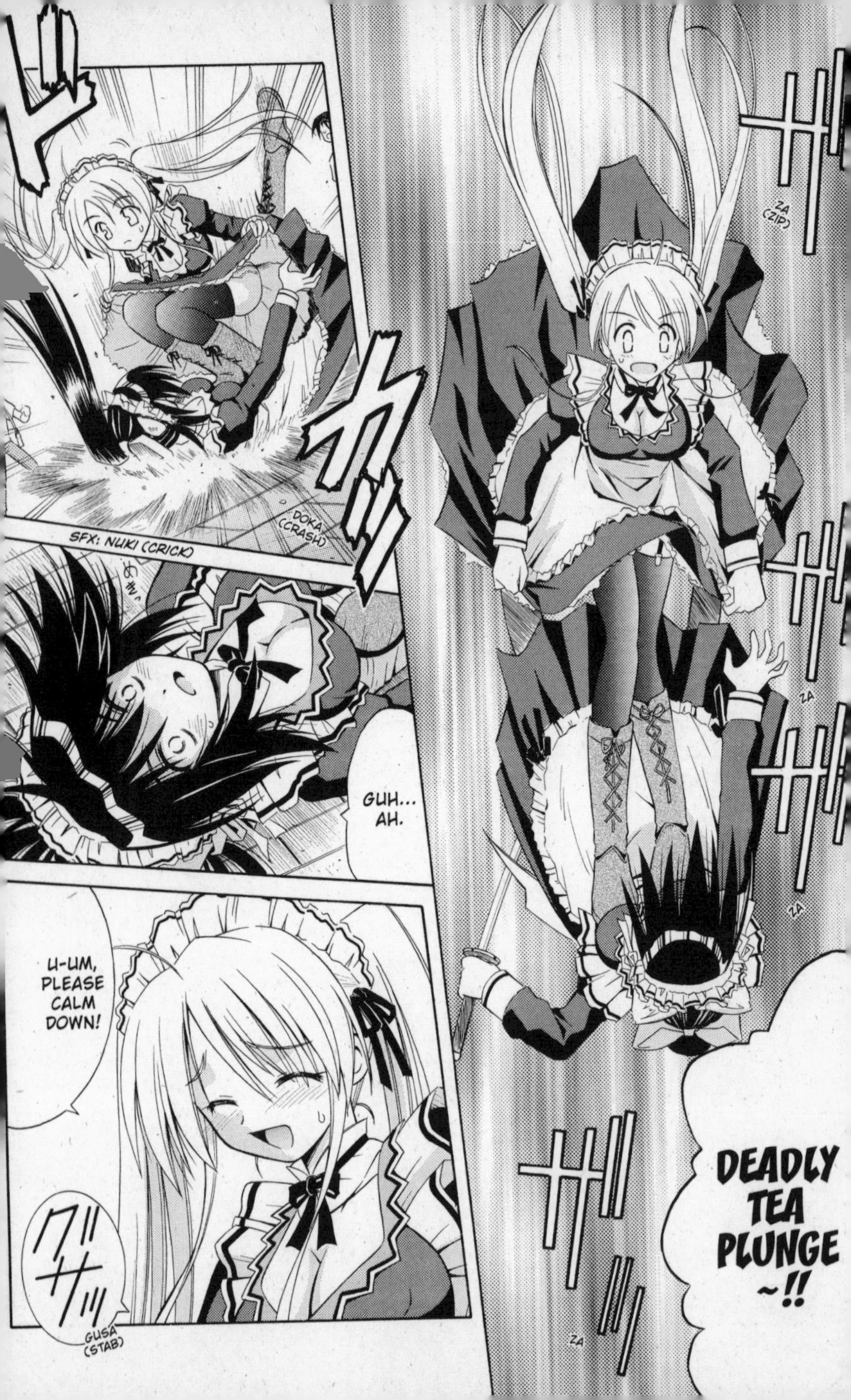
ZA (ZIP)
ZA
ZA
DEADLY TEA PLUNGE ~!!
ZA
DOKA (CRASH)
SFX: NUKI (CRICK)
GUH... AH.
U-UM, PLEASE CALM DOWN!
GUSA (STAB)

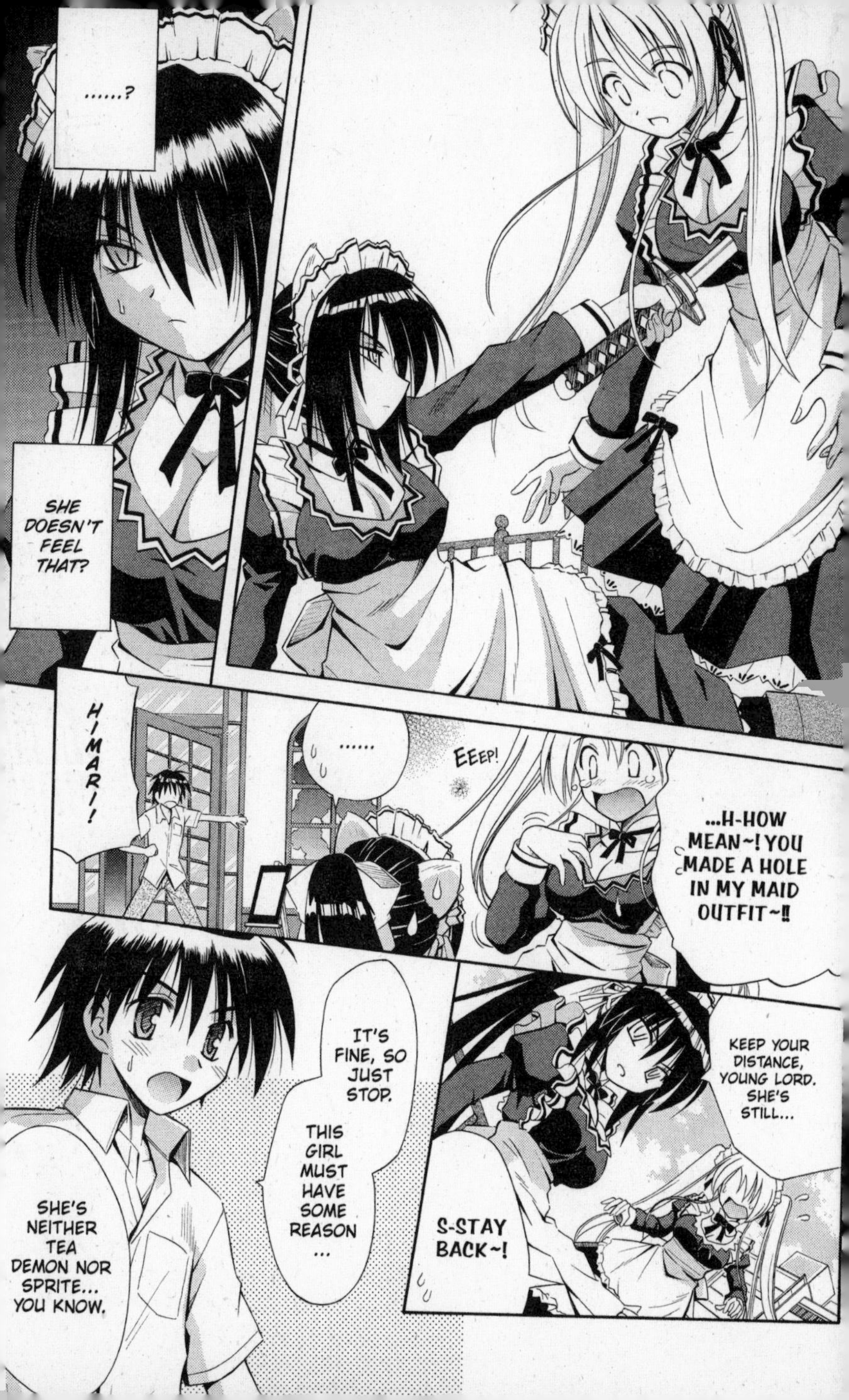
......?
SHE DOESN'T FEEL THAT?
...H-HOW MEAN~! YOU MADE A HOLE IN MY MAID OUTFIT~!!
EEEP!
......
HIMARI!
KEEP YOUR DISTANCE, YOUNG LORD. SHE'S STILL...
S-STAY BACK~!
IT'S FINE, SO JUST STOP.
THIS GIRL MUST HAVE SOME REASON ...
SHE'S NEITHER TEA DEMON NOR SPRITE... YOU KNOW.

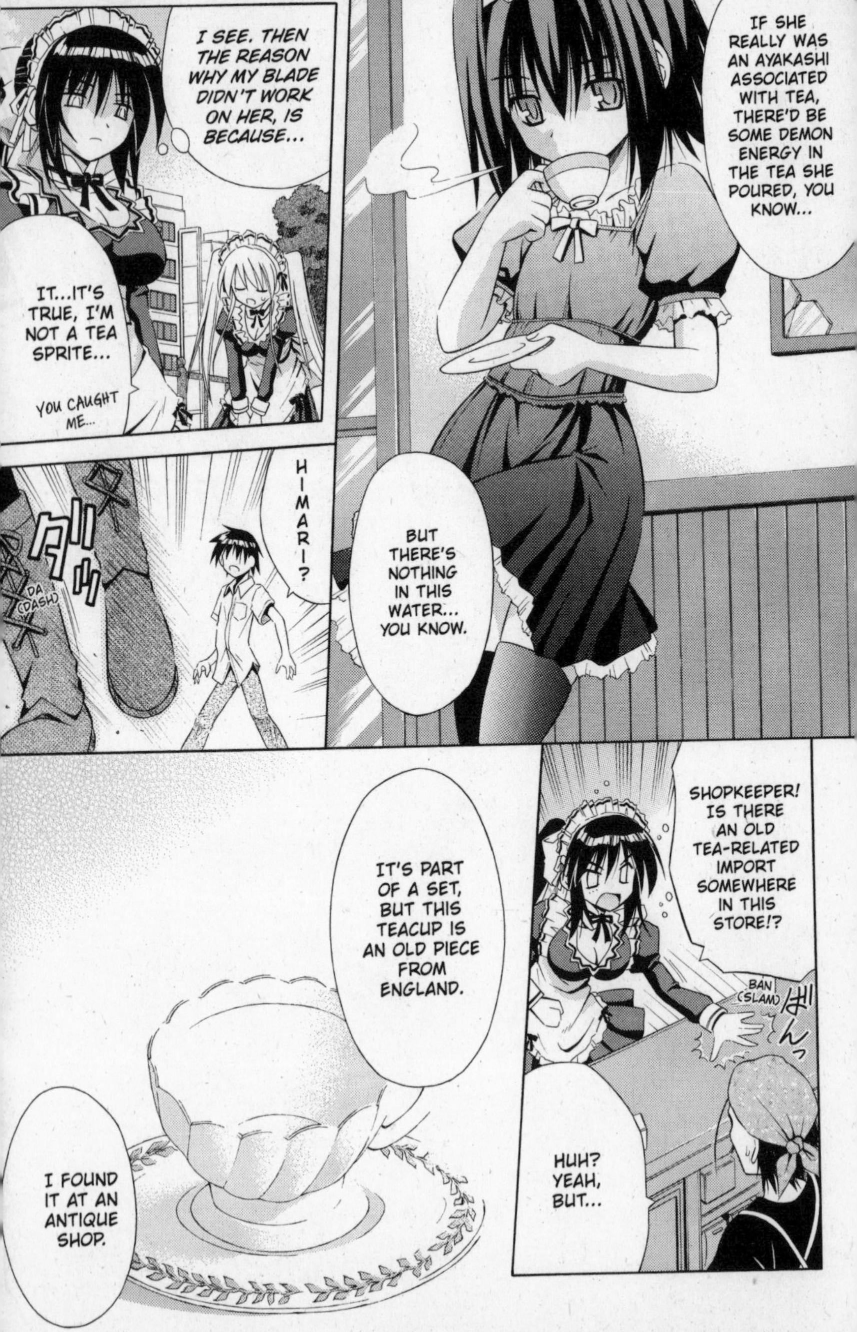
IF SHE REALLY WAS AN AYAKASHI ASSOCIATED WITH TEA, THERE'D BE SOME DEMON ENERGY IN THE TEA SHE POURED, YOU KNOW...
BUT THERE'S NOTHING IN THIS WATER... YOU KNOW.
I SEE. THEN THE REASON WHY MY BLADE DIDN'T WORK ON HER, IS BECAUSE...
IT...IT'S TRUE, I'M NOT A TEA SPRITE...
YOU CAUGHT ME...
HIMARI?
ダッ
DA (DASH)
SHOPKEEPER! IS THERE AN OLD TEA-RELATED IMPORT SOMEWHERE IN THIS STORE!?
BAN (SLAM)
ばんっ
HUH? YEAH, BUT...
IT'S PART OF A SET, BUT THIS TEACUP IS AN OLD PIECE FROM ENGLAND.
I FOUND IT AT AN ANTIQUE SHOP.

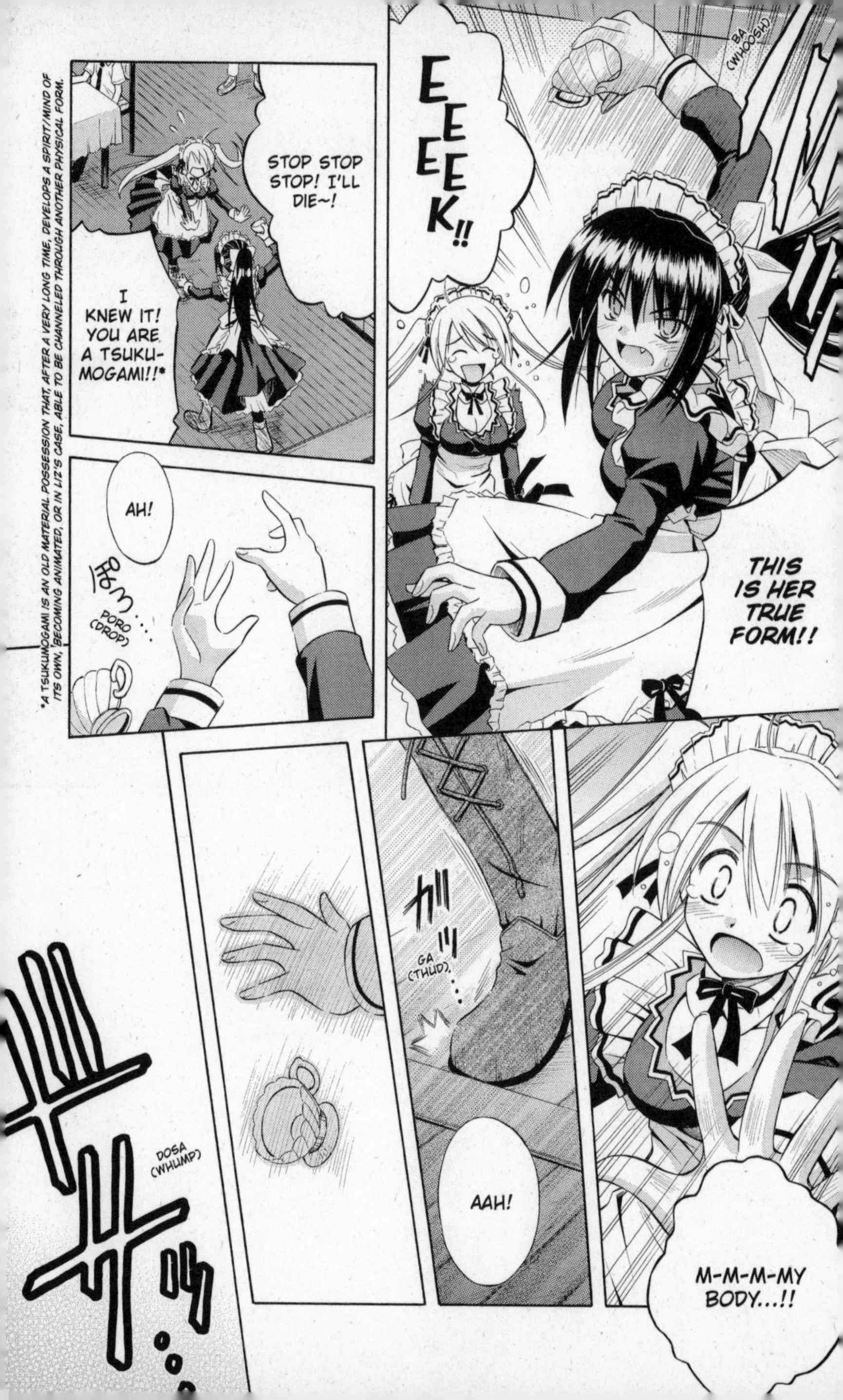

BA (WHOOSH)
EEEK!!
THIS IS HER TRUE FORM!!
STOP STOP STOP! I'LL DIE~!
I KNEW IT! YOU ARE A TSUKUMOGAMI!!*
AH!
PORO (DROP)
M-M-M-MY BODY...!!
GA (THUD)
AAH!
DOSA (WHUMP)

*A TSUKUMOGAMI IS AN OLD MATERIAL POSSESSION THAT, AFTER A VERY LONG TIME, DEVELOPS A SPIRIT/MIND OF ITS OWN, BECOMING ANIMATED, OR IN LIZ'S CASE, ABLE TO BE CHANNELED THROUGH ANOTHER PHYSICAL FORM.

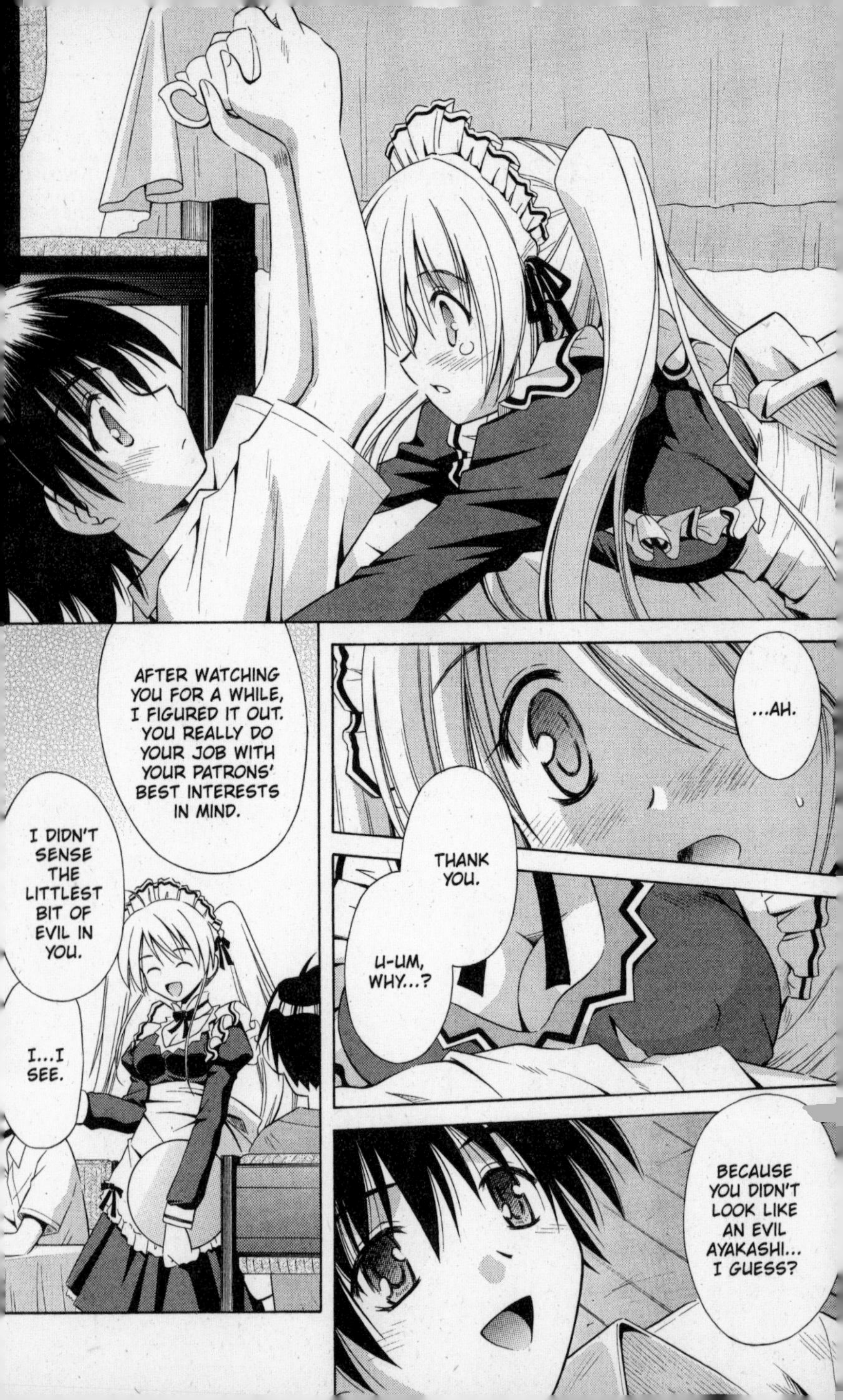
...AH.
THANK YOU.
U-UM, WHY...?
BECAUSE YOU DIDN'T LOOK LIKE AN EVIL AYAKASHI... I GUESS?
AFTER WATCHING YOU FOR A WHILE, I FIGURED IT OUT. YOU REALLY DO YOUR JOB WITH YOUR PATRONS' BEST INTERESTS IN MIND.
I DIDN'T SENSE THE LITTLEST BIT OF EVIL IN YOU.
I...I SEE.

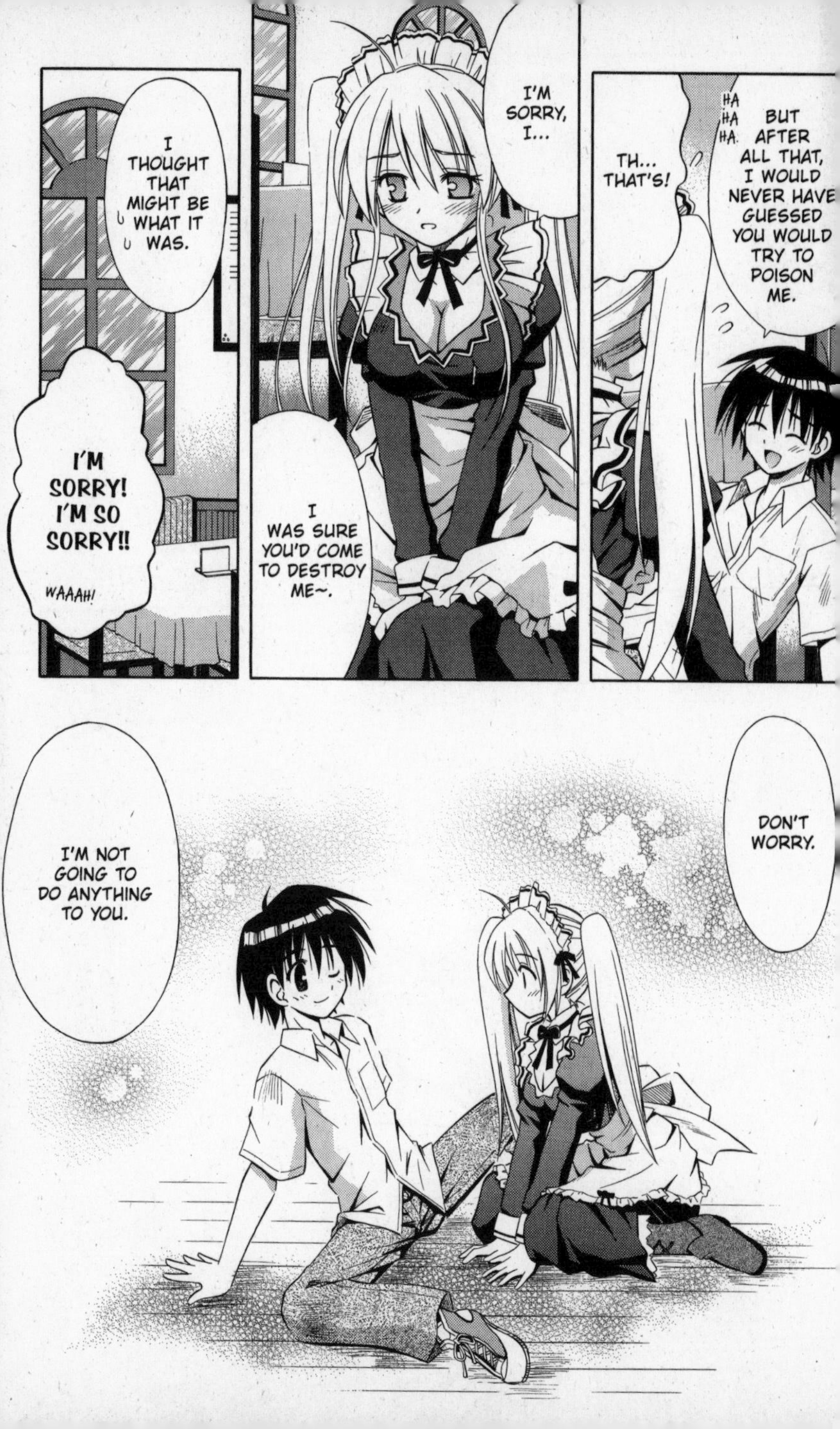
HA HA HA
BUT AFTER ALL THAT, I WOULD NEVER HAVE GUESSED YOU WOULD TRY TO POISON ME.
TH... THAT'S!
I'M SORRY, I...
I WAS SURE YOU'D COME TO DESTROY ME~.
I THOUGHT THAT MIGHT BE WHAT IT WAS.
I'M SORRY! I'M SO SORRY!!
WAAAH!
DON'T WORRY.
I'M NOT GOING TO DO ANYTHING TO YOU.

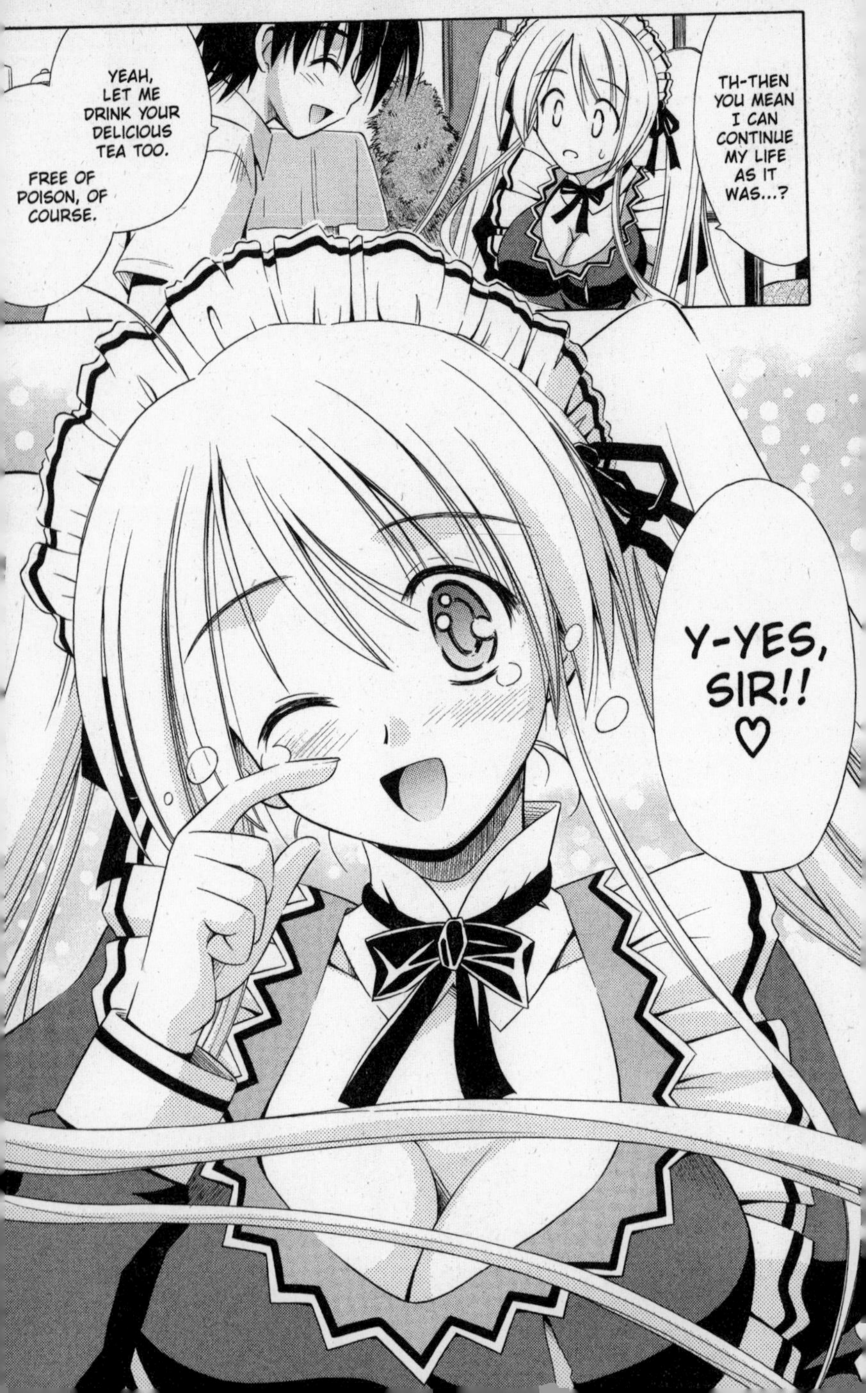
TH-THEN YOU MEAN I CAN CONTINUE MY LIFE AS IT WAS...?
YEAH, LET ME DRINK YOUR DELICIOUS TEA TOO.
FREE OF POISON, OF COURSE.
Y-YES, SIR!! ♡

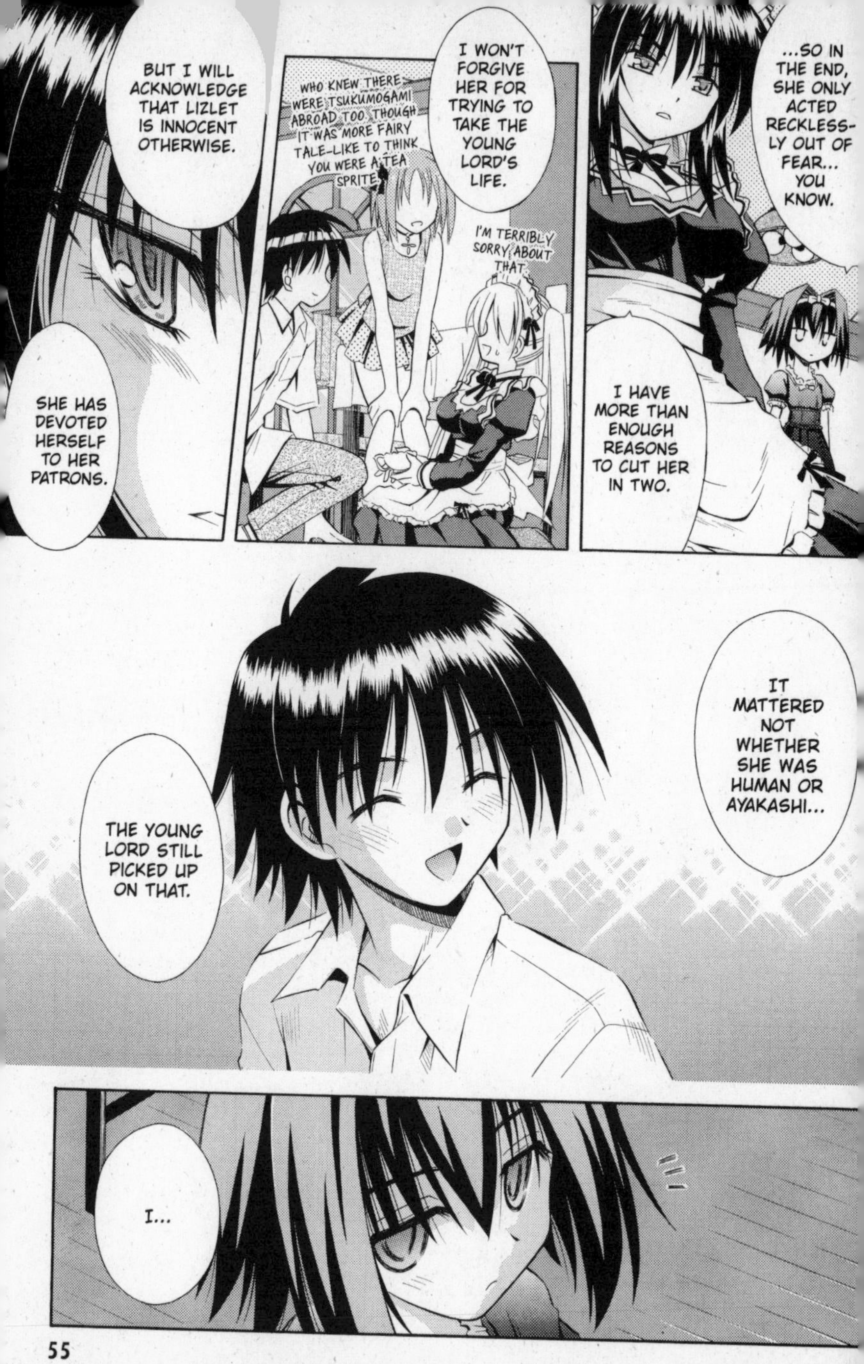
...SO IN THE END, SHE ONLY ACTED RECKLESS-LY OUT OF FEAR... YOU KNOW.
I HAVE MORE THAN ENOUGH REASONS TO CUT HER IN TWO.
I WON'T FORGIVE HER FOR TRYING TO TAKE THE YOUNG LORD'S LIFE.
WHO KNEW THERE WERE TSUKUMOGAMI ABROAD TOO. THOUGH IT WAS MORE FAIRY TALE-LIKE TO THINK YOU WERE A TEA SPRITE.
I'M TERRIBLY SORRY ABOUT THAT.
BUT I WILL ACKNOWLEDGE THAT LIZLET IS INNOCENT OTHERWISE.
SHE HAS DEVOTED HERSELF TO HER PATRONS.
IT MATTERED NOT WHETHER SHE WAS HUMAN OR AYAKASHI...
THE YOUNG LORD STILL PICKED UP ON THAT.
I...

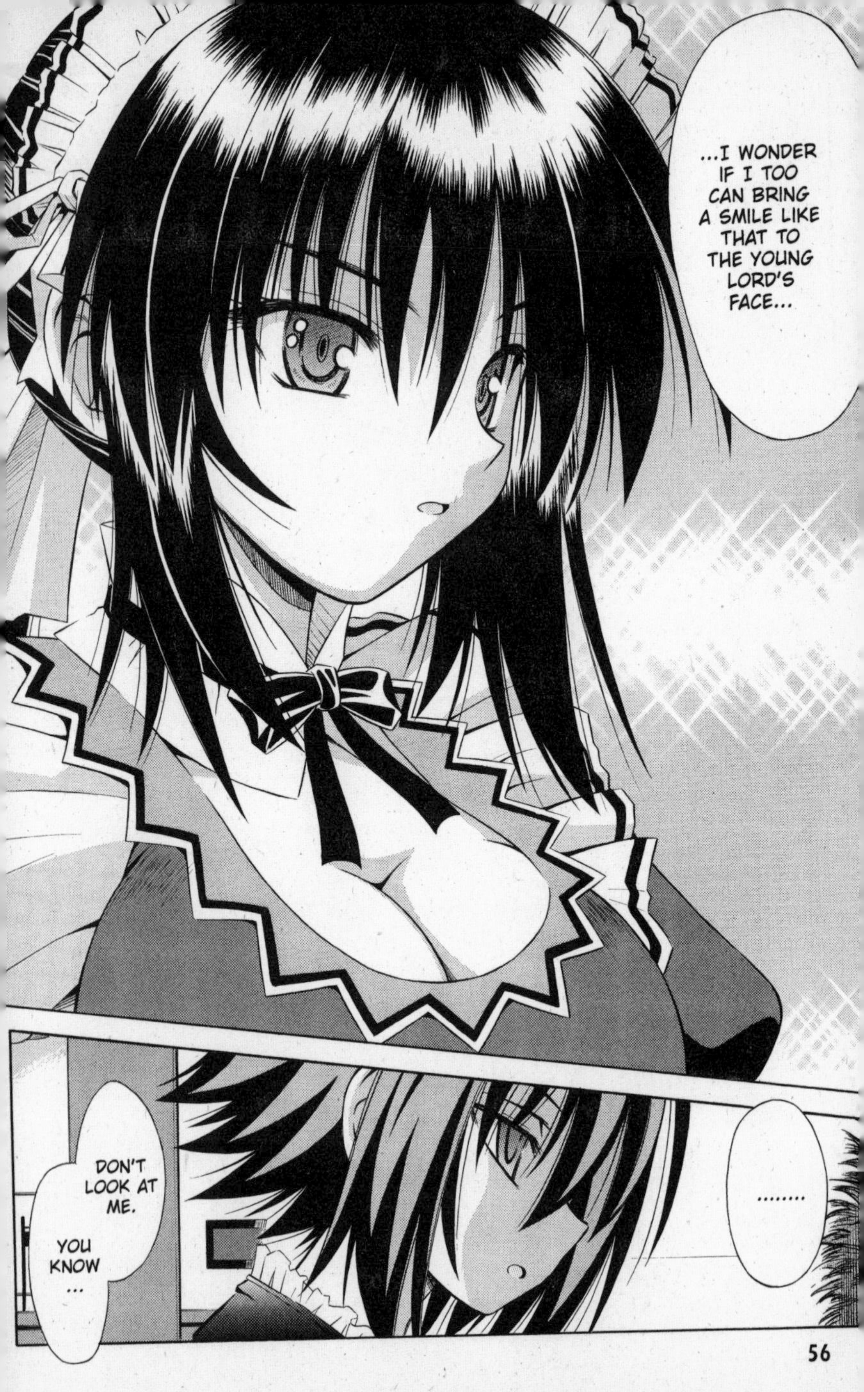
...I WONDER IF I TOO CAN BRING A SMILE LIKE THAT TO THE YOUNG LORD'S FACE...
....
DON'T LOOK AT ME.
YOU KNOW ...

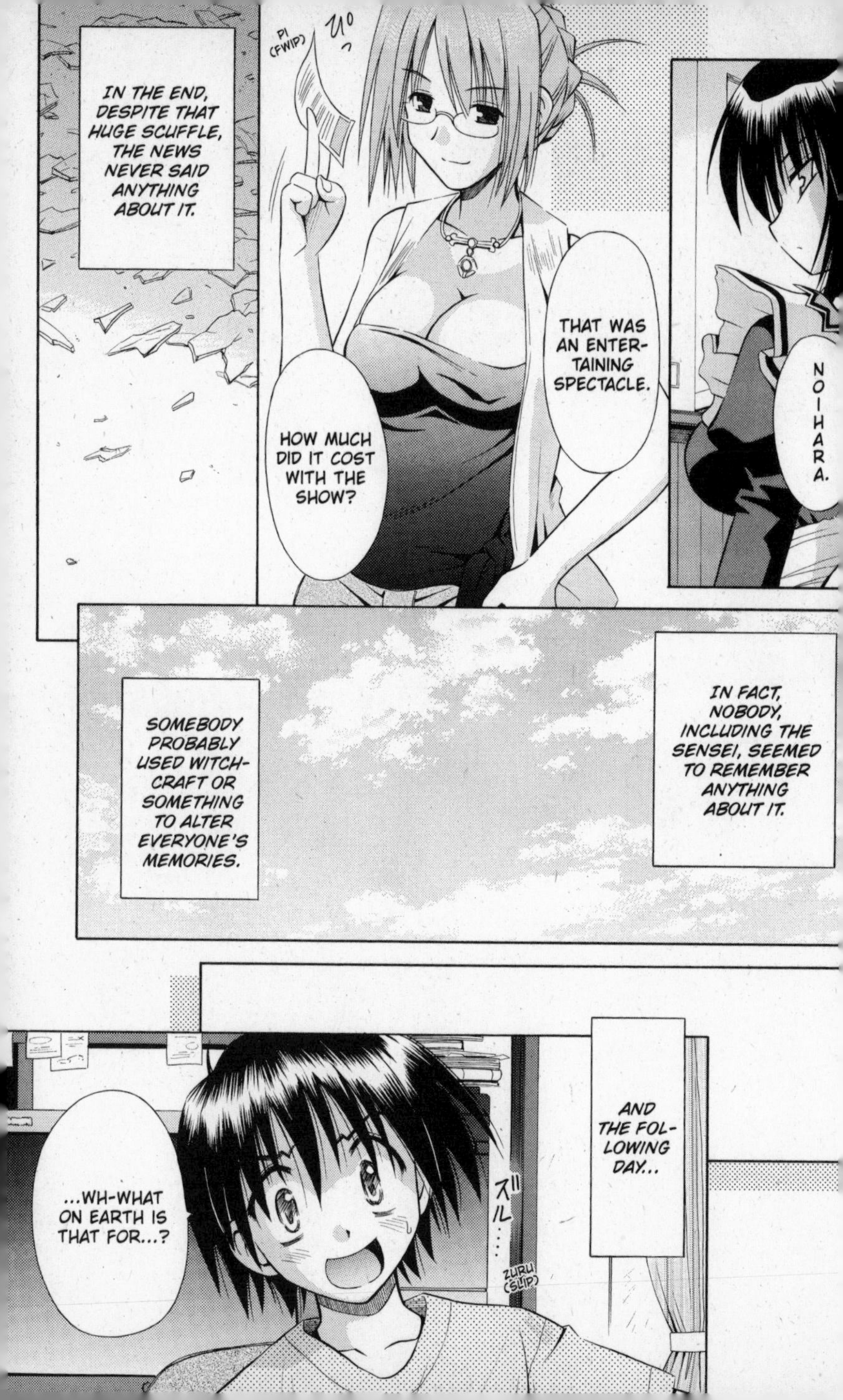
NOIHARA.
PI (FWIP)
THAT WAS AN ENTERTAINING SPECTACLE.
HOW MUCH DID IT COST WITH THE SHOW?
IN THE END, DESPITE THAT HUGE SCUFFLE, THE NEWS NEVER SAID ANYTHING ABOUT IT.
IN FACT, NOBODY, INCLUDING THE SENSEI, SEEMED TO REMEMBER ANYTHING ABOUT IT.
SOMEBODY PROBABLY USED WITCHCRAFT OR SOMETHING TO ALTER EVERYONE'S MEMORIES.
AND THE FOLLOWING DAY...
ズル…
ZURU (SLIP)
...WH-WHAT ON EARTH IS THAT FOR...?

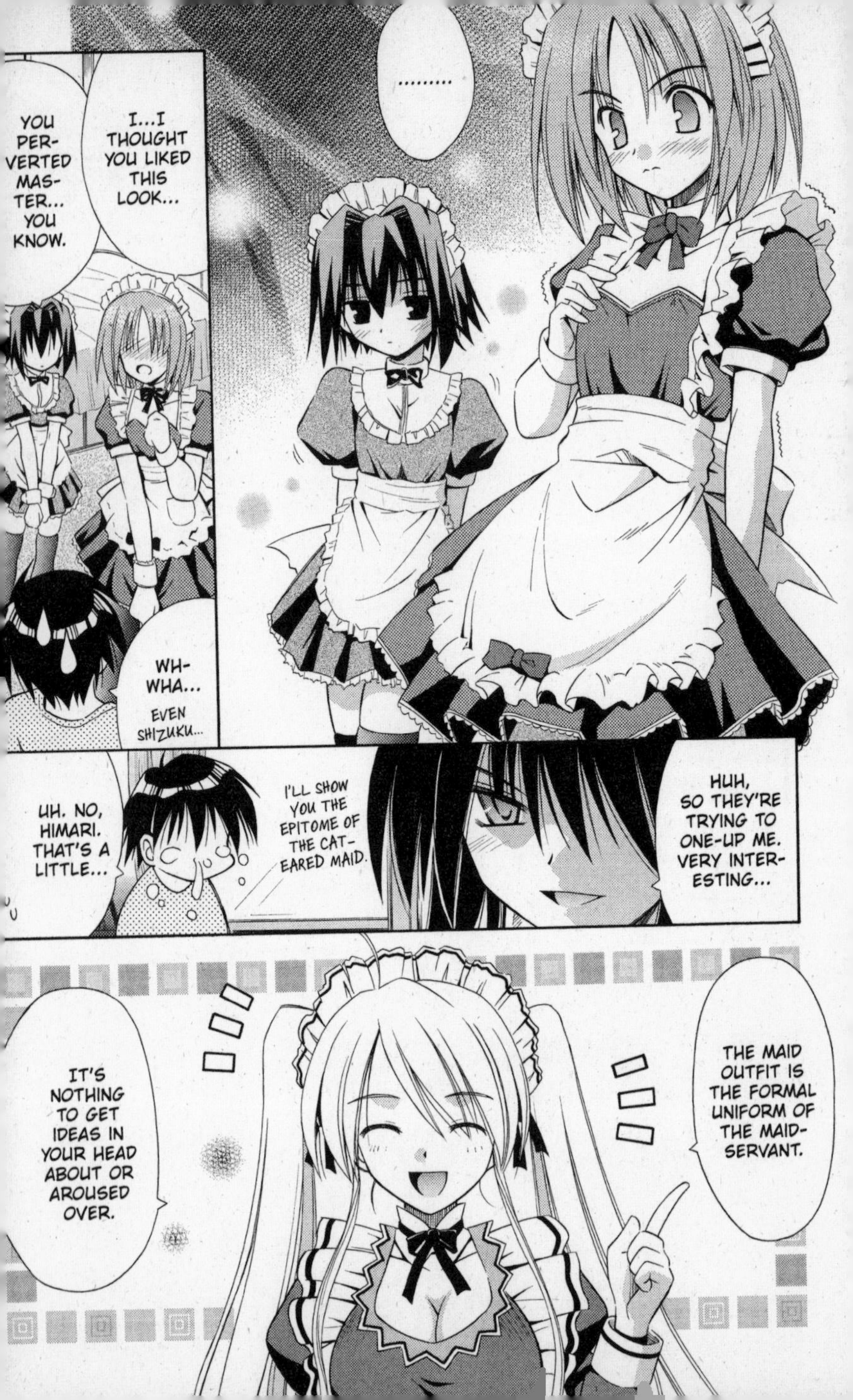
....
I...I THOUGHT YOU LIKED THIS LOOK...
YOU PER-VERTED MAS-TER... YOU KNOW.
WH- WHA...
EVEN SHIZUKU...
HUH, SO THEY'RE TRYING TO ONE-UP ME. VERY INTER-ESTING...
I'LL SHOW YOU THE EPITOME OF THE CAT-EARED MAID.
UH. NO, HIMARI. THAT'S A LITTLE...
THE MAID OUTFIT IS THE FORMAL UNIFORM OF THE MAID-SERVANT.
IT'S NOTHING TO GET IDEAS IN YOUR HEAD ABOUT OR AROUSED OVER.

MENAGERIE 9: THE RED RIBBON OF THE CAT-LOVING GIRL

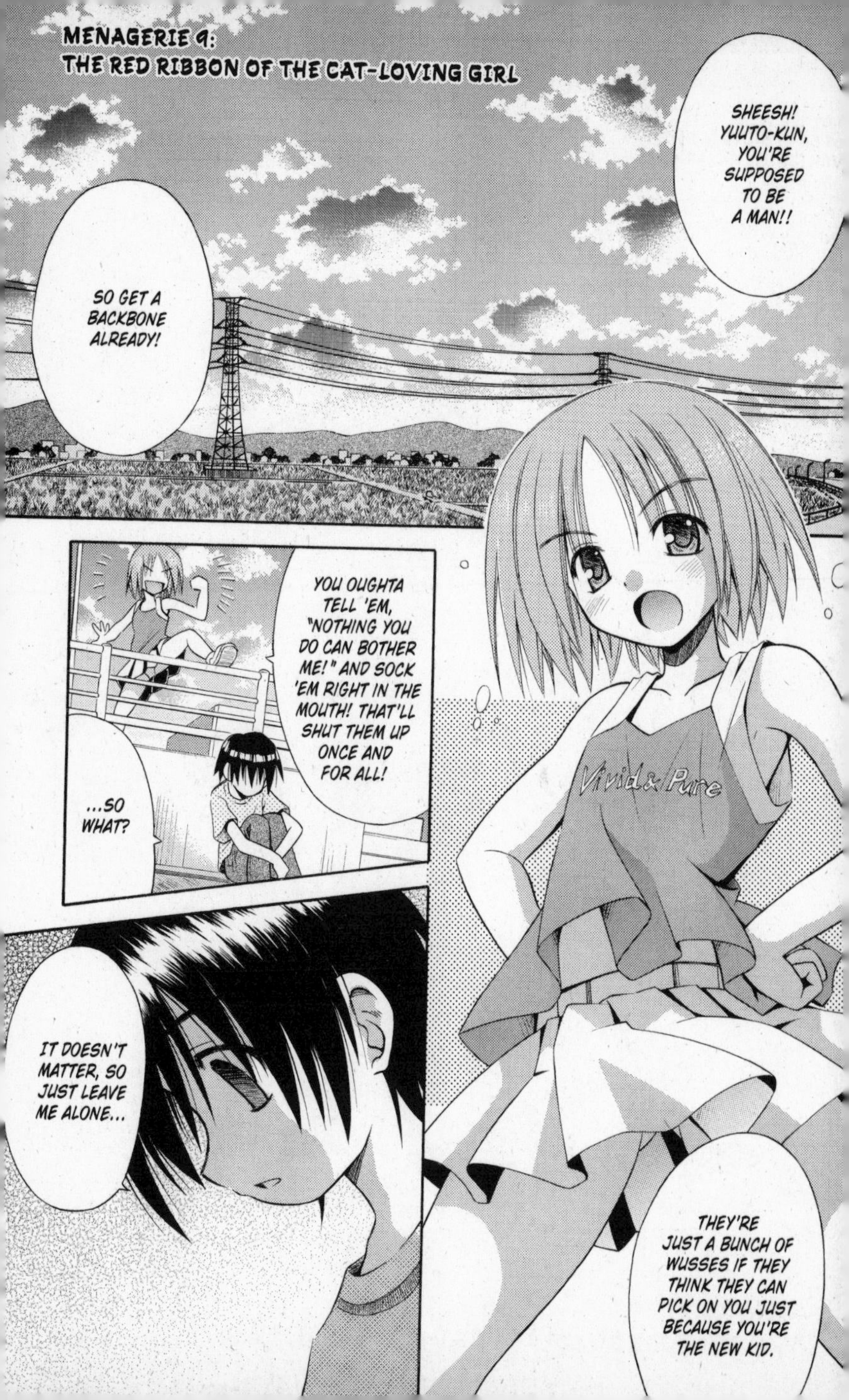
SHEESH! YUUTO-KUN, YOU'RE SUPPOSED TO BE A MAN!!
SO GET A BACKBONE ALREADY!
THEY'RE JUST A BUNCH OF WUSSES IF THEY THINK THEY CAN PICK ON YOU JUST BECAUSE YOU'RE THE NEW KID.
YOU OUGHTA TELL 'EM, "NOTHING YOU DO CAN BOTHER ME!" AND SOCK 'EM RIGHT IN THE MOUTH! THAT'LL SHUT THEM UP ONCE AND FOR ALL!
...SO WHAT?
IT DOESN'T MATTER, SO JUST LEAVE ME ALONE...
Vivid & Pure

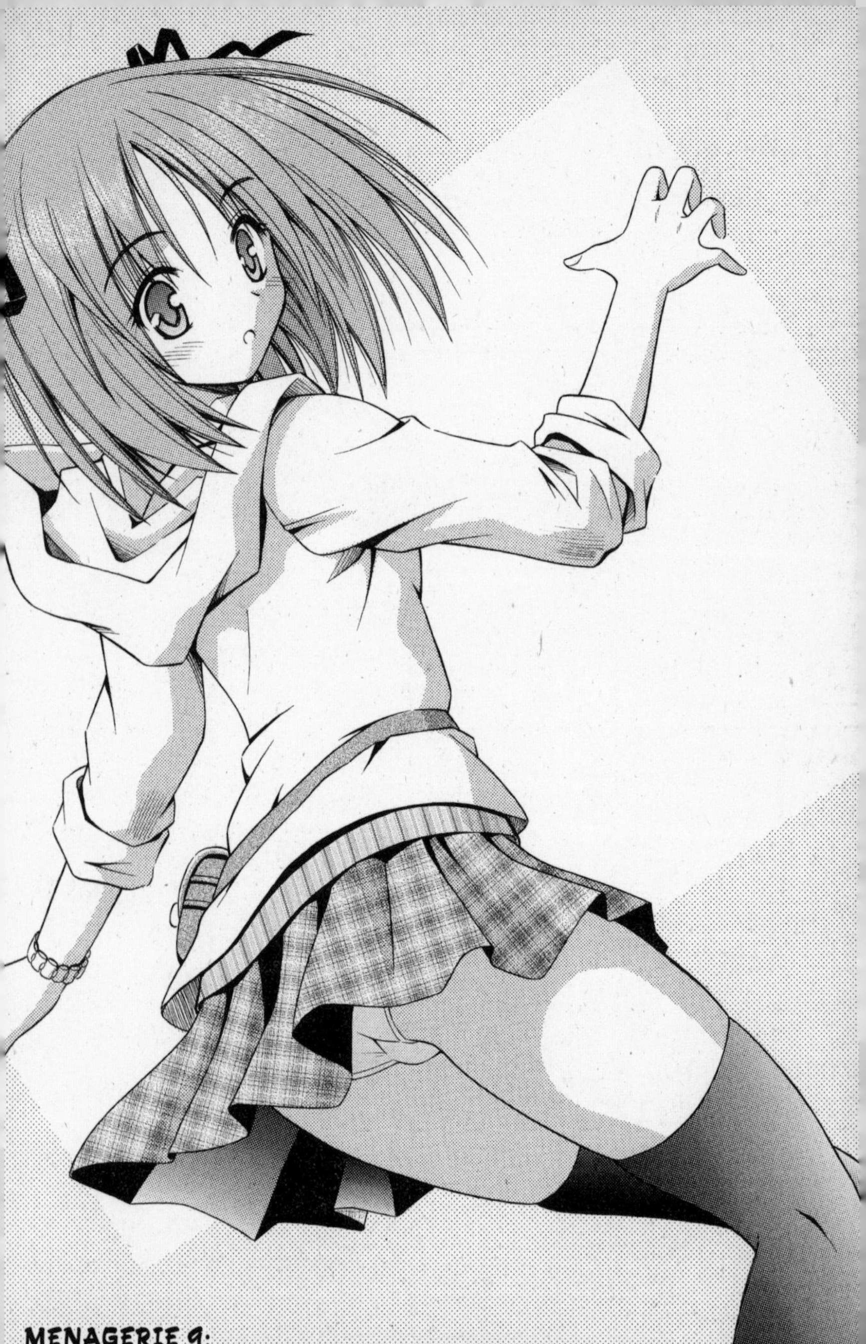

MENAGERIE 9:
THE RED RIBBON OF THE CAT-LOVING GIRL

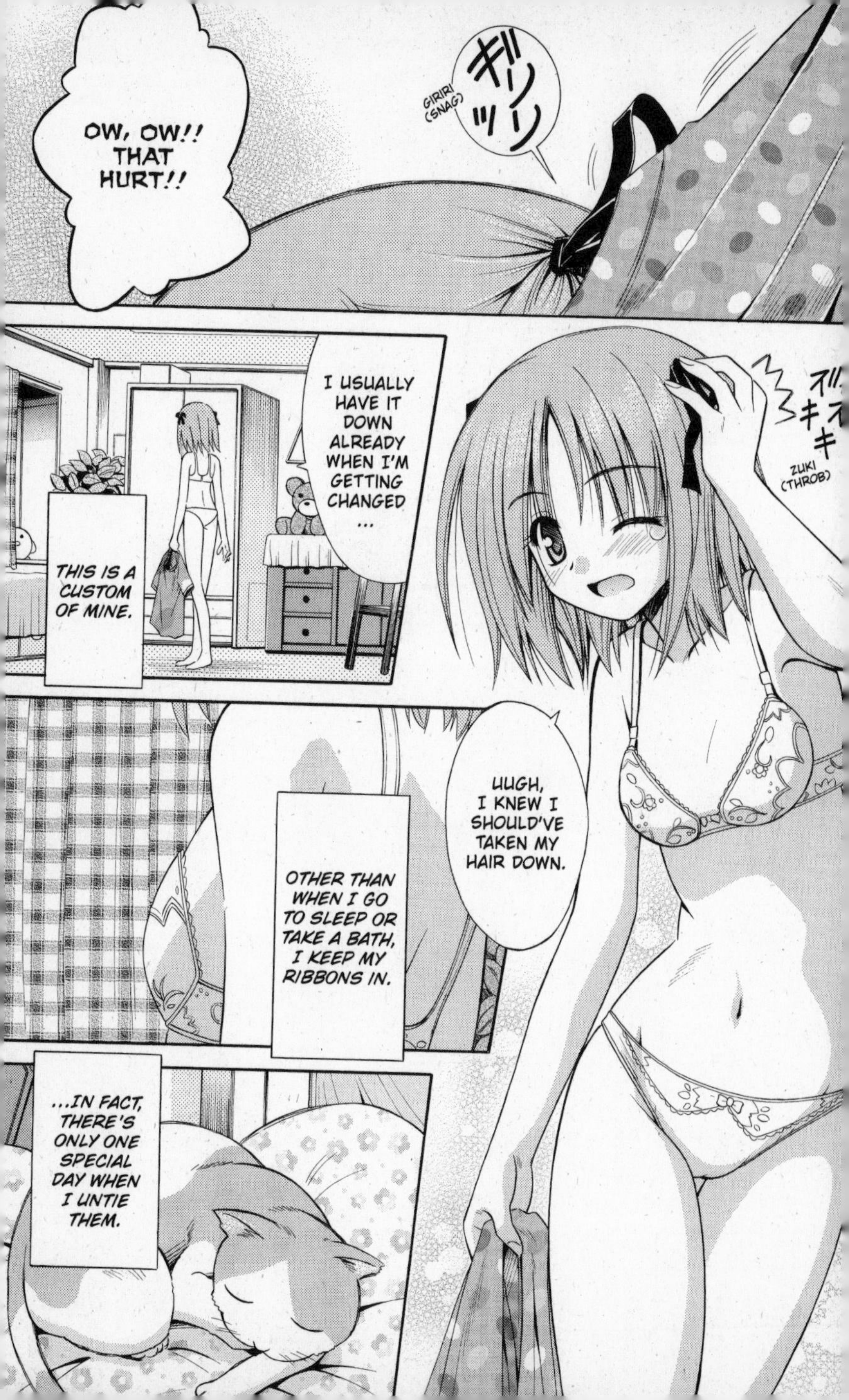
ギリッ
GIRIRI (SNAG)
OW, OW!! THAT HURT!!
ズキズキ
ZUKI (THROB)
UUGH, I KNEW I SHOULD'VE TAKEN MY HAIR DOWN.
I USUALLY HAVE IT DOWN ALREADY WHEN I'M GETTING CHANGED ...
THIS IS A CUSTOM OF MINE.
OTHER THAN WHEN I GO TO SLEEP OR TAKE A BATH, I KEEP MY RIBBONS IN.
...IN FACT, THERE'S ONLY ONE SPECIAL DAY WHEN I UNTIE THEM.

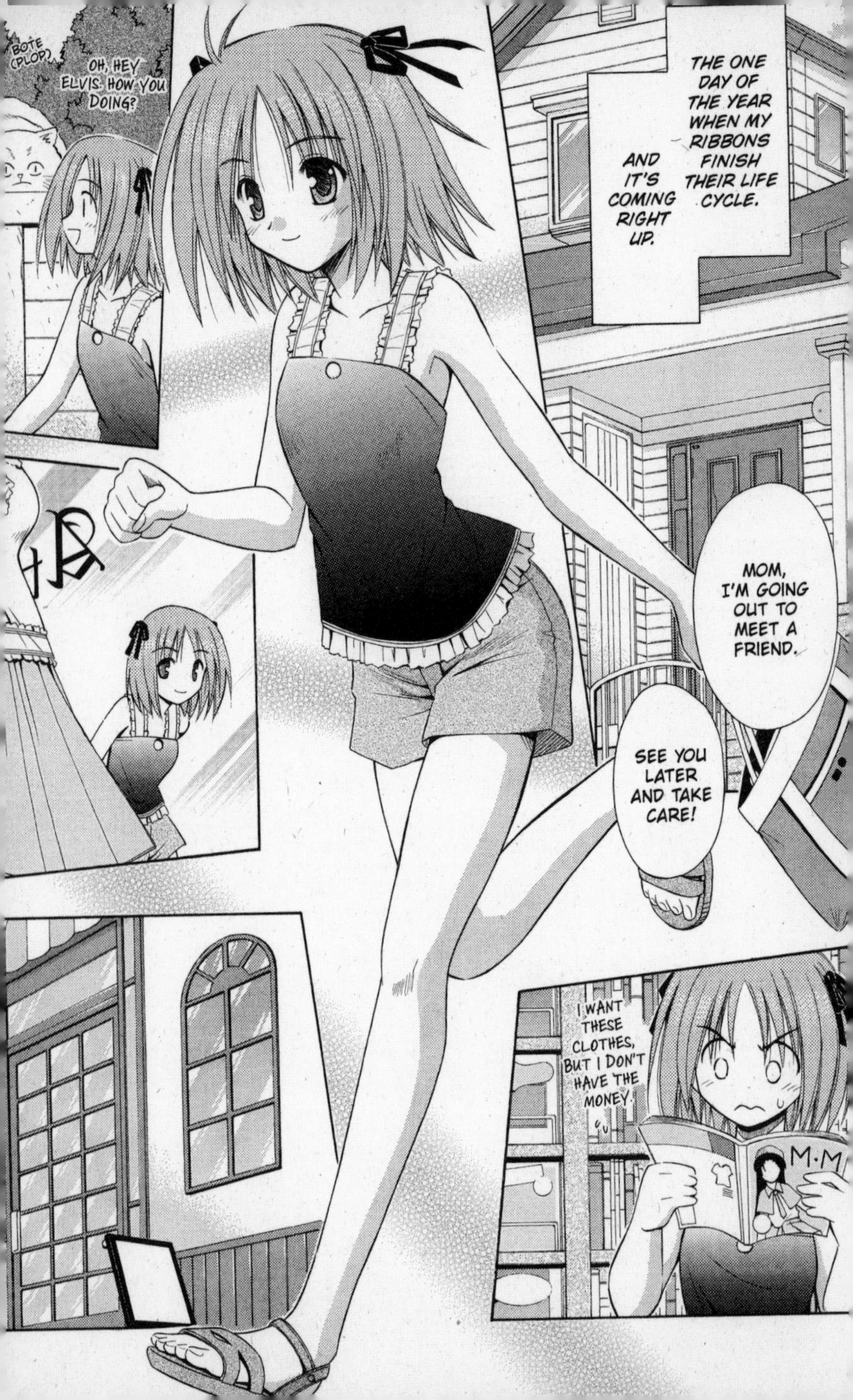
THE ONE DAY OF THE YEAR WHEN MY RIBBONS FINISH THEIR LIFE CYCLE.
AND IT'S COMING RIGHT UP.
BOTE (PLOP)
OH, HEY ELVIS. HOW YOU DOING?
MOM, I'M GOING OUT TO MEET A FRIEND.
SEE YOU LATER AND TAKE CARE!
I WANT THESE CLOTHES, BUT I DON'T HAVE THE MONEY.
M·M

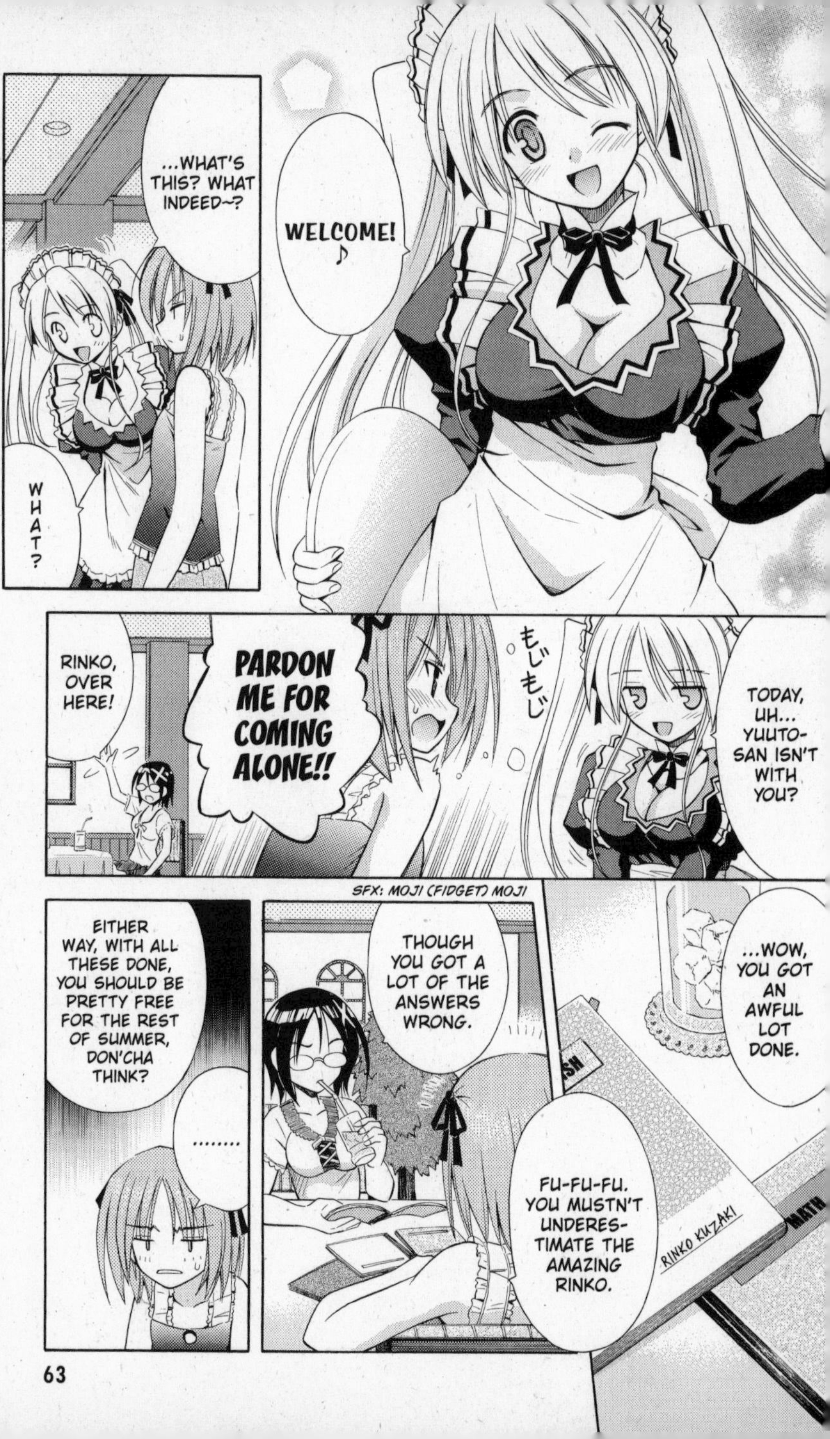
WELCOME! ♪
...WHAT'S THIS? WHAT INDEED~?
WHAT?
TODAY, UH... YUUTO-SAN ISN'T WITH YOU?
もじもじ
PARDON ME FOR COMING ALONE!!
RINKO, OVER HERE!
SFX: MOJI (FIDGET) MOJI
...WOW, YOU GOT AN AWFUL LOT DONE.
FU-FU-FU. YOU MUSTN'T UNDERES-TIMATE THE AMAZING RINKO.
RINKO KUZAKI
MATH
SH
THOUGH YOU GOT A LOT OF THE ANSWERS WRONG.
EITHER WAY, WITH ALL THESE DONE, YOU SHOULD BE PRETTY FREE FOR THE REST OF SUMMER, DON'CHA THINK?
....

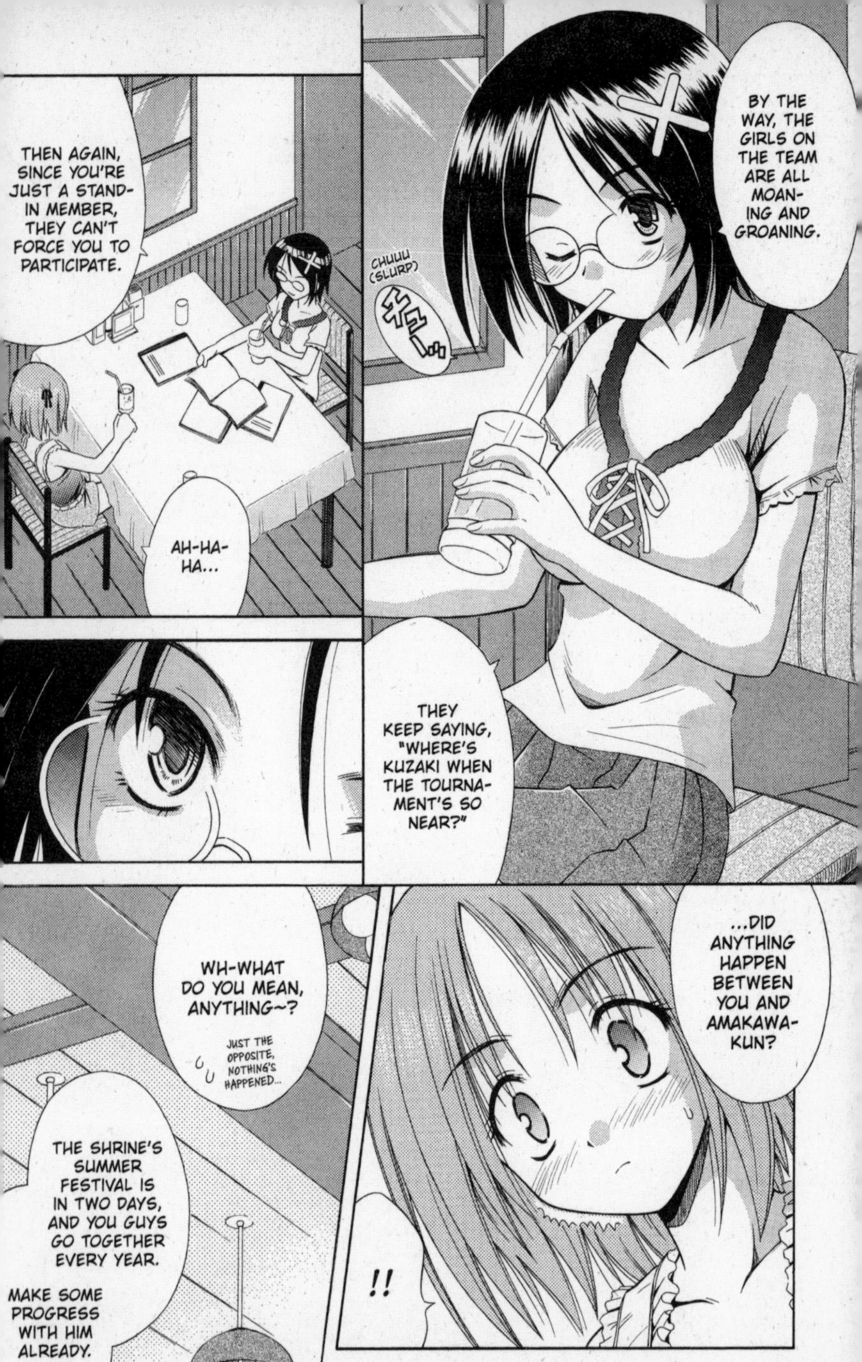
BY THE WAY, THE GIRLS ON THE TEAM ARE ALL MOANING AND GROANING.
CHUUU (SLURP)
THEY KEEP SAYING, "WHERE'S KUZAKI WHEN THE TOURNAMENT'S SO NEAR?"
THEN AGAIN, SINCE YOU'RE JUST A STAND-IN MEMBER, THEY CAN'T FORCE YOU TO PARTICIPATE.
AH-HA-HA...
...DID ANYTHING HAPPEN BETWEEN YOU AND AMAKAWA-KUN?
!!
WH-WHAT DO YOU MEAN, ANYTHING~?
JUST THE OPPOSITE, NOTHING'S HAPPENED...
THE SHRINE'S SUMMER FESTIVAL IS IN TWO DAYS, AND YOU GUYS GO TOGETHER EVERY YEAR.
MAKE SOME PROGRESS WITH HIM ALREADY.

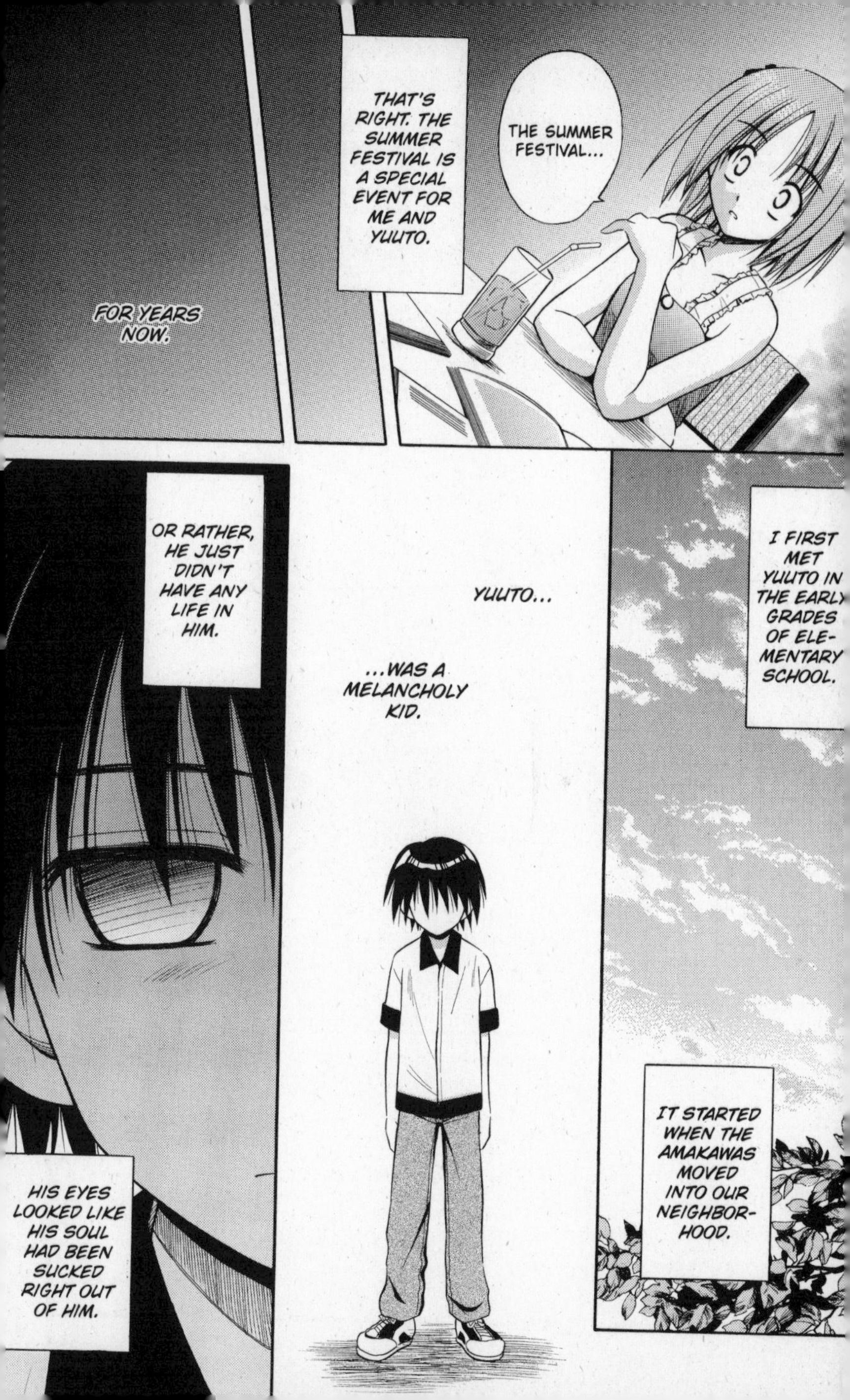
THE SUMMER FESTIVAL...
THAT'S RIGHT. THE SUMMER FESTIVAL IS A SPECIAL EVENT FOR ME AND YUUTO.
FOR YEARS NOW.
I FIRST MET YUUTO IN THE EARLY GRADES OF ELE-MENTARY SCHOOL.
IT STARTED WHEN THE AMAKAWAS MOVED INTO OUR NEIGHBOR-HOOD.
YUUTO...
...WAS A MELANCHOLY KID.
OR RATHER, HE JUST DIDN'T HAVE ANY LIFE IN HIM.
HIS EYES LOOKED LIKE HIS SOUL HAD BEEN SUCKED RIGHT OUT OF HIM.

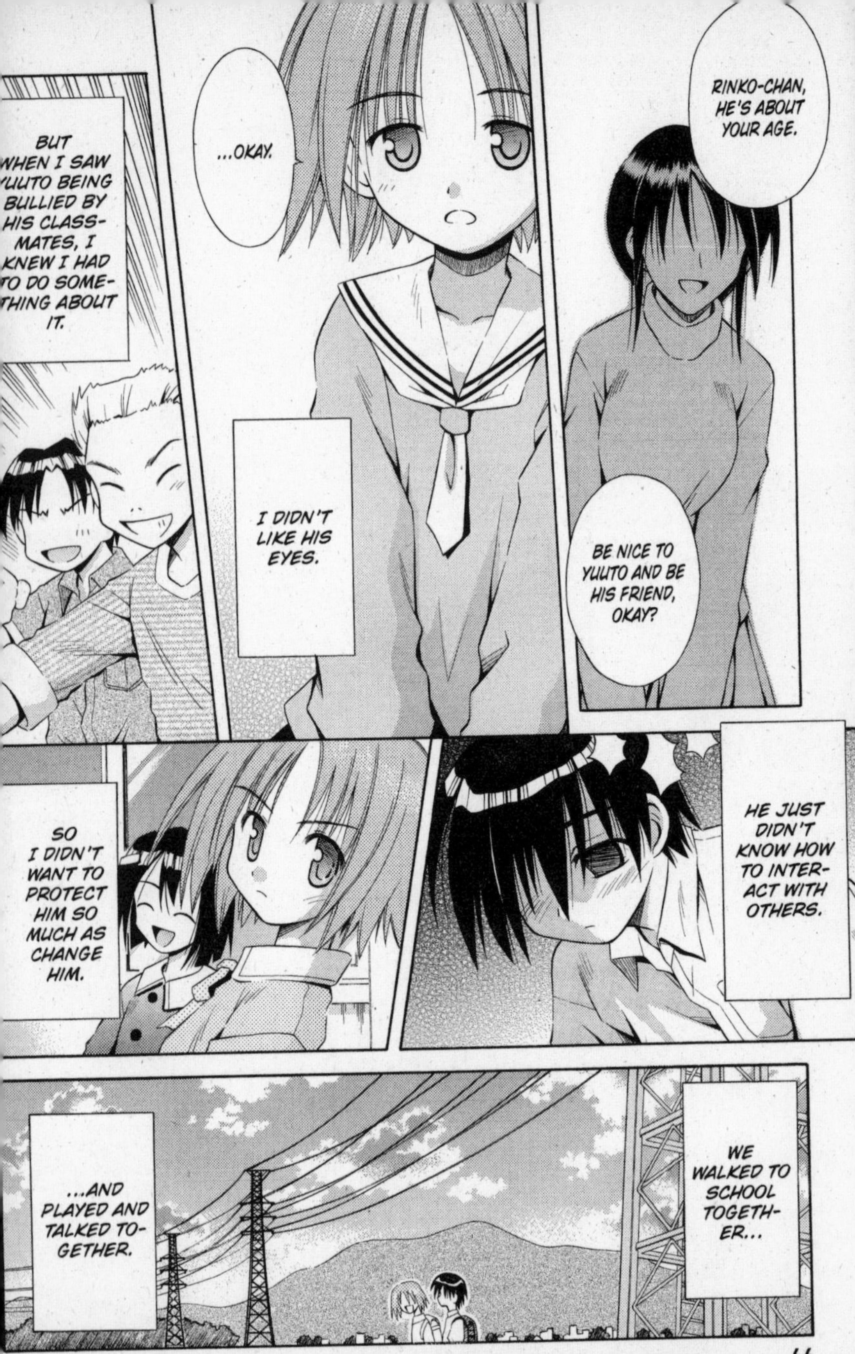
RINKO-CHAN, HE'S ABOUT YOUR AGE.
BE NICE TO YUUTO AND BE HIS FRIEND, OKAY?
...OKAY.
I DIDN'T LIKE HIS EYES.
BUT WHEN I SAW YUUTO BEING BULLIED BY HIS CLASSMATES, I KNEW I HAD TO DO SOMETHING ABOUT IT.
HE JUST DIDN'T KNOW HOW TO INTERACT WITH OTHERS.
SO I DIDN'T WANT TO PROTECT HIM SO MUCH AS CHANGE HIM.
WE WALKED TO SCHOOL TOGETHER...
...AND PLAYED AND TALKED TOGETHER.

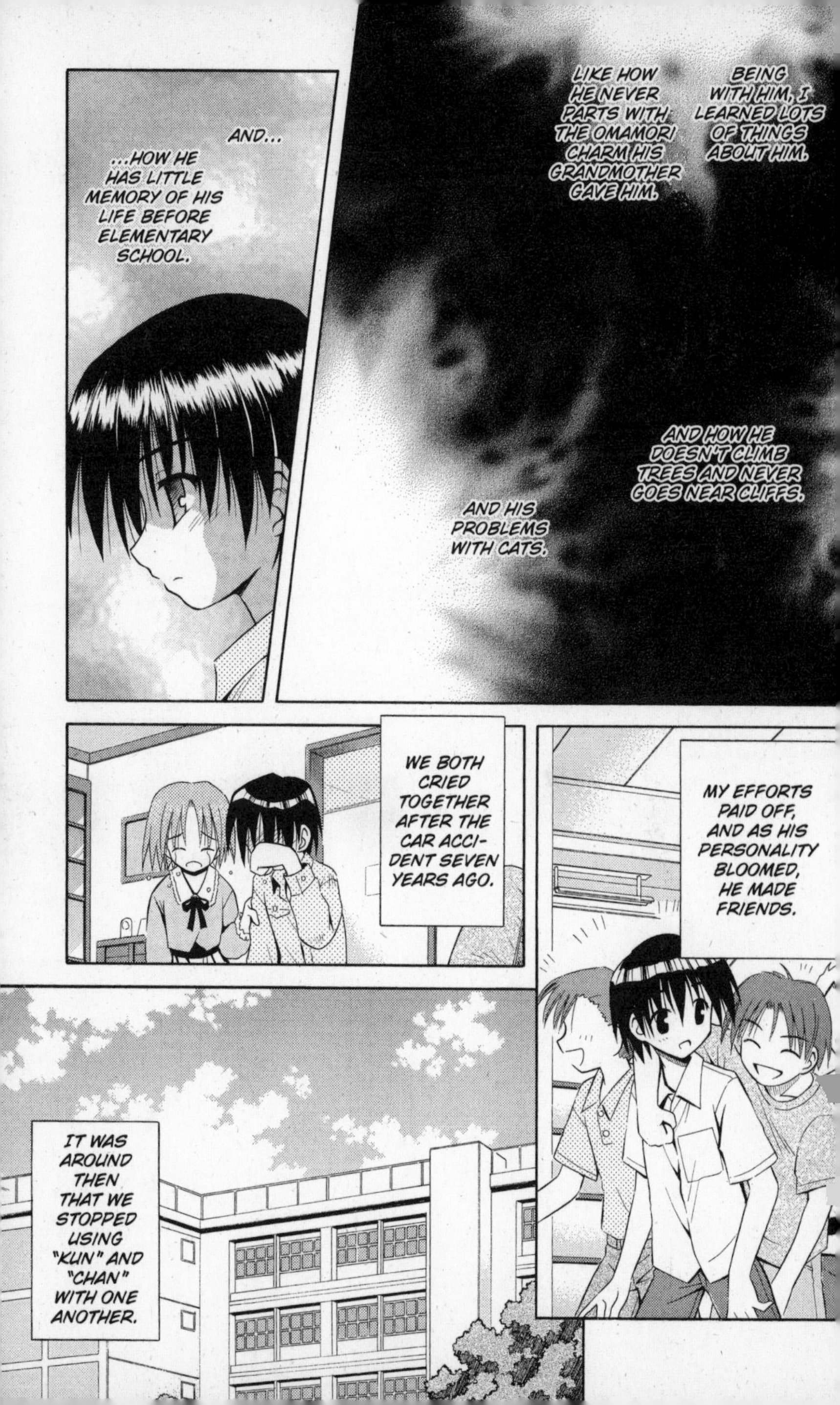
BEING WITH HIM, I LEARNED LOTS OF THINGS ABOUT HIM.
LIKE HOW HE NEVER PARTS WITH THE OMAMORI CHARM HIS GRANDMOTHER GAVE HIM.
AND HOW HE DOESN'T CLIMB TREES AND NEVER GOES NEAR CLIFFS.
AND HIS PROBLEMS WITH CATS.
AND...
...HOW HE HAS LITTLE MEMORY OF HIS LIFE BEFORE ELEMENTARY SCHOOL.
MY EFFORTS PAID OFF, AND AS HIS PERSONALITY BLOOMED, HE MADE FRIENDS.
WE BOTH CRIED TOGETHER AFTER THE CAR ACCI-DENT SEVEN YEARS AGO.
IT WAS AROUND THEN THAT WE STOPPED USING "KUN" AND "CHAN" WITH ONE ANOTHER.

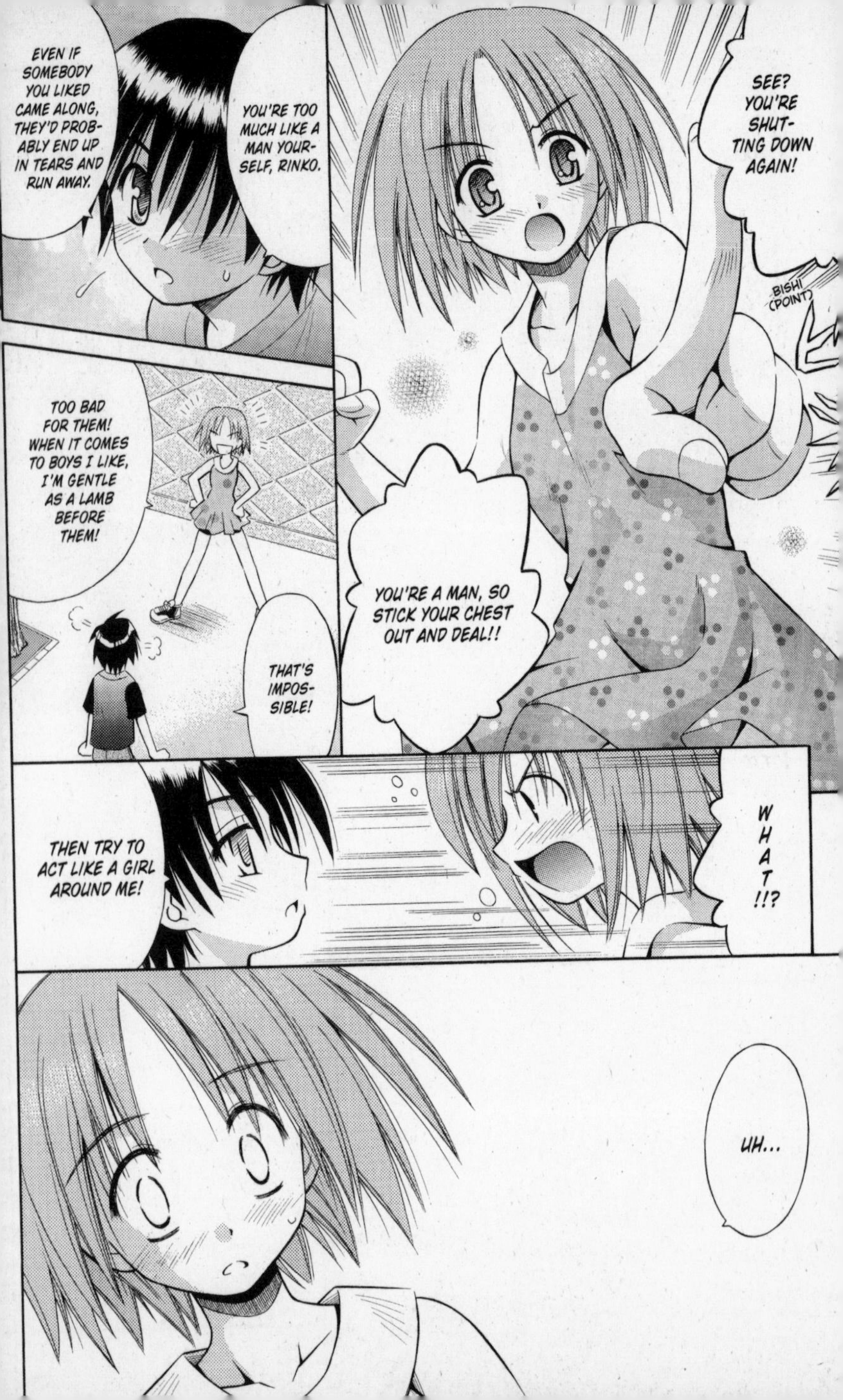
SEE? YOU'RE SHUT-TING DOWN AGAIN!
BISHI (POINT)
YOU'RE A MAN, SO STICK YOUR CHEST OUT AND DEAL!!
YOU'RE TOO MUCH LIKE A MAN YOUR-SELF, RINKO.
EVEN IF SOMEBODY YOU LIKED CAME ALONG, THEY'D PROB-ABLY END UP IN TEARS AND RUN AWAY.
TOO BAD FOR THEM! WHEN IT COMES TO BOYS I LIKE, I'M GENTLE AS A LAMB BEFORE THEM!
THAT'S IMPOS-SIBLE!
THEN TRY TO ACT LIKE A GIRL AROUND ME!
WHAT!!?
UH...

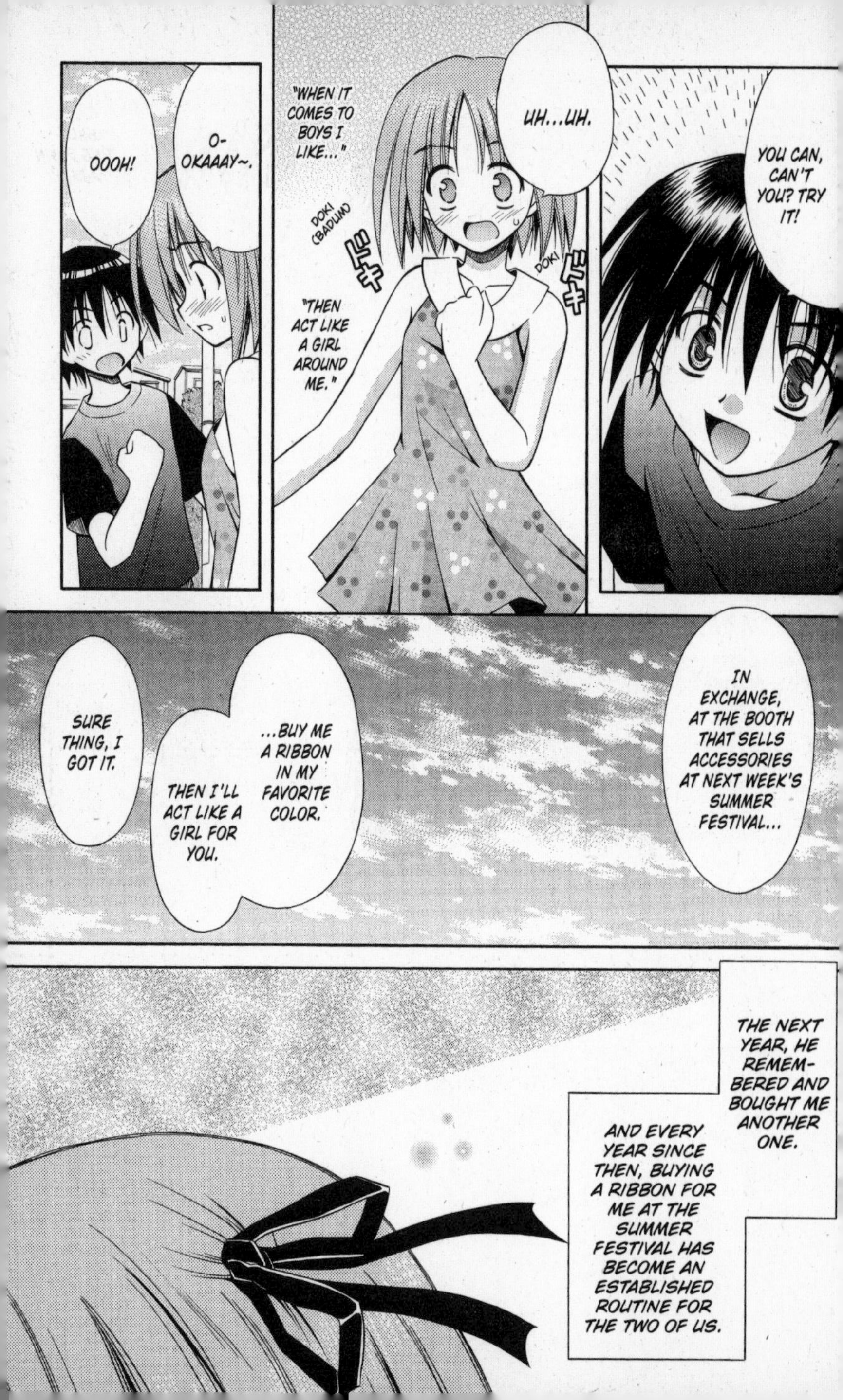
YOU CAN, CAN'T YOU? TRY IT!
UH...UH.
DOKI
"WHEN IT COMES TO BOYS I LIKE..."
DOKI (BADUM)
"THEN ACT LIKE A GIRL AROUND ME."
O-OKAAAY~.
OOOH!
IN EXCHANGE, AT THE BOOTH THAT SELLS ACCESSORIES AT NEXT WEEK'S SUMMER FESTIVAL...
...BUY ME A RIBBON IN MY FAVORITE COLOR.
THEN I'LL ACT LIKE A GIRL FOR YOU.
SURE THING, I GOT IT.
THE NEXT YEAR, HE REMEMBERED AND BOUGHT ME ANOTHER ONE.
AND EVERY YEAR SINCE THEN, BUYING A RIBBON FOR ME AT THE SUMMER FESTIVAL HAS BECOME AN ESTABLISHED ROUTINE FOR THE TWO OF US.

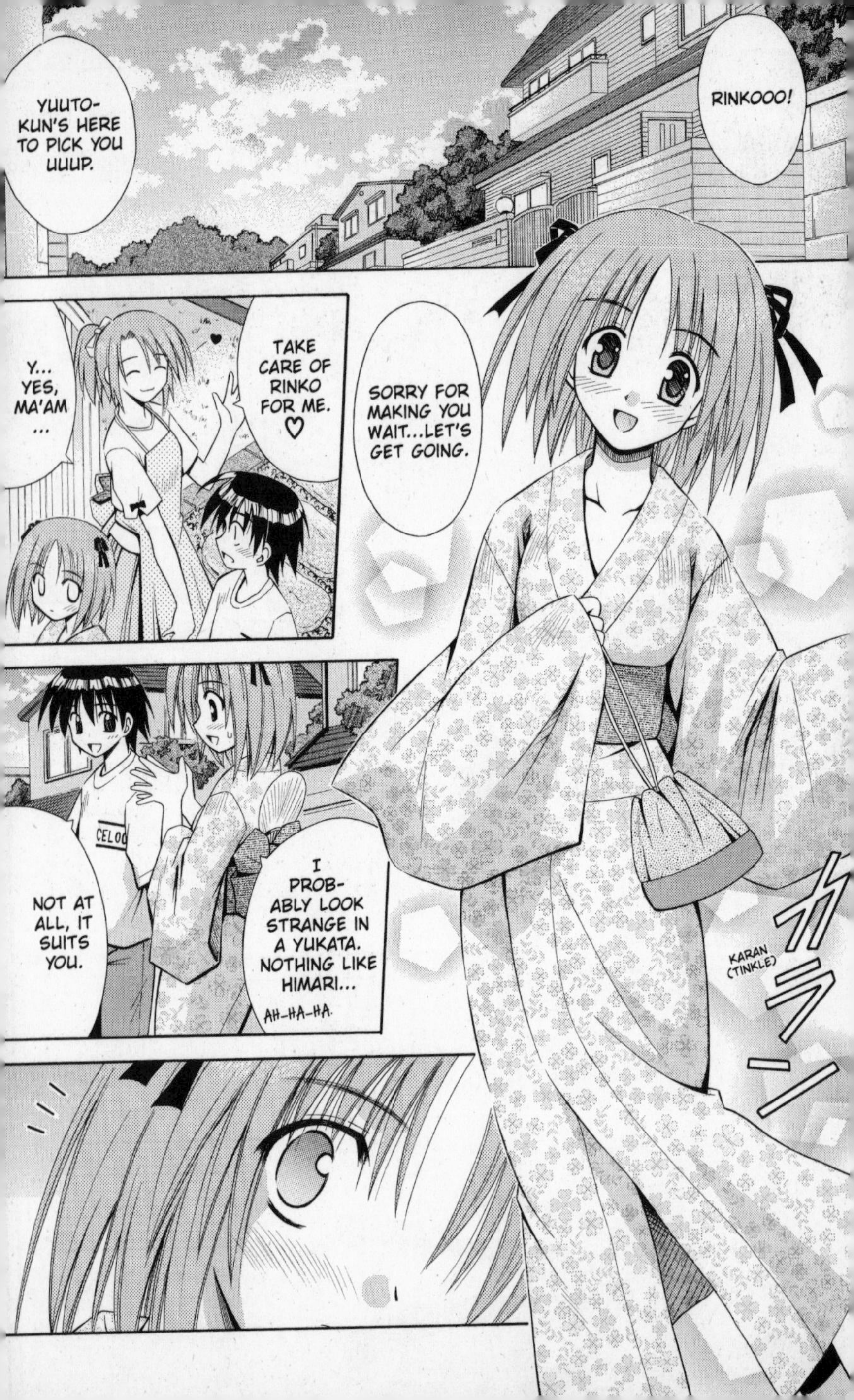
RINKOOO!
YUUTO-KUN'S HERE TO PICK YOU UUUP.
SORRY FOR MAKING YOU WAIT...LET'S GET GOING.
KARAN (TINKLE)
TAKE CARE OF RINKO FOR ME. ♡
Y... YES, MA'AM ...
I PROBABLY LOOK STRANGE IN A YUKATA. NOTHING LIKE HIMARI...
AH-HA-HA.
NOT AT ALL, IT SUITS YOU.

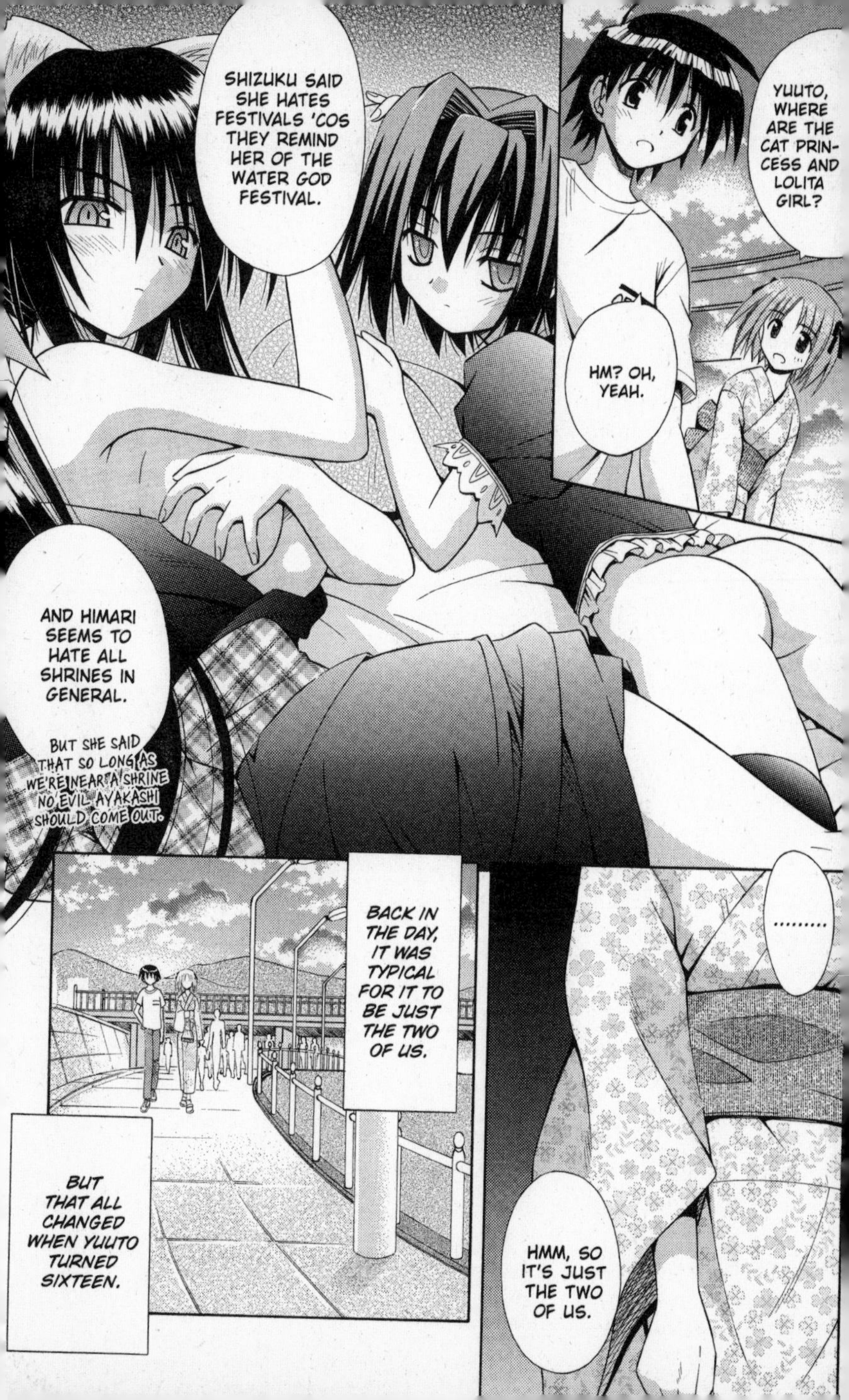
YUUTO, WHERE ARE THE CAT PRIN-CESS AND LOLITA GIRL?
HM? OH, YEAH.
SHIZUKU SAID SHE HATES FESTIVALS 'COS THEY REMIND HER OF THE WATER GOD FESTIVAL.
AND HIMARI SEEMS TO HATE ALL SHRINES IN GENERAL.
BUT SHE SAID THAT SO LONG AS WE'RE NEAR A SHRINE NO EVIL AYAKASHI SHOULD COME OUT.
....
HMM, SO IT'S JUST THE TWO OF US.
BACK IN THE DAY, IT WAS TYPICAL FOR IT TO BE JUST THE TWO OF US.
BUT THAT ALL CHANGED WHEN YUUTO TURNED SIXTEEN.

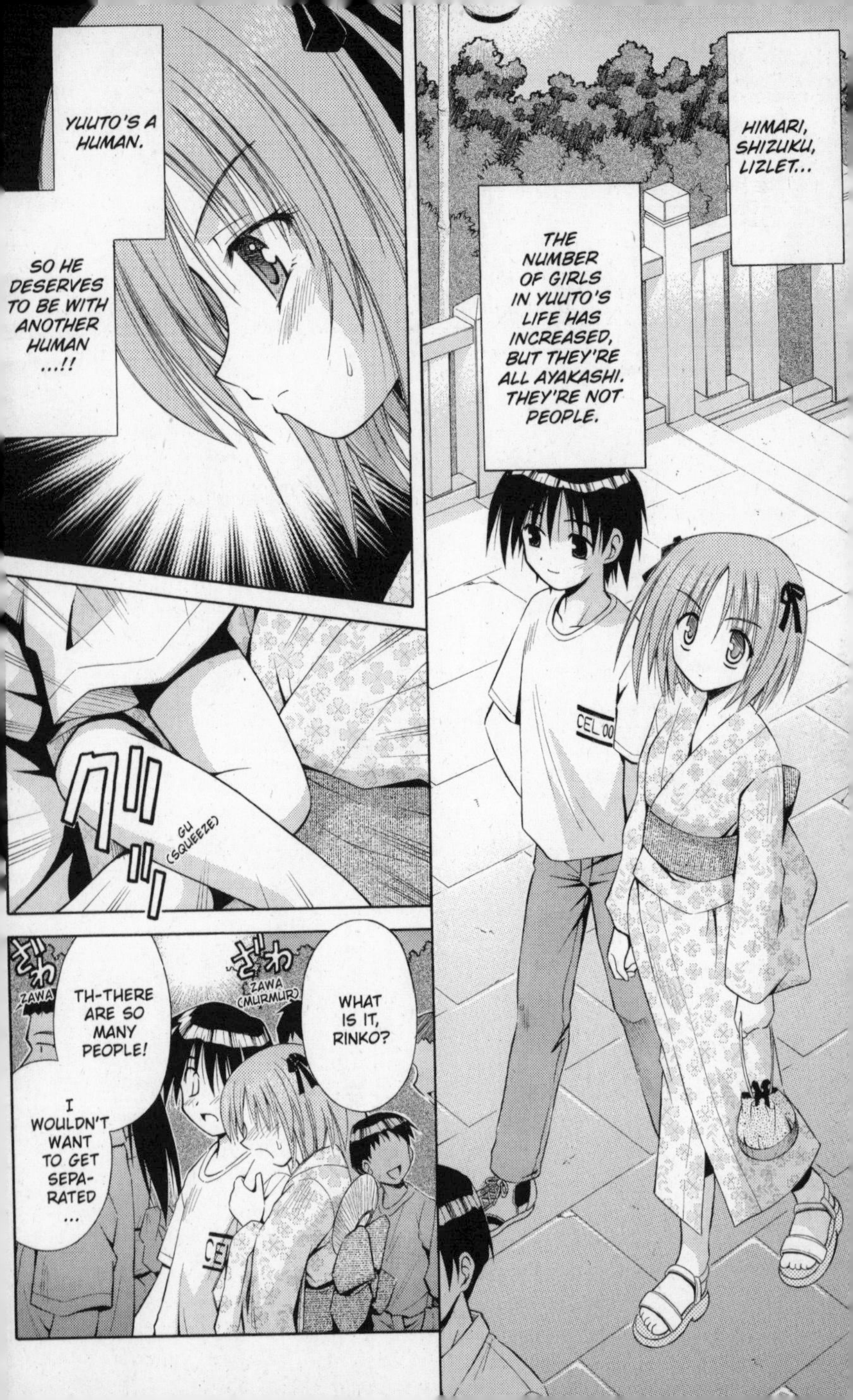

HIMARI, SHIZUKU, LIZLET...
THE NUMBER OF GIRLS IN YUUTO'S LIFE HAS INCREASED, BUT THEY'RE ALL AYAKASHI. THEY'RE NOT PEOPLE.
YUUTO'S A HUMAN.
SO HE DESERVES TO BE WITH ANOTHER HUMAN ...!!
GU (SQUEEZE)
ZAWA (MURMUR)
WHAT IS IT, RINKO?
ZAWA
TH-THERE ARE SO MANY PEOPLE!
I WOULDN'T WANT TO GET SEPA-RATED ...

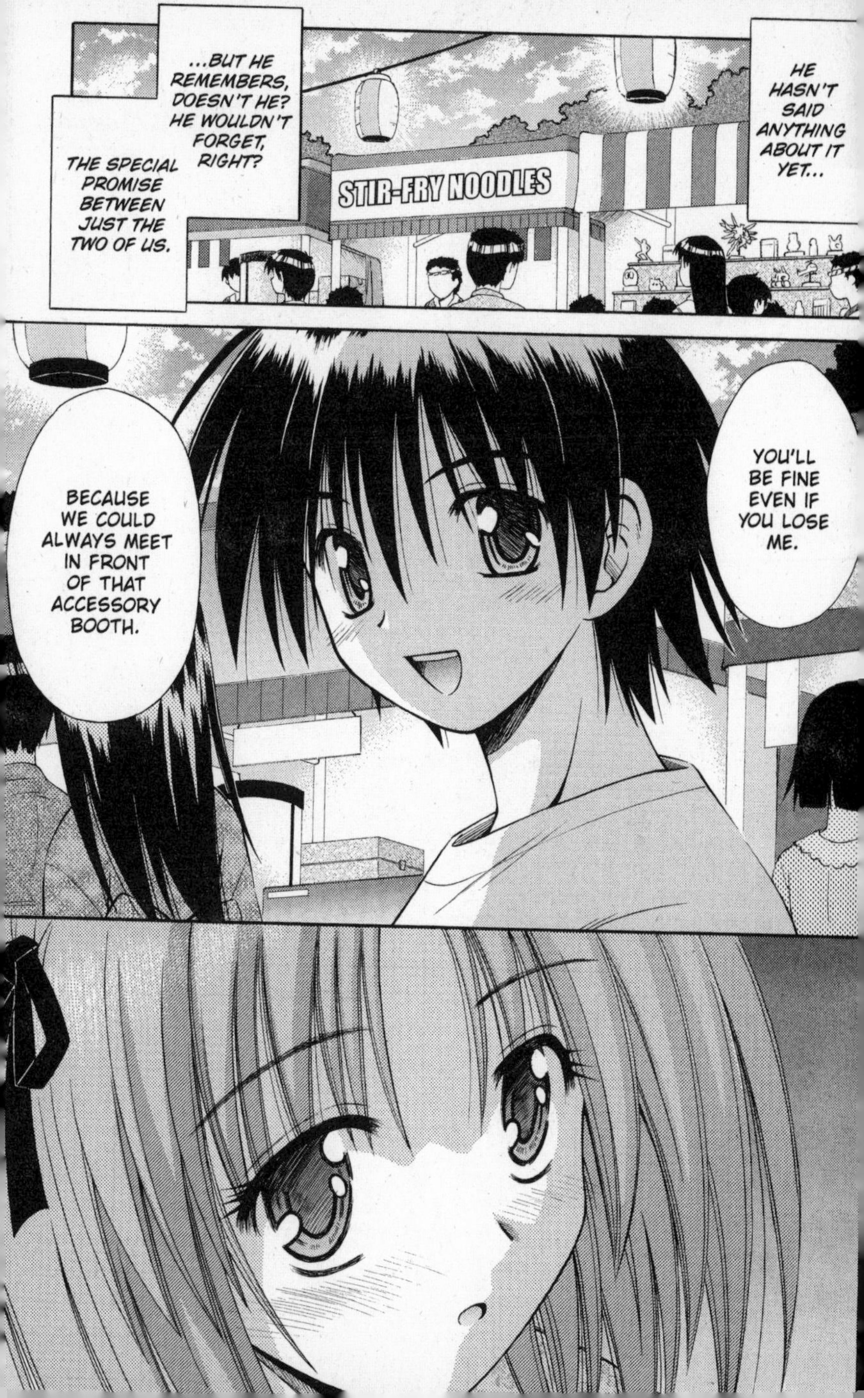
HE HASN'T SAID ANYTHING ABOUT IT YET...
...BUT HE REMEMBERS, DOESN'T HE? HE WOULDN'T FORGET, RIGHT?
STIR-FRY NOODLES
THE SPECIAL PROMISE BETWEEN JUST THE TWO OF US.
YOU'LL BE FINE EVEN IF YOU LOSE ME.
BECAUSE WE COULD ALWAYS MEET IN FRONT OF THAT ACCESSORY BOOTH.

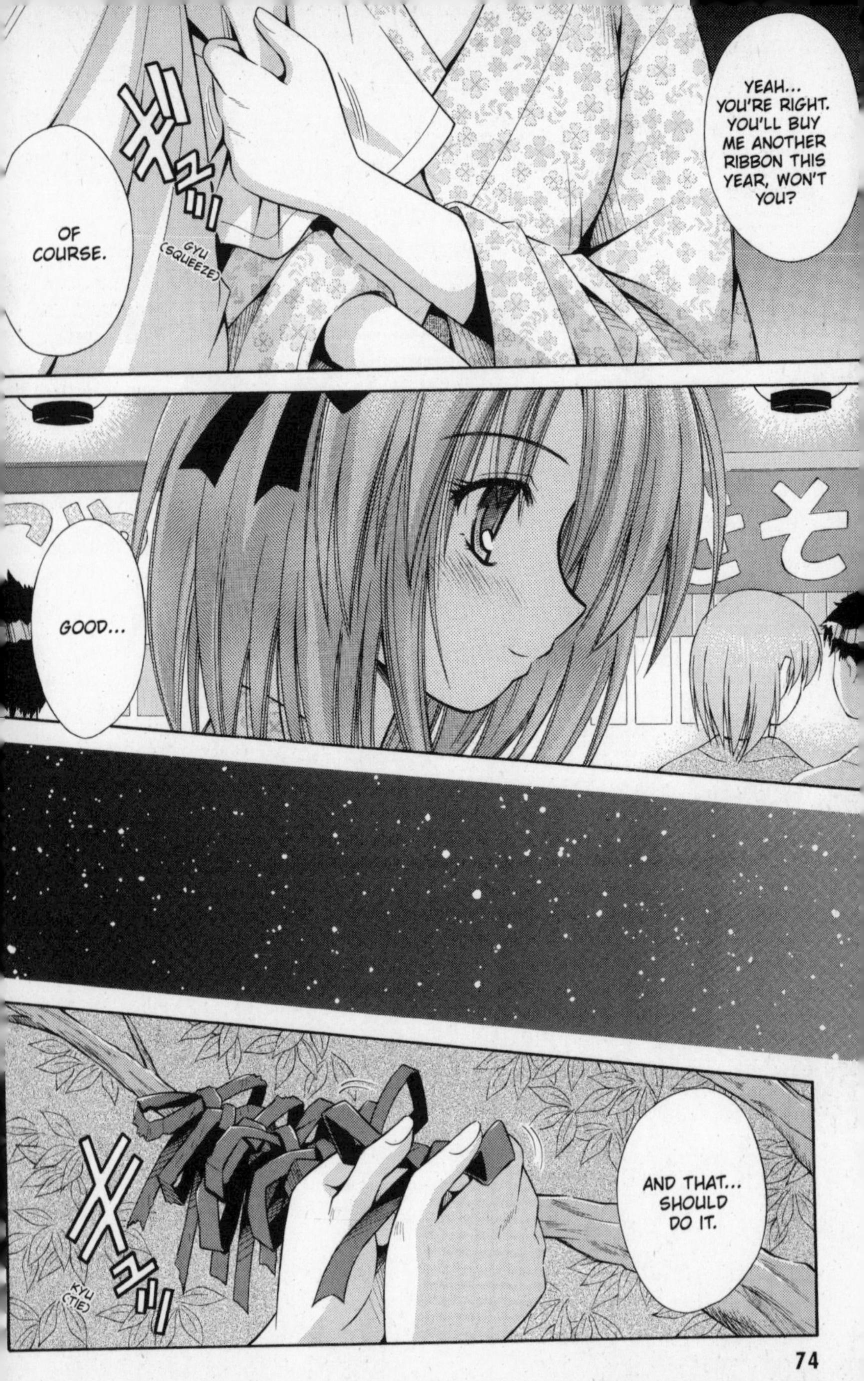
YEAH... YOU'RE RIGHT. YOU'LL BUY ME ANOTHER RIBBON THIS YEAR, WON'T YOU?
GYU (SQUEEZE)
OF COURSE.
GOOD...
AND THAT... SHOULD DO IT.
KYU (TIE)

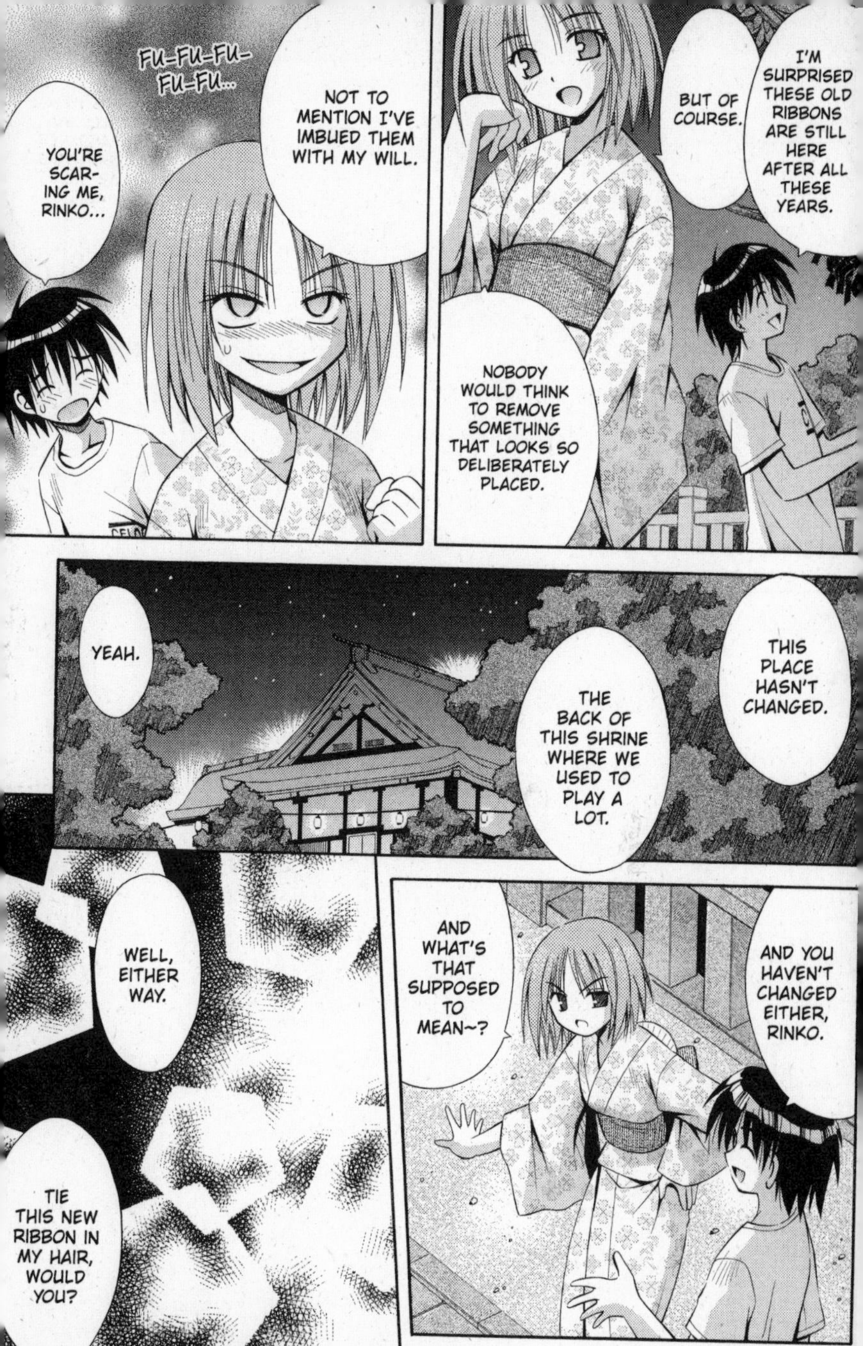
I'M SURPRISED THESE OLD RIBBONS ARE STILL HERE AFTER ALL THESE YEARS.
BUT OF COURSE.
NOBODY WOULD THINK TO REMOVE SOMETHING THAT LOOKS SO DELIBERATELY PLACED.
NOT TO MENTION I'VE IMBUED THEM WITH MY WILL.
FU-FU-FU-FU-FU...
YOU'RE SCAR-ING ME, RINKO...
THIS PLACE HASN'T CHANGED.
THE BACK OF THIS SHRINE WHERE WE USED TO PLAY A LOT.
YEAH.
AND YOU HAVEN'T CHANGED EITHER, RINKO.
AND WHAT'S THAT SUPPOSED TO MEAN~?
WELL, EITHER WAY.
TIE THIS NEW RIBBON IN MY HAIR, WOULD YOU?

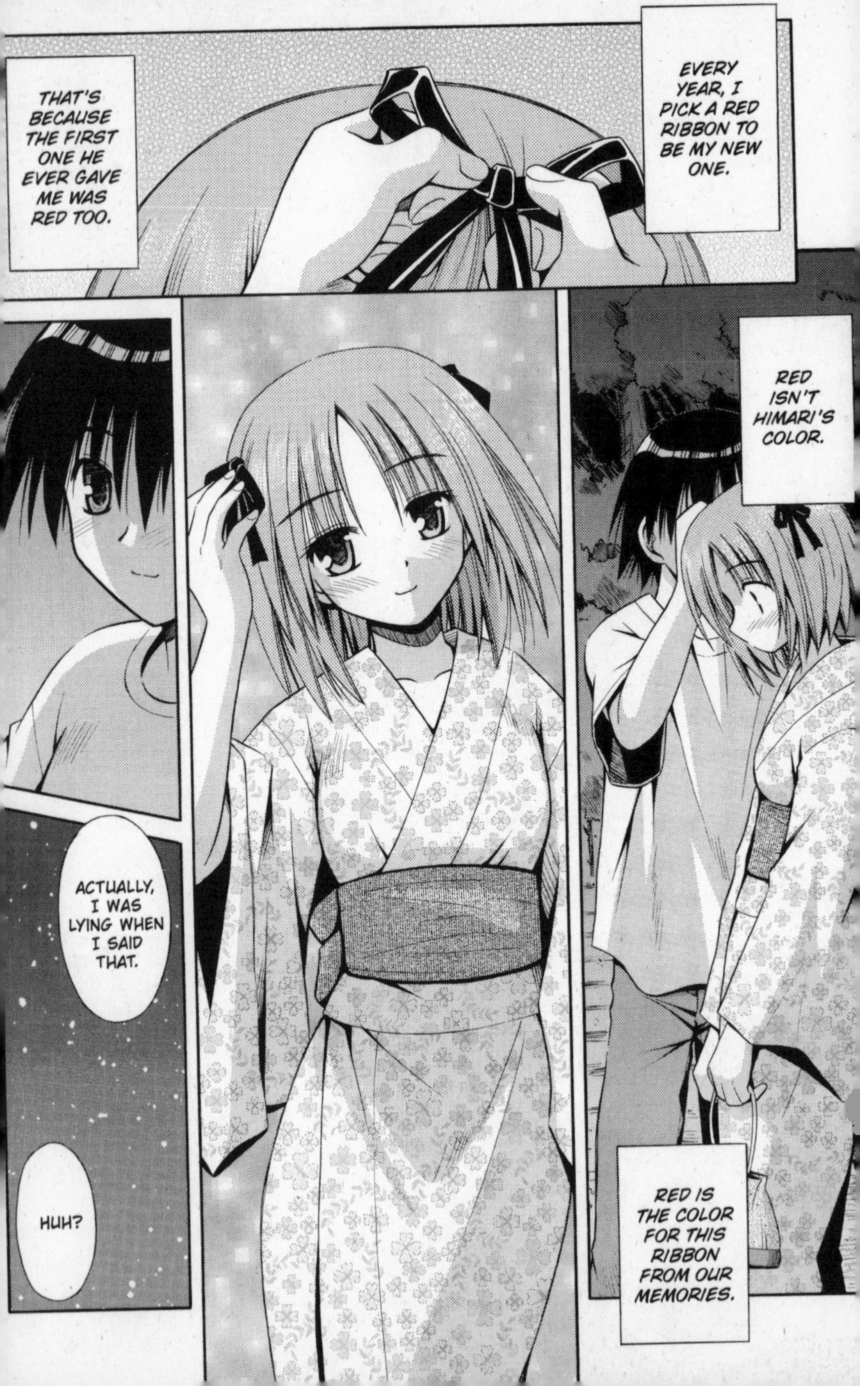
EVERY YEAR, I PICK A RED RIBBON TO BE MY NEW ONE.
THAT'S BECAUSE THE FIRST ONE HE EVER GAVE ME WAS RED TOO.
RED ISN'T HIMARI'S COLOR.
RED IS THE COLOR FOR THIS RIBBON FROM OUR MEMORIES.
ACTUALLY, I WAS LYING WHEN I SAID THAT.
HUH?

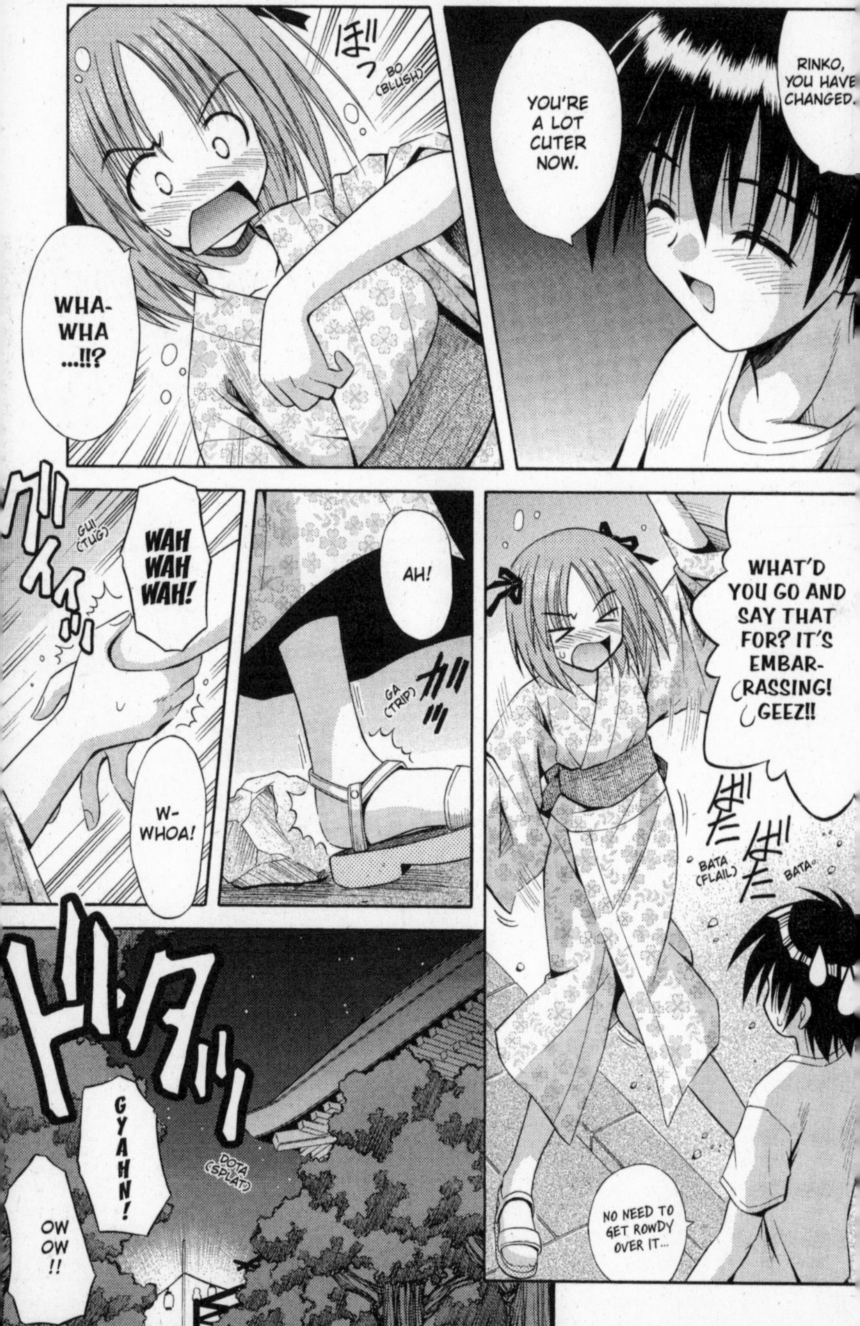

RINKO, YOU HAVE CHANGED.
YOU'RE A LOT CUTER NOW.
ぼっ
BO (BLUSH)
WHA-WHA ...!!?
WHAT'D YOU GO AND SAY THAT FOR? IT'S EMBAR-RASSING! GEEZ!!
BATA (FLAIL)
BATA
NO NEED TO GET ROWDY OVER IT...
AH!
GA (TRIP)
GUI (TUG)
WAH WAH WAH!
W-WHOA!
DOTA (SPLAT)
GYAHN!
OW OW !!

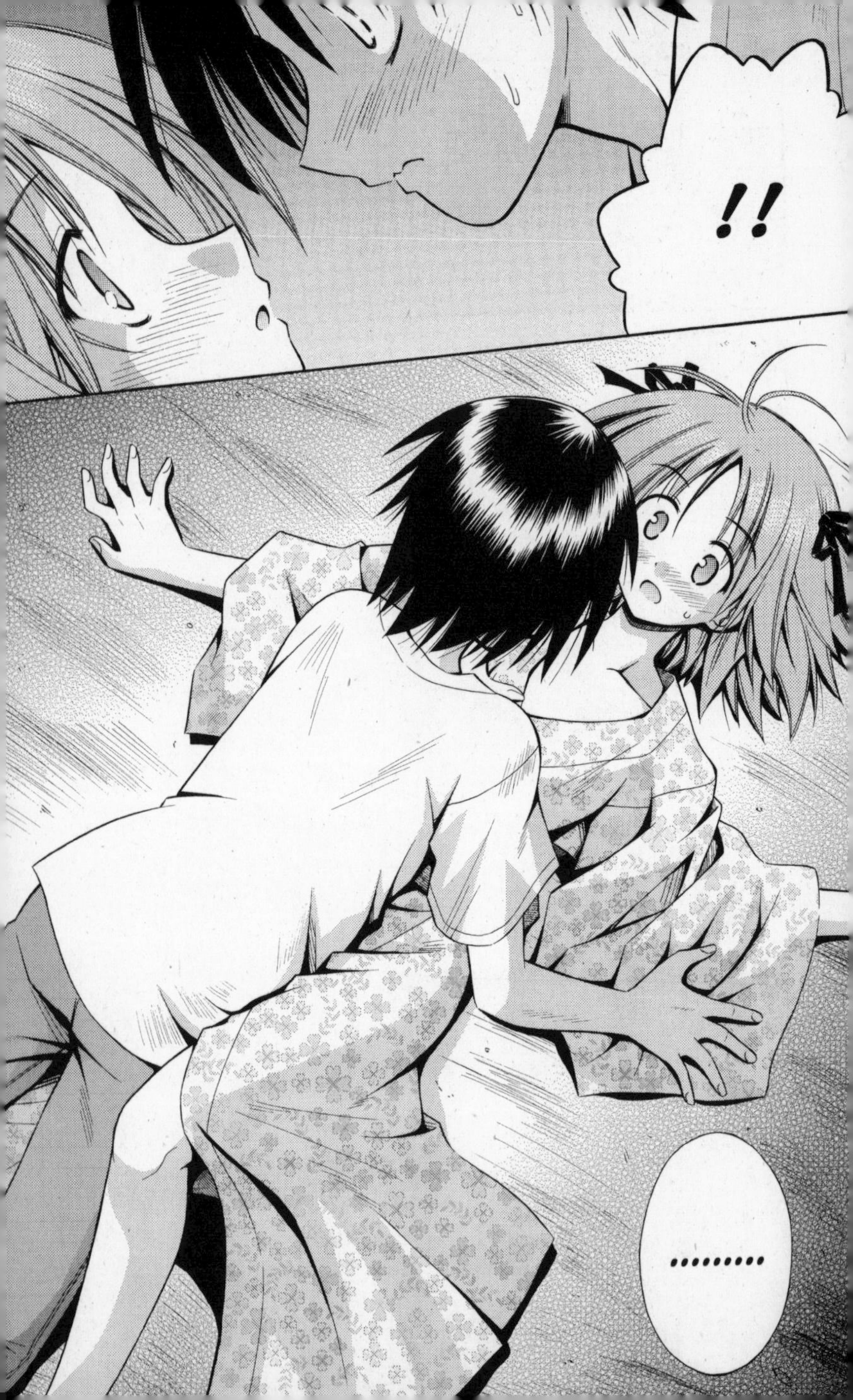
!!
....

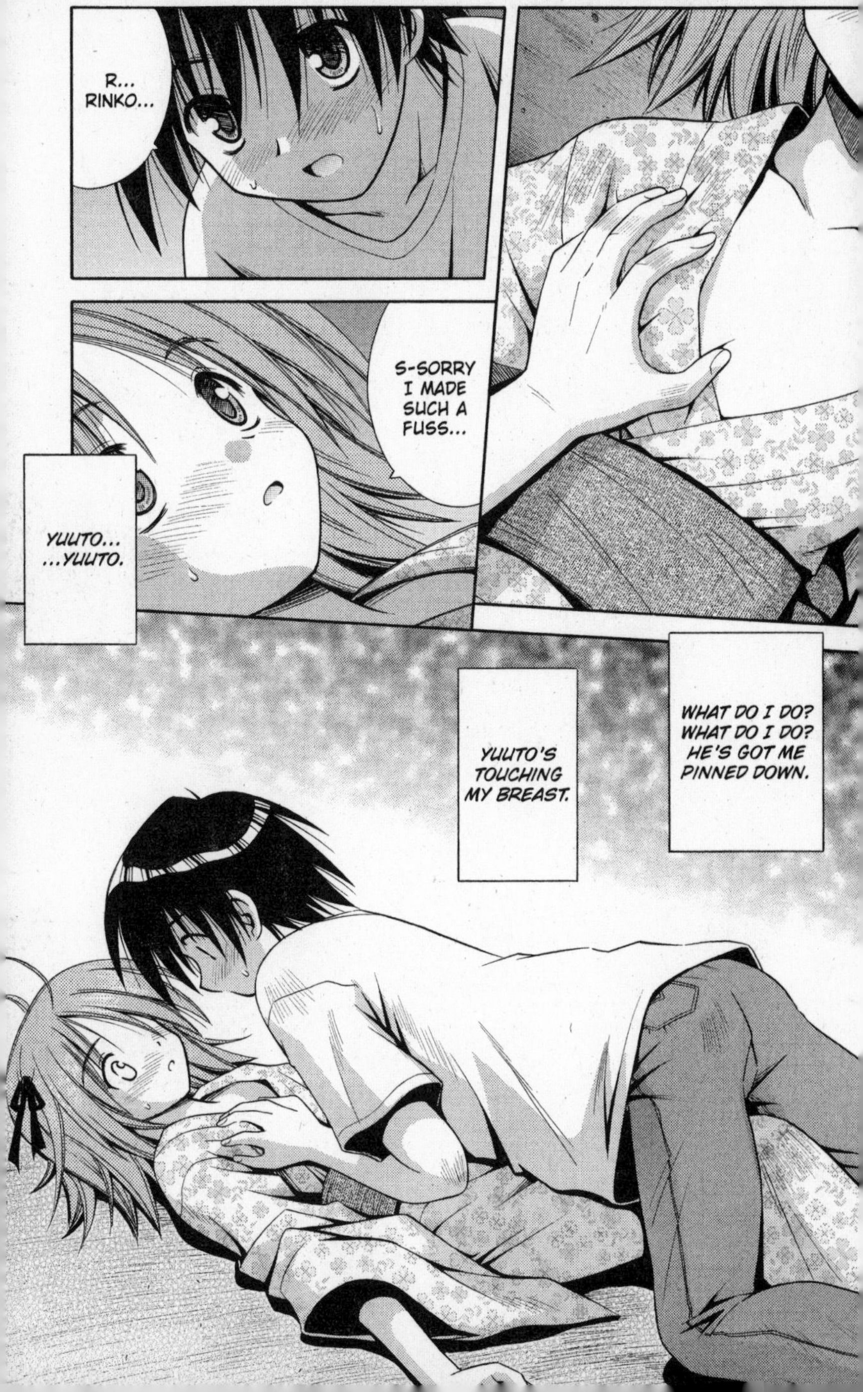

R... RINKO...
S-SORRY I MADE SUCH A FUSS...
YUUTO... ...YUUTO.
WHAT DO I DO? WHAT DO I DO? HE'S GOT ME PINNED DOWN.
YUUTO'S TOUCHING MY BREAST.

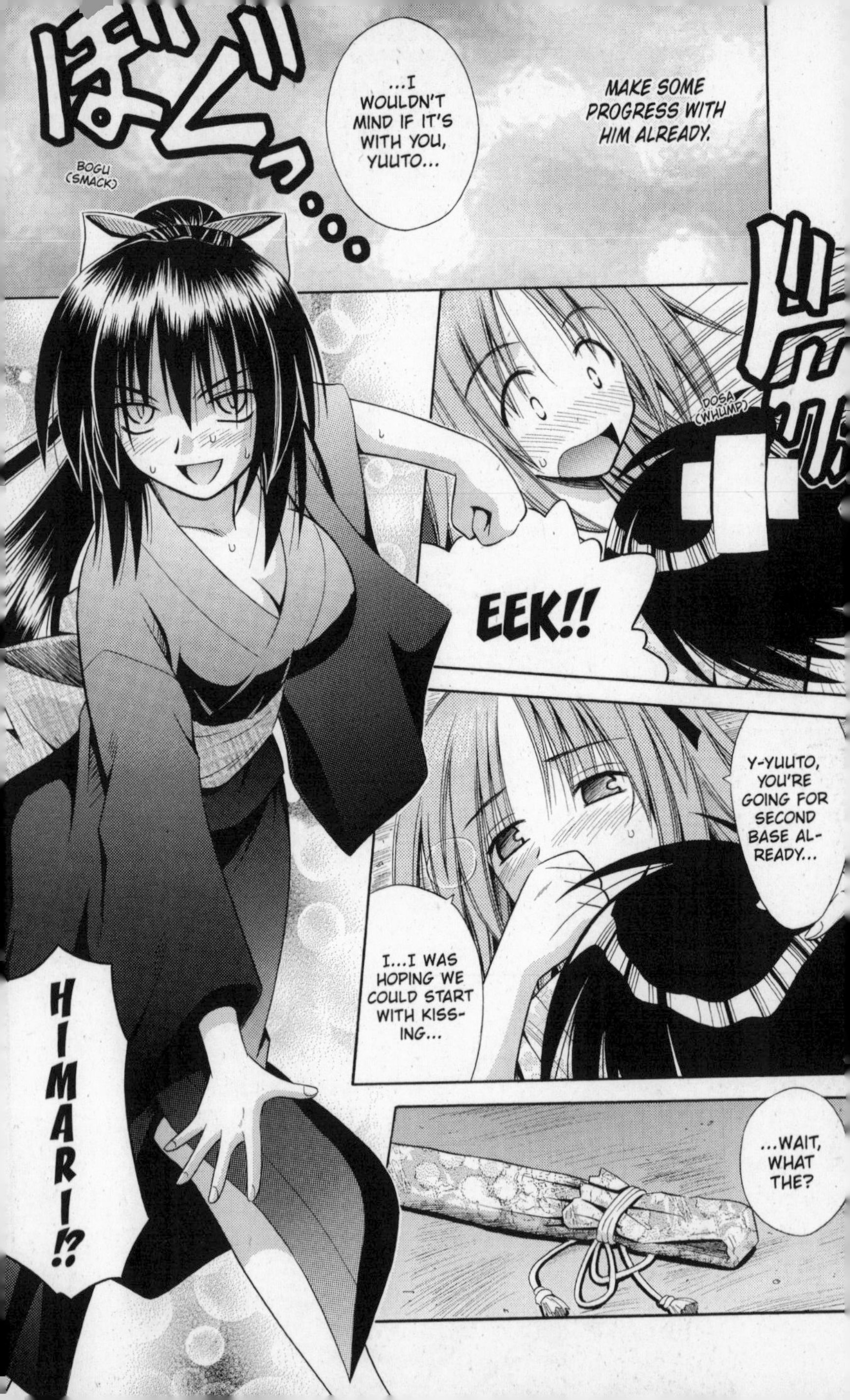
MAKE SOME PROGRESS WITH HIM ALREADY.
...I WOULDN'T MIND IF IT'S WITH YOU, YUUTO...
BOGU (SMACK)
DOSA (WHUMP)
EEK!!
Y-YUUTO, YOU'RE GOING FOR SECOND BASE AL-READY...
I...I WAS HOPING WE COULD START WITH KISS-ING...
...WAIT, WHAT THE?
HIMARI!?

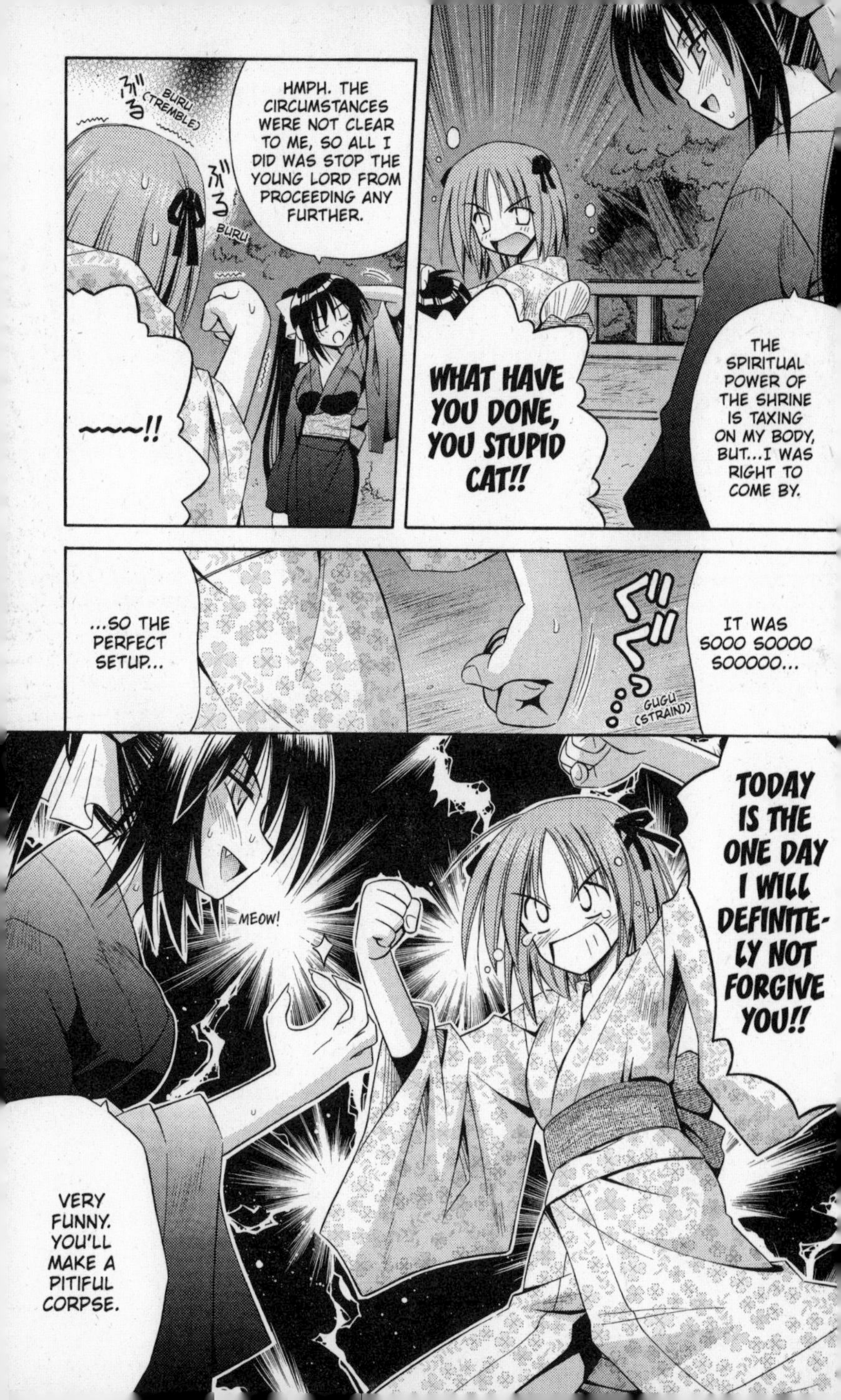
THE SPIRITUAL POWER OF THE SHRINE IS TAXING ON MY BODY, BUT...I WAS RIGHT TO COME BY.
WHAT HAVE YOU DONE, YOU STUPID CAT!!
HMPH. THE CIRCUMSTANCES WERE NOT CLEAR TO ME, SO ALL I DID WAS STOP THE YOUNG LORD FROM PROCEEDING ANY FURTHER.
ぶる BURU (TREMBLE)
ぶる BURU
~~~!!
IT WAS SOOO SOOOO SOOOOO...
ぐぐ GUGU (STRAIN)
...SO THE PERFECT SETUP...
TODAY IS THE ONE DAY I WILL DEFINITE-LY NOT FORGIVE YOU!!
MEOW!
VERY FUNNY. YOU'LL MAKE A PITIFUL CORPSE.
~~~

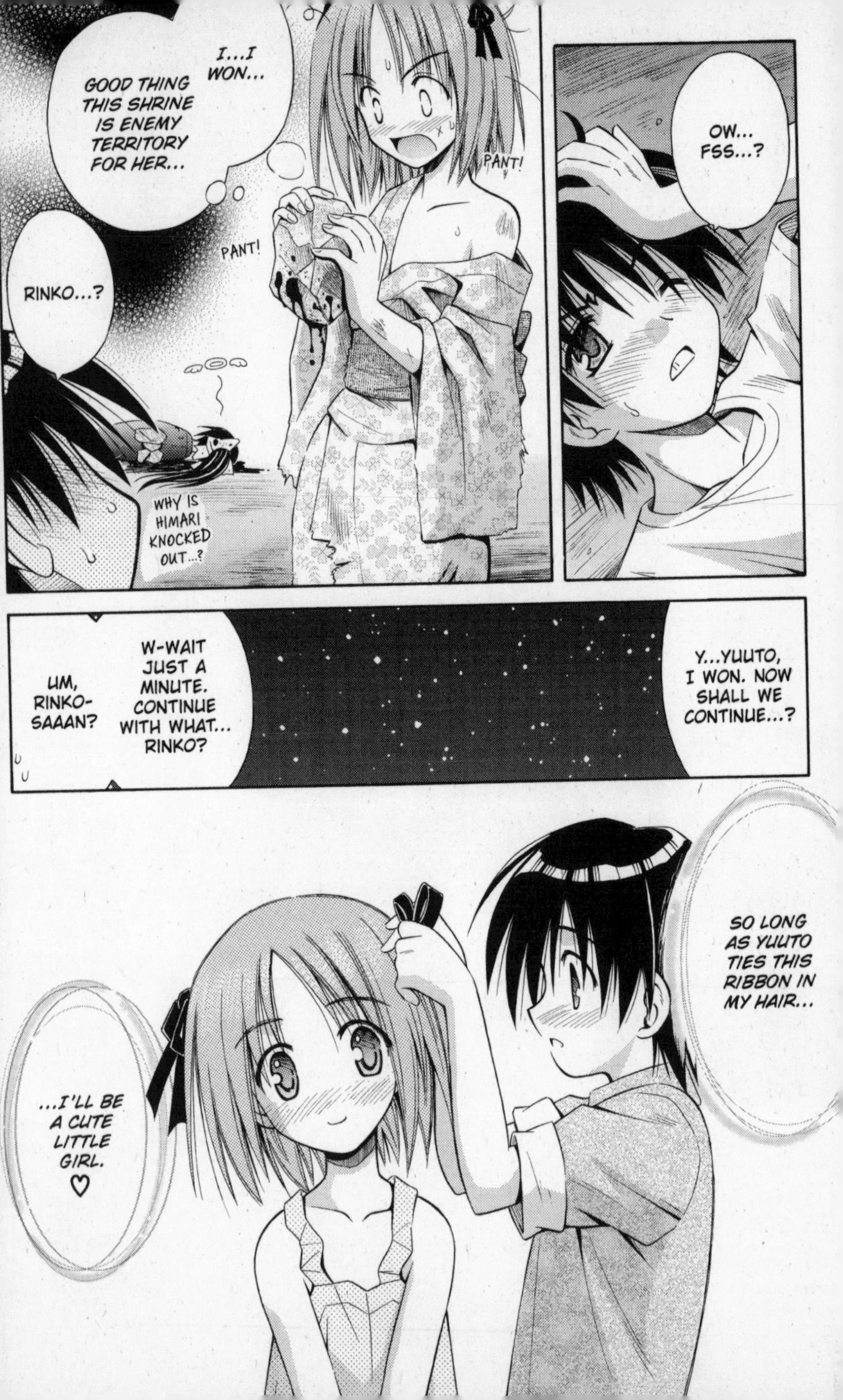
OW... FSS...?
I...I WON...
GOOD THING THIS SHRINE IS ENEMY TERRITORY FOR HER...
PANT!
PANT!
RINKO...?
WHY IS HIMARI KNOCKED OUT...?
Y...YUUTO, I WON. NOW SHALL WE CONTINUE...?
W-WAIT JUST A MINUTE. CONTINUE WITH WHAT... RINKO?
UM, RINKO-SAAAN?
SO LONG AS YUUTO TIES THIS RIBBON IN MY HAIR...
...I'LL BE A CUTE LITTLE GIRL. ♥

MENAGERIE 10: TWILIGHT KITTY OF TEMPTATION

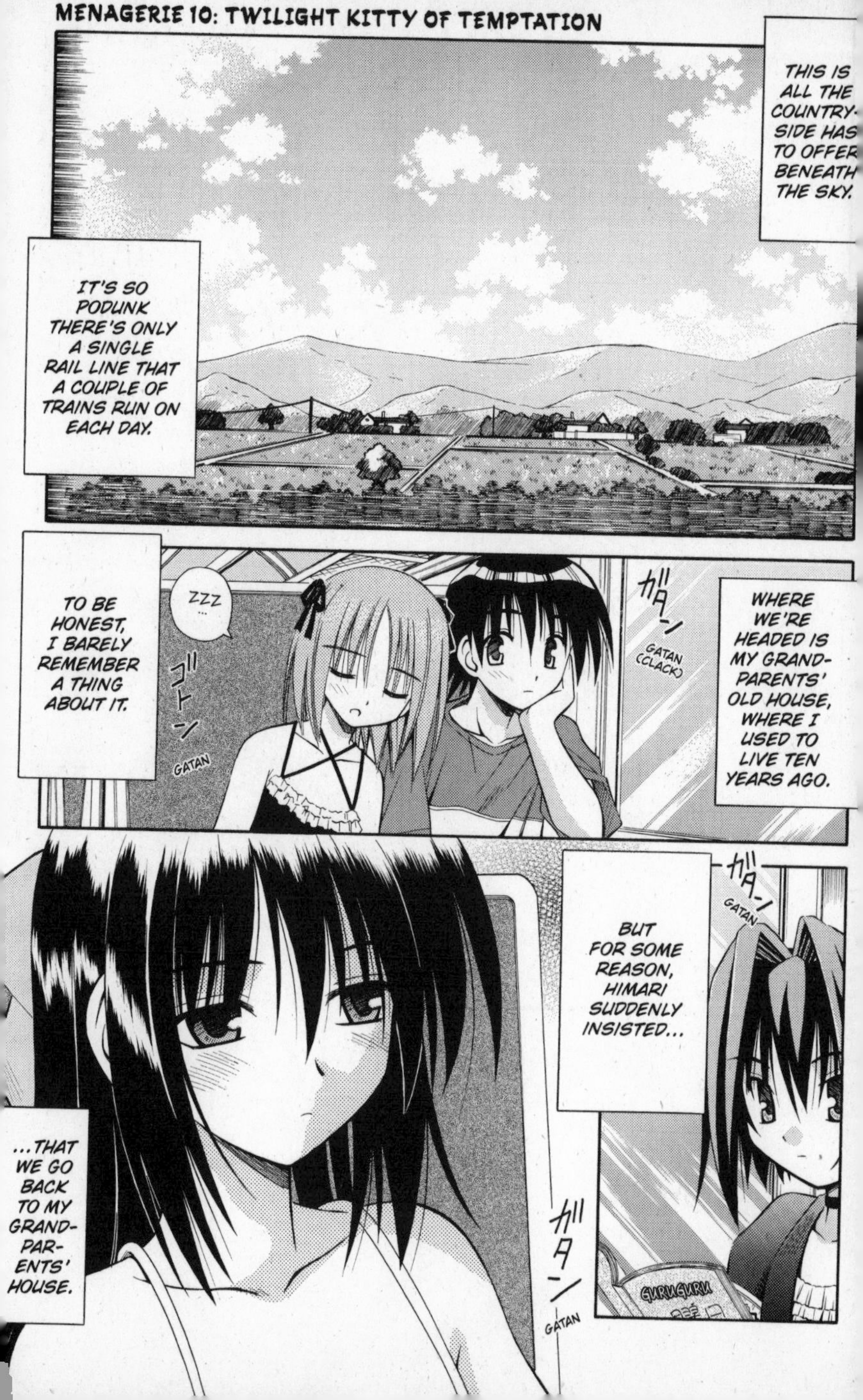
THIS IS ALL THE COUNTRY-SIDE HAS TO OFFER BENEATH THE SKY.
IT'S SO PODUNK THERE'S ONLY A SINGLE RAIL LINE THAT A COUPLE OF TRAINS RUN ON EACH DAY.
WHERE WE'RE HEADED IS MY GRAND-PARENTS' OLD HOUSE, WHERE I USED TO LIVE TEN YEARS AGO.
GATAN (CLACK)
ZZZ ...
GATAN
TO BE HONEST, I BARELY REMEMBER A THING ABOUT IT.
GATAN
BUT FOR SOME REASON, HIMARI SUDDENLY INSISTED...
GURUGURU
GATAN
...THAT WE GO BACK TO MY GRAND-PAR-ENTS' HOUSE.

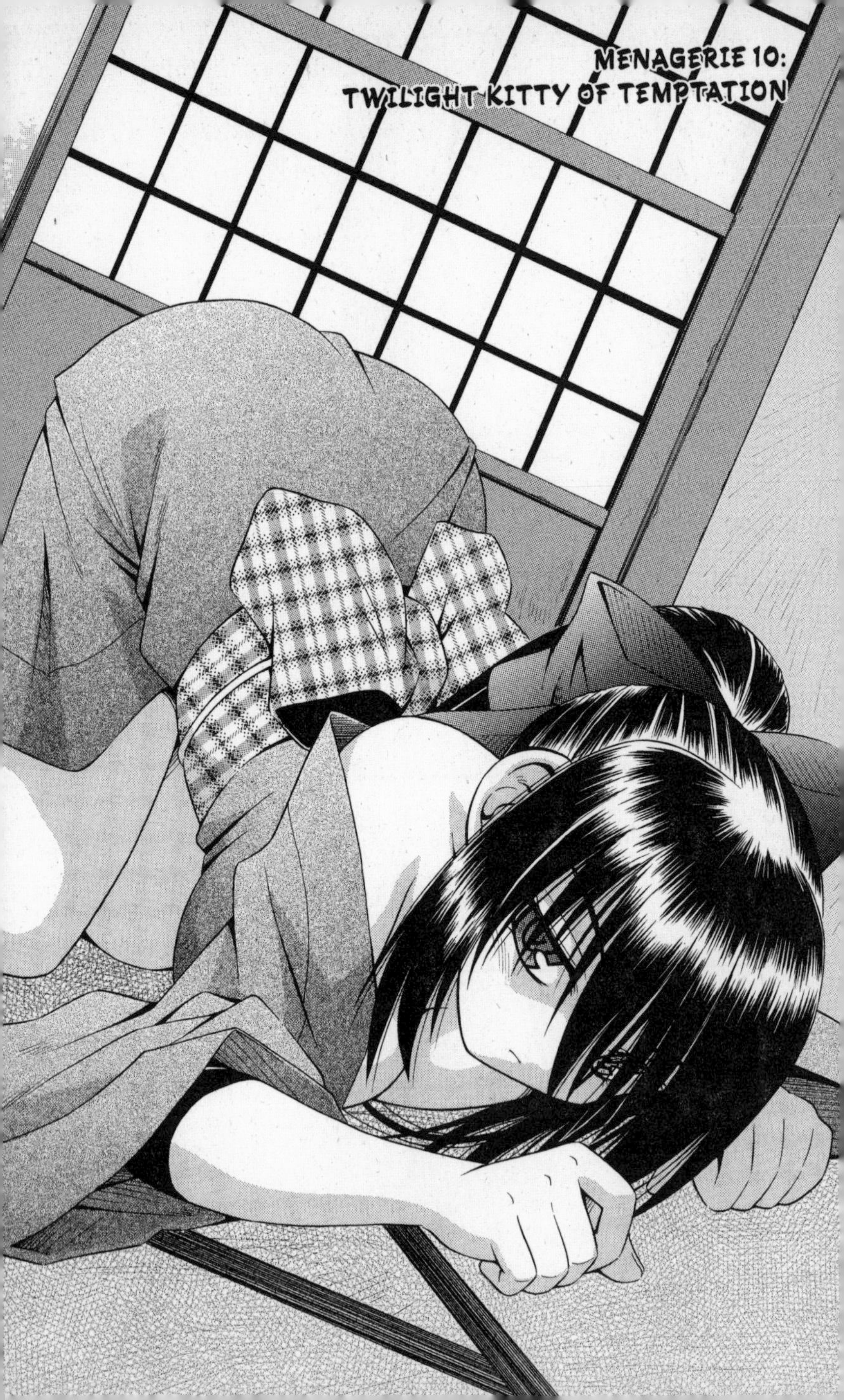
MENAGERIE 10:
TWILIGHT KITTY OF TEMPTATION

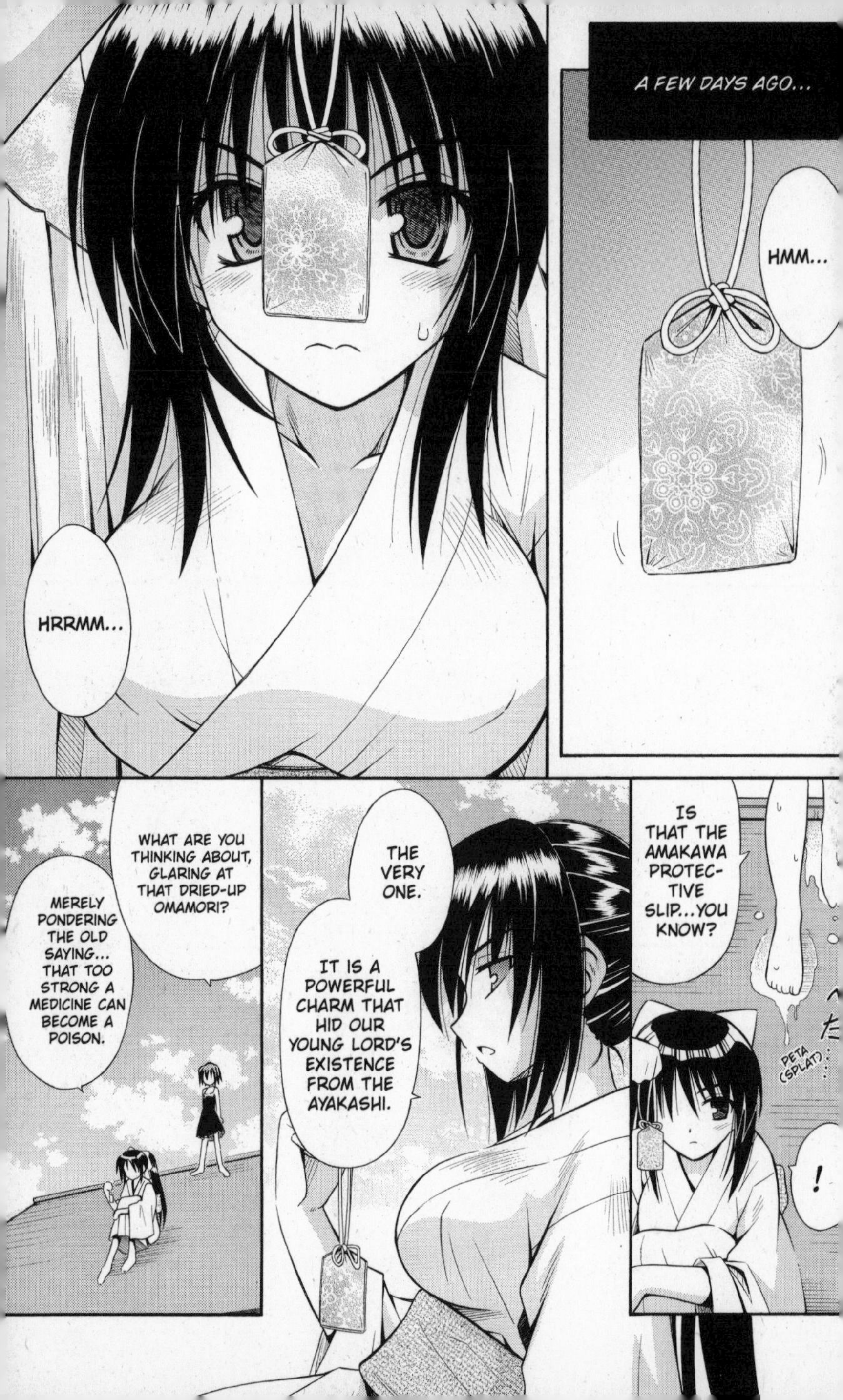

A FEW DAYS AGO...
HMM...
HRRMM...
IS THAT THE AMAKAWA PROTECTIVE SLIP...YOU KNOW?
PETA (SPLAT)...
!
THE VERY ONE.
IT IS A POWERFUL CHARM THAT HID OUR YOUNG LORD'S EXISTENCE FROM THE AYAKASHI.
WHAT ARE YOU THINKING ABOUT, GLARING AT THAT DRIED-UP OMAMORI?
MERELY PONDERING THE OLD SAYING... THAT TOO STRONG A MEDICINE CAN BECOME A POISON.

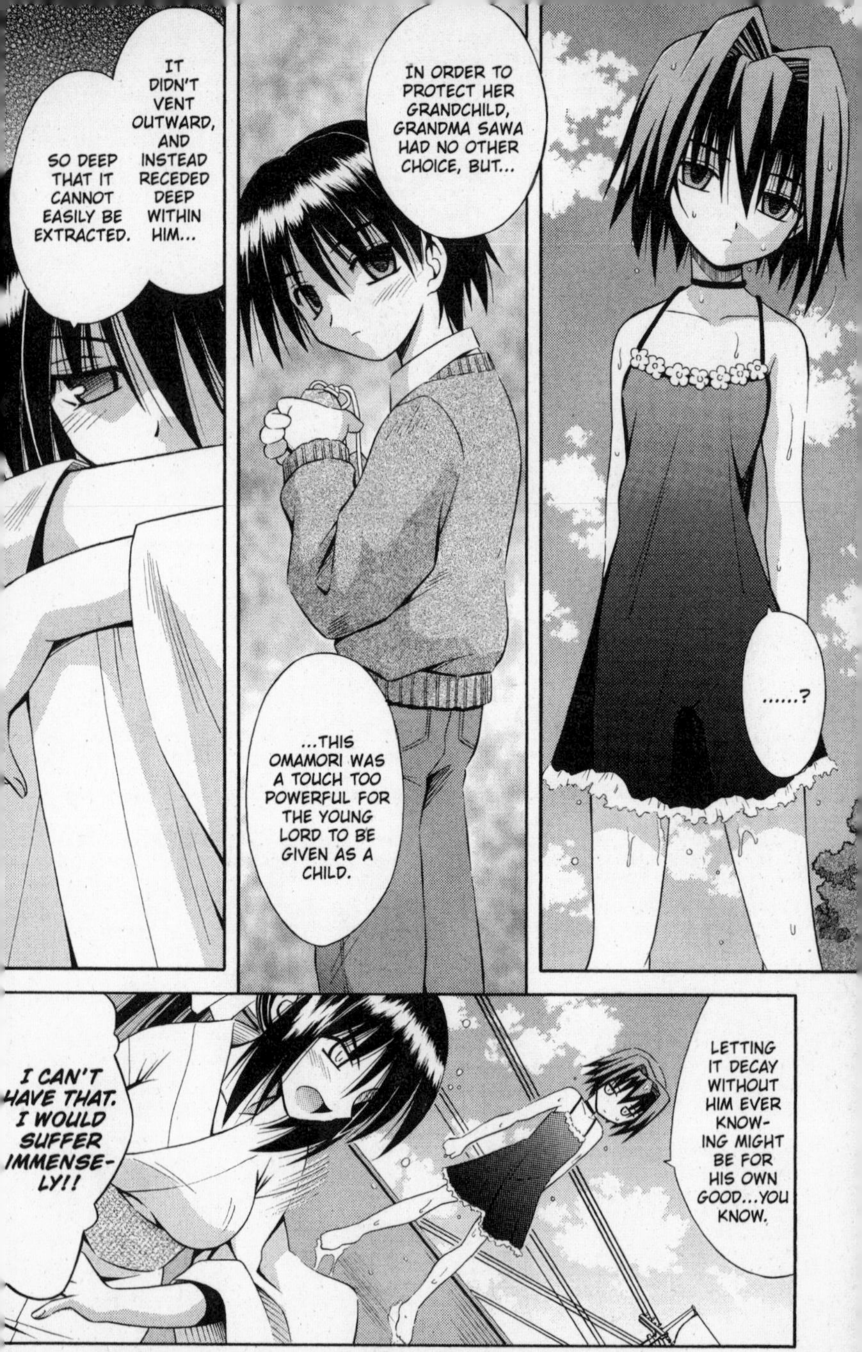
......?
IN ORDER TO PROTECT HER GRANDCHILD, GRANDMA SAWA HAD NO OTHER CHOICE, BUT...
...THIS OMAMORI WAS A TOUCH TOO POWERFUL FOR THE YOUNG LORD TO BE GIVEN AS A CHILD.
IT DIDN'T VENT OUTWARD, AND INSTEAD RECEDED DEEP WITHIN HIM...
SO DEEP THAT IT CANNOT EASILY BE EXTRACTED.
LETTING IT DECAY WITHOUT HIM EVER KNOWING MIGHT BE FOR HIS OWN GOOD...YOU KNOW.
I CAN'T HAVE THAT. I WOULD SUFFER IMMENSELY!!

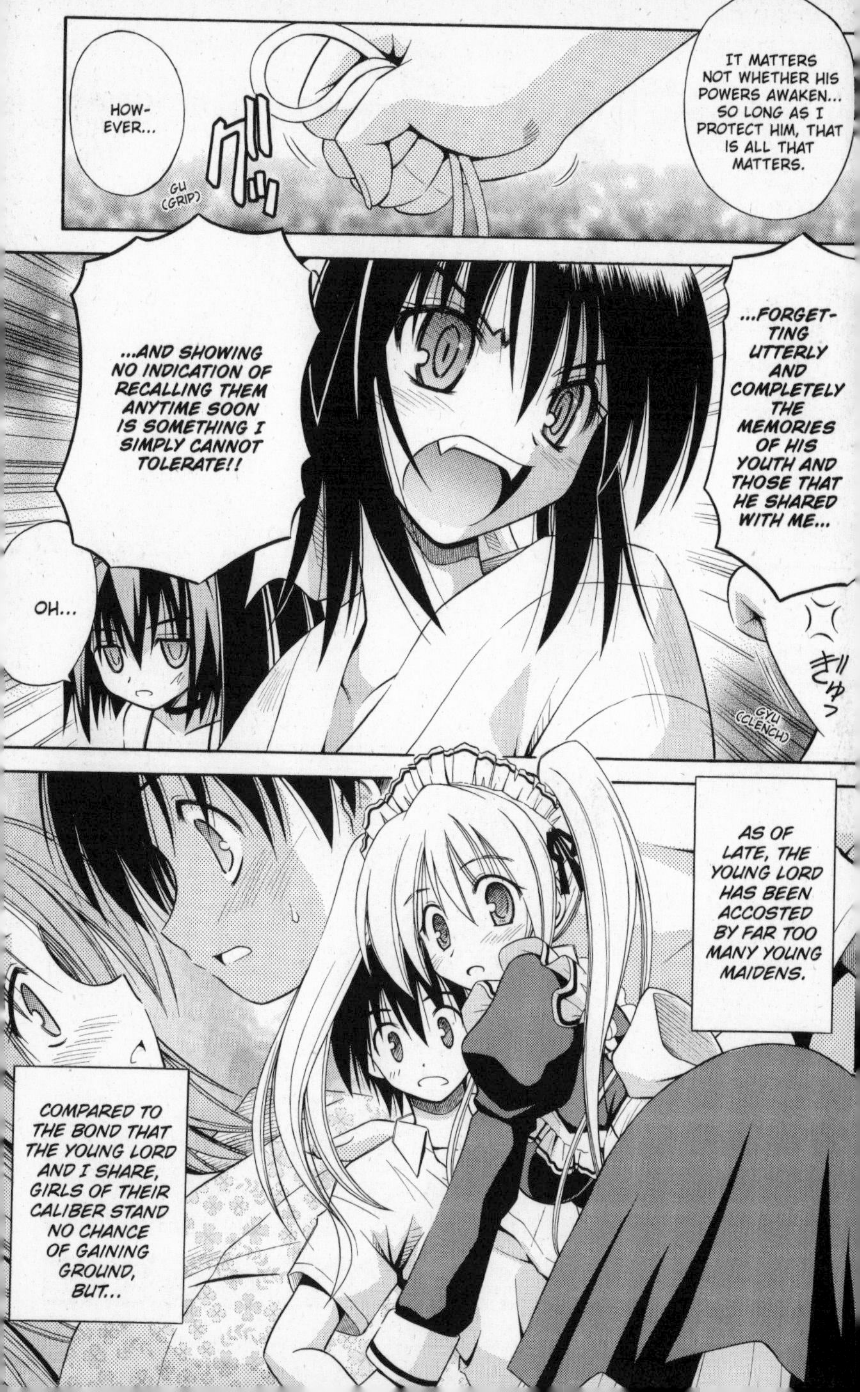
IT MATTERS NOT WHETHER HIS POWERS AWAKEN... SO LONG AS I PROTECT HIM, THAT IS ALL THAT MATTERS.
HOW-EVER...
GU (GRIP)
...FORGETTING UTTERLY AND COMPLETELY THE MEMORIES OF HIS YOUTH AND THOSE THAT HE SHARED WITH ME...
...AND SHOWING NO INDICATION OF RECALLING THEM ANYTIME SOON IS SOMETHING I SIMPLY CANNOT TOLERATE!!
OH...
GYU (CLENCH)
AS OF LATE, THE YOUNG LORD HAS BEEN ACCOSTED BY FAR TOO MANY YOUNG MAIDENS.
COMPARED TO THE BOND THAT THE YOUNG LORD AND I SHARE, GIRLS OF THEIR CALIBER STAND NO CHANCE OF GAINING GROUND, BUT...

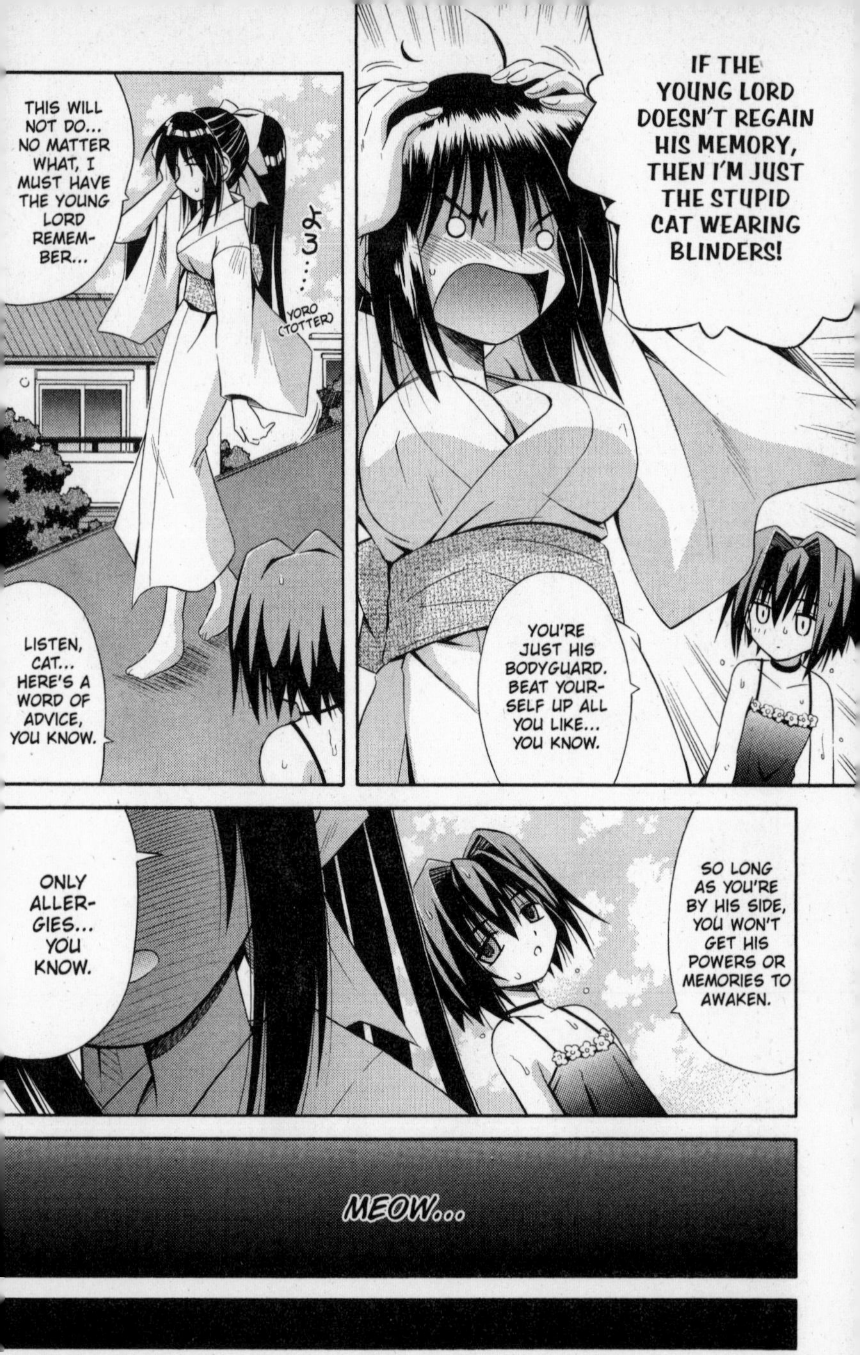
IF THE YOUNG LORD DOESN'T REGAIN HIS MEMORY, THEN I'M JUST THE STUPID CAT WEARING BLINDERS!
YOU'RE JUST HIS BODYGUARD. BEAT YOURSELF UP ALL YOU LIKE... YOU KNOW.
THIS WILL NOT DO... NO MATTER WHAT, I MUST HAVE THE YOUNG LORD REMEMBER...
よろ...
YORO (TOTTER)
LISTEN, CAT... HERE'S A WORD OF ADVICE, YOU KNOW.
SO LONG AS YOU'RE BY HIS SIDE, YOU WON'T GET HIS POWERS OR MEMORIES TO AWAKEN.
ONLY ALLERGIES... YOU KNOW.
MEOW...

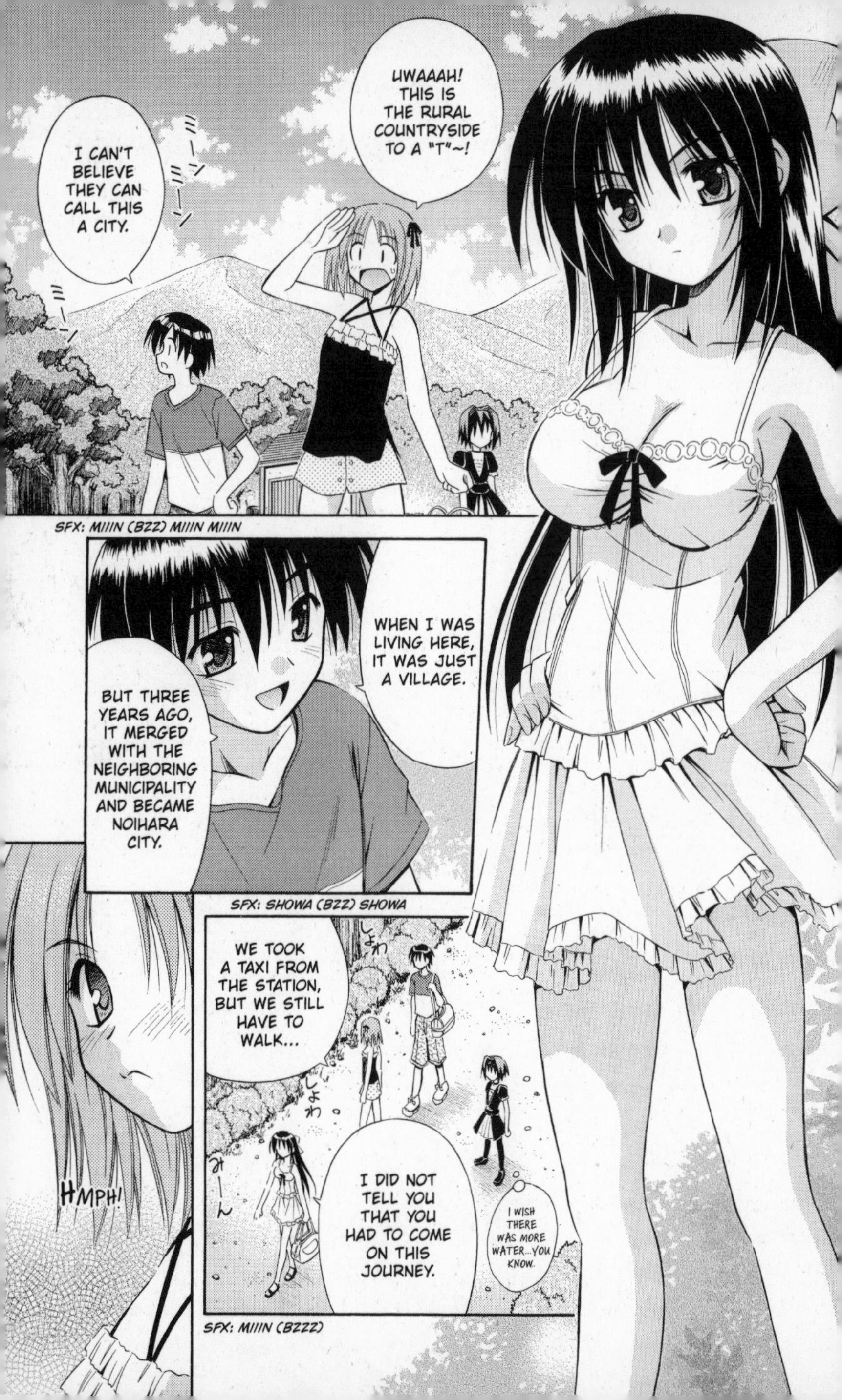
UWAAAH! THIS IS THE RURAL COUNTRYSIDE TO A "T"~!
ミーン
ミーン
I CAN'T BELIEVE THEY CAN CALL THIS A CITY.
ミーン
SFX: MIIIN (BZZ) MIIIN MIIIN
WHEN I WAS LIVING HERE, IT WAS JUST A VILLAGE.
BUT THREE YEARS AGO, IT MERGED WITH THE NEIGHBORING MUNICIPALITY AND BECAME NOIHARA CITY.
SFX: SHOWA (BZZ) SHOWA
しょわ
WE TOOK A TAXI FROM THE STATION, BUT WE STILL HAVE TO WALK...
しょわ
I WISH THERE WAS MORE WATER...YOU KNOW.
I DID NOT TELL YOU THAT YOU HAD TO COME ON THIS JOURNEY.
みーん
SFX: MIIIN (BZZZ)
HMPH!

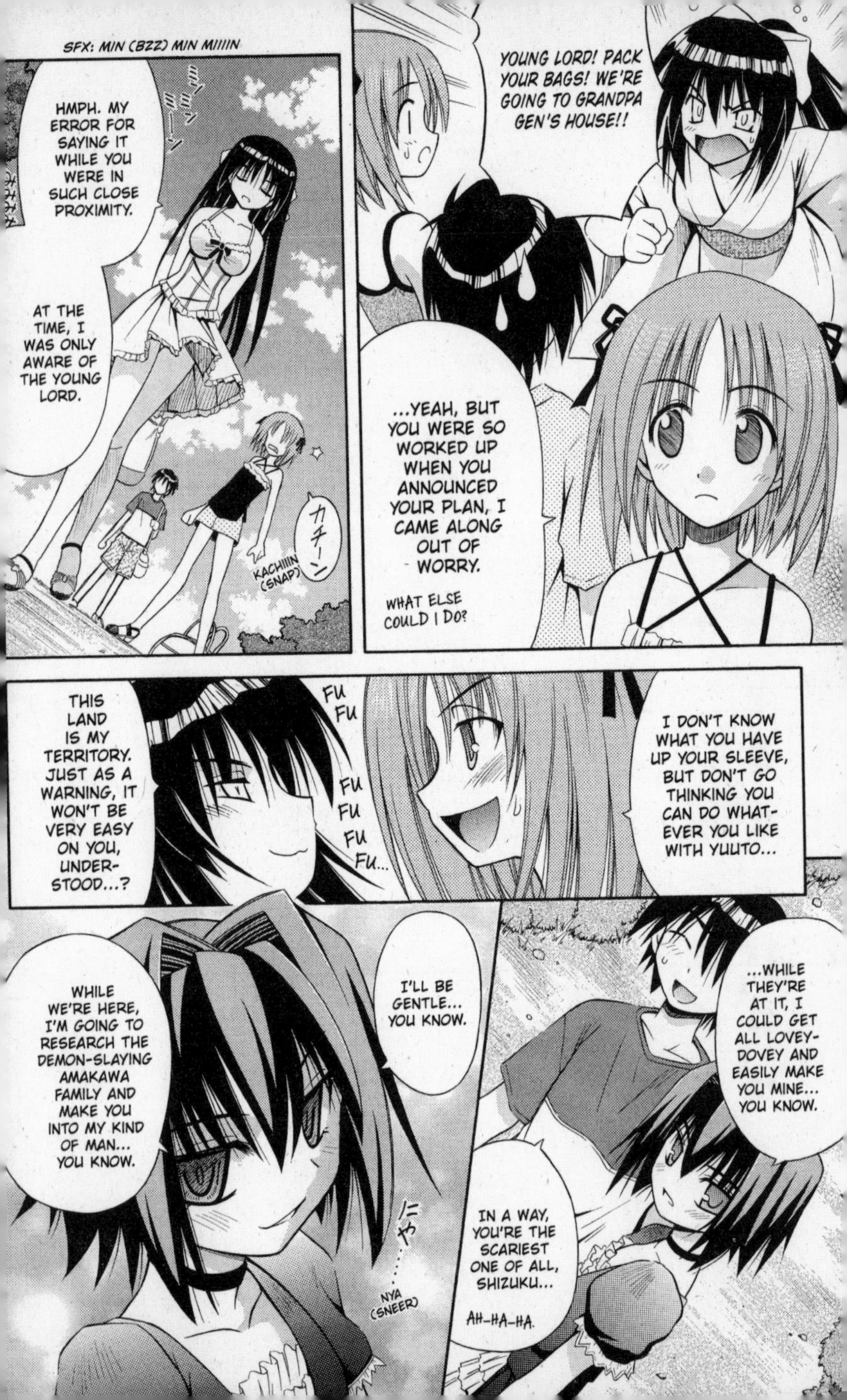
YOUNG LORD! PACK YOUR BAGS! WE'RE GOING TO GRANDPA GEN'S HOUSE!!
...YEAH, BUT YOU WERE SO WORKED UP WHEN YOU ANNOUNCED YOUR PLAN, I CAME ALONG OUT OF WORRY.
WHAT ELSE COULD I DO?
SFX: MIN (BZZ) MIN MIIIIN
ミンミンミーン
HMPH. MY ERROR FOR SAYING IT WHILE YOU WERE IN SUCH CLOSE PROXIMITY.
AT THE TIME, I WAS ONLY AWARE OF THE YOUNG LORD.
カチーン
KACHIIIN (SNAP)
I DON'T KNOW WHAT YOU HAVE UP YOUR SLEEVE, BUT DON'T GO THINKING YOU CAN DO WHATEVER YOU LIKE WITH YUUTO...
FU FU FU FU FU FU...
THIS LAND IS MY TERRITORY. JUST AS A WARNING, IT WON'T BE VERY EASY ON YOU, UNDERSTOOD...?
...WHILE THEY'RE AT IT, I COULD GET ALL LOVEY-DOVEY AND EASILY MAKE YOU MINE... YOU KNOW.
IN A WAY, YOU'RE THE SCARIEST ONE OF ALL, SHIZUKU...
AH-HA-HA.
I'LL BE GENTLE... YOU KNOW.
WHILE WE'RE HERE, I'M GOING TO RESEARCH THE DEMON-SLAYING AMAKAWA FAMILY AND MAKE YOU INTO MY KIND OF MAN... YOU KNOW.
にや
NYA (SNEER)

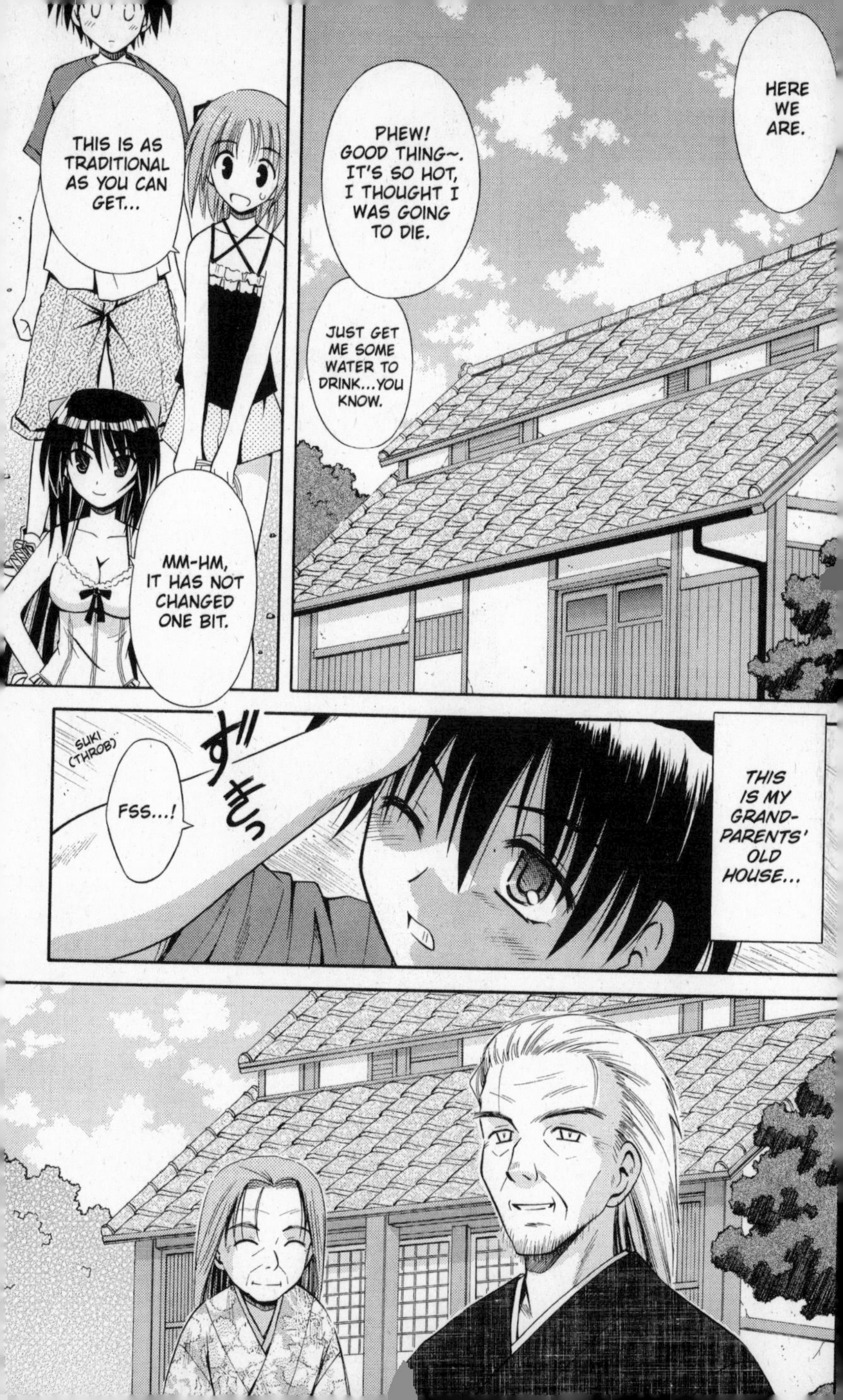
HERE WE ARE.
PHEW! GOOD THING~. IT'S SO HOT, I THOUGHT I WAS GOING TO DIE.
JUST GET ME SOME WATER TO DRINK...YOU KNOW.
THIS IS AS TRADITIONAL AS YOU CAN GET...
MM-HM, IT HAS NOT CHANGED ONE BIT.
THIS IS MY GRAND-PARENTS' OLD HOUSE...
SUKI (THROB)
FSS...!

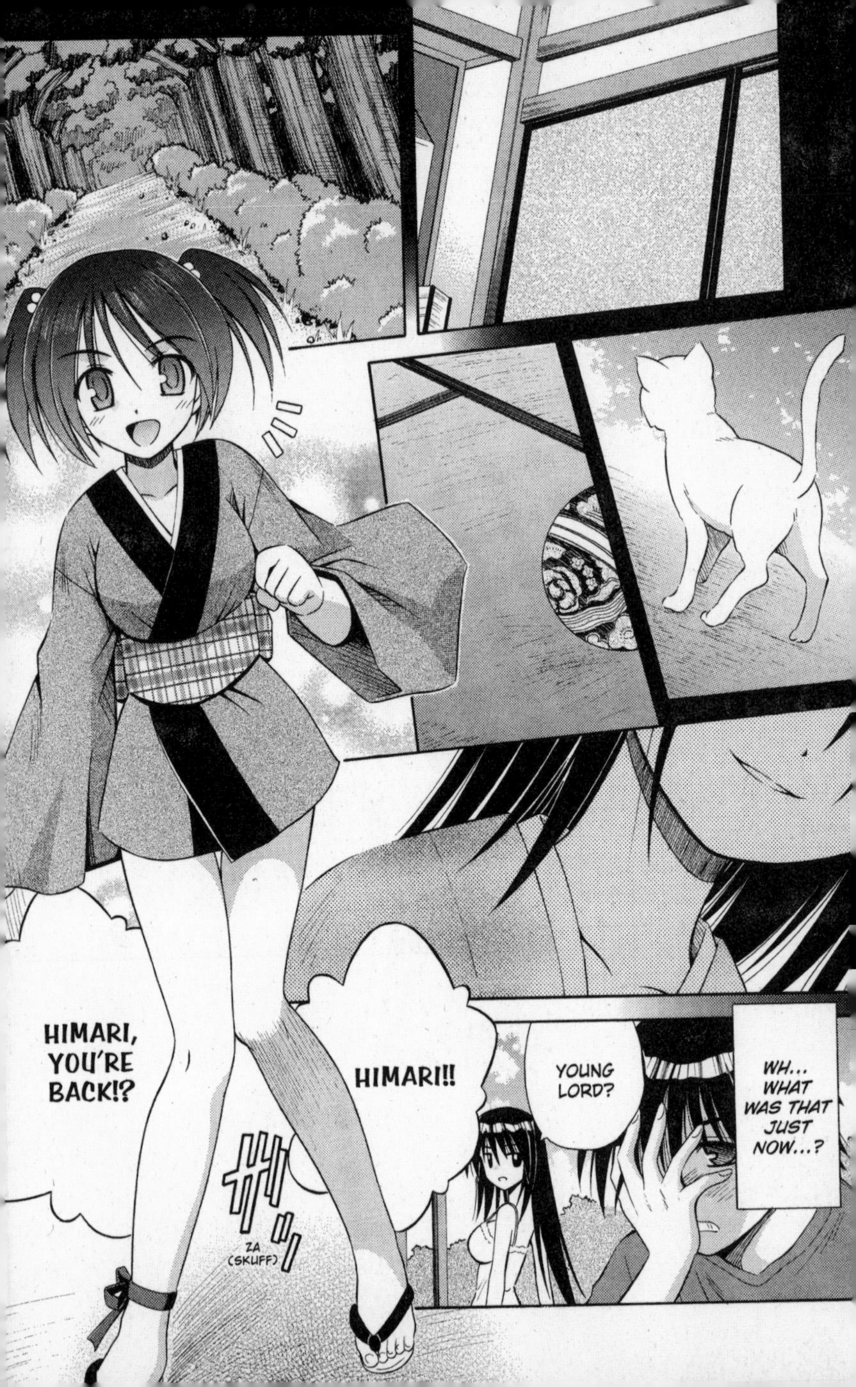
WH... WHAT WAS THAT JUST NOW...?
YOUNG LORD?
HIMARI!!
HIMARI, YOU'RE BACK!?
ZA (SKUFF)

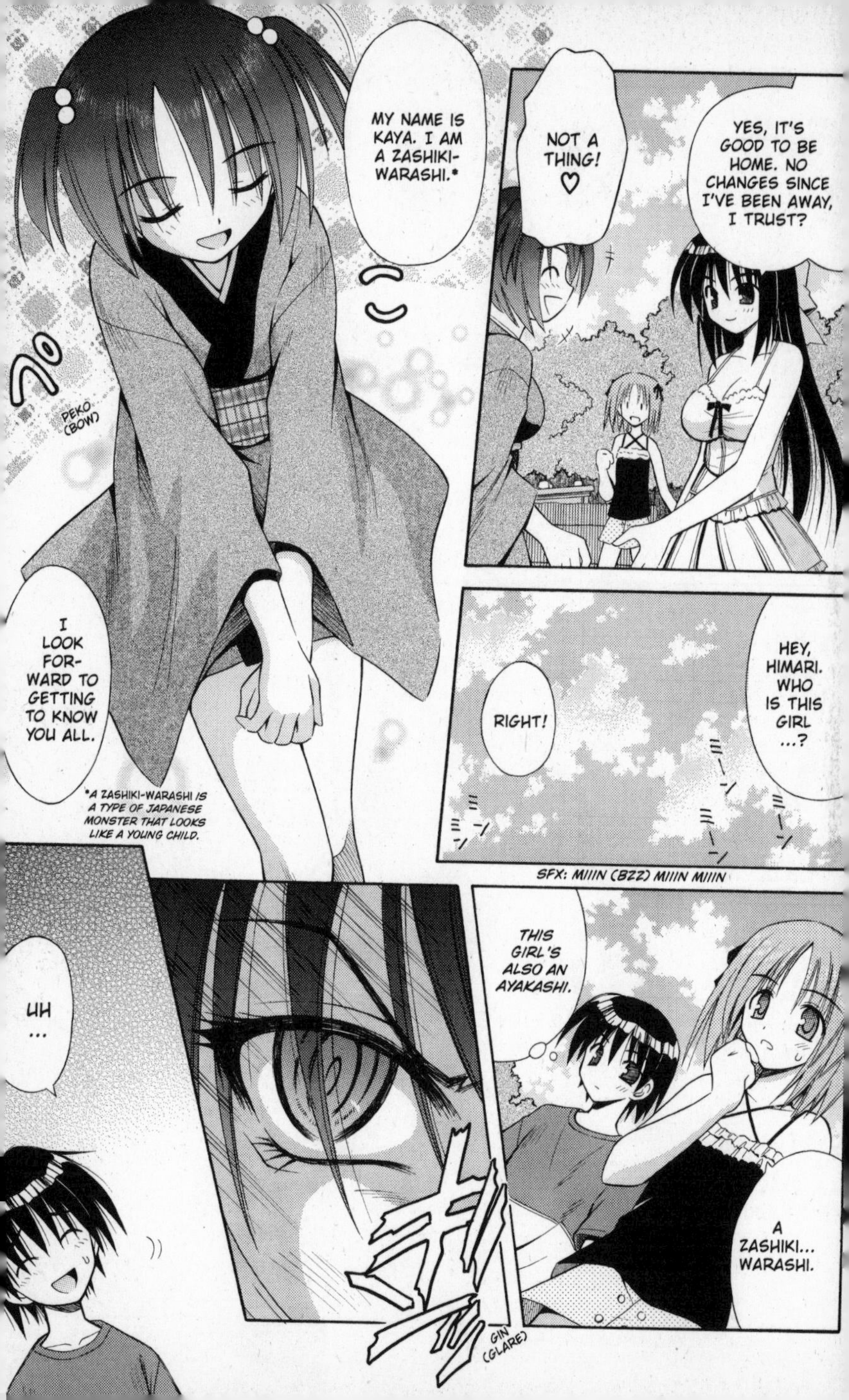
YES, IT'S GOOD TO BE HOME. NO CHANGES SINCE I'VE BEEN AWAY, I TRUST?
NOT A THING! ♡
HEY, HIMARI. WHO IS THIS GIRL ...?
RIGHT!
SFX: MIIIN (BZZ) MIIIN MIIIN
MY NAME IS KAYA. I AM A ZASHIKI-WARASHI.*
PEKO (BOW)
I LOOK FOR-WARD TO GETTING TO KNOW YOU ALL.
THIS GIRL'S ALSO AN AYAKASHI.
A ZASHIKI... WARASHI.
GIN (GLARE)
UH ...
*A ZASHIKI-WARASHI IS A TYPE OF JAPANESE MONSTER THAT LOOKS LIKE A YOUNG CHILD.

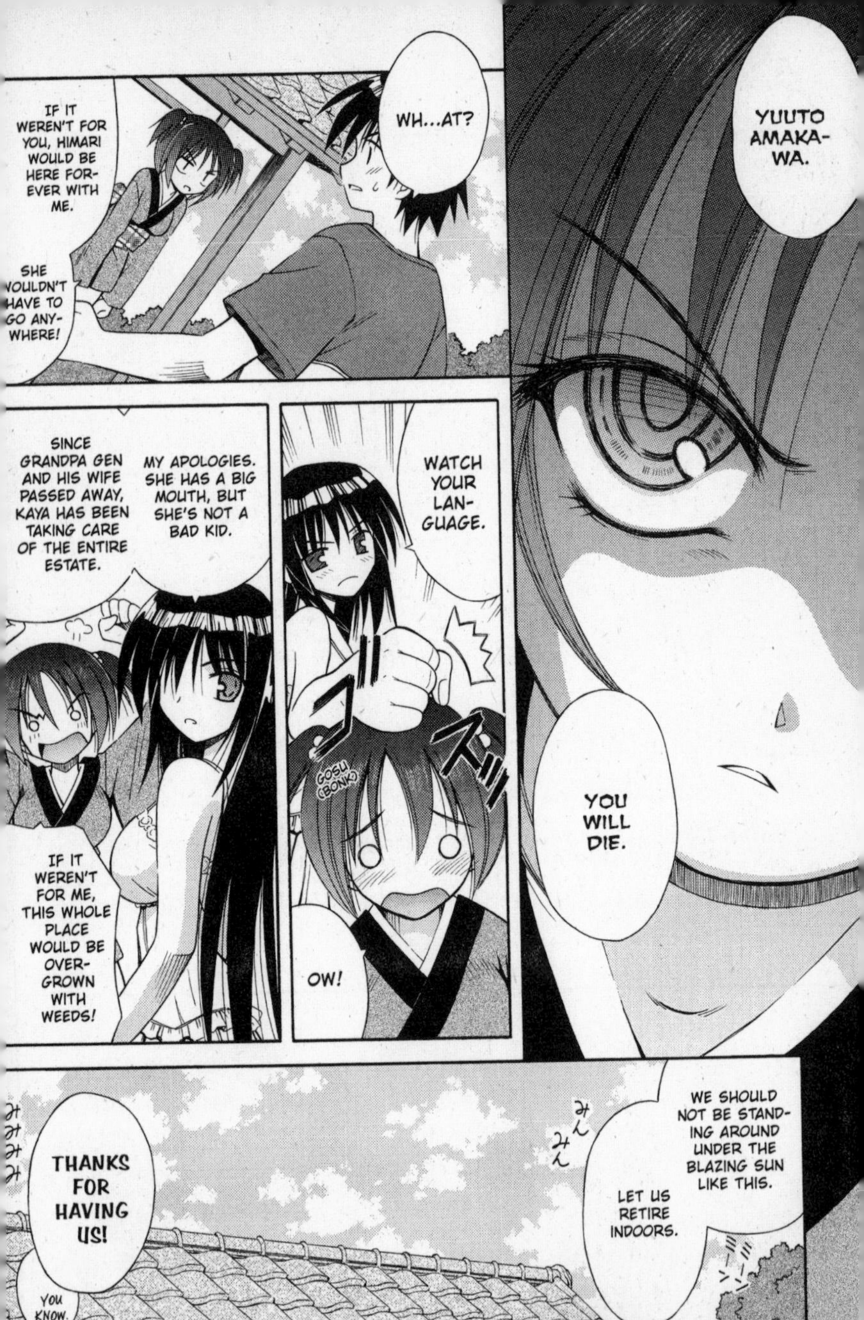
YUUTO AMAKAWA.
YOU WILL DIE.
WH...AT?
IF IT WEREN'T FOR YOU, HIMARI WOULD BE HERE FOREVER WITH ME.
SHE WOULDN'T HAVE TO GO ANYWHERE!
WATCH YOUR LANGUAGE.
GOSU (BONK)
OW!
MY APOLOGIES. SHE HAS A BIG MOUTH, BUT SHE'S NOT A BAD KID.
SINCE GRANDPA GEN AND HIS WIFE PASSED AWAY, KAYA HAS BEEN TAKING CARE OF THE ENTIRE ESTATE.
IF IT WEREN'T FOR ME, THIS WHOLE PLACE WOULD BE OVERGROWN WITH WEEDS!
WE SHOULD NOT BE STANDING AROUND UNDER THE BLAZING SUN LIKE THIS.
LET US RETIRE INDOORS.
みんみん
THANKS FOR HAVING US!
YOU KNOW.
みみみみ
SFX: MIN (BZZ) MIN MIN MIN MIN MIN

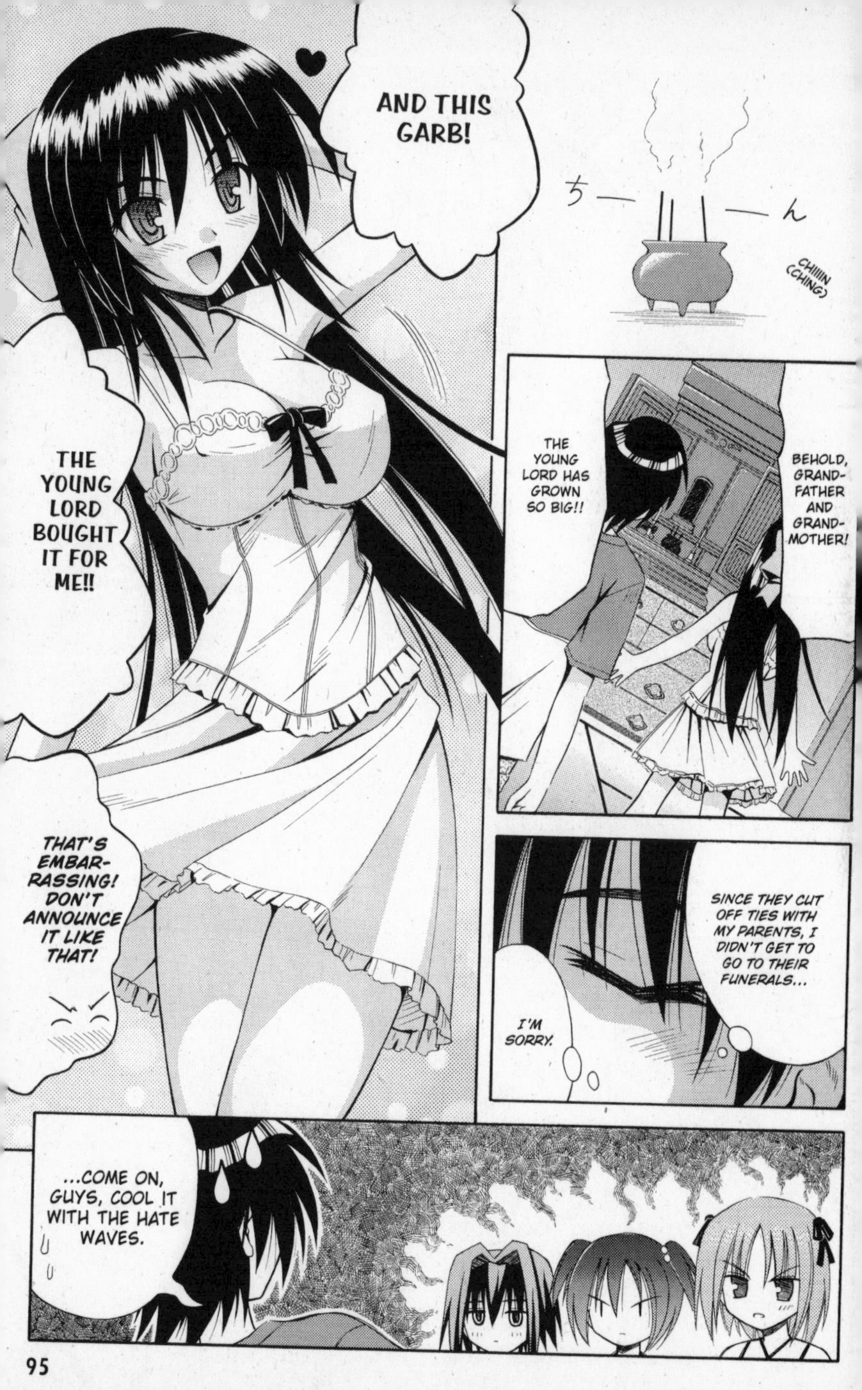
ちーーん
CHIIIN (CHING)
BEHOLD, GRAND-FATHER AND GRAND-MOTHER!
THE YOUNG LORD HAS GROWN SO BIG!!
SINCE THEY CUT OFF TIES WITH MY PARENTS, I DIDN'T GET TO GO TO THEIR FUNERALS...
I'M SORRY.
AND THIS GARB!
THE YOUNG LORD BOUGHT IT FOR ME!!
THAT'S EMBAR-RASSING! DON'T ANNOUNCE IT LIKE THAT!
...COME ON, GUYS, COOL IT WITH THE HATE WAVES.

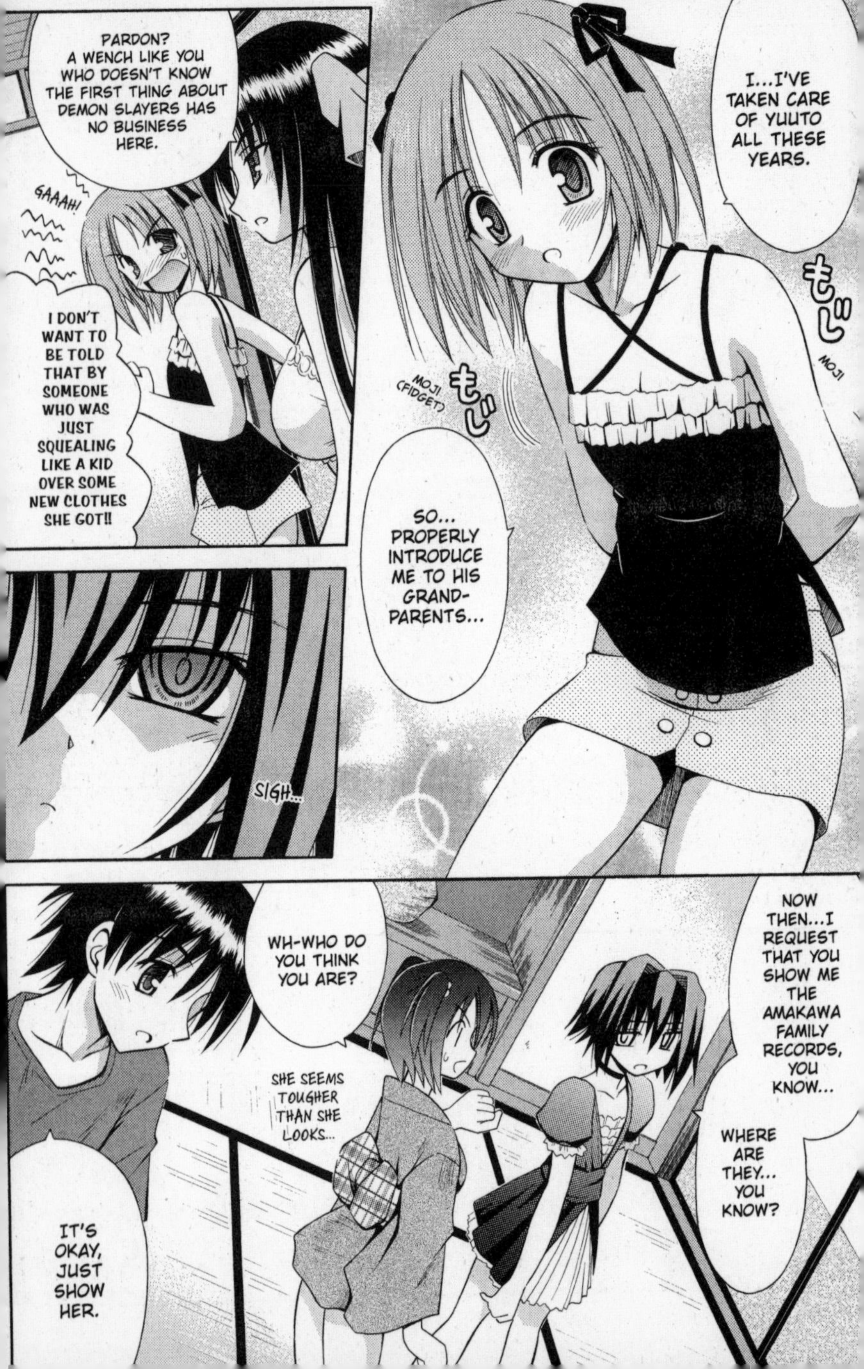
I...I'VE TAKEN CARE OF YUUTO ALL THESE YEARS.
もじ
MOJI
もじ
MOJI (FIDGET)
SO... PROPERLY INTRODUCE ME TO HIS GRAND-PARENTS...
PARDON? A WENCH LIKE YOU WHO DOESN'T KNOW THE FIRST THING ABOUT DEMON SLAYERS HAS NO BUSINESS HERE.
GAAAH!
I DON'T WANT TO BE TOLD THAT BY SOMEONE WHO WAS JUST SQUEALING LIKE A KID OVER SOME NEW CLOTHES SHE GOT!!
SIGH...
NOW THEN...I REQUEST THAT YOU SHOW ME THE AMAKAWA FAMILY RECORDS, YOU KNOW...
WHERE ARE THEY... YOU KNOW?
WH-WHO DO YOU THINK YOU ARE?
SHE SEEMS TOUGHER THAN SHE LOOKS...
IT'S OKAY, JUST SHOW HER.

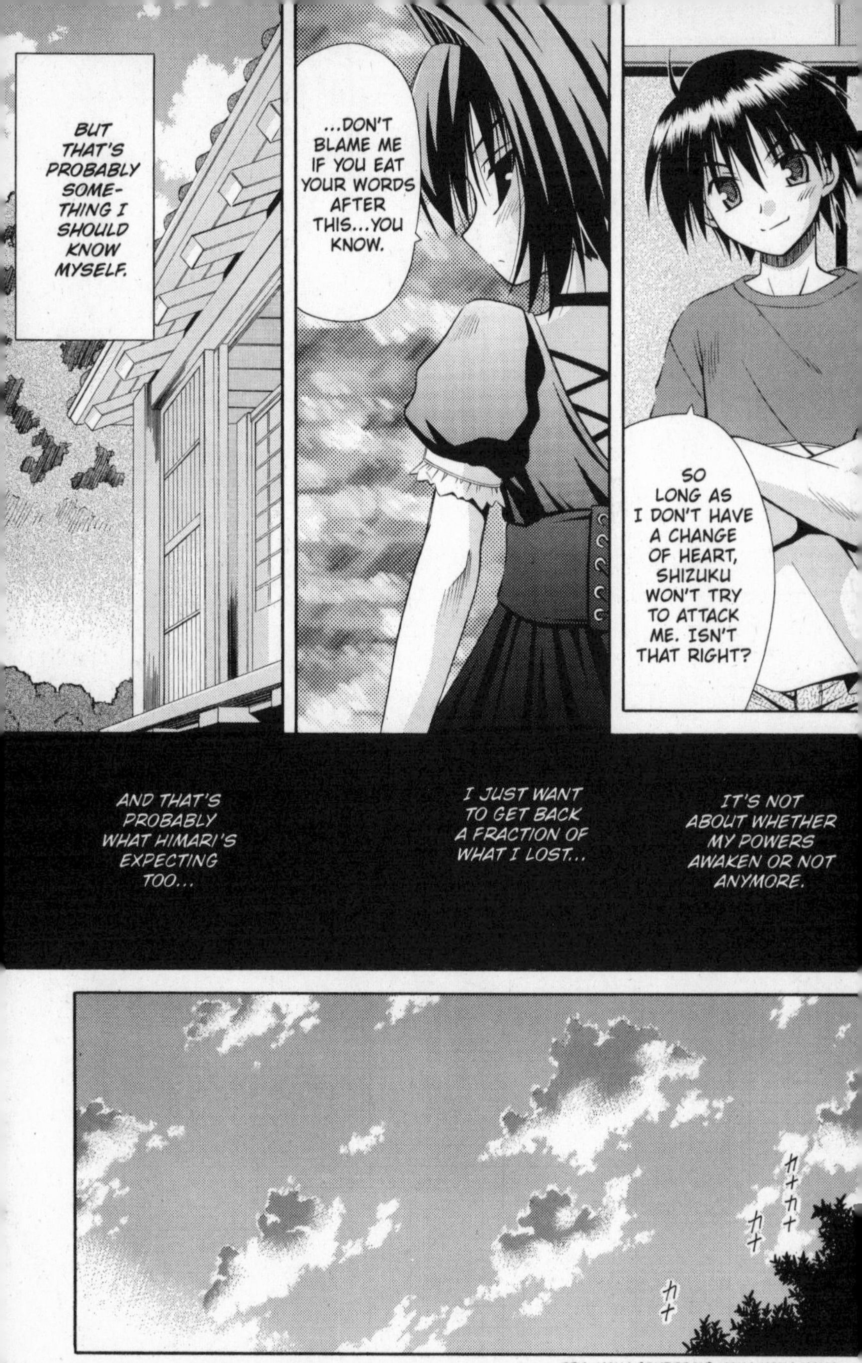
SO LONG AS I DON'T HAVE A CHANGE OF HEART, SHIZUKU WON'T TRY TO ATTACK ME. ISN'T THAT RIGHT?
...DON'T BLAME ME IF YOU EAT YOUR WORDS AFTER THIS...YOU KNOW.
BUT THAT'S PROBABLY SOME-THING I SHOULD KNOW MYSELF.
IT'S NOT ABOUT WHETHER MY POWERS AWAKEN OR NOT ANYMORE.
I JUST WANT TO GET BACK A FRACTION OF WHAT I LOST...
AND THAT'S PROBABLY WHAT HIMARI'S EXPECTING TOO...
カナカナ
カナ
カナ

SFX: KANA (SKREECH) KANA KANA KANA

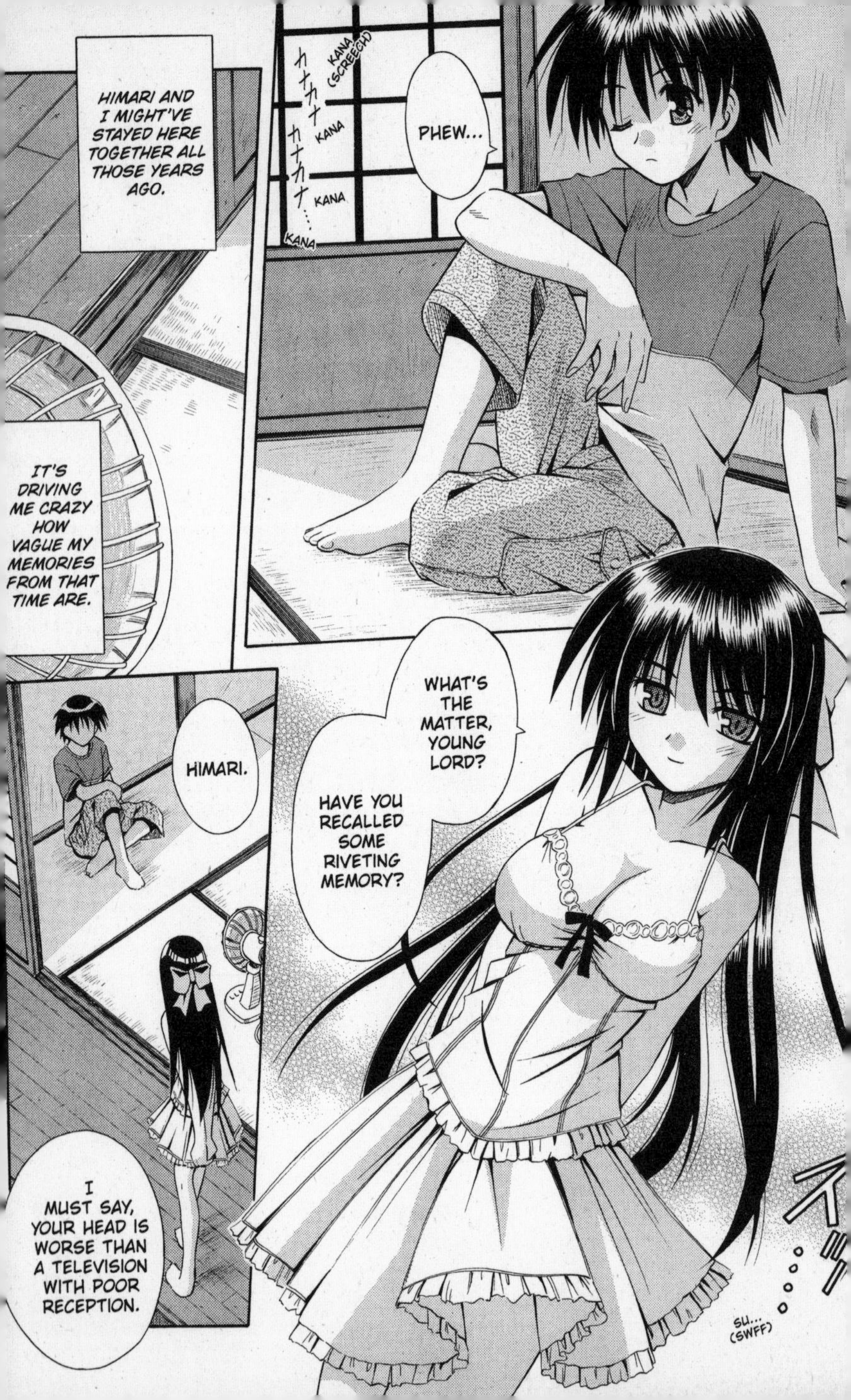

カナカナ
KANA (SCREECH)
カナカナ
KANA
カナカナ…
KANA
KANA
PHEW...
HIMARI AND I MIGHT'VE STAYED HERE TOGETHER ALL THOSE YEARS AGO.
IT'S DRIVING ME CRAZY HOW VAGUE MY MEMORIES FROM THAT TIME ARE.
WHAT'S THE MATTER, YOUNG LORD?
HAVE YOU RECALLED SOME RIVETING MEMORY?
SU... (SWFF)
HIMARI.
I MUST SAY, YOUR HEAD IS WORSE THAN A TELEVISION WITH POOR RECEPTION.

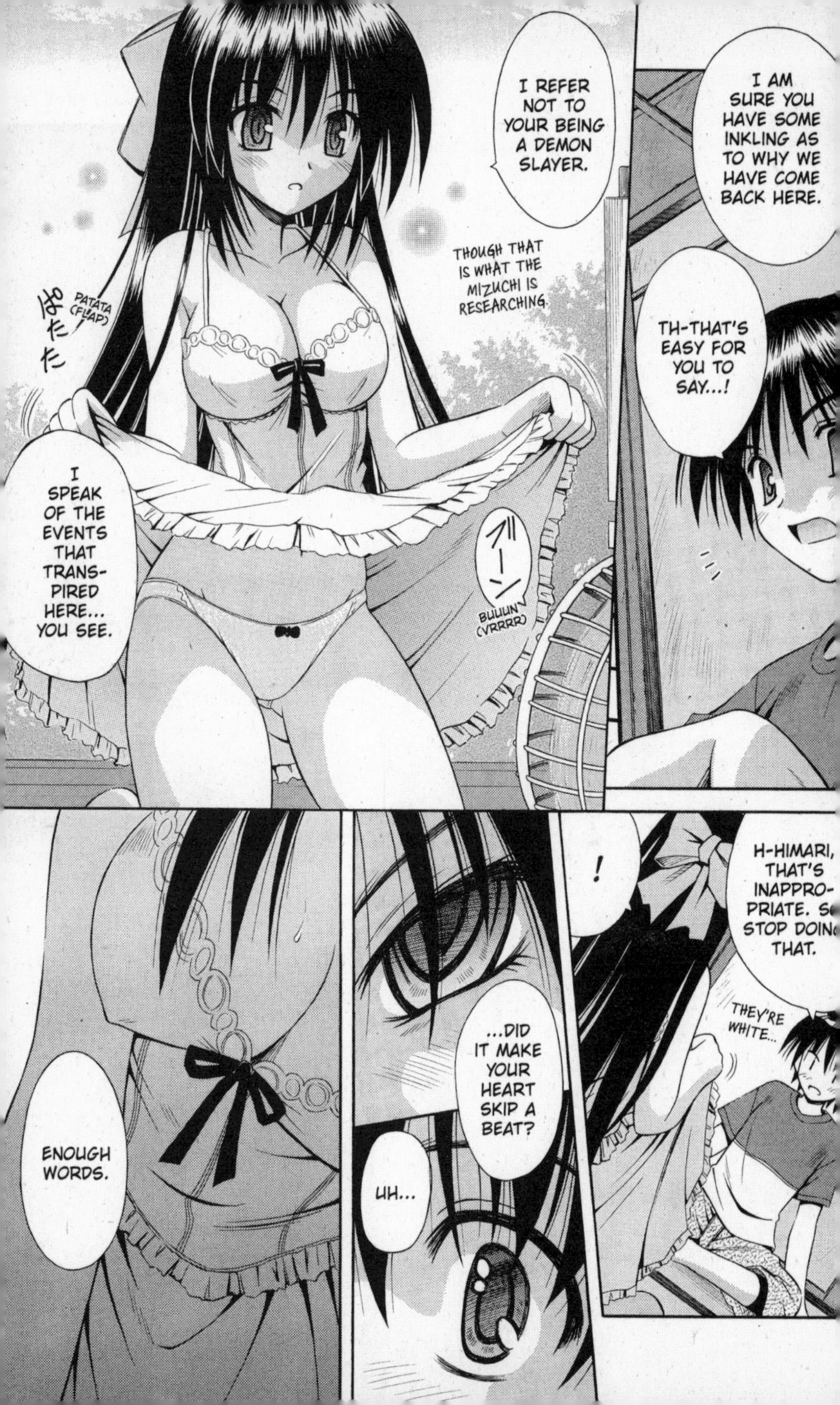
I AM SURE YOU HAVE SOME INKLING AS TO WHY WE HAVE COME BACK HERE.
TH-THAT'S EASY FOR YOU TO SAY...!
I REFER NOT TO YOUR BEING A DEMON SLAYER.
THOUGH THAT IS WHAT THE MIZUCHI IS RESEARCHING.
ぱたた
PATATA (FLAP)
I SPEAK OF THE EVENTS THAT TRANSPIRED HERE... YOU SEE.
ブーン
BUUUN (VRRRR)
H-HIMARI, THAT'S INAPPROPRIATE. S STOP DOIN THAT.
THEY'RE WHITE...
!
...DID IT MAKE YOUR HEART SKIP A BEAT?
UH...
ENOUGH WORDS.

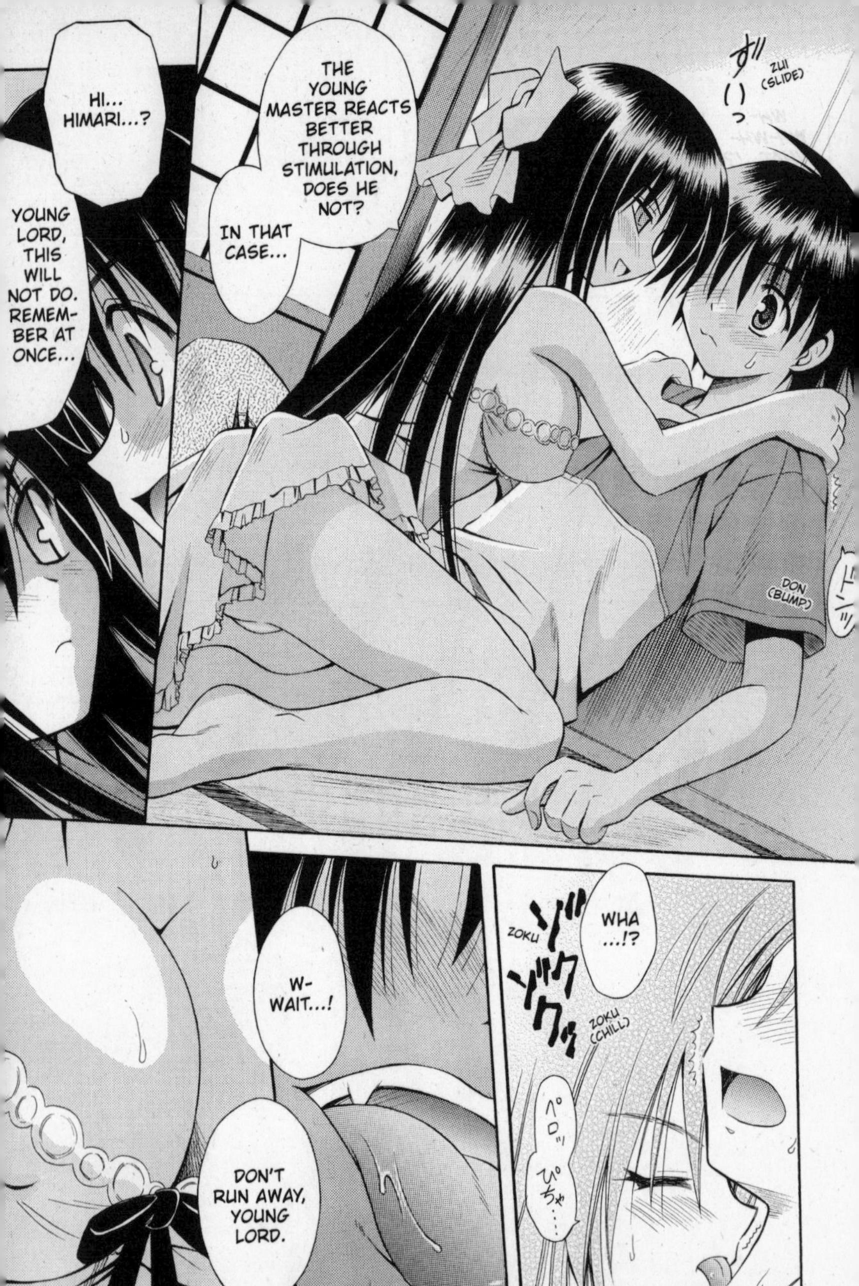
ZUI (SLIDE)
THE YOUNG MASTER REACTS BETTER THROUGH STIMULATION, DOES HE NOT?
IN THAT CASE...
DON (BUMP)
HI... HIMARI...?
YOUNG LORD, THIS WILL NOT DO. REMEMBER AT ONCE...
WHA ...!?
ZOKU
ZOKU (CHILL)
W- WAIT...!
DON'T RUN AWAY, YOUNG LORD.

SFX: PERO (LAP), PICHA (SLICK)

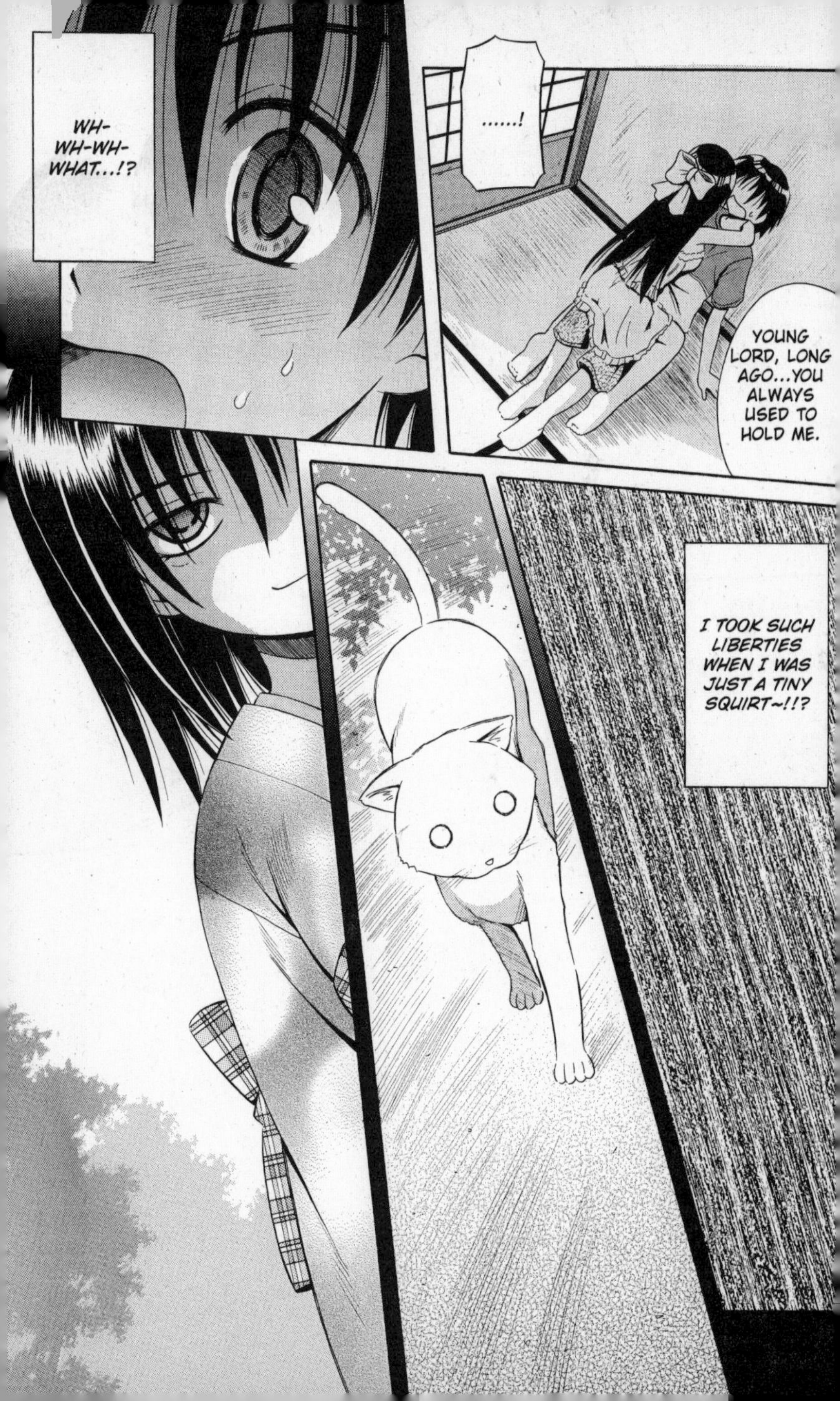
......!
YOUNG LORD, LONG AGO...YOU ALWAYS USED TO HOLD ME.
WH-WH-WH-WHAT...!?
I TOOK SUCH LIBERTIES WHEN I WAS JUST A TINY SQUIRT~!!?

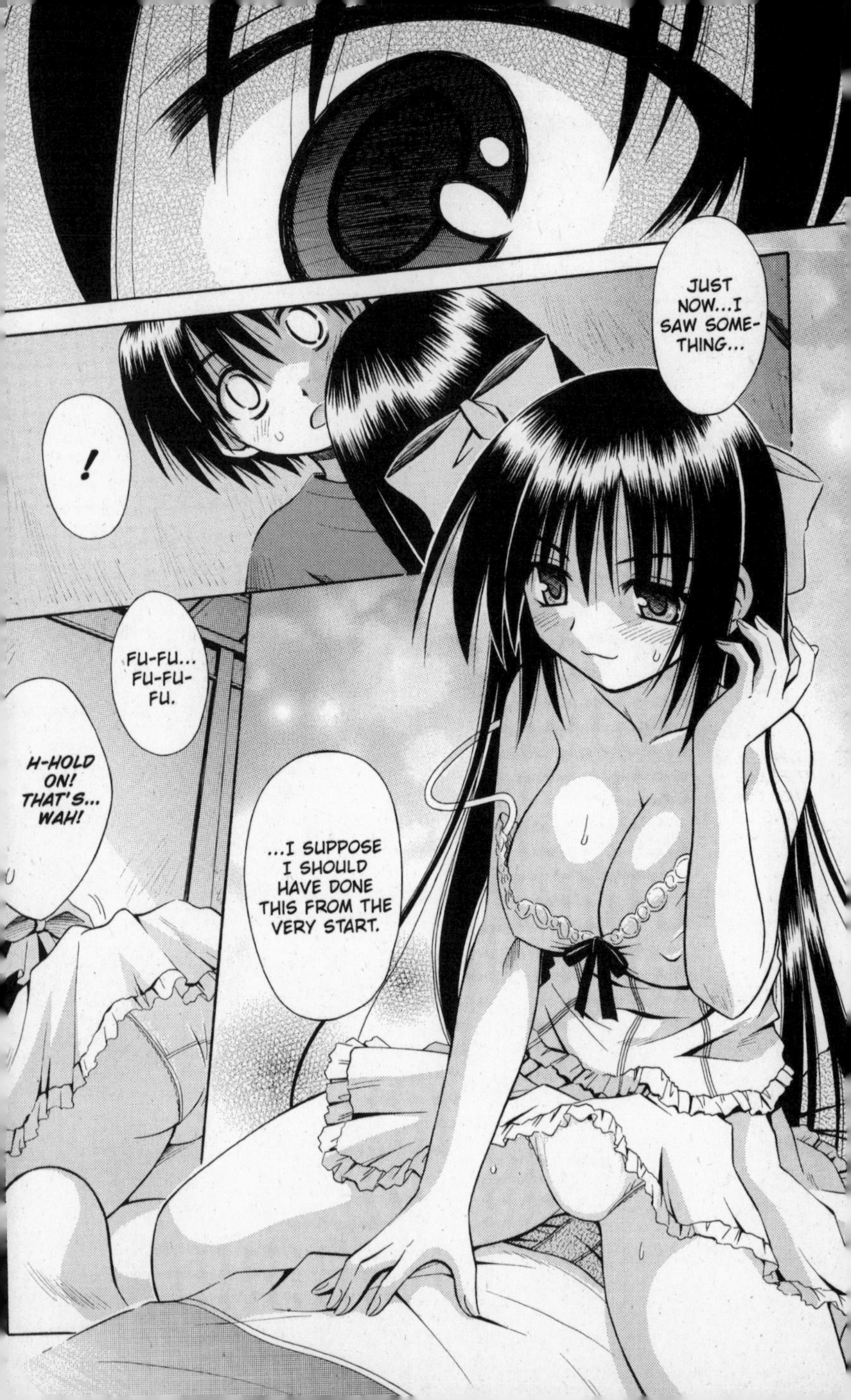
JUST NOW...I SAW SOME-THING...
!
FU-FU... FU-FU-FU.
...I SUPPOSE I SHOULD HAVE DONE THIS FROM THE VERY START.
H-HOLD ON! THAT'S... WAH!

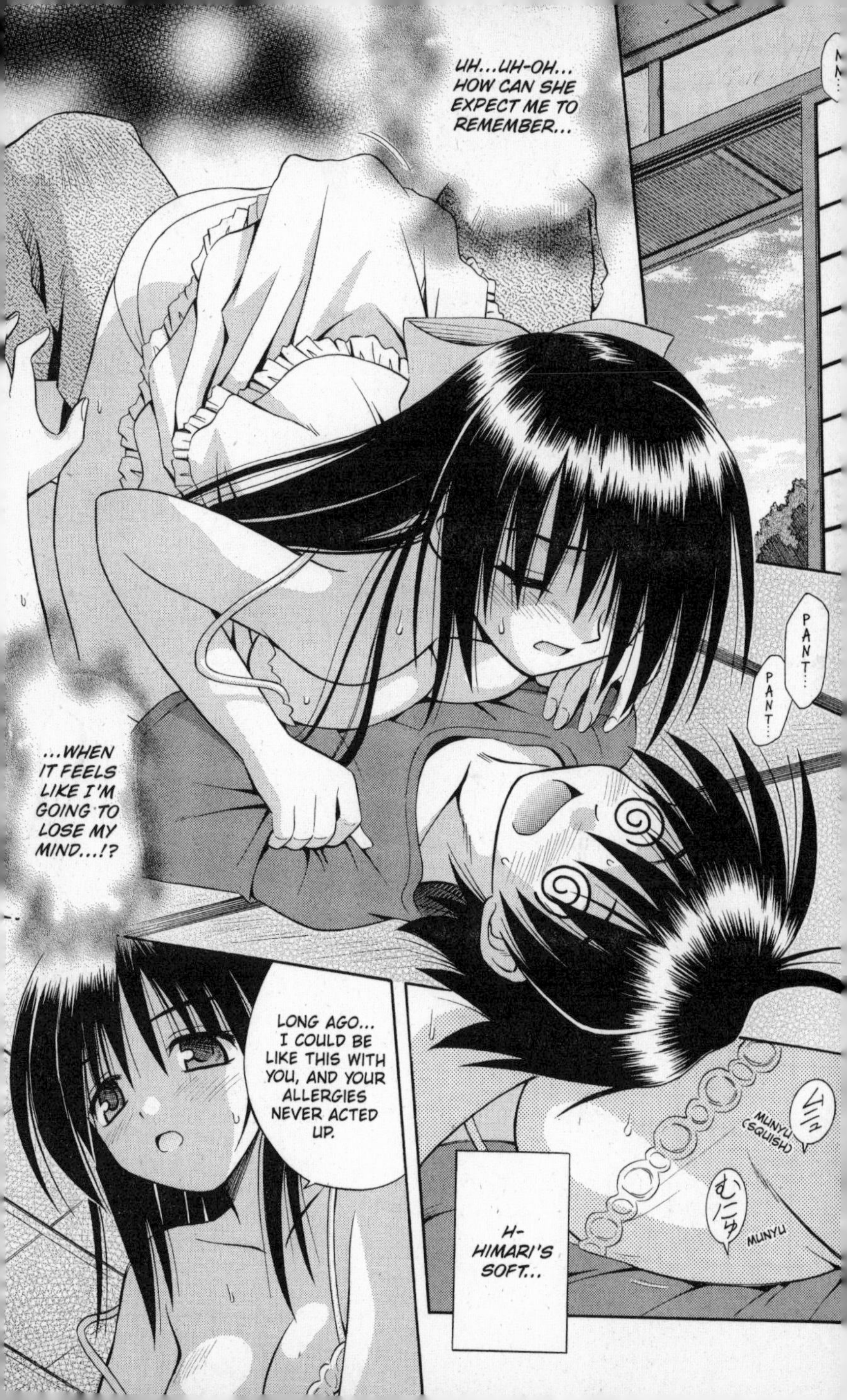
NN...
UH...UH-OH... HOW CAN SHE EXPECT ME TO REMEMBER...
PANT...
PANT...
...WHEN IT FEELS LIKE I'M GOING TO LOSE MY MIND...!?
むにゅ
MUNYU (SQUISH)
むにゅ
MUNYU
H-HIMARI'S SOFT...
LONG AGO... I COULD BE LIKE THIS WITH YOU, AND YOUR ALLERGIES NEVER ACTED UP.

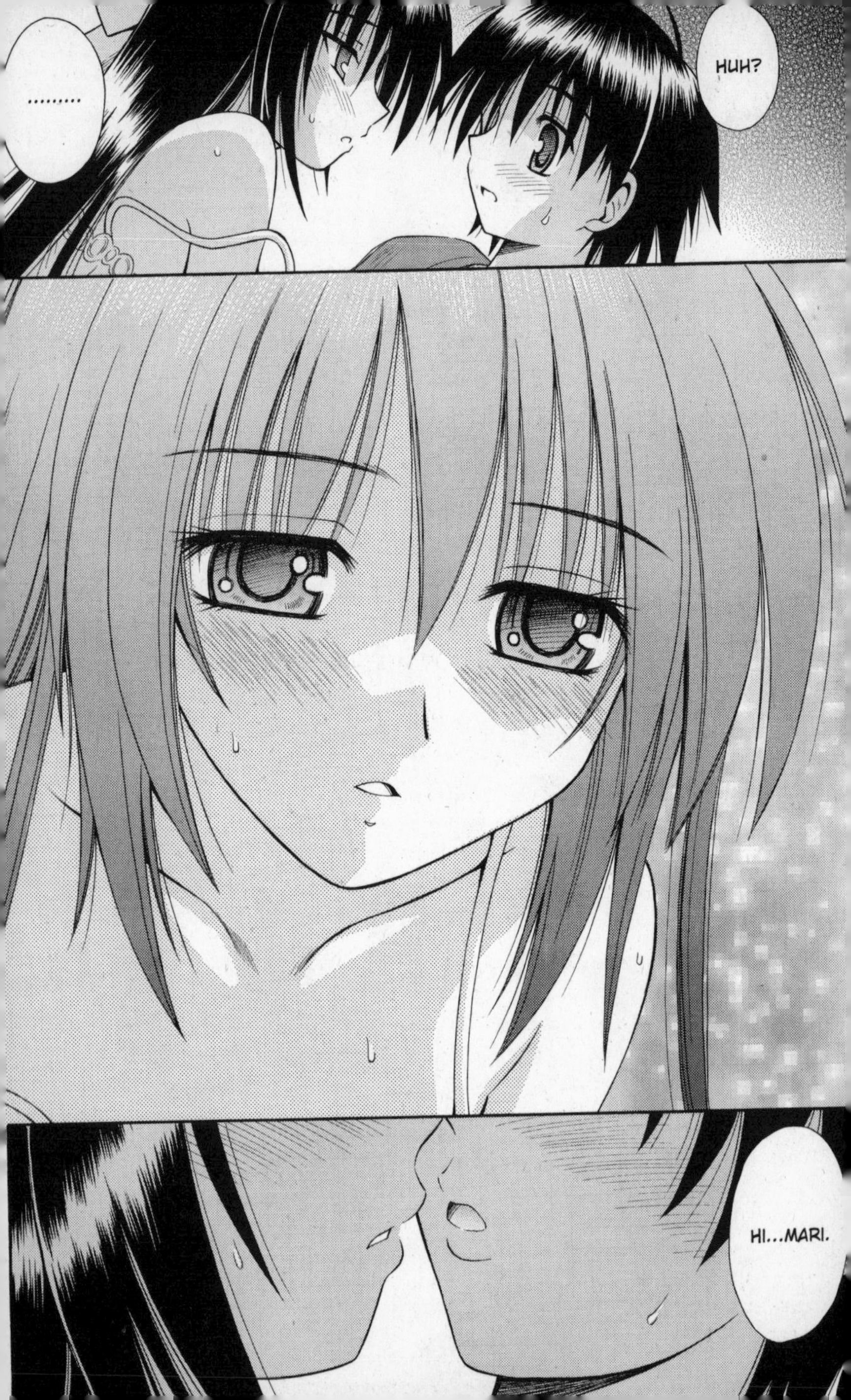
HUH?
....
HI...MARI.

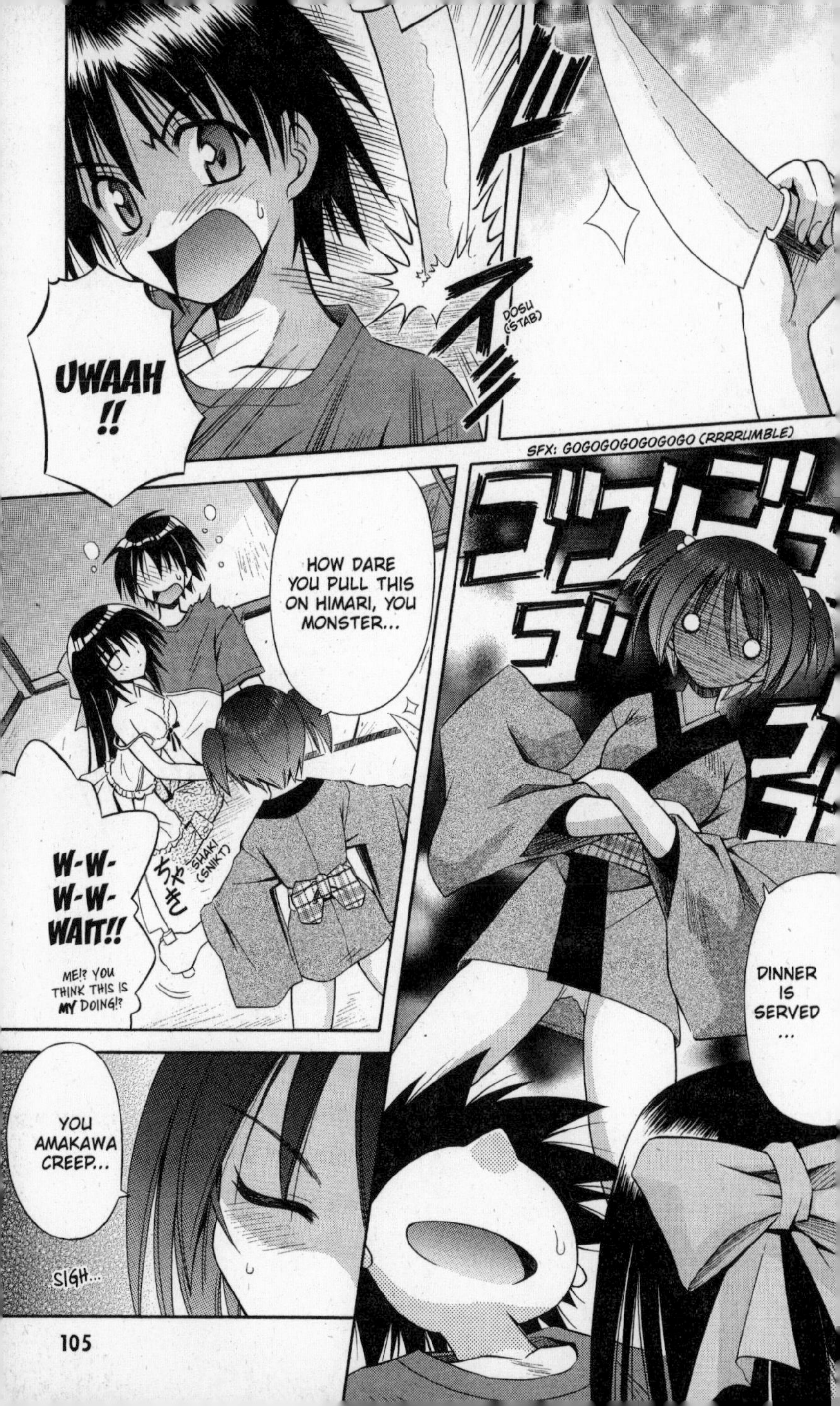

DOSU (STAB)
UWAAH!!
SFX: GOGOGOGOGOGOGO (RRRRUMBLE)
DINNER IS SERVED...
HOW DARE YOU PULL THIS ON HIMARI, YOU MONSTER...
SHAKI (SNIKT)
W-W-W-W-WAIT!!
ME!? YOU THINK THIS IS MY DOING!?
YOU AMAKAWA CREEP...
SIGH...

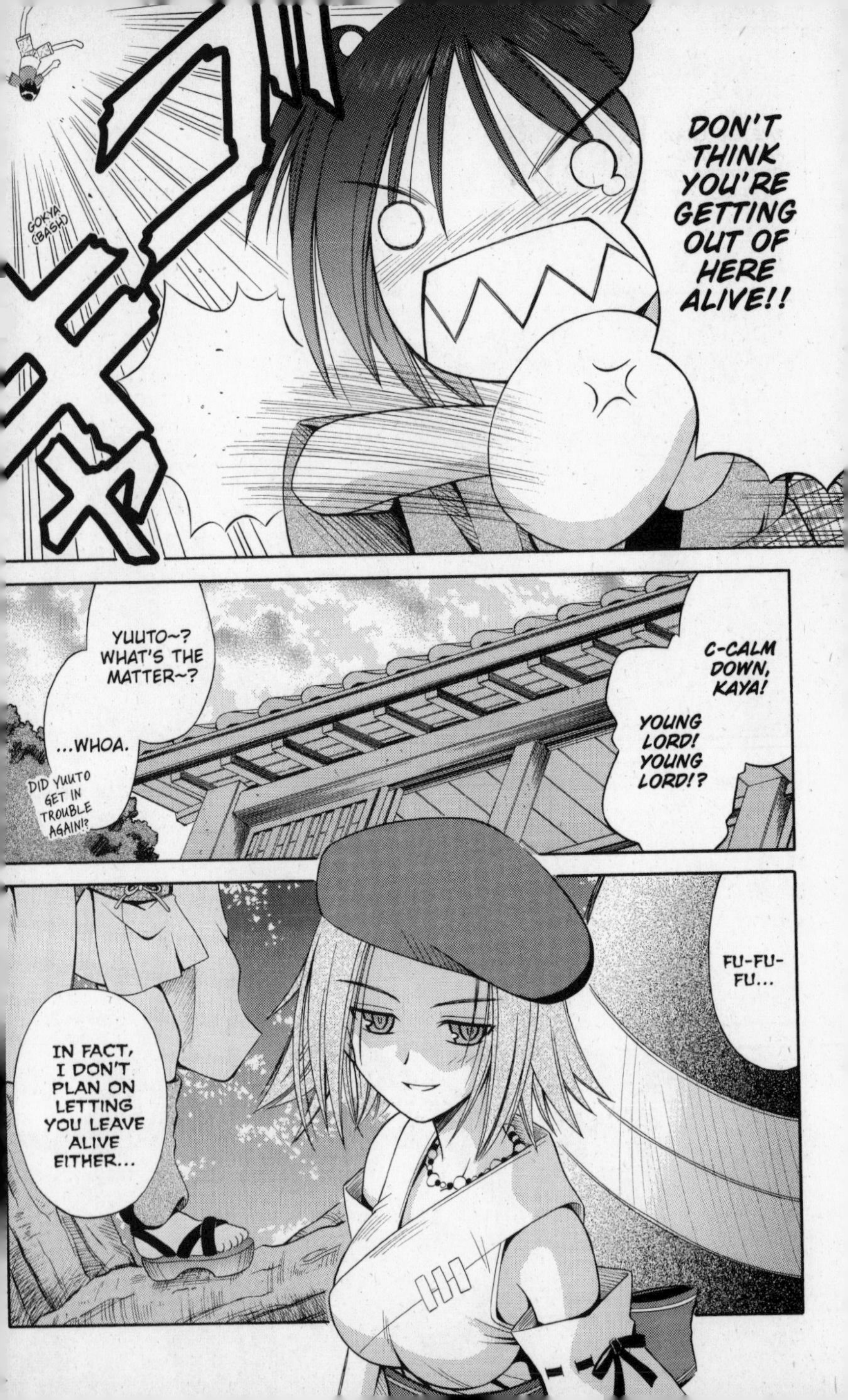
DON'T THINK YOU'RE GETTING OUT OF HERE ALIVE!!
GOKYA (BASH)
C-CALM DOWN, KAYA!
YOUNG LORD! YOUNG LORD!?
YUUTO~? WHAT'S THE MATTER~?
...WHOA.
DID YUUTO GET IN TROUBLE AGAIN!?
FU-FU-FU...
IN FACT, I DON'T PLAN ON LETTING YOU LEAVE ALIVE EITHER...

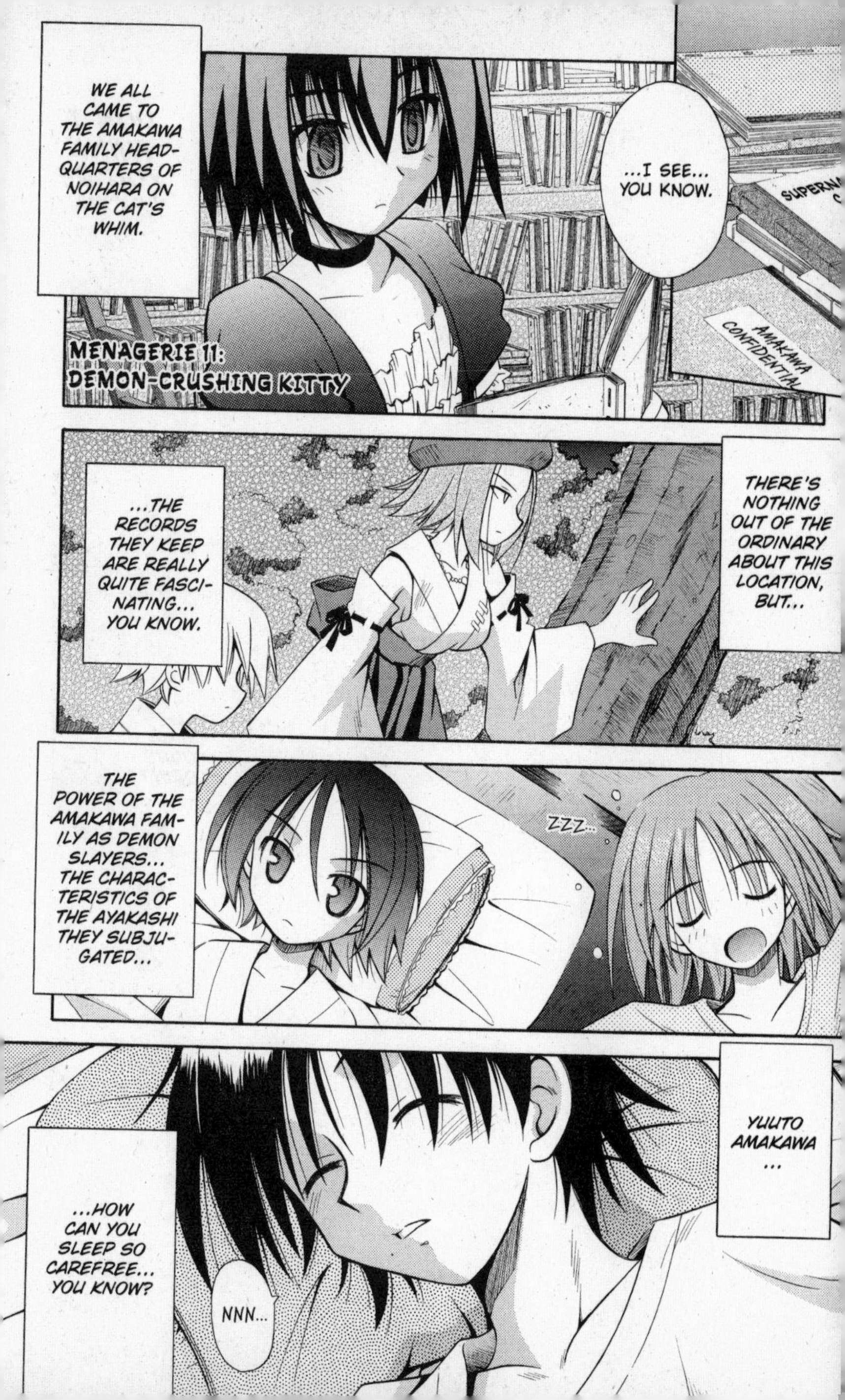
SUPERNA
AMAKAWA CONFIDENTIAL
...I SEE... YOU KNOW.
WE ALL CAME TO THE AMAKAWA FAMILY HEAD-QUARTERS OF NOIHARA ON THE CAT'S WHIM.
MENAGERIE 11: DEMON-CRUSHING KITTY
THERE'S NOTHING OUT OF THE ORDINARY ABOUT THIS LOCATION, BUT...
...THE RECORDS THEY KEEP ARE REALLY QUITE FASCI-NATING... YOU KNOW.
ZZZ...
THE POWER OF THE AMAKAWA FAM-ILY AS DEMON SLAYERS... THE CHARAC-TERISTICS OF THE AYAKASHI THEY SUBJU-GATED...
YUUTO AMAKAWA ...
...HOW CAN YOU SLEEP SO CAREFREE... YOU KNOW?
NNN...

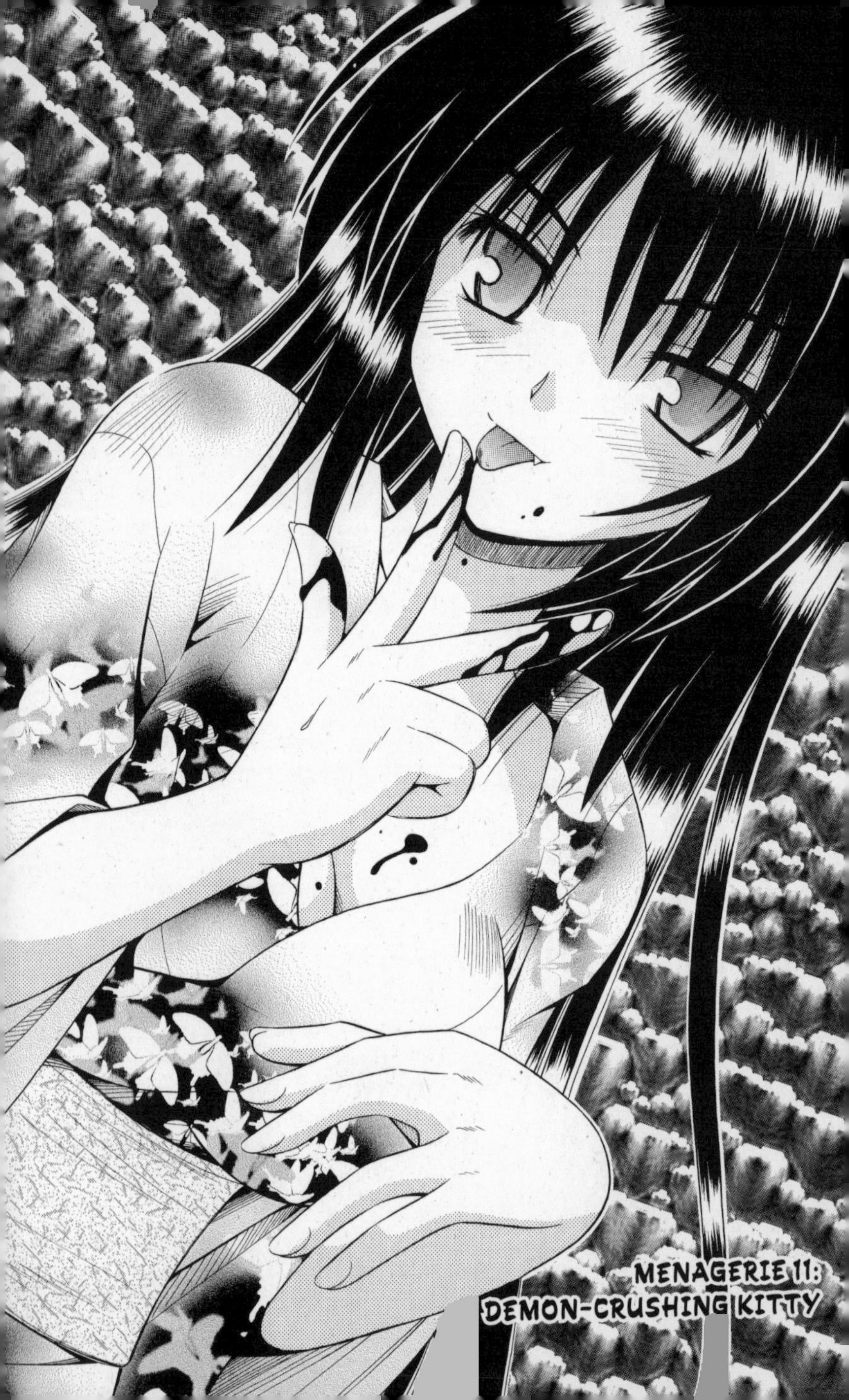
MENAGERIE 11:
DEMON-CRUSHING KITTY

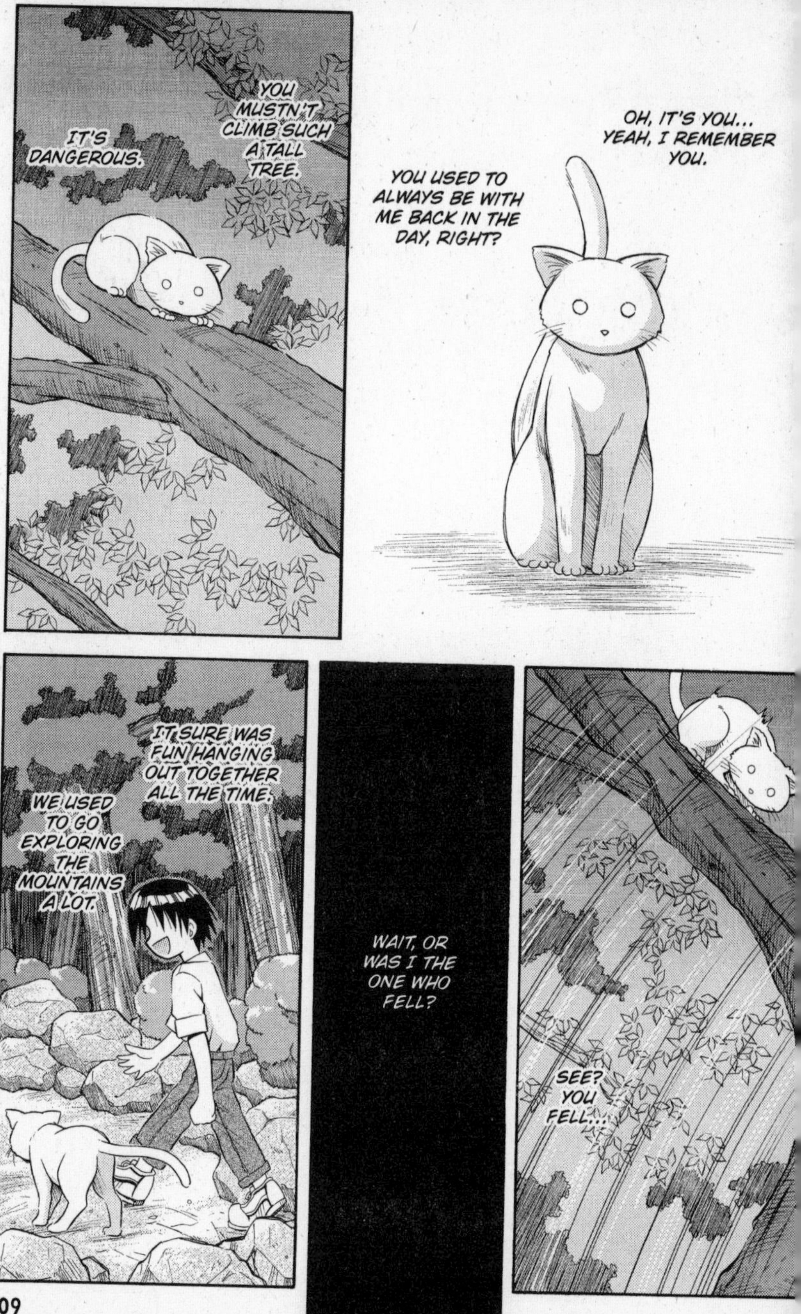
OH, IT'S YOU... YEAH, I REMEMBER YOU.
YOU USED TO ALWAYS BE WITH ME BACK IN THE DAY, RIGHT?
YOU MUSTN'T CLIMB SUCH A TALL TREE.
IT'S DANGEROUS.
SEE? YOU FELL...
WAIT, OR WAS I THE ONE WHO FELL?
IT SURE WAS FUN HANGING OUT TOGETHER ALL THE TIME.
WE USED TO GO EXPLORING THE MOUNTAINS A LOT.

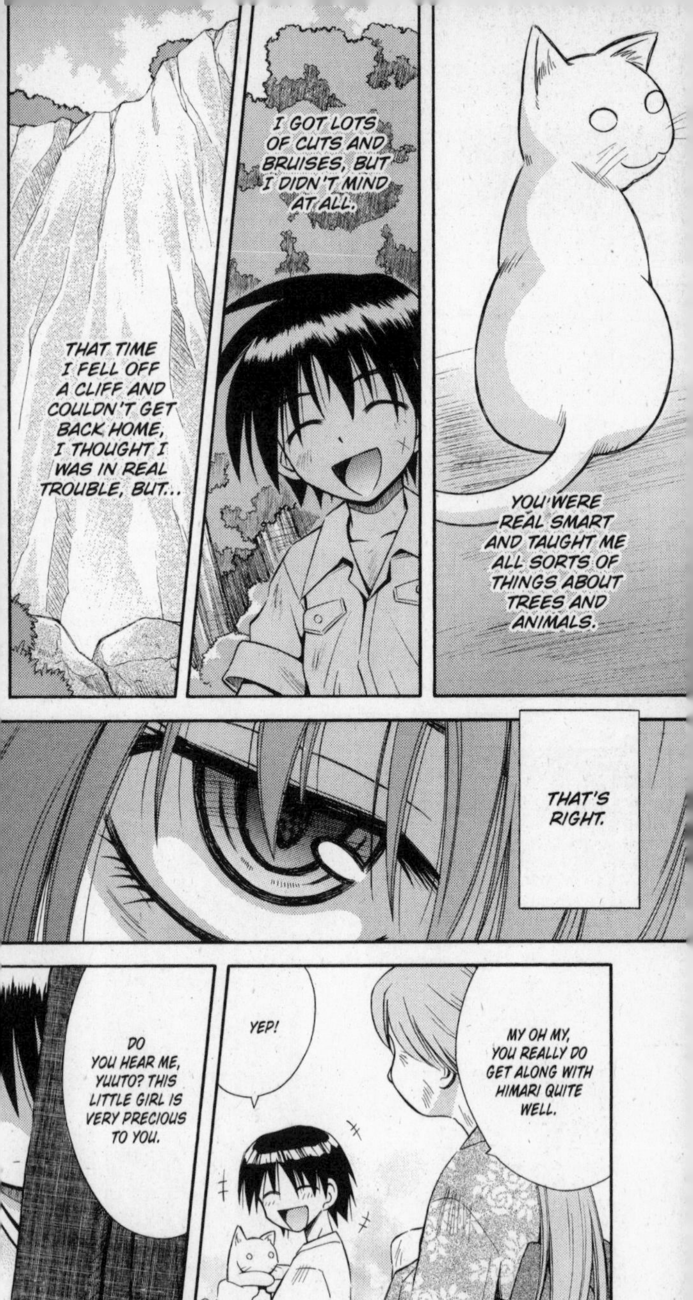
YOU WERE REAL SMART AND TAUGHT ME ALL SORTS OF THINGS ABOUT TREES AND ANIMALS.
I GOT LOTS OF CUTS AND BRUISES, BUT I DIDN'T MIND AT ALL.
THAT TIME I FELL OFF A CLIFF AND COULDN'T GET BACK HOME, I THOUGHT I WAS IN REAL TROUBLE, BUT...
THAT'S RIGHT.
MY OH MY, YOU REALLY DO GET ALONG WITH HIMARI QUITE WELL.
YEP!
DO YOU HEAR ME, YUUTO? THIS LITTLE GIRL IS VERY PRECIOUS TO YOU.

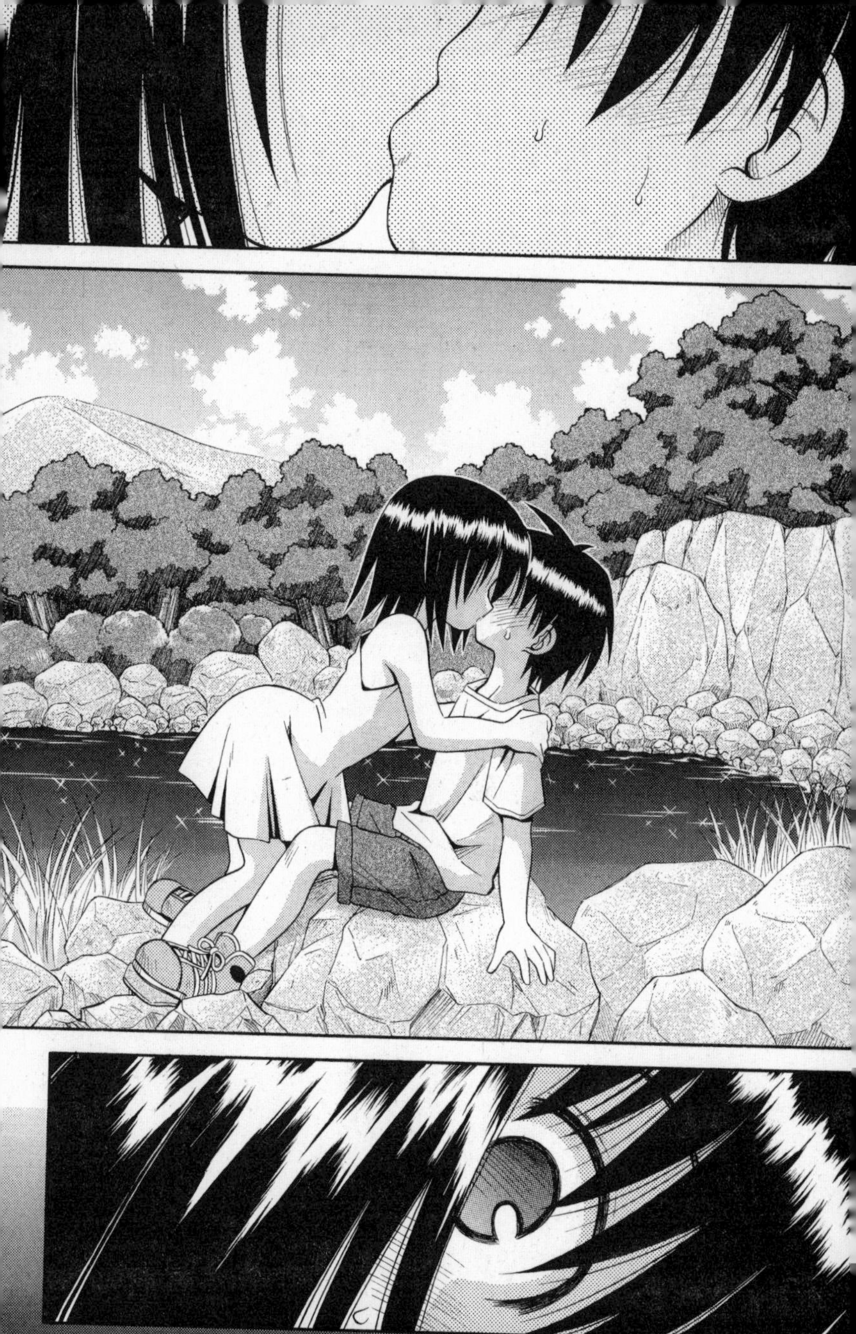

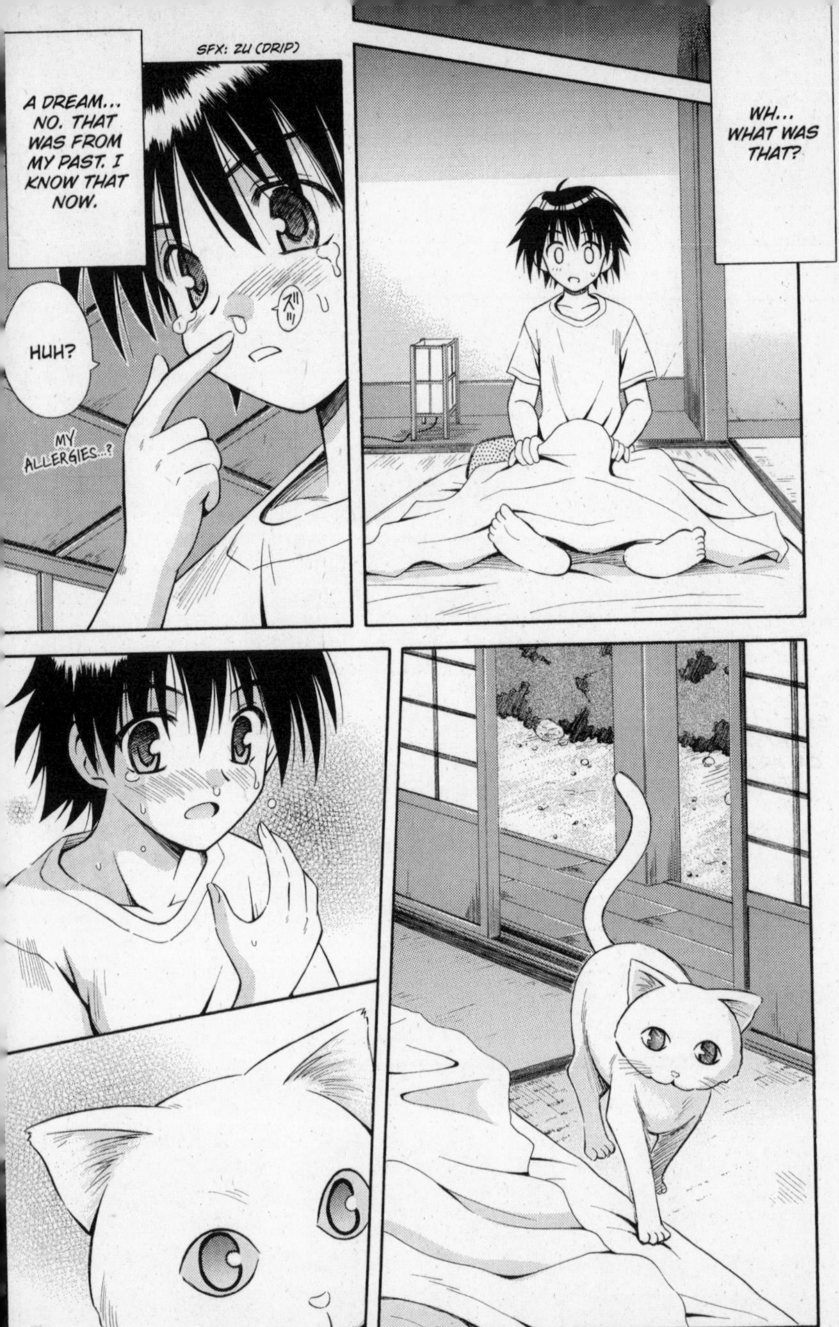
WH... WHAT WAS THAT?
SFX: ZU (DRIP)
A DREAM... NO. THAT WAS FROM MY PAST. I KNOW THAT NOW.
HUH?
MY ALLERGIES...?

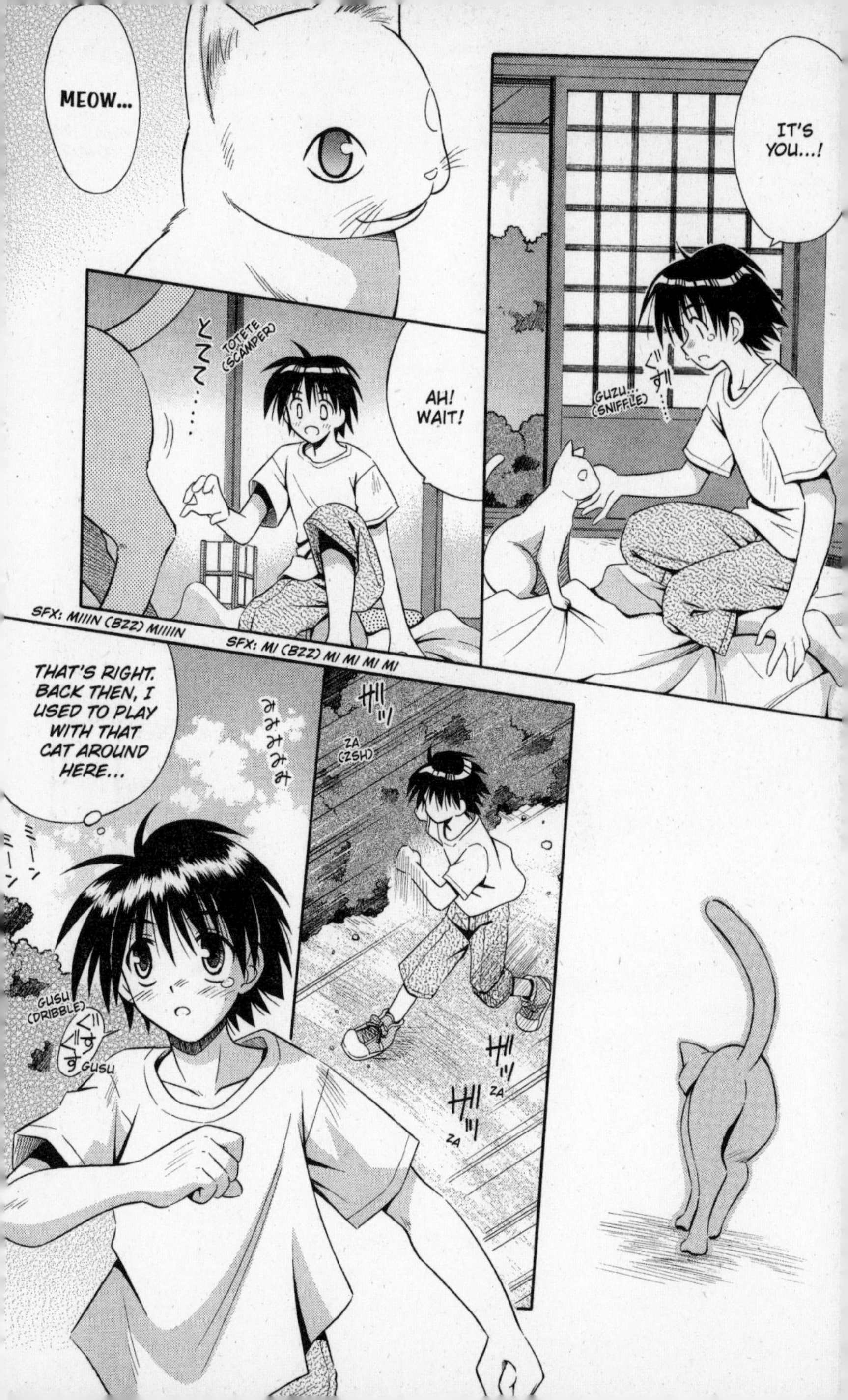
IT'S YOU...!
GUZU... (SNIFFLE)
MEOW...
AH! WAIT!
とてて
TOTETE (SCAMPER)
SFX: MIIIN (BZZ) MIIIN
SFX: MI (BZZ) MI MI MI MI
ザッ
ZA (ZSH)
ザッ
ZA
ザッ
ZA
みみみみみ
THAT'S RIGHT. BACK THEN, I USED TO PLAY WITH THAT CAT AROUND HERE...
ミーン
ぐすぐす
GUSU (DRIBBLE)
GUSU

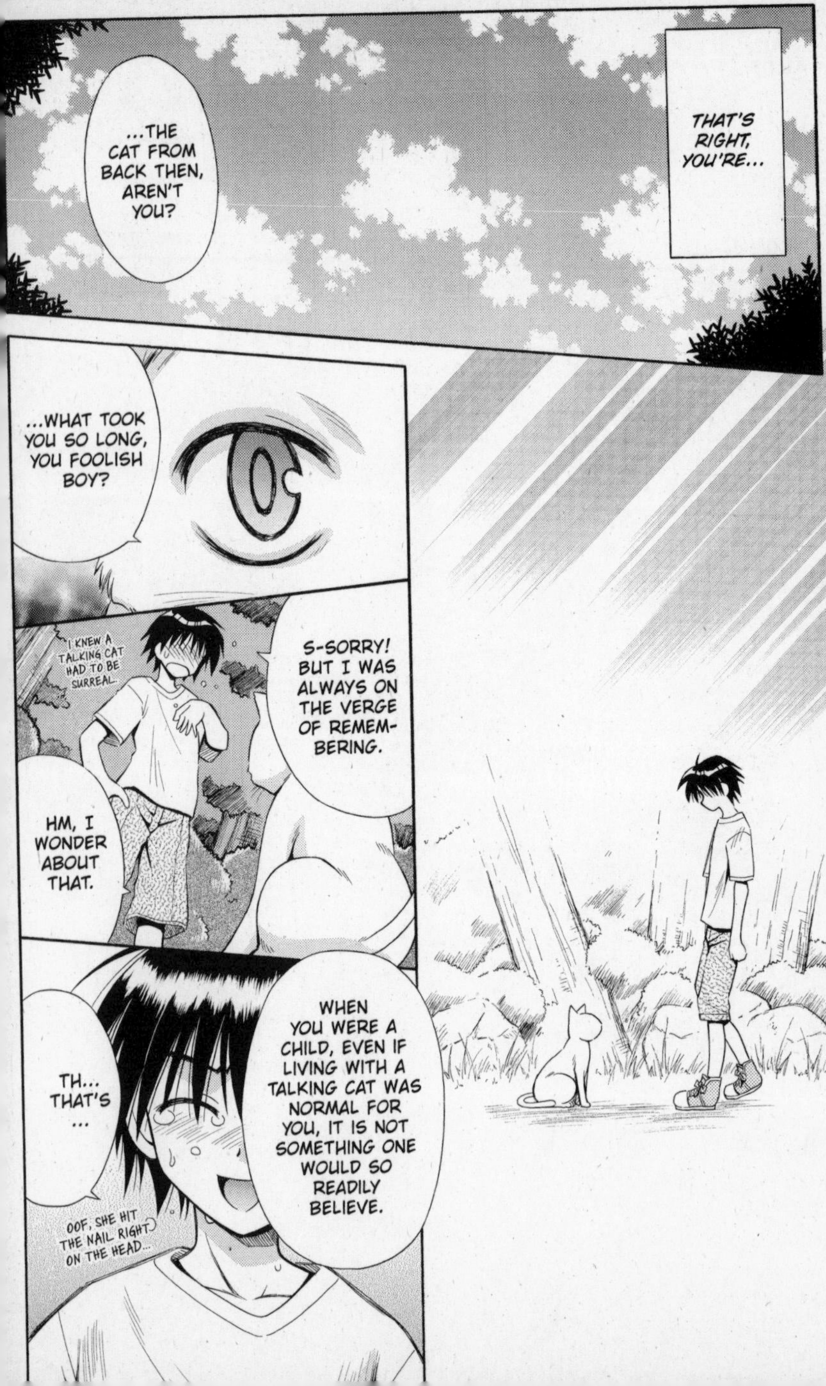
THAT'S RIGHT, YOU'RE...
...THE CAT FROM BACK THEN, AREN'T YOU?
...WHAT TOOK YOU SO LONG, YOU FOOLISH BOY?
S-SORRY! BUT I WAS ALWAYS ON THE VERGE OF REMEM-BERING.
I KNEW A TALKING CAT HAD TO BE SURREAL.
HM, I WONDER ABOUT THAT.
WHEN YOU WERE A CHILD, EVEN IF LIVING WITH A TALKING CAT WAS NORMAL FOR YOU, IT IS NOT SOMETHING ONE WOULD SO READILY BELIEVE.
TH... THAT'S ...
OOF, SHE HIT THE NAIL RIGHT ON THE HEAD...

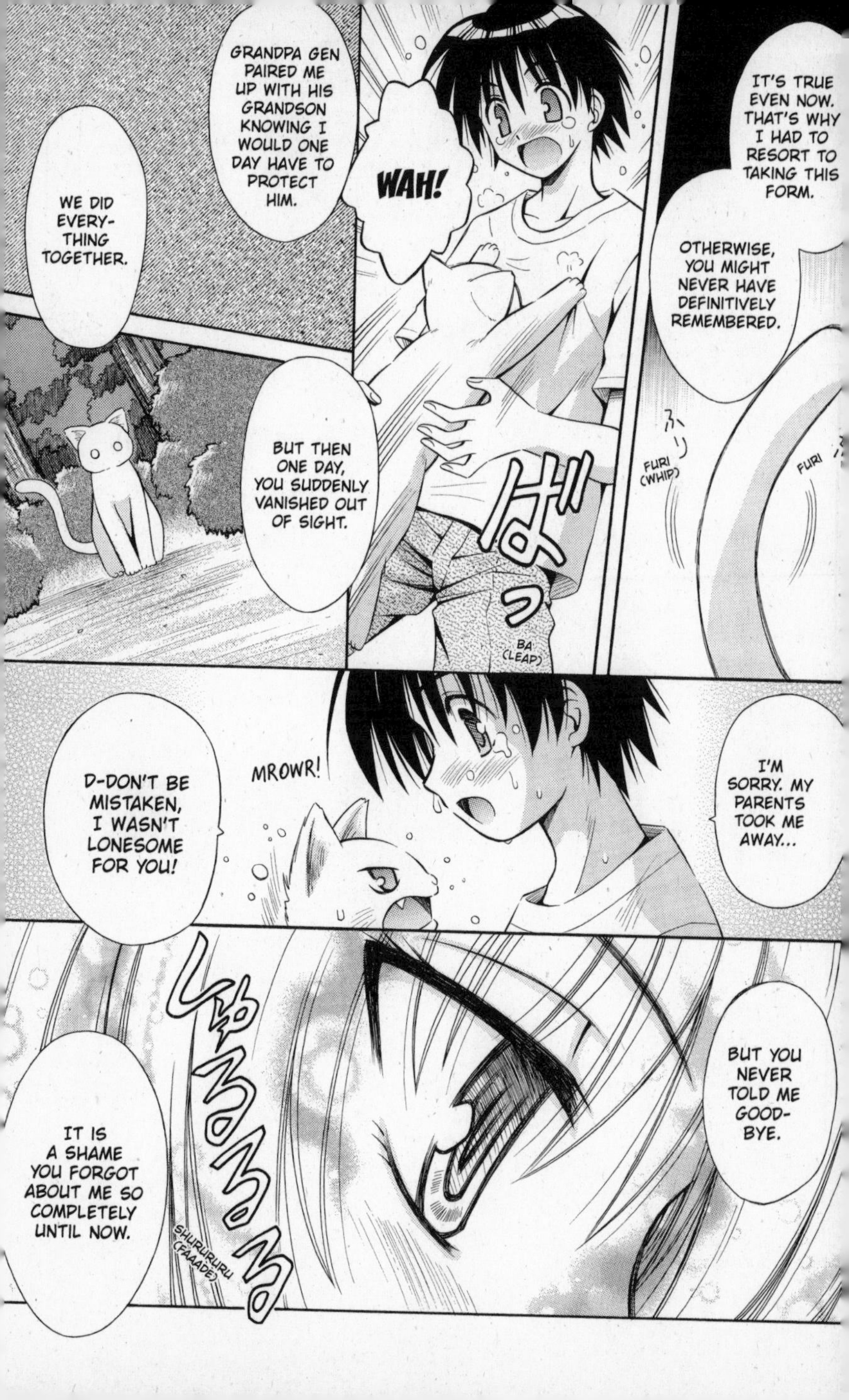
IT'S TRUE EVEN NOW. THAT'S WHY I HAD TO RESORT TO TAKING THIS FORM.
OTHERWISE, YOU MIGHT NEVER HAVE DEFINITIVELY REMEMBERED.
ふり
FURI (WHIP)
FURI
WAH!
GRANDPA GEN PAIRED ME UP WITH HIS GRANDSON KNOWING I WOULD ONE DAY HAVE TO PROTECT HIM.
WE DID EVERY-THING TOGETHER.
BUT THEN ONE DAY, YOU SUDDENLY VANISHED OUT OF SIGHT.
ばっ
BA (LEAP)
I'M SORRY. MY PARENTS TOOK ME AWAY...
MROWR!
D-DON'T BE MISTAKEN, I WASN'T LONESOME FOR YOU!
BUT YOU NEVER TOLD ME GOOD-BYE.
しゅるるるる
SHURURURU (FAAADE)
IT IS A SHAME YOU FORGOT ABOUT ME SO COMPLETELY UNTIL NOW.

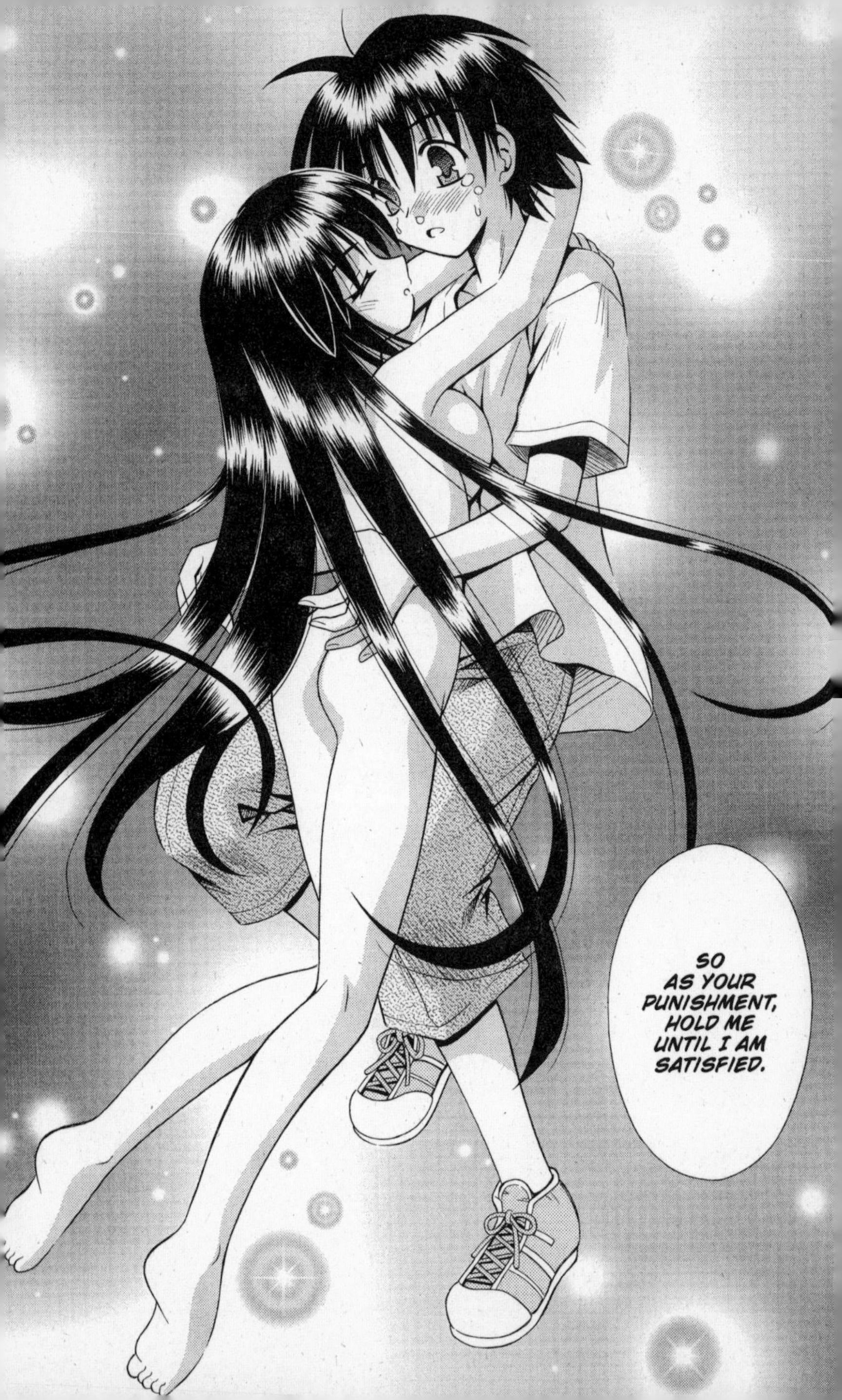
SO AS YOUR PUNISHMENT, HOLD ME UNTIL I AM SATISFIED.

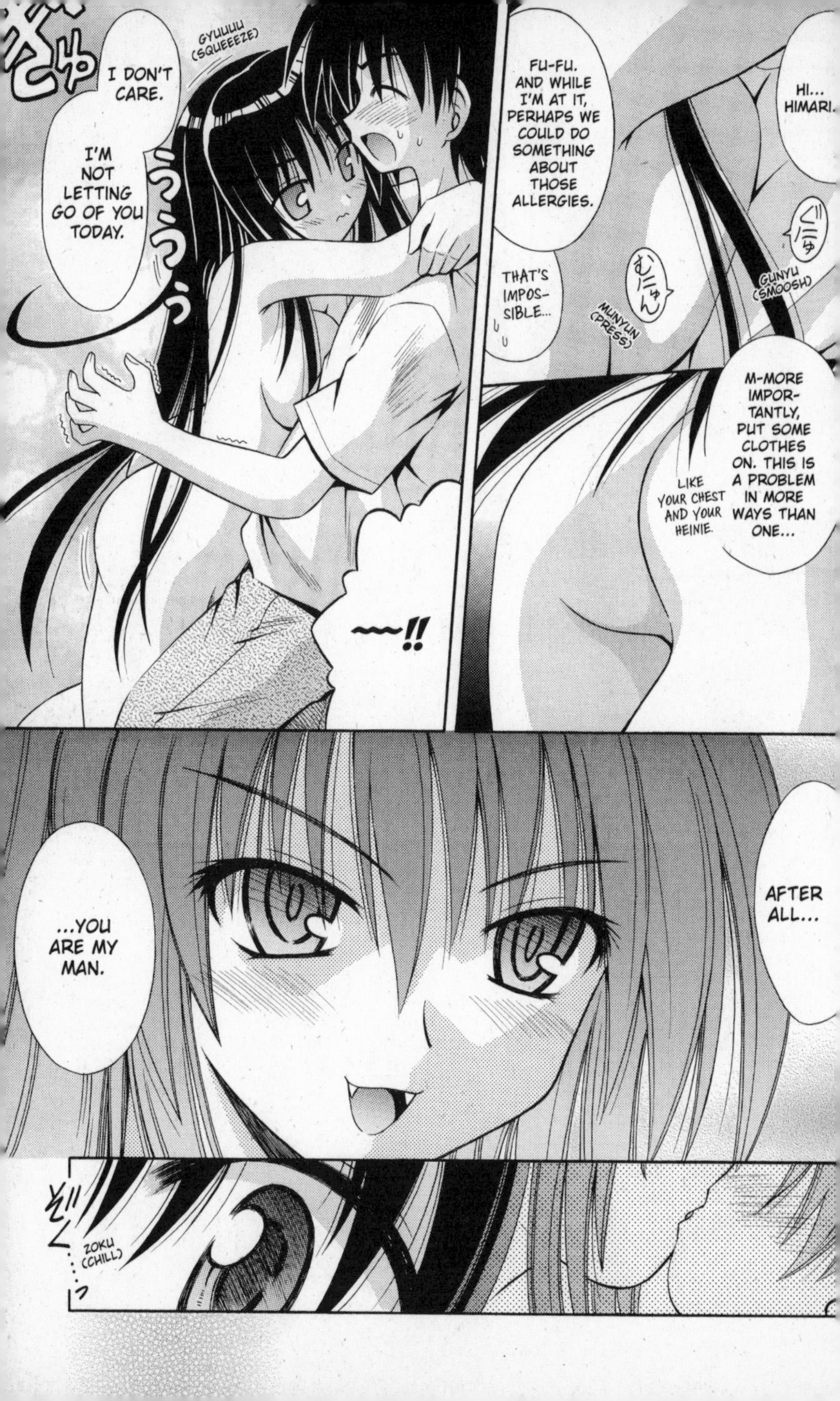

HI... HIMARI.
FU-FU. AND WHILE I'M AT IT, PERHAPS WE COULD DO SOMETHING ABOUT THOSE ALLERGIES.
ぐにゅ
GUNYU (SMOOSH)
むにゅん
MUNYUN (PRESS)
THAT'S IMPOSSIBLE...
M-MORE IMPORTANTLY, PUT SOME CLOTHES ON. THIS IS A PROBLEM IN MORE WAYS THAN ONE...
LIKE YOUR CHEST AND YOUR HEINIE.
ぎゅ
GYUUUU (SQUEEEZE)
I DON'T CARE.
I'M NOT LETTING GO OF YOU TODAY.
~~~!!
AFTER ALL...
...YOU ARE MY MAN.
ぞくっ
ZOKU (CHILL)
~~~

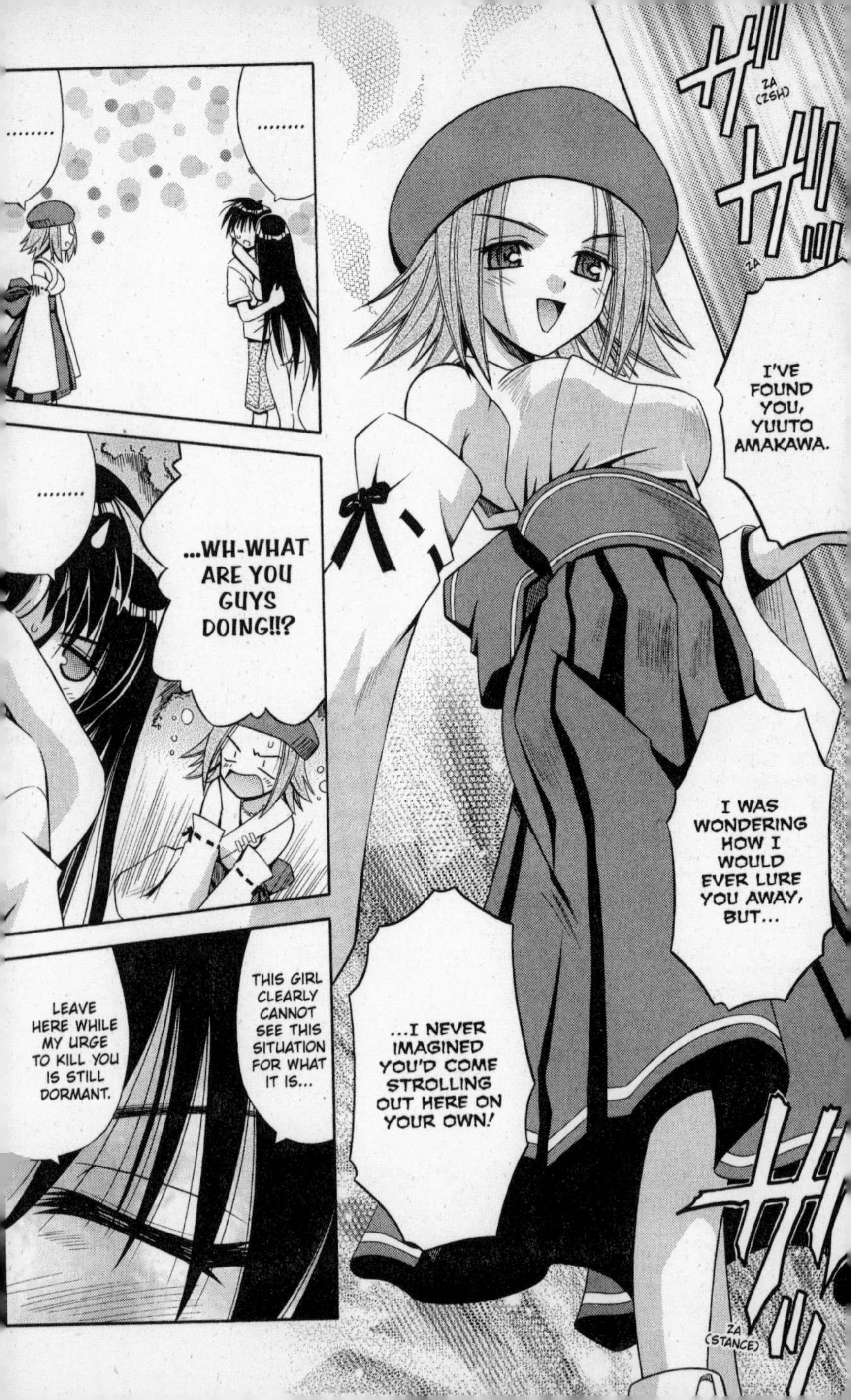
ZA (ZSH)
ZA
I'VE FOUND YOU, YUUTO AMAKAWA.
I WAS WONDERING HOW I WOULD EVER LURE YOU AWAY, BUT...
...I NEVER IMAGINED YOU'D COME STROLLING OUT HERE ON YOUR OWN!
ZA (STANCE)
....
....
...WH-WHAT ARE YOU GUYS DOING!!?
....
THIS GIRL CLEARLY CANNOT SEE THIS SITUATION FOR WHAT IT IS...
LEAVE HERE WHILE MY URGE TO KILL YOU IS STILL DORMANT.

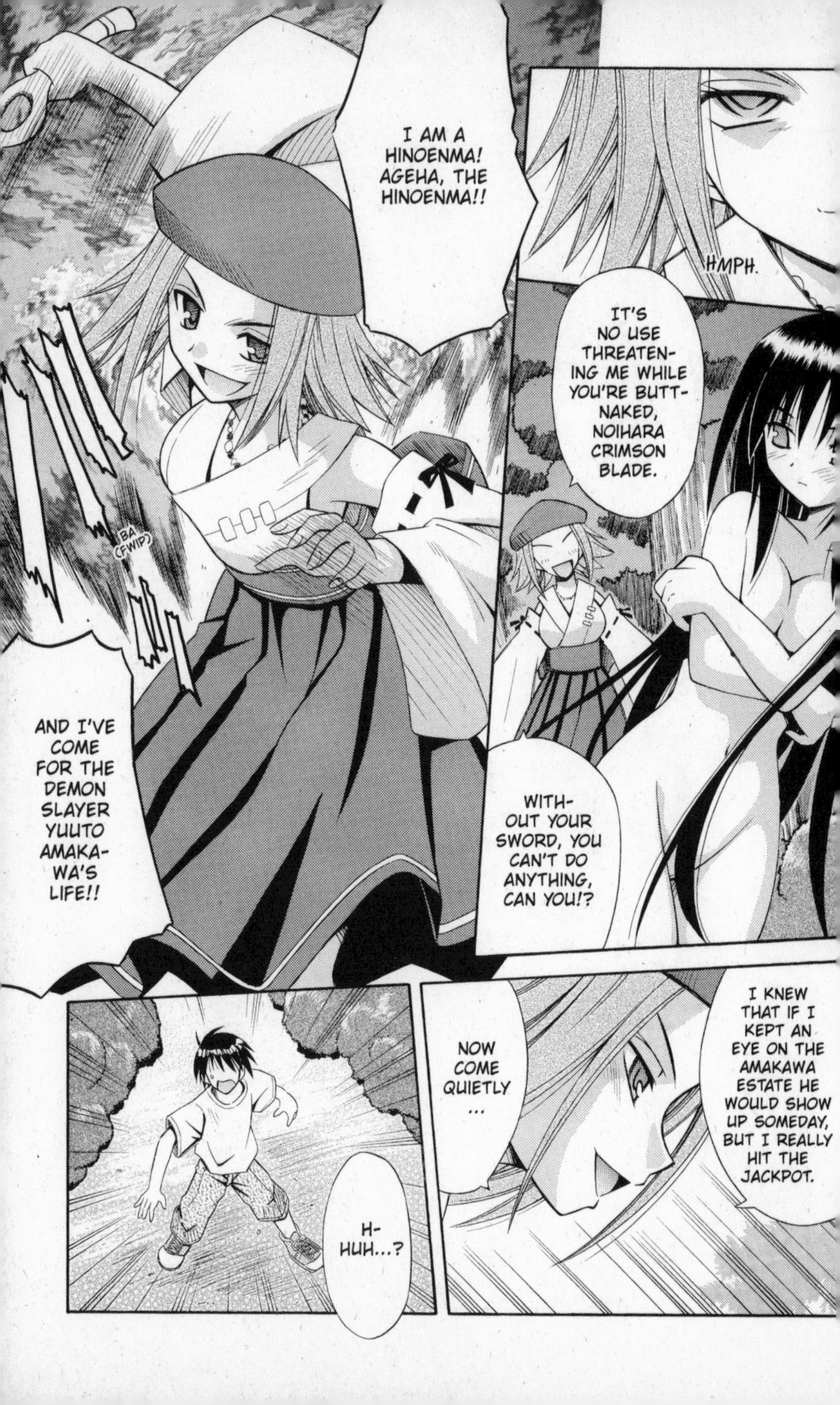
HMPH.
IT'S NO USE THREATEN-ING ME WHILE YOU'RE BUTT-NAKED, NOIHARA CRIMSON BLADE.
WITH-OUT YOUR SWORD, YOU CAN'T DO ANYTHING, CAN YOU!?
I AM A HINOENMA! AGEHA, THE HINOENMA!!
BA (FWIP)
AND I'VE COME FOR THE DEMON SLAYER YUUTO AMAKA-WA'S LIFE!!
I KNEW THAT IF I KEPT AN EYE ON THE AMAKAWA ESTATE HE WOULD SHOW UP SOMEDAY, BUT I REALLY HIT THE JACKPOT.
NOW COME QUIETLY ...
H-HUH...?

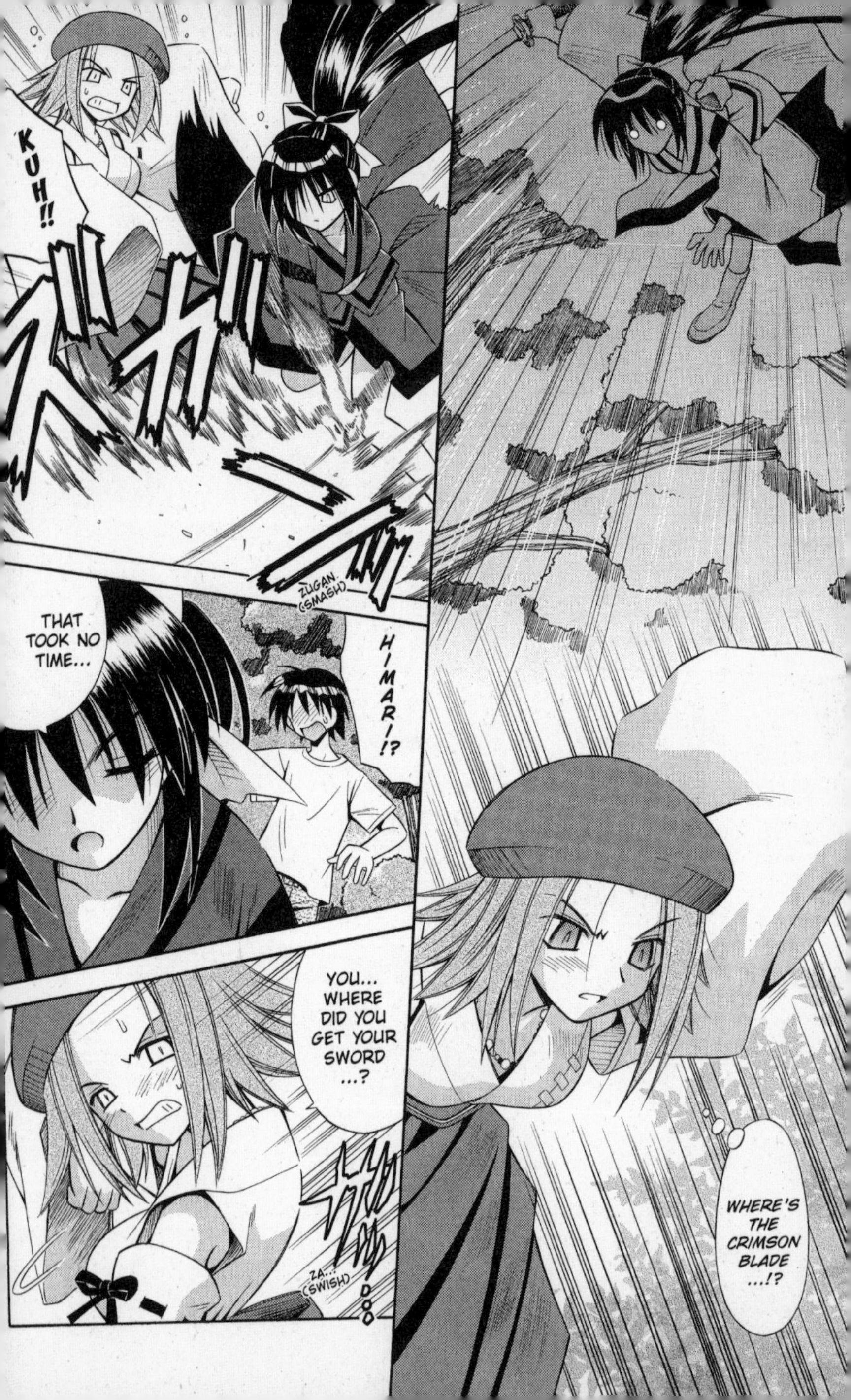
WHERE'S THE CRIMSON BLADE ...!?
KUH!!
ZUGAN (SMASH)
HIMARI!?
THAT TOOK NO TIME...
YOU... WHERE DID YOU GET YOUR SWORD ...?
ZA... (SWISH)
DOO

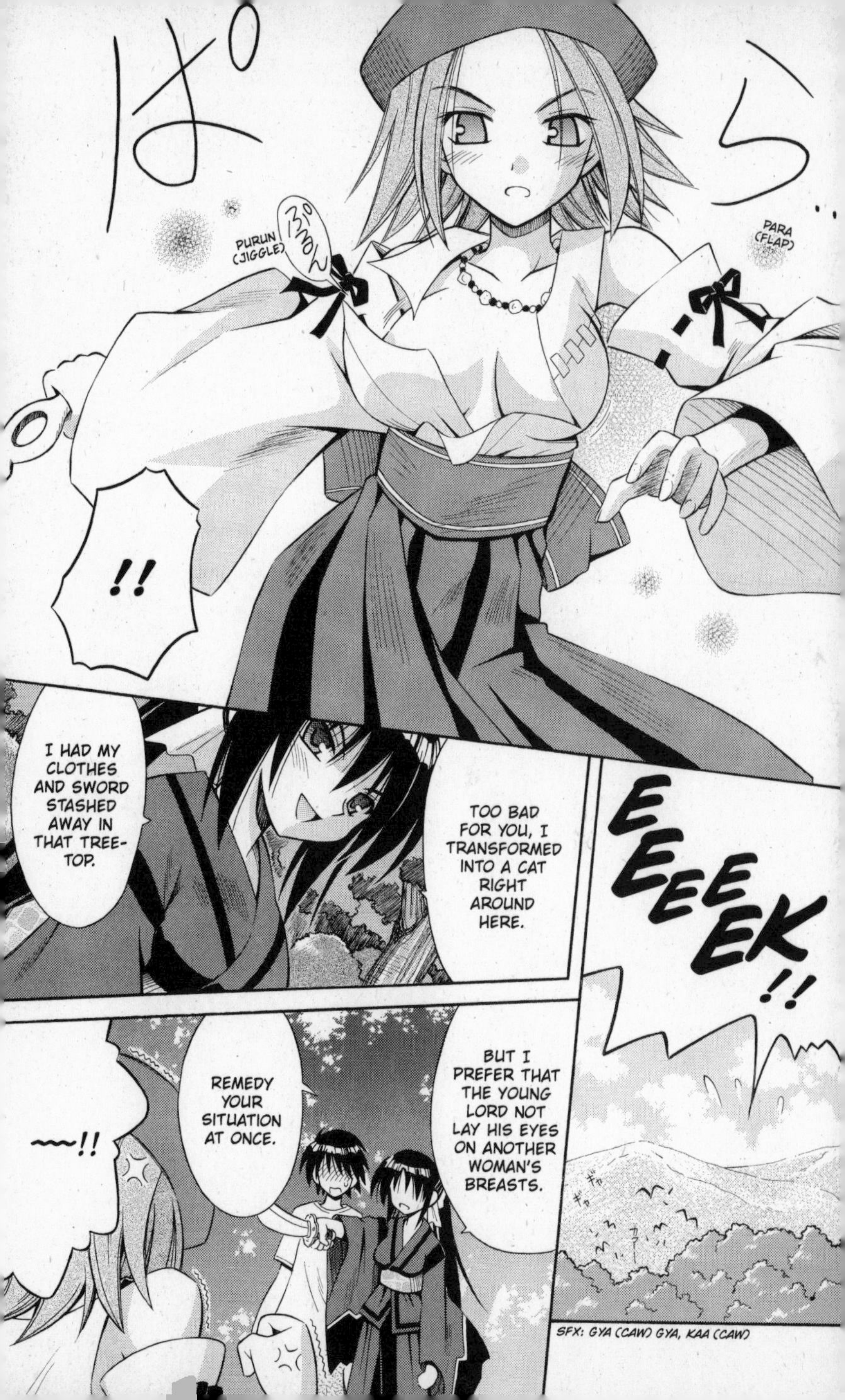
ぱら
PARA (FLAP)
ぷるん
PURUN (JIGGLE)
!!
EEEEEK!!
SFX: GYA (CAW) GYA, KAA (CAW)
TOO BAD FOR YOU, I TRANSFORMED INTO A CAT RIGHT AROUND HERE.
I HAD MY CLOTHES AND SWORD STASHED AWAY IN THAT TREE-TOP.
BUT I PREFER THAT THE YOUNG LORD NOT LAY HIS EYES ON ANOTHER WOMAN'S BREASTS.
REMEDY YOUR SITUATION AT ONCE.
~~!!

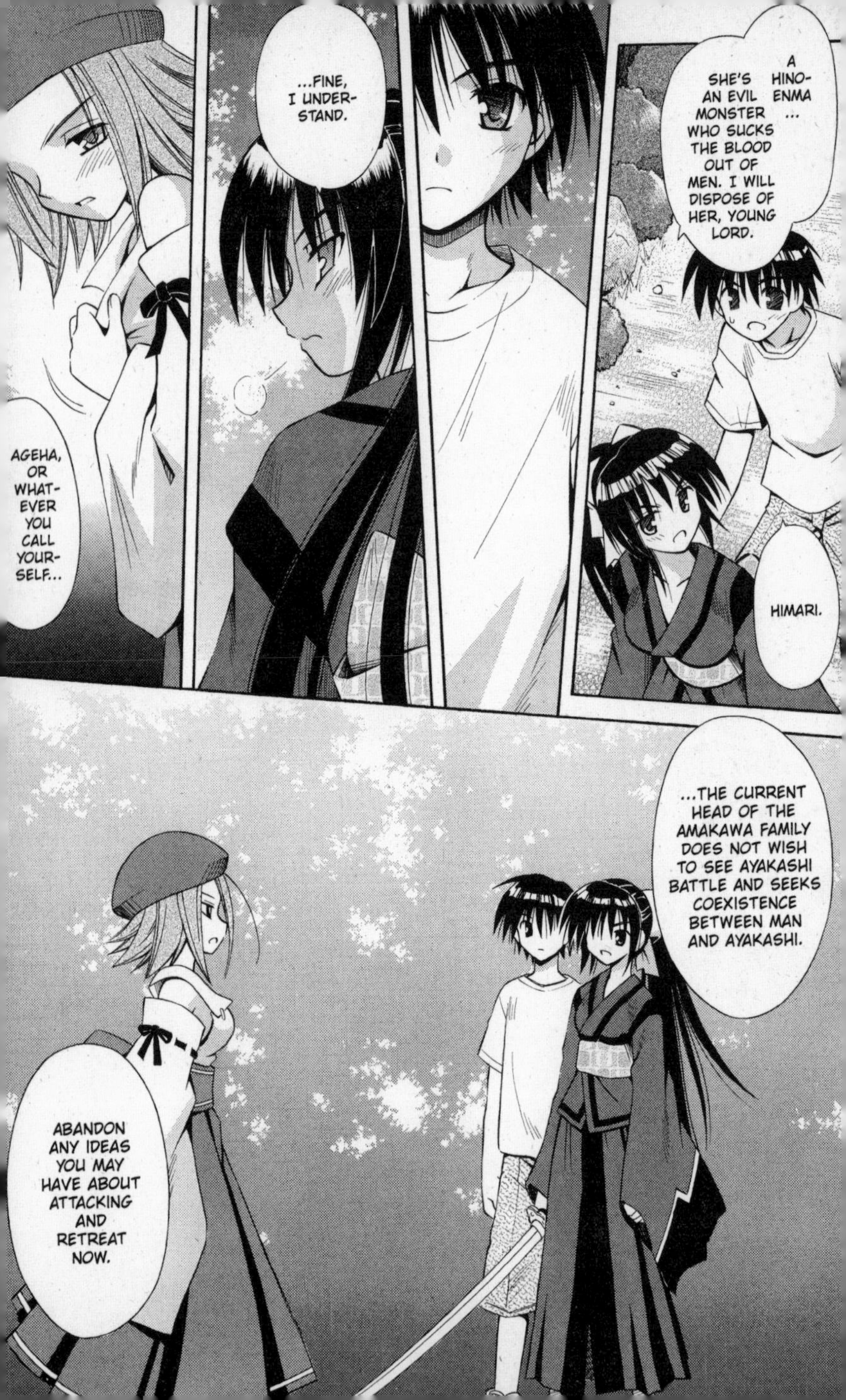
A HINOENMA...
SHE'S AN EVIL MONSTER WHO SUCKS THE BLOOD OUT OF MEN. I WILL DISPOSE OF HER, YOUNG LORD.
HIMARI.
...FINE, I UNDERSTAND.
AGEHA, OR WHATEVER YOU CALL YOURSELF...
...THE CURRENT HEAD OF THE AMAKAWA FAMILY DOES NOT WISH TO SEE AYAKASHI BATTLE AND SEEKS COEXISTENCE BETWEEN MAN AND AYAKASHI.
ABANDON ANY IDEAS YOU MAY HAVE ABOUT ATTACKING AND RETREAT NOW.

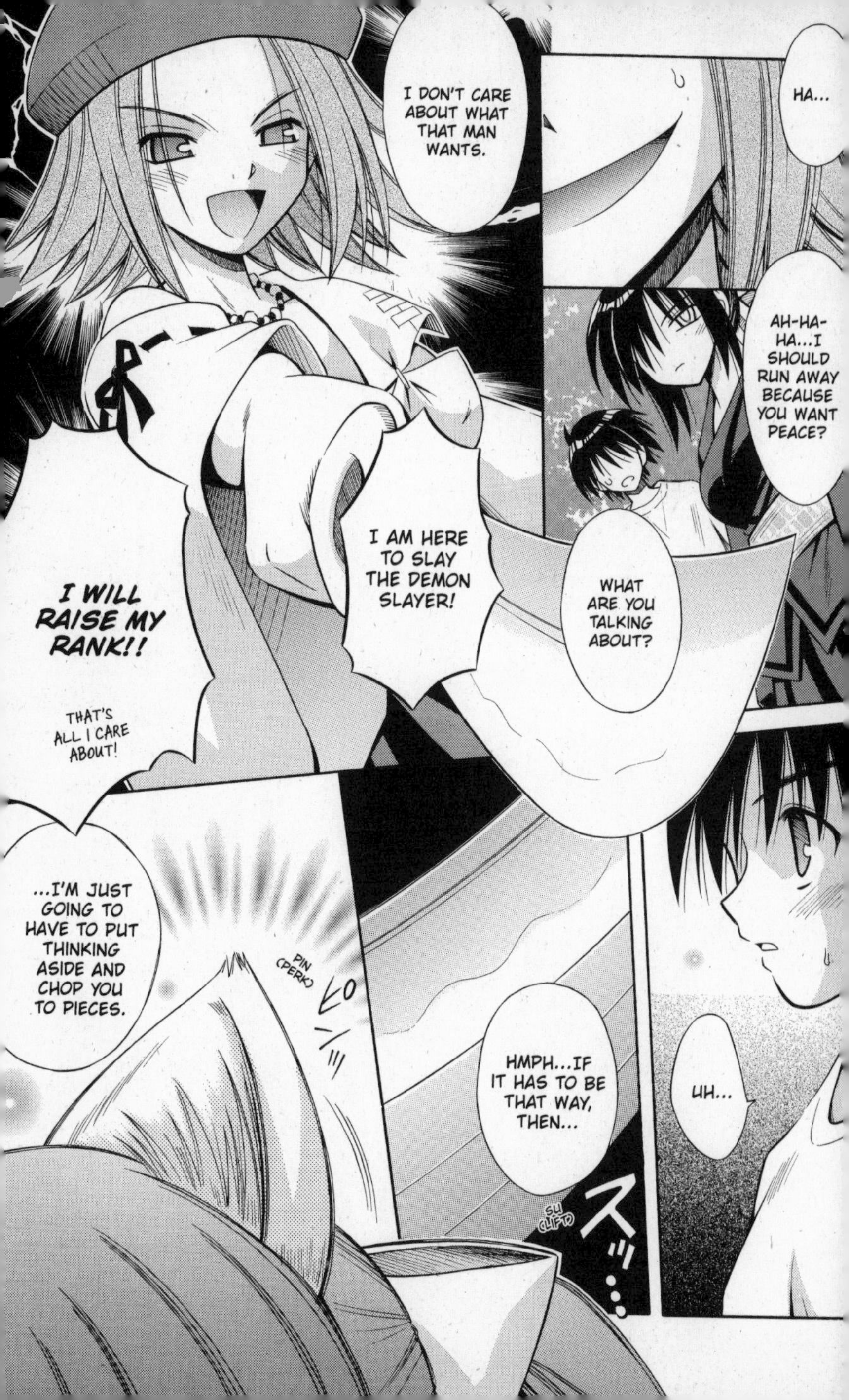
HA...
AH-HA-HA...I SHOULD RUN AWAY BECAUSE YOU WANT PEACE?
WHAT ARE YOU TALKING ABOUT?
I DON'T CARE ABOUT WHAT THAT MAN WANTS.
I AM HERE TO SLAY THE DEMON SLAYER!
I WILL RAISE MY RANK!!
THAT'S ALL I CARE ABOUT!
UH...
SU (LIFT)
HMPH...IF IT HAS TO BE THAT WAY, THEN...
PIN (PERK)
...I'M JUST GOING TO HAVE TO PUT THINKING ASIDE AND CHOP YOU TO PIECES.

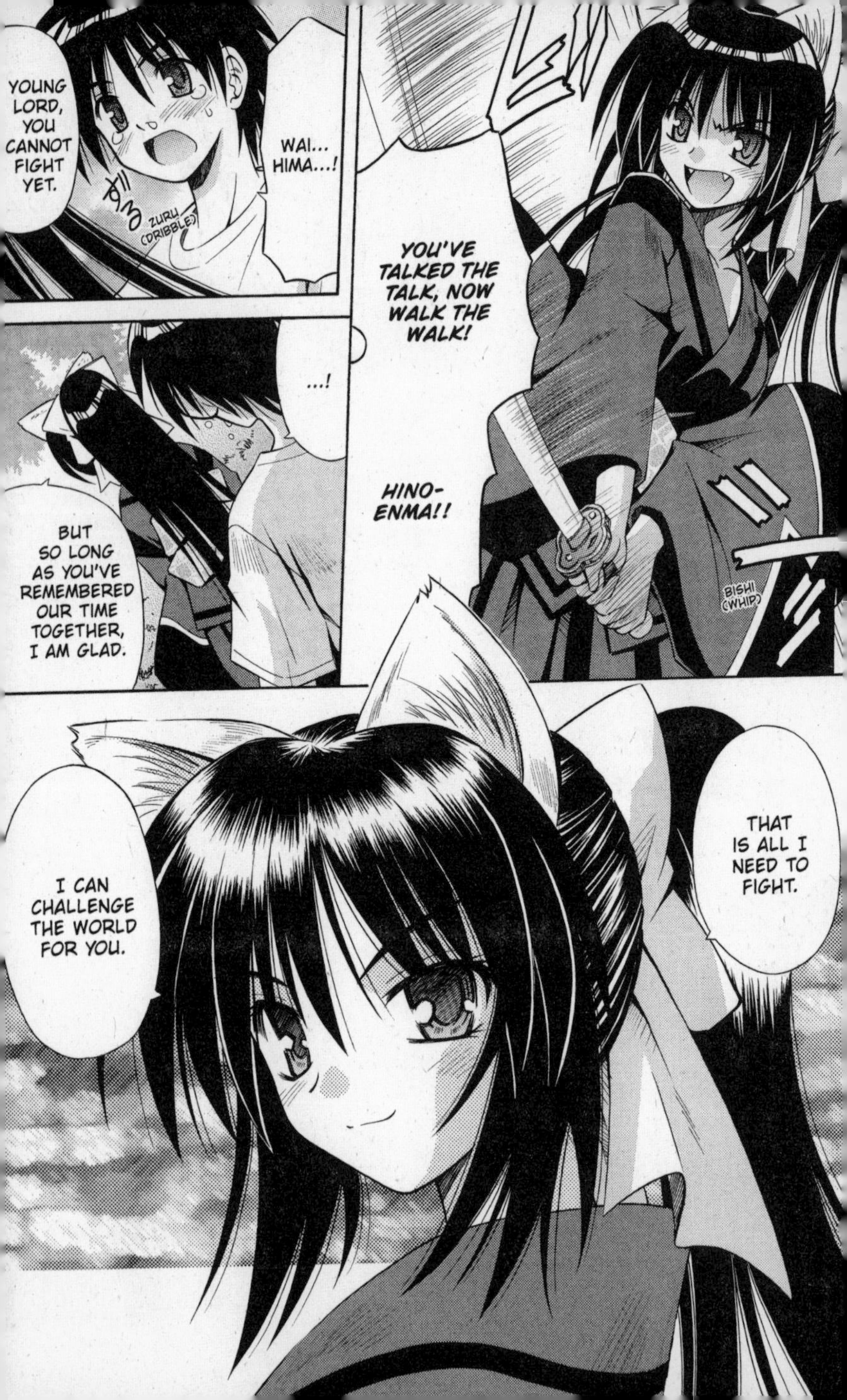
YOU'VE TALKED THE TALK, NOW WALK THE WALK!
HINO-ENMA!!
BISHI (WHIP)
WAI... HIMA...!
YOUNG LORD, YOU CANNOT FIGHT YET.
ZURU (DRIBBLE)
...!
BUT SO LONG AS YOU'VE REMEMBERED OUR TIME TOGETHER, I AM GLAD.
THAT IS ALL I NEED TO FIGHT.
I CAN CHALLENGE THE WORLD FOR YOU.

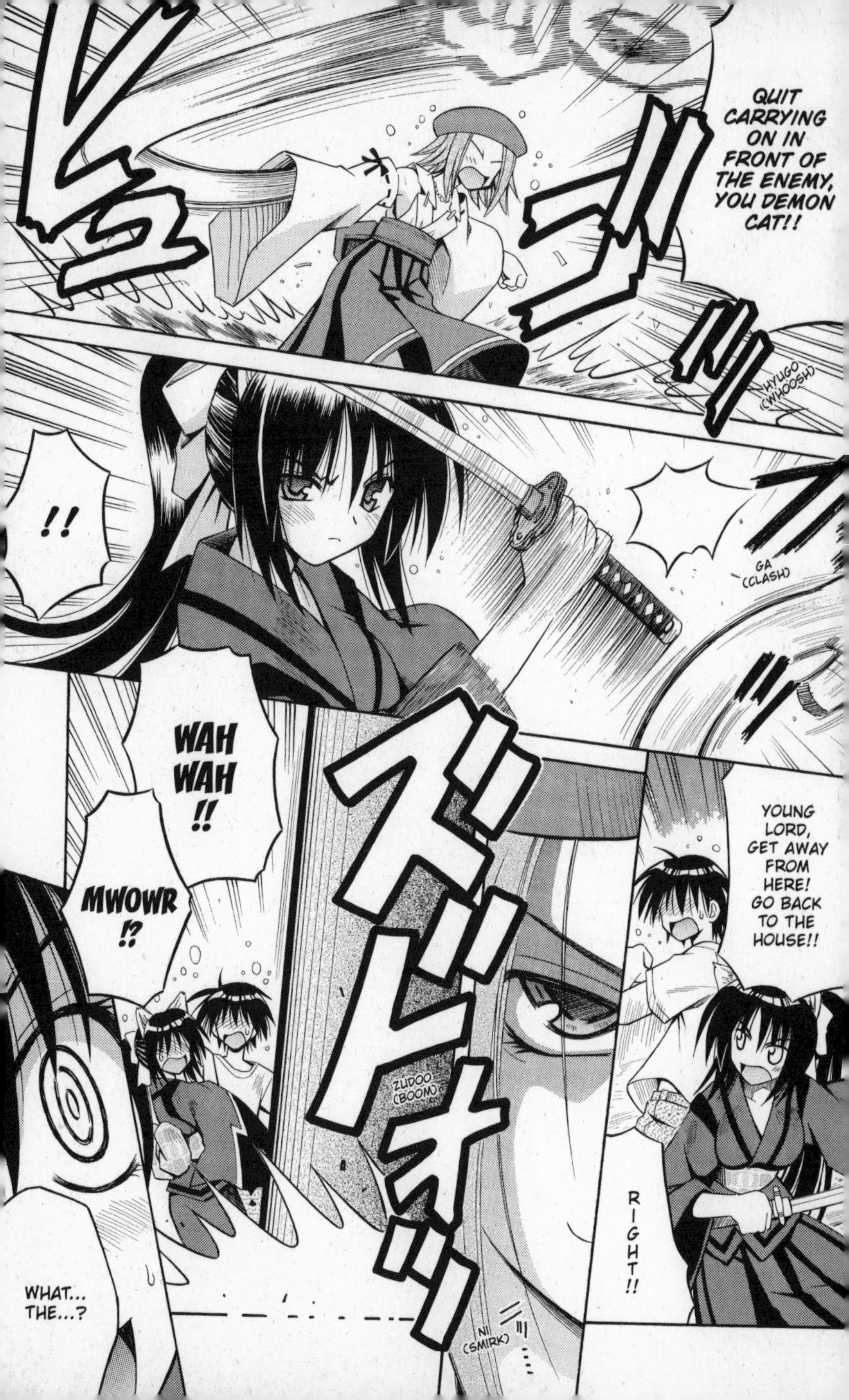
QUIT CARRYING ON IN FRONT OF THE ENEMY, YOU DEMON CAT!!
HYUGO (WHOOSH)
GA (CLASH)
!!
YOUNG LORD, GET AWAY FROM HERE! GO BACK TO THE HOUSE!!
RIGHT!!
ZUDOO (BOOM)
NI (SMIRK)
WAH WAH!!
MWOWR!?
WHAT... THE...?

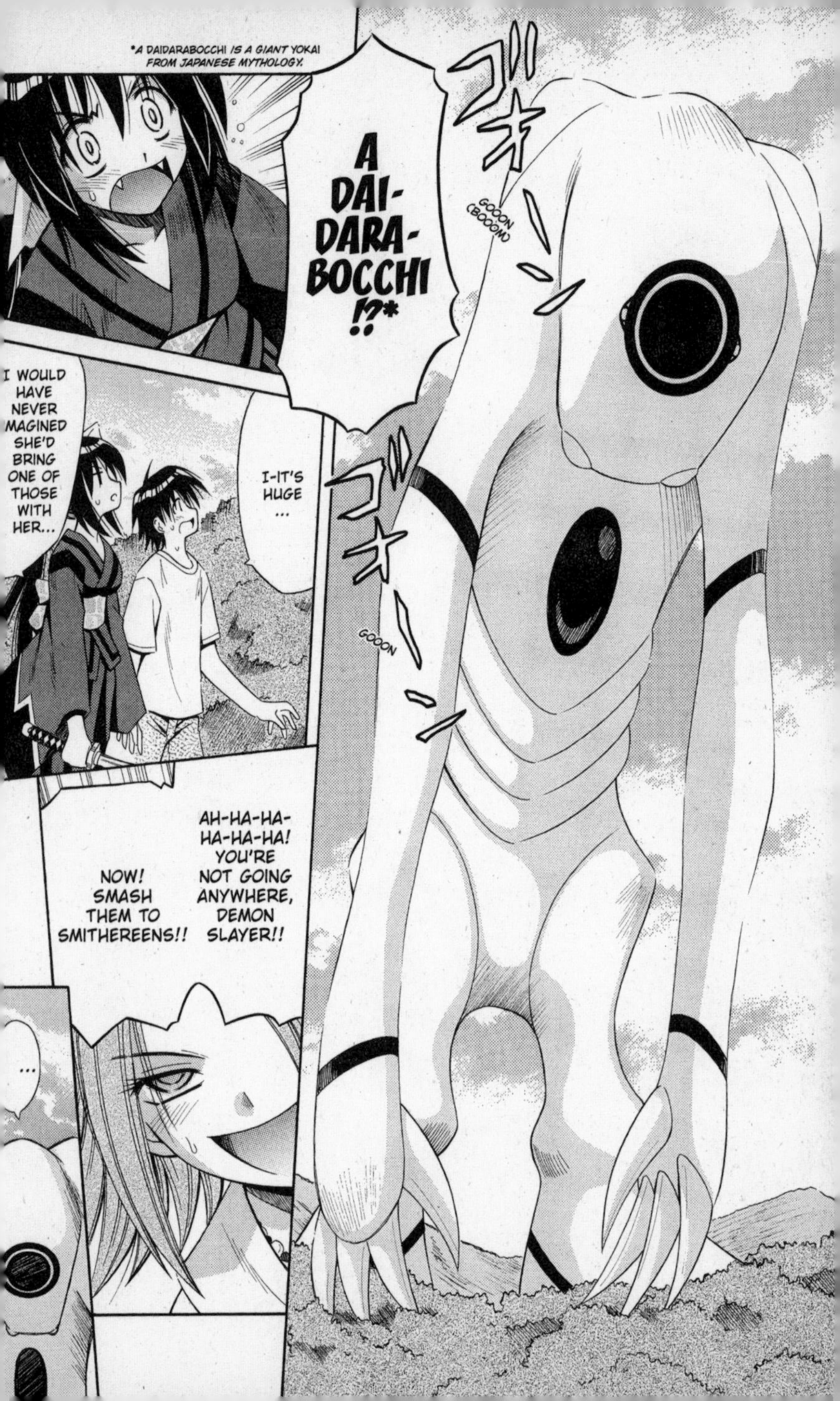

GOOON (BOOOM)
GOOON
A DAIDARABOCCHI!?*
*A DAIDARABOCCHI IS A GIANT YOKAI FROM JAPANESE MYTHOLOGY.
I-IT'S HUGE...
I WOULD HAVE NEVER MAGINED SHE'D BRING ONE OF THOSE WITH HER...
AH-HA-HA-HA-HA-HA! YOU'RE NOT GOING ANYWHERE, DEMON SLAYER!!
NOW! SMASH THEM TO SMITHEREENS!!
...

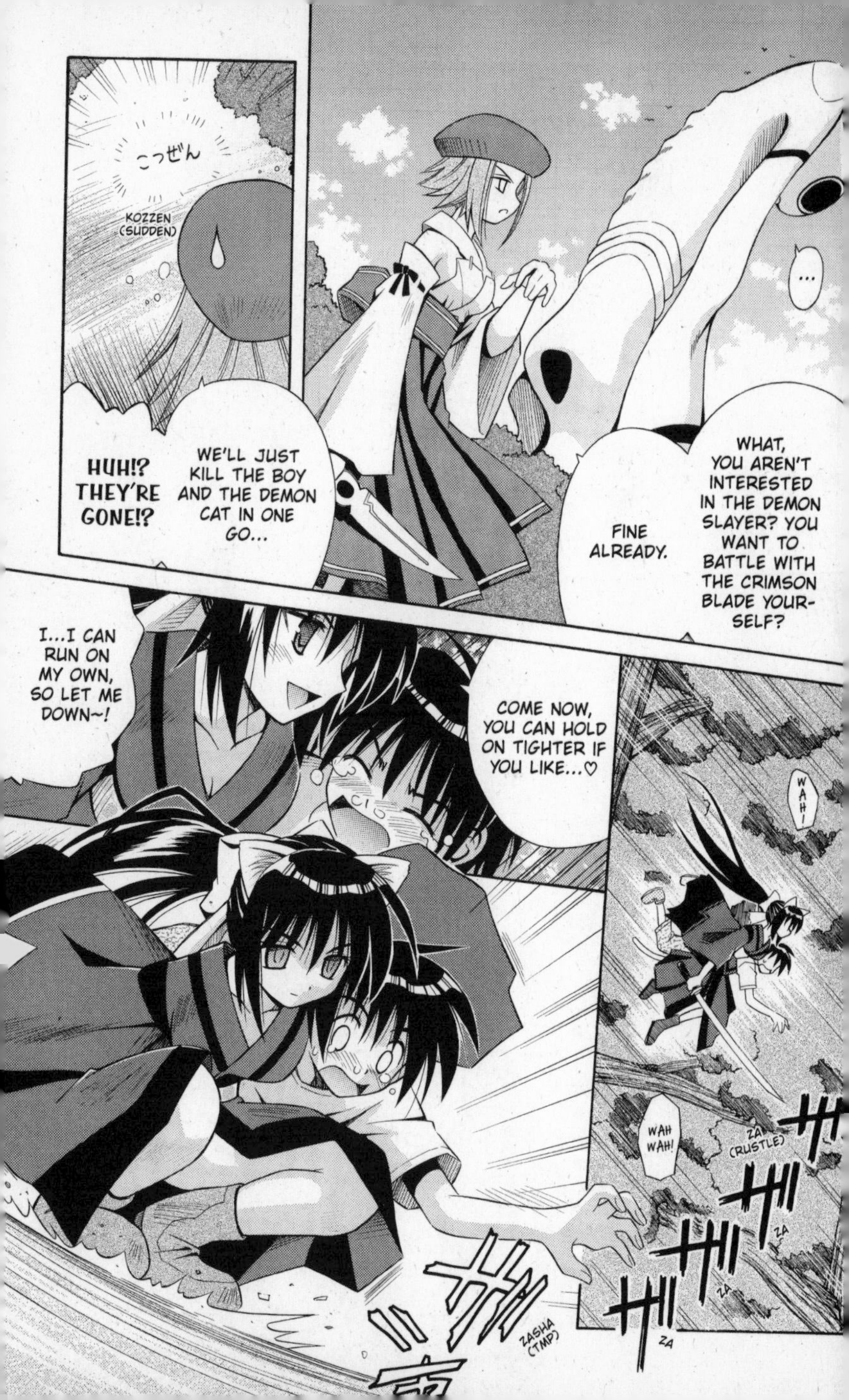
...
WHAT, YOU AREN'T INTERESTED IN THE DEMON SLAYER? YOU WANT TO BATTLE WITH THE CRIMSON BLADE YOUR-SELF?
FINE ALREADY.
こつぜん
KOZZEN (SUDDEN)
WE'LL JUST KILL THE BOY AND THE DEMON CAT IN ONE GO...
HUH!? THEY'RE GONE!?
WAH!
WAH WAH!
ZA (RUSTLE)
ZA
ZA
ZA
COME NOW, YOU CAN HOLD ON TIGHTER IF YOU LIKE...♡
I...I CAN RUN ON MY OWN, SO LET ME DOWN~!
ZASHA (TMP)

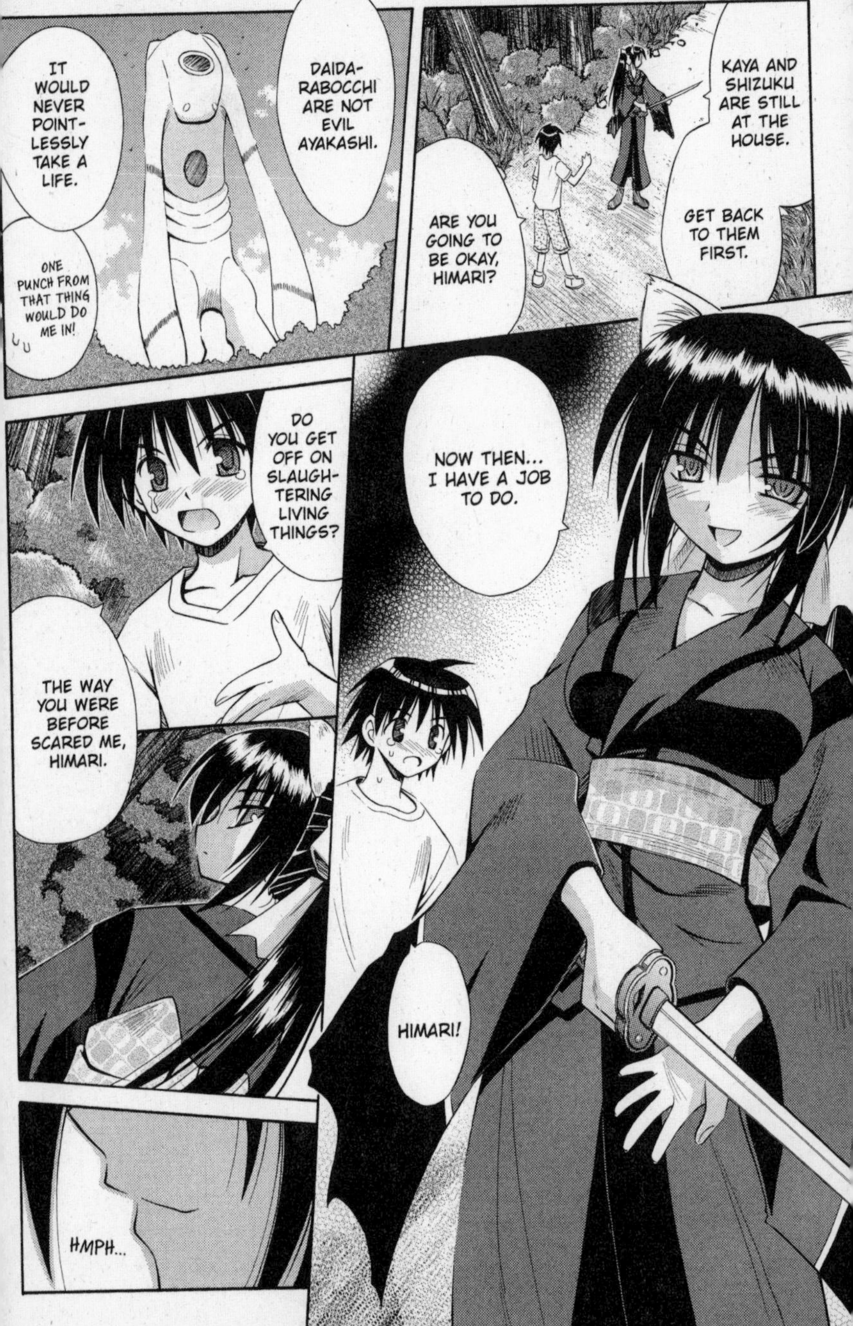
KAYA AND SHIZUKU ARE STILL AT THE HOUSE.
GET BACK TO THEM FIRST.
ARE YOU GOING TO BE OKAY, HIMARI?
DAIDA-RABOCCHI ARE NOT EVIL AYAKASHI.
IT WOULD NEVER POINTLESSLY TAKE A LIFE.
ONE PUNCH FROM THAT THING WOULD DO ME IN!
NOW THEN... I HAVE A JOB TO DO.
HIMARI!
DO YOU GET OFF ON SLAUGHTERING LIVING THINGS?
THE WAY YOU WERE BEFORE SCARED ME, HIMARI.
HMPH...

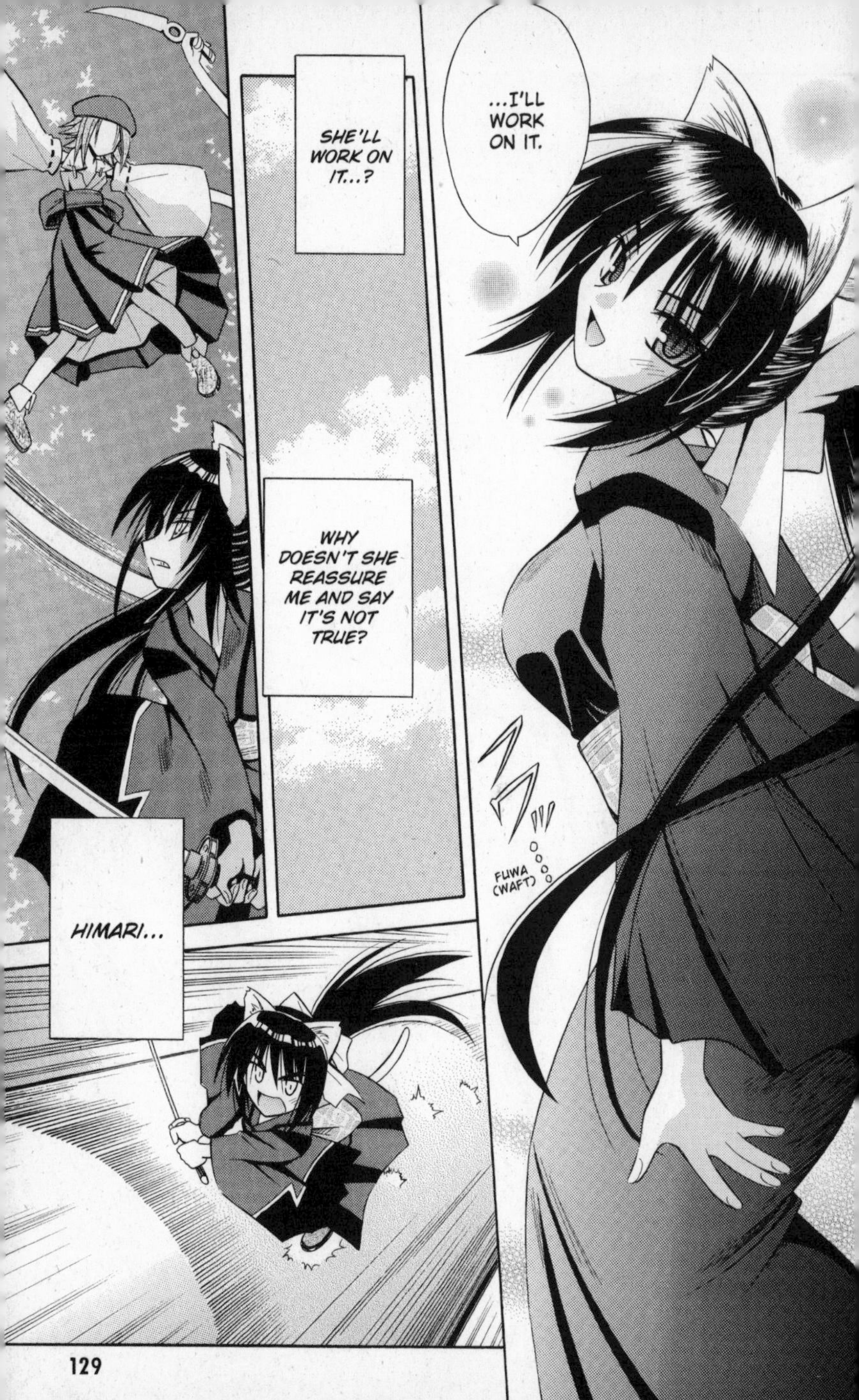
...I'LL WORK ON IT.
FUWA (WAFT)
SHE'LL WORK ON IT...?
WHY DOESN'T SHE REASSURE ME AND SAY IT'S NOT TRUE?
HIMARI...

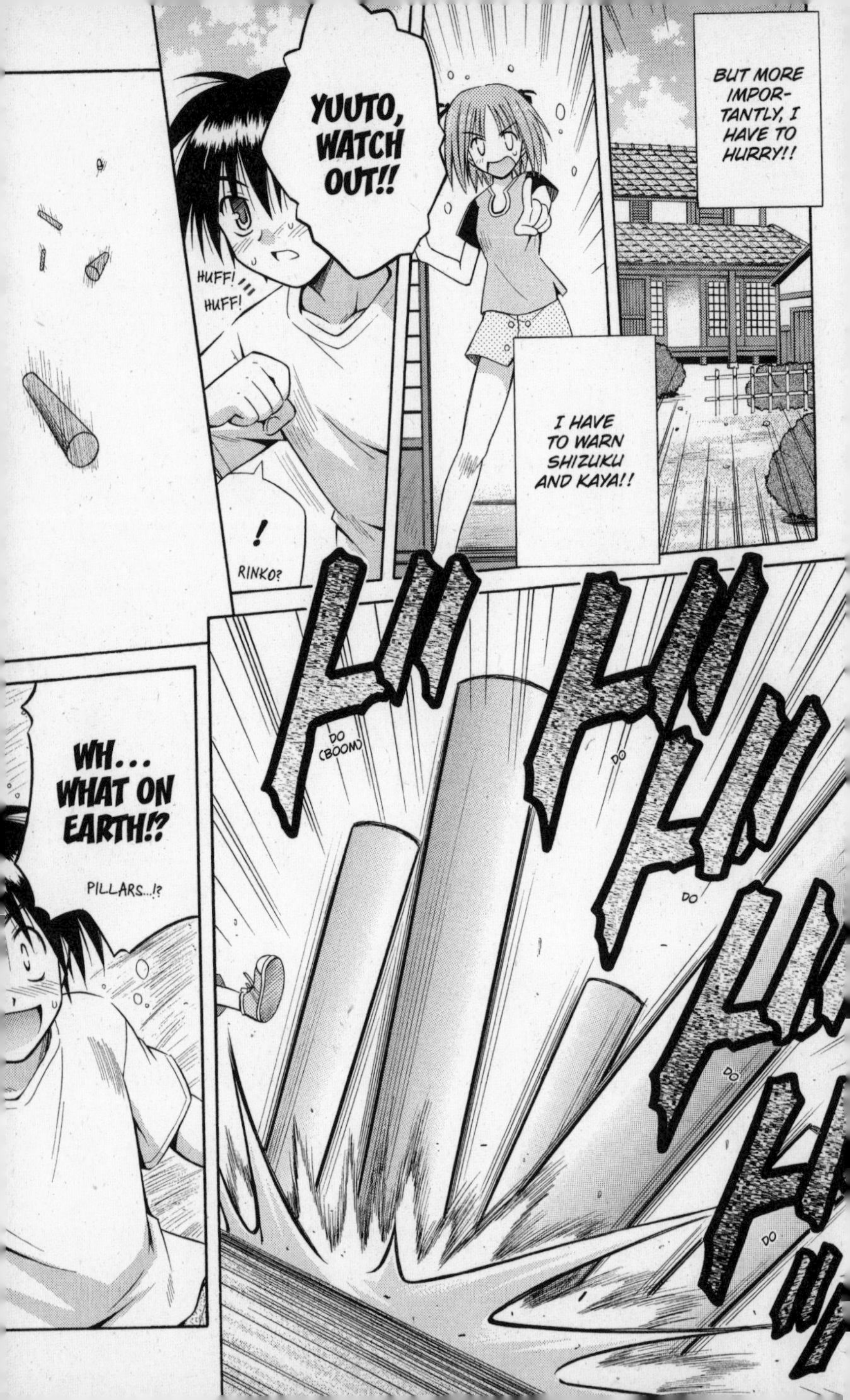
BUT MORE IMPOR-TANTLY, I HAVE TO HURRY!!
I HAVE TO WARN SHIZUKU AND KAYA!!
YUUTO, WATCH OUT!!
HUFF! HUFF!
!
RINKO?
DO (BOOM)
DO
DO
DO
DO
WH... WHAT ON EARTH!?
PILLARS...!?

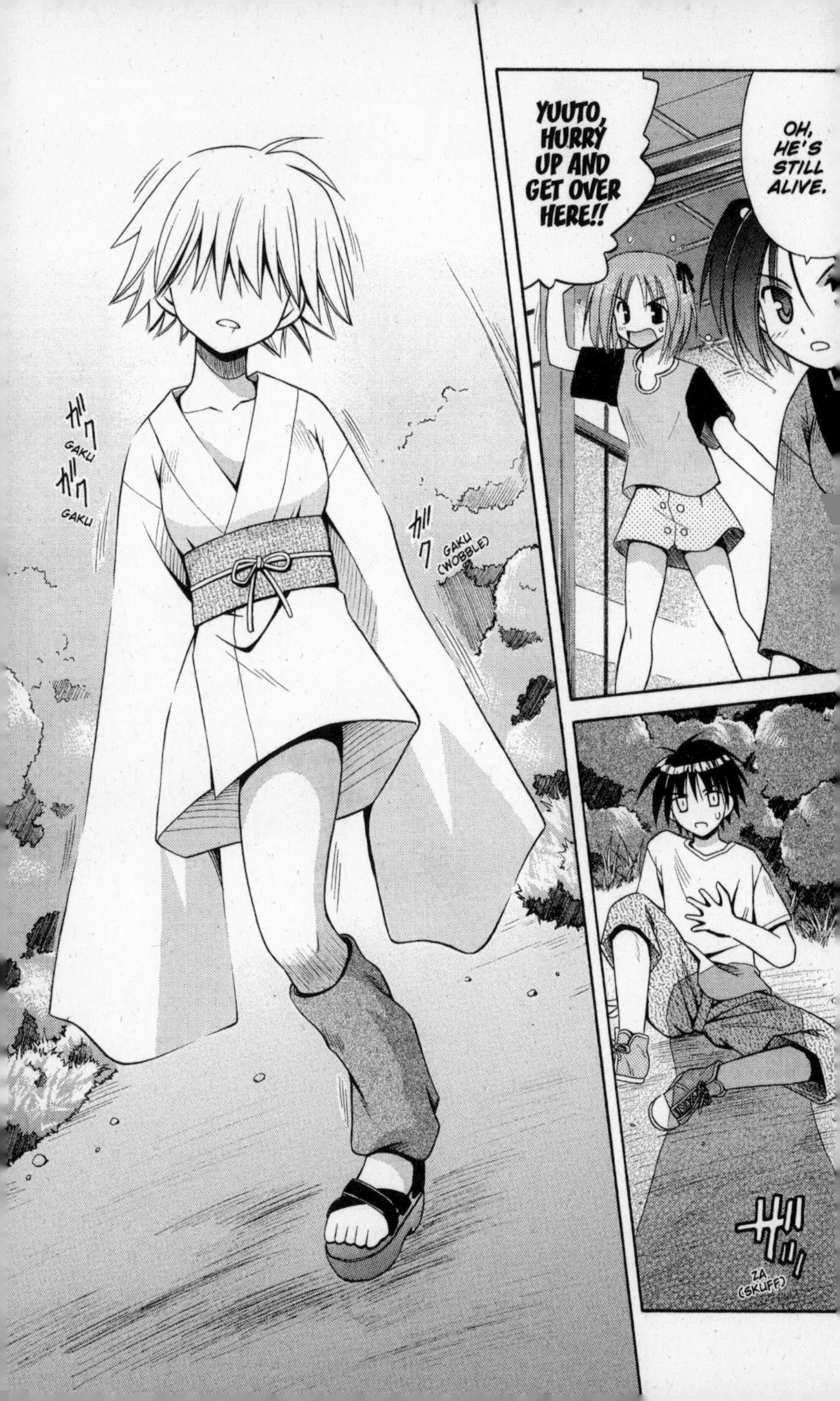
OH, HE'S STILL ALIVE.
YUUTO, HURRY UP AND GET OVER HERE!!
ザッ
ZA (SKUFF)
ガク
GAKU (WOBBLE)
ガク
GAKU
ガク
GAKU

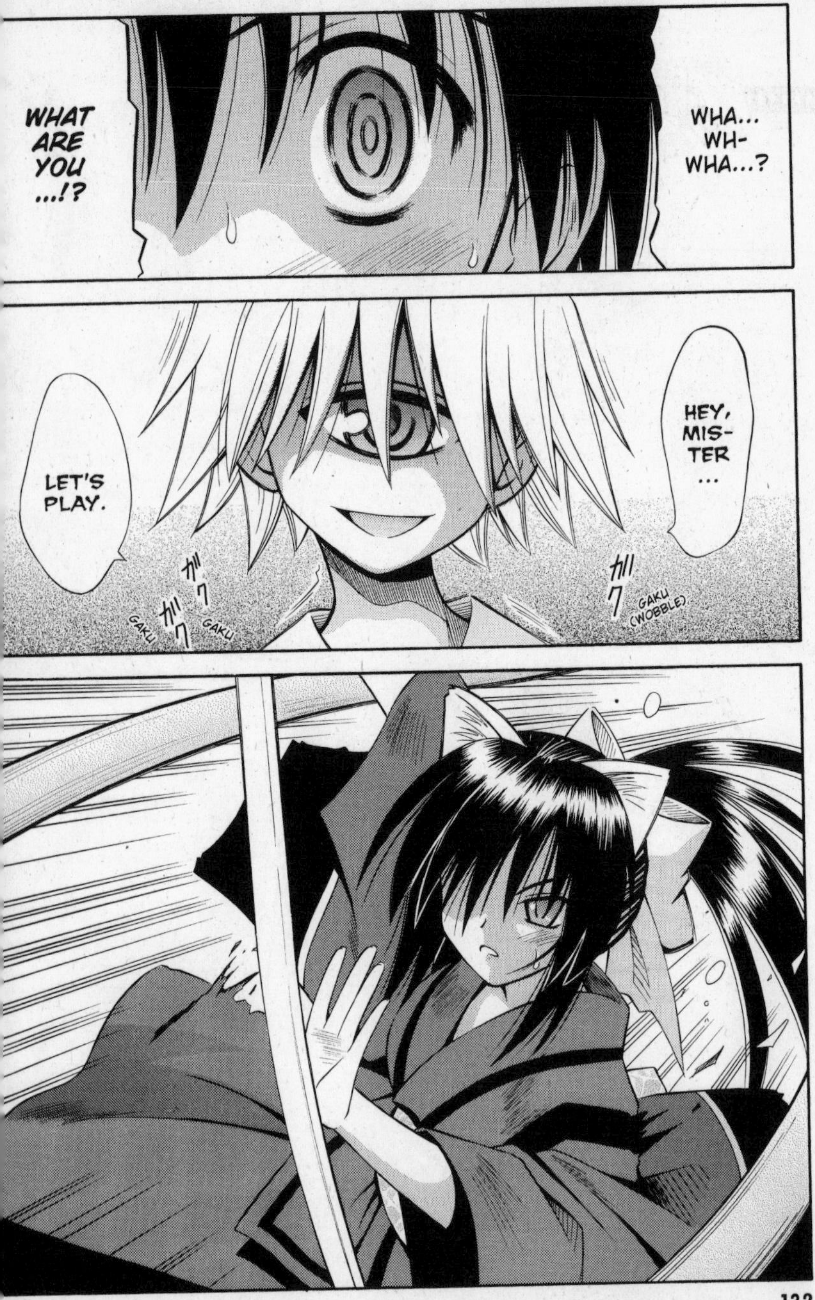
WHA... WH-WHA...?
WHAT ARE YOU ...!?
HEY, MIS-TER ...
ガク
GAKU (WOBBLE)
LET'S PLAY.
ガク
GAKU
ガク
GAKU

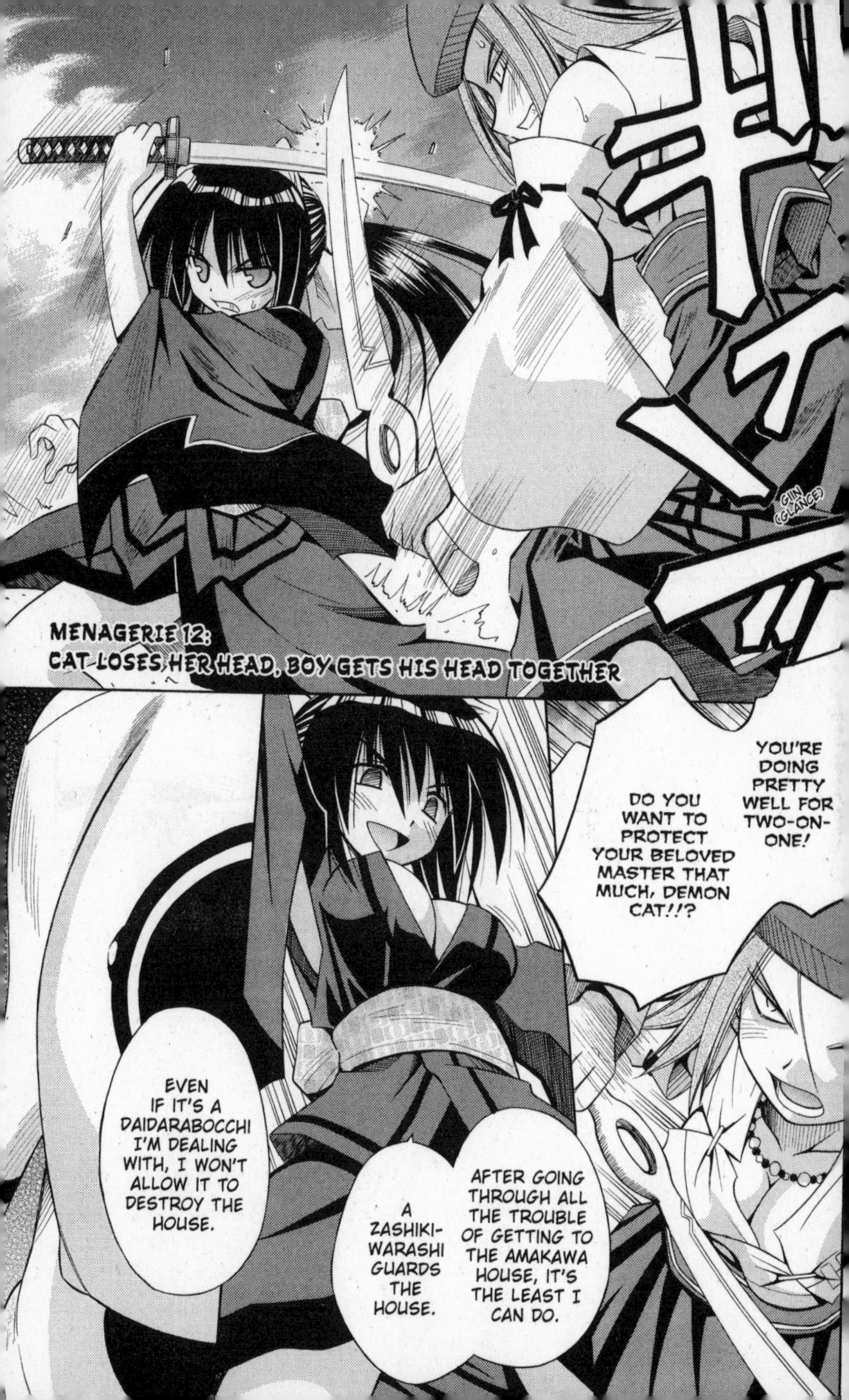
GIIN (GLANCE)
MENAGERIE 12:
CAT LOSES HER HEAD, BOY GETS HIS HEAD TOGETHER
YOU'RE DOING PRETTY WELL FOR TWO-ON-ONE!
DO YOU WANT TO PROTECT YOUR BELOVED MASTER THAT MUCH, DEMON CAT!!?
AFTER GOING THROUGH ALL THE TROUBLE OF GETTING TO THE AMAKAWA HOUSE, IT'S THE LEAST I CAN DO.
A ZASHIKI-WARASHI GUARDS THE HOUSE.
EVEN IF IT'S A DAIDARABOCCHI I'M DEALING WITH, I WON'T ALLOW IT TO DESTROY THE HOUSE.

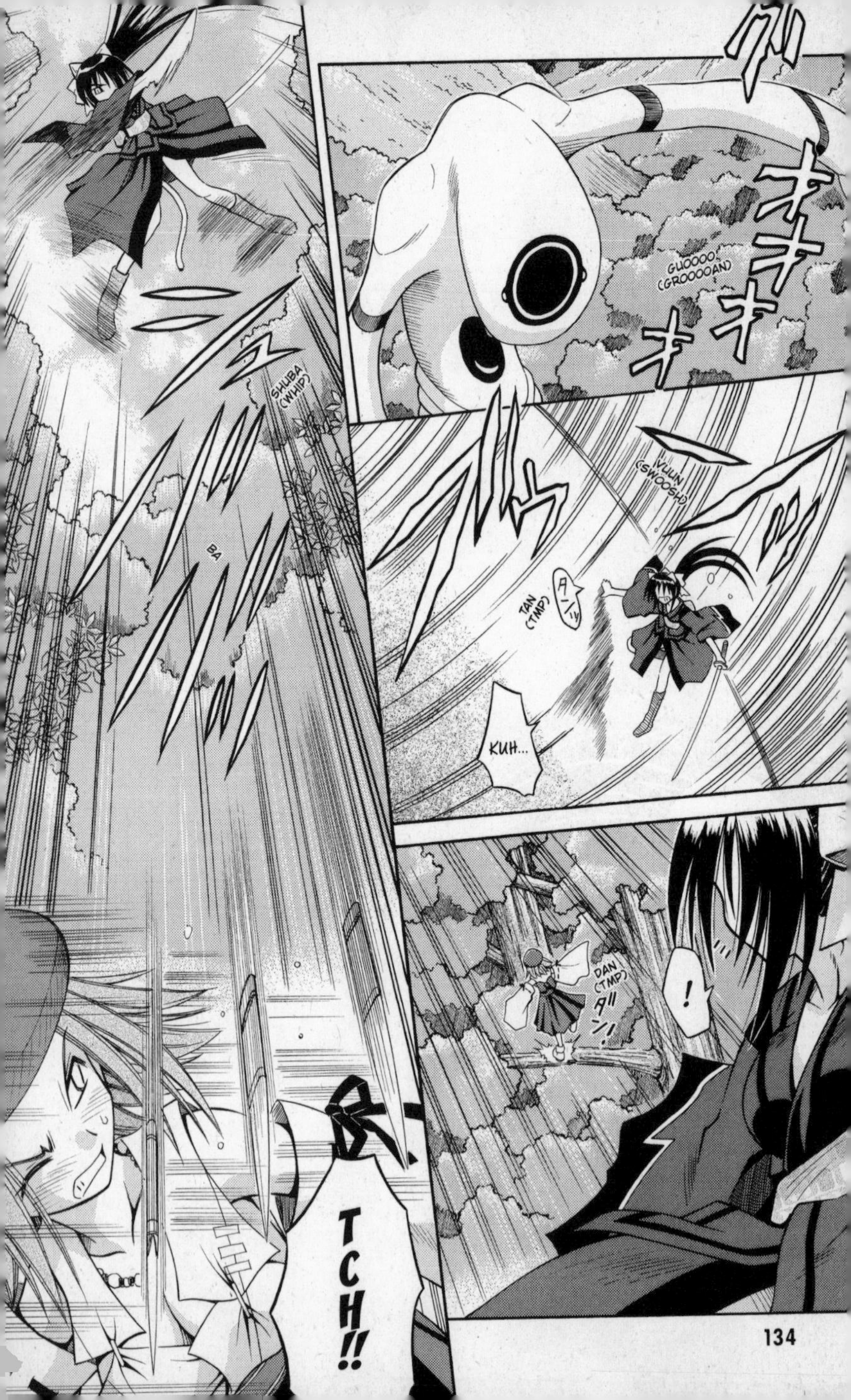
GUOOOO (GROOOOAN)
VUUN (SWOOSH)
ダンッ
TAN (TMP)
KUH...
!
DAN (TMP)
ダン!
SHUBA (WHIP)
BA
TCH!!

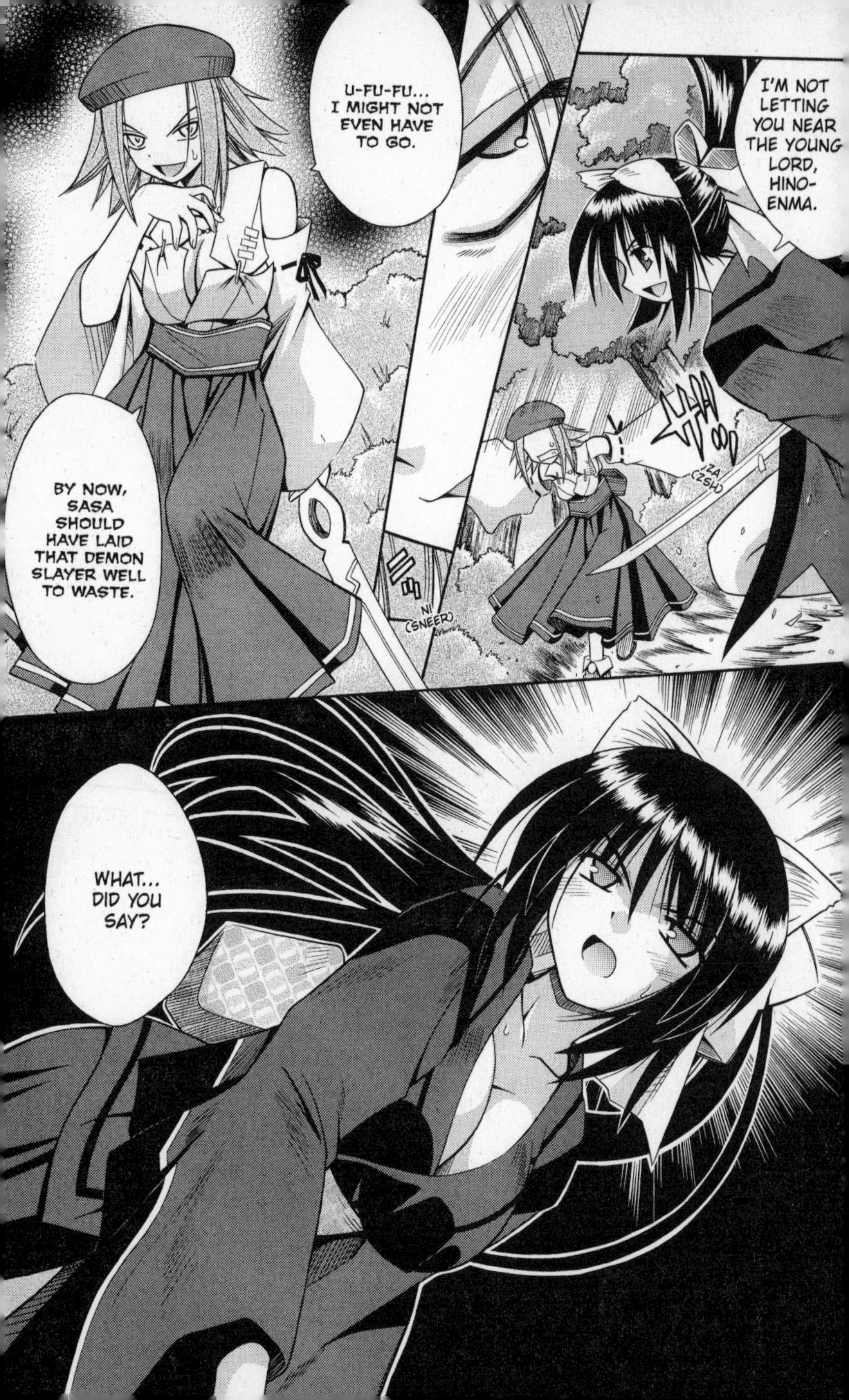
I'M NOT LETTING YOU NEAR THE YOUNG LORD, HINO-ENMA.
ZA (ZSH)
U-FU-FU... I MIGHT NOT EVEN HAVE TO GO.
NI (SNEER)
BY NOW, SASA SHOULD HAVE LAID THAT DEMON SLAYER WELL TO WASTE.
WHAT... DID YOU SAY?

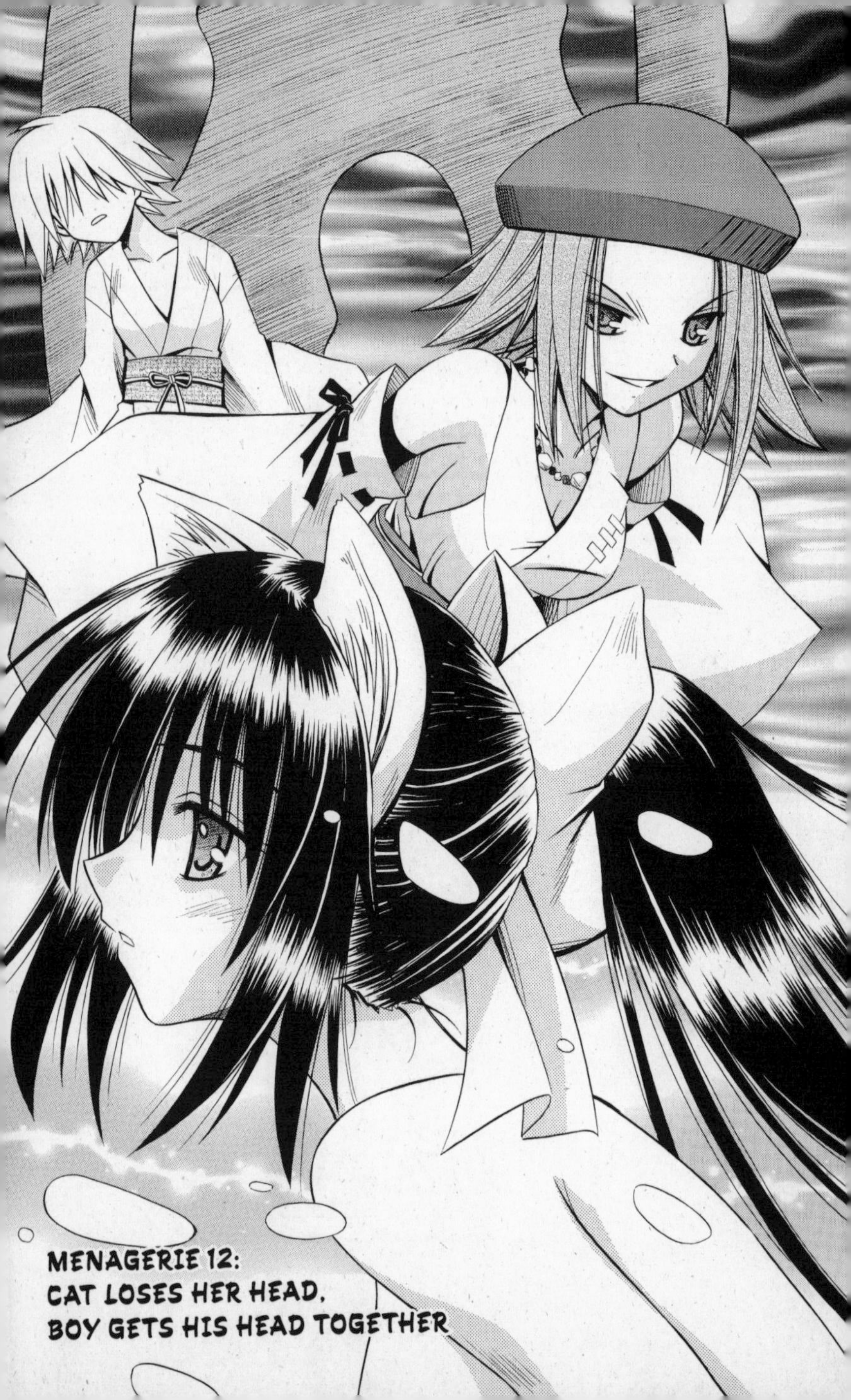
MENAGERIE 12:
CAT LOSES HER HEAD,
BOY GETS HIS HEAD TOGETHER

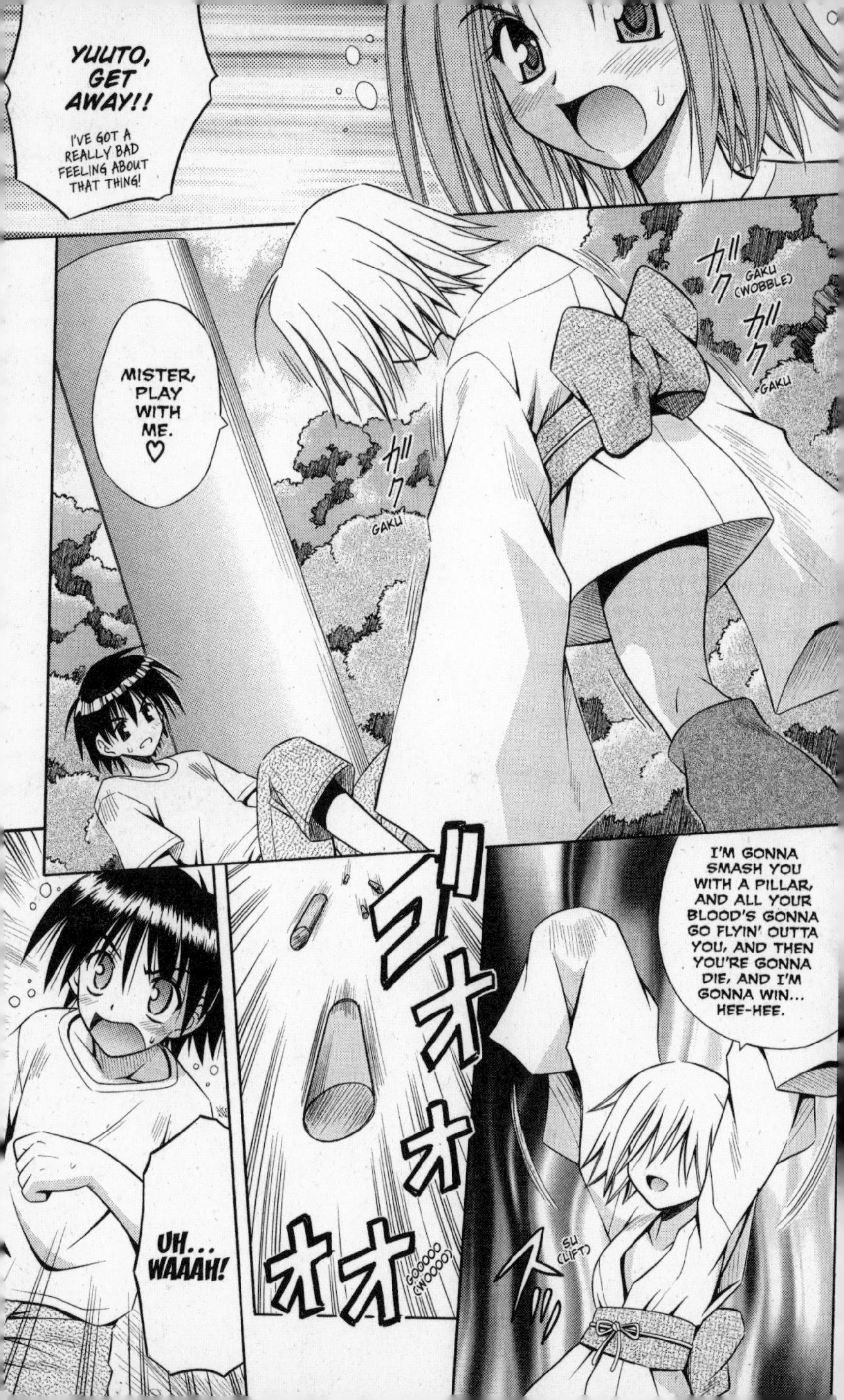
YUUTO, GET AWAY!!
I'VE GOT A REALLY BAD FEELING ABOUT THAT THING!
ガク GAKU (WOBBLE)
ガク GAKU
MISTER, PLAY WITH ME. ♡
ガク GAKU
I'M GONNA SMASH YOU WITH A PILLAR, AND ALL YOUR BLOOD'S GONNA GO FLYIN' OUTTA YOU, AND THEN YOU'RE GONNA DIE, AND I'M GONNA WIN... HEE-HEE.
ス SU (LIFT)
ゴオオオオ GOOOOO (WOOOO)
UH... WAAAH!

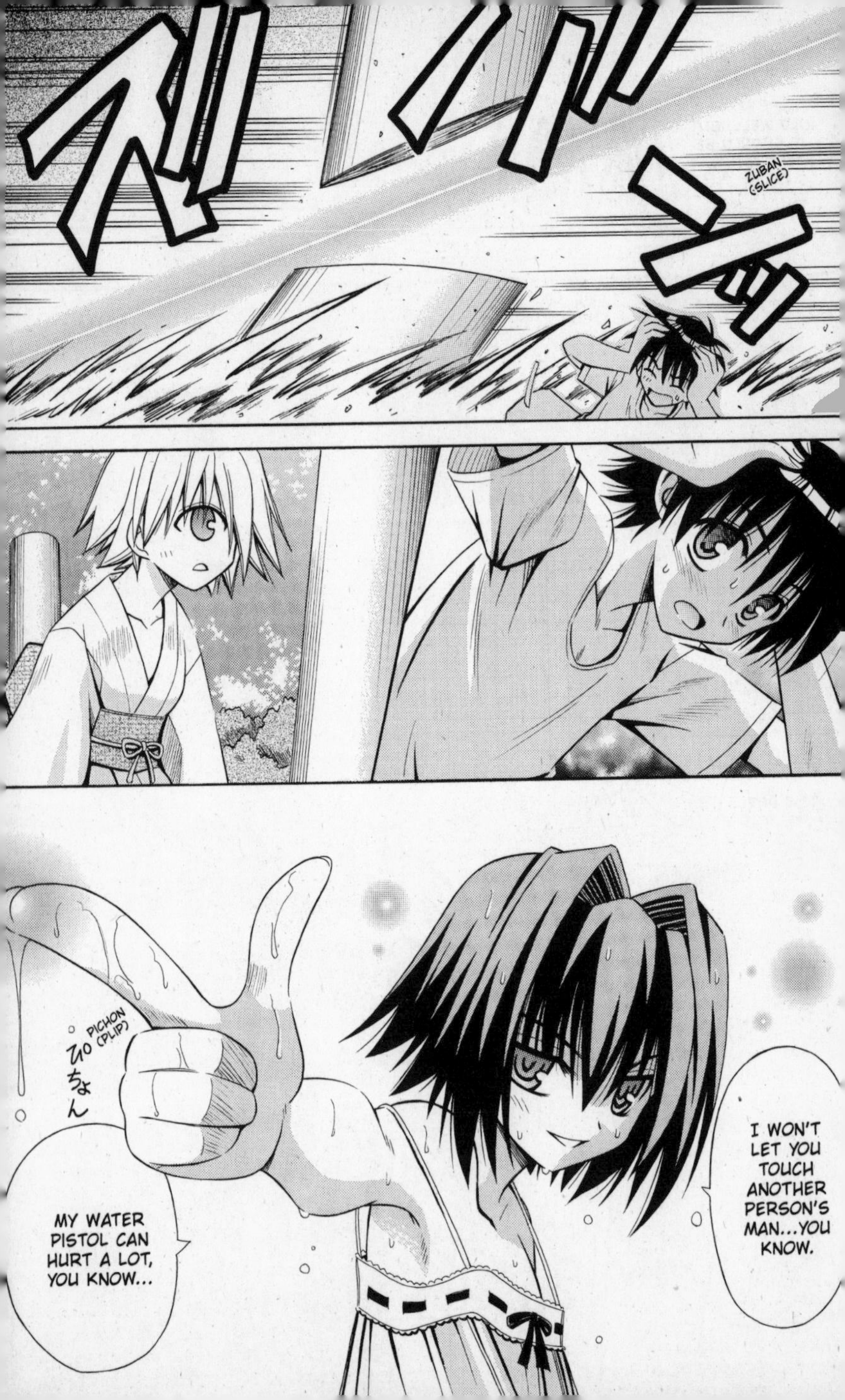
ZUBAN (SLICE)
PICHON (PLIP)
ぴちょん
I WON'T LET YOU TOUCH ANOTHER PERSON'S MAN...YOU KNOW.
MY WATER PISTOL CAN HURT A LOT, YOU KNOW...

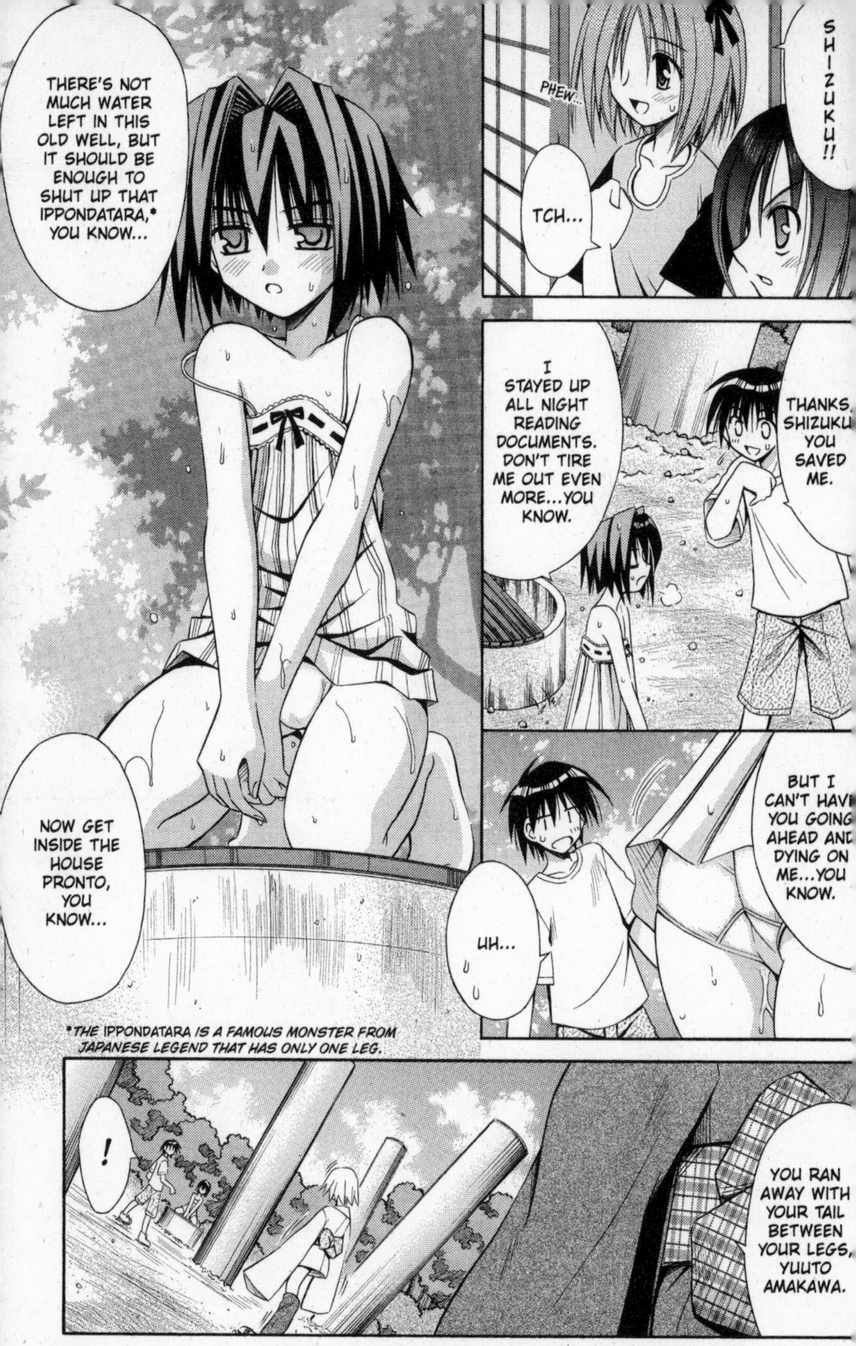
SHIZUKU!!
PHEW...
TCH...
THANKS, SHIZUKU YOU SAVED ME.
I STAYED UP ALL NIGHT READING DOCUMENTS. DON'T TIRE ME OUT EVEN MORE...YOU KNOW.
BUT I CAN'T HAVE YOU GOING AHEAD AND DYING ON ME...YOU KNOW.
UH...
THERE'S NOT MUCH WATER LEFT IN THIS OLD WELL, BUT IT SHOULD BE ENOUGH TO SHUT UP THAT IPPONDATARA,* YOU KNOW...
NOW GET INSIDE THE HOUSE PRONTO, YOU KNOW...
YOU RAN AWAY WITH YOUR TAIL BETWEEN YOUR LEGS, YUUTO AMAKAWA.
!
*THE IPPONDATARA IS A FAMOUS MONSTER FROM JAPANESE LEGEND THAT HAS ONLY ONE LEG.

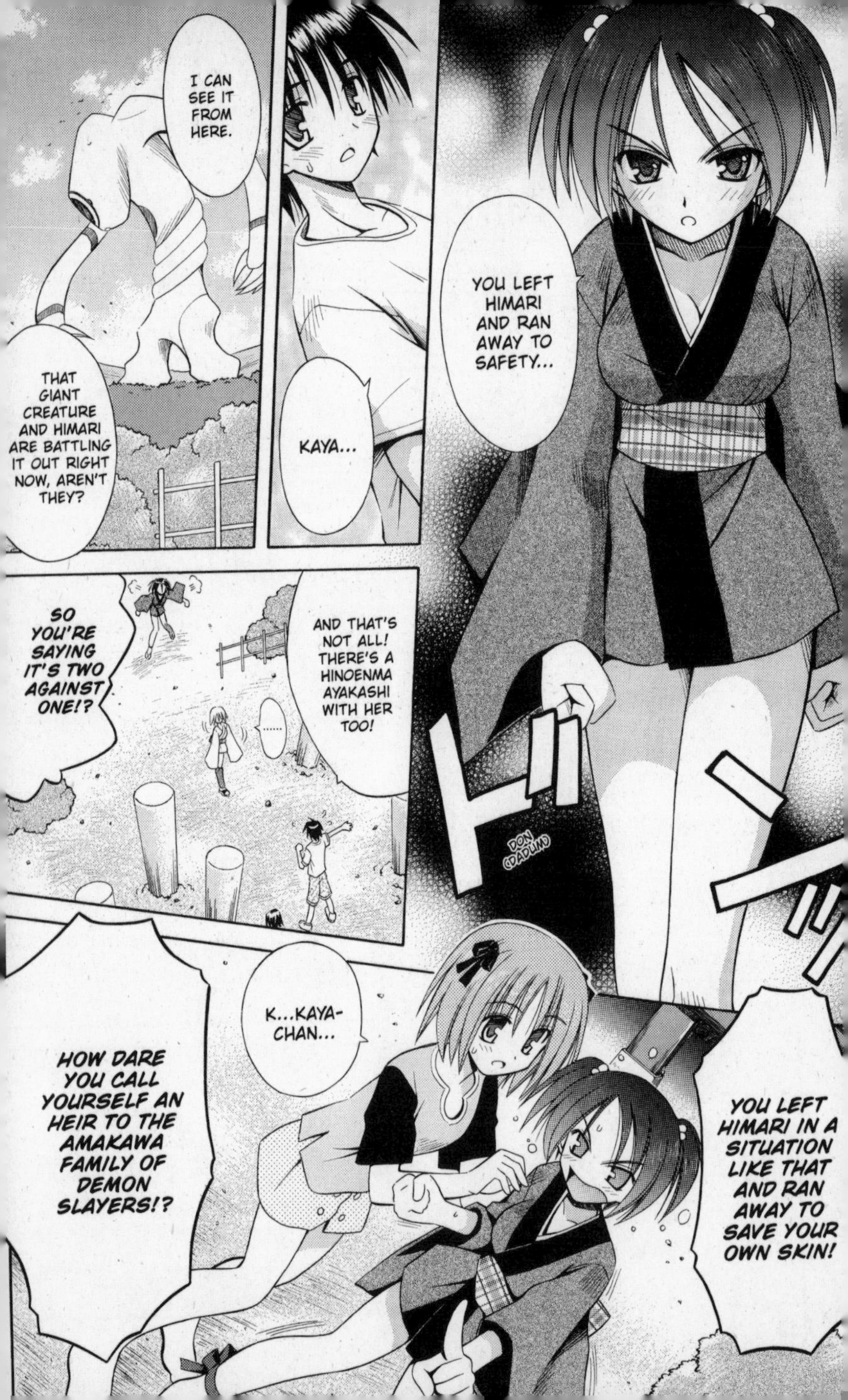
YOU LEFT HIMARI AND RAN AWAY TO SAFETY...
DON (DADUM)
KAYA...
I CAN SEE IT FROM HERE.
THAT GIANT CREATURE AND HIMARI ARE BATTLING IT OUT RIGHT NOW, AREN'T THEY?
AND THAT'S NOT ALL! THERE'S A HINOENMA AYAKASHI WITH HER TOO!
......
SO YOU'RE SAYING IT'S TWO AGAINST ONE!?
YOU LEFT HIMARI IN A SITUATION LIKE THAT AND RAN AWAY TO SAVE YOUR OWN SKIN!
K...KAYA-CHAN...
HOW DARE YOU CALL YOURSELF AN HEIR TO THE AMAKAWA FAMILY OF DEMON SLAYERS!?

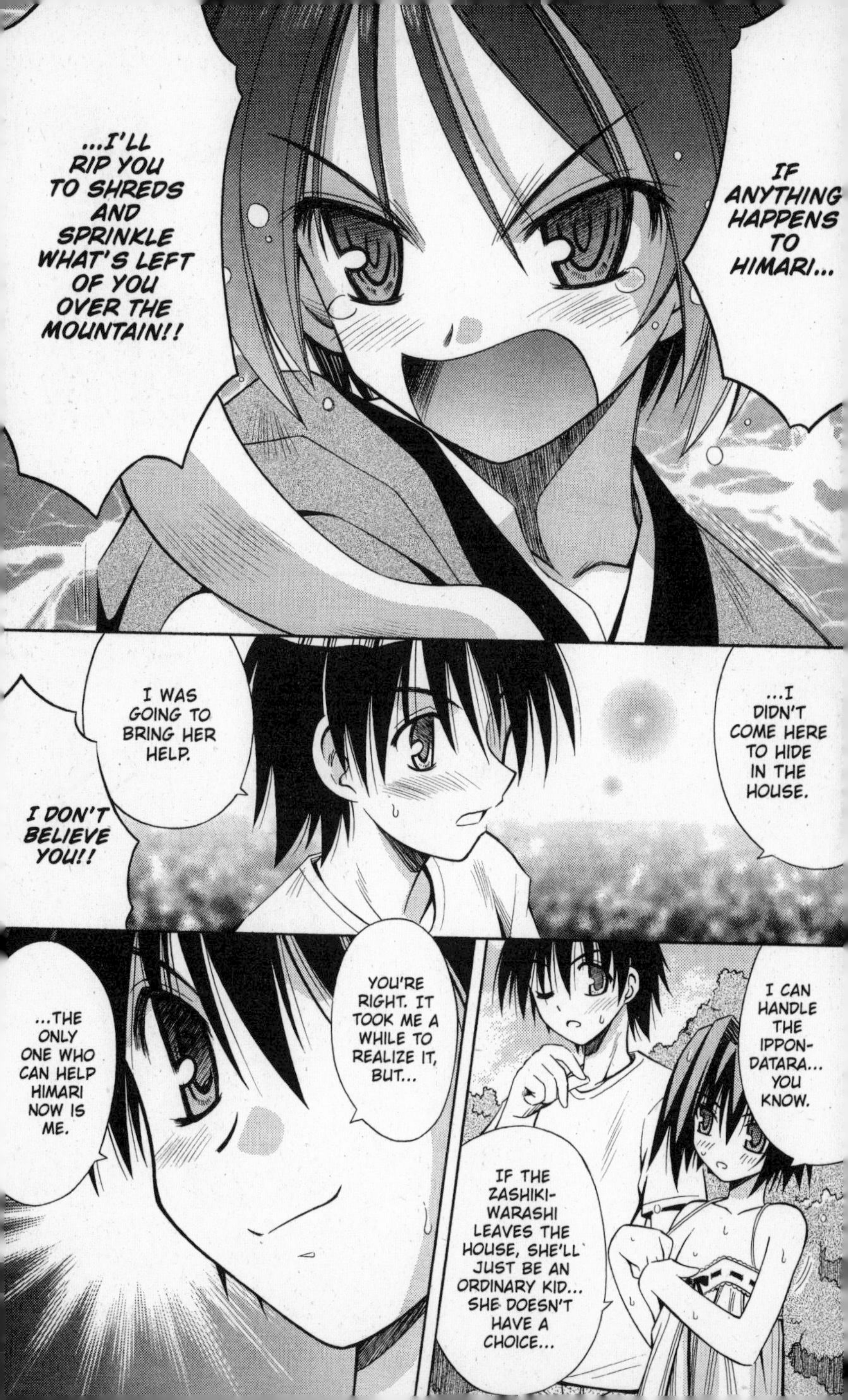
IF ANYTHING HAPPENS TO HIMARI...
...I'LL RIP YOU TO SHREDS AND SPRINKLE WHAT'S LEFT OF YOU OVER THE MOUNTAIN!!
...I DIDN'T COME HERE TO HIDE IN THE HOUSE.
I WAS GOING TO BRING HER HELP.
I DON'T BELIEVE YOU!!
I CAN HANDLE THE IPPON-DATARA... YOU KNOW.
IF THE ZASHIKI-WARASHI LEAVES THE HOUSE, SHE'LL JUST BE AN ORDINARY KID... SHE DOESN'T HAVE A CHOICE...
YOU'RE RIGHT. IT TOOK ME A WHILE TO REALIZE IT, BUT...
...THE ONLY ONE WHO CAN HELP HIMARI NOW IS ME.

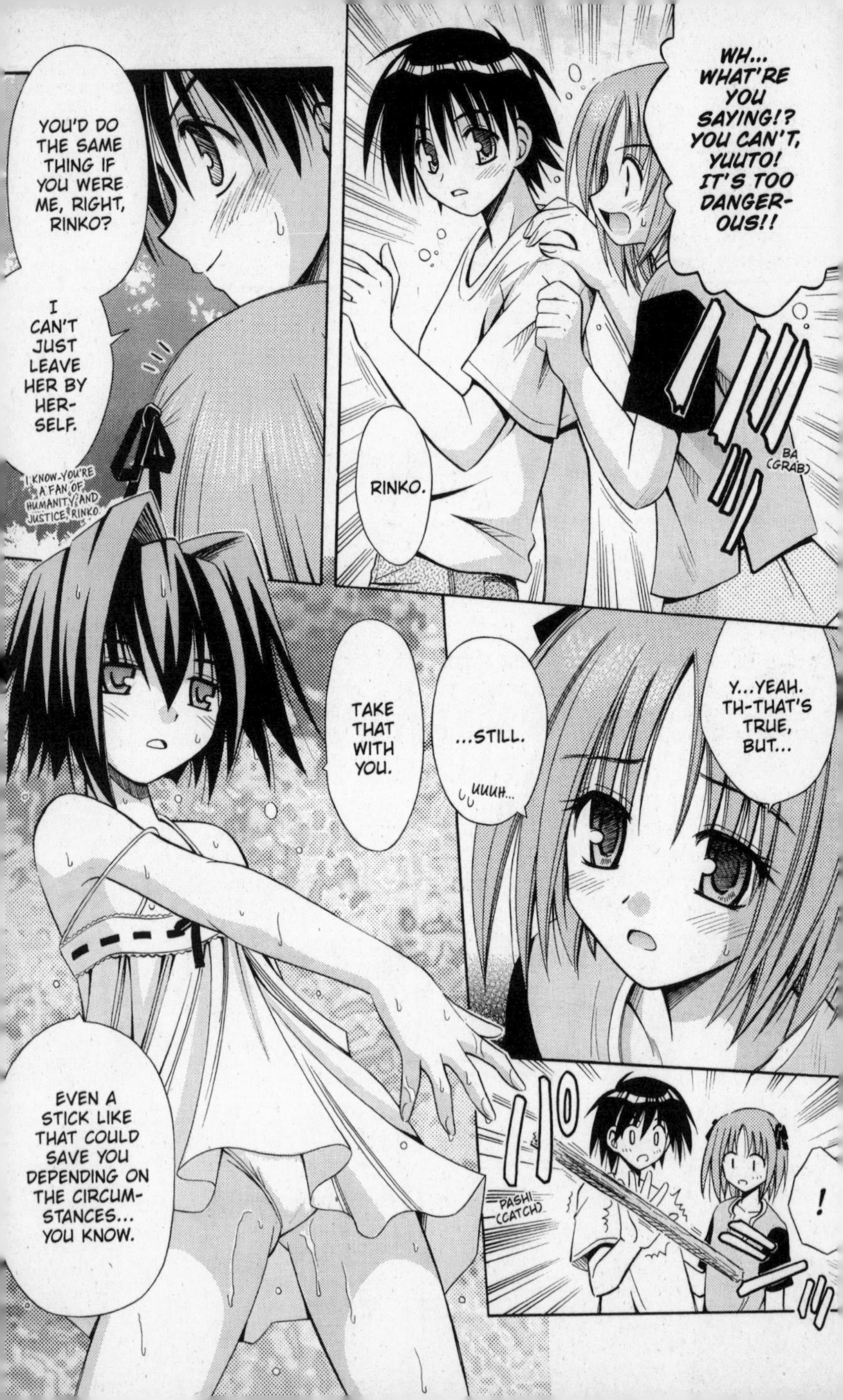
WH... WHAT'RE YOU SAYING!? YOU CAN'T, YUUTO! IT'S TOO DANGER-OUS!!
BA (GRAB)
RINKO.
YOU'D DO THE SAME THING IF YOU WERE ME, RIGHT, RINKO?
I CAN'T JUST LEAVE HER BY HER-SELF.
I KNOW YOU'RE A FAN OF HUMANITY AND JUSTICE, RINKO.
Y...YEAH. TH-THAT'S TRUE, BUT...
...STILL.
UUUH...
PASHI (CATCH)
!
TAKE THAT WITH YOU.
EVEN A STICK LIKE THAT COULD SAVE YOU DEPENDING ON THE CIRCUM-STANCES... YOU KNOW.

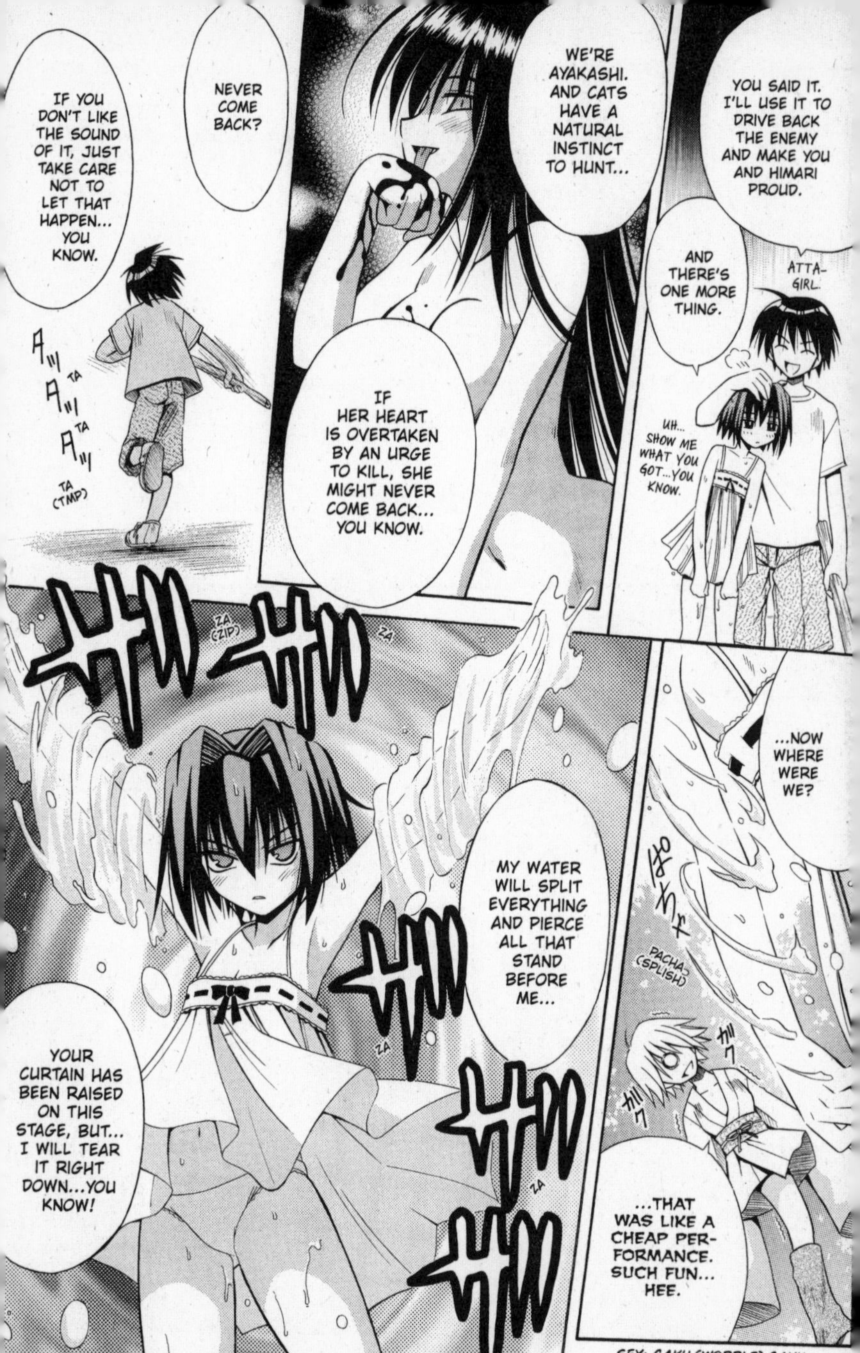
YOU SAID IT. I'LL USE IT TO DRIVE BACK THE ENEMY AND MAKE YOU AND HIMARI PROUD.
ATTA-GIRL.
AND THERE'S ONE MORE THING.
UH... SHOW ME WHAT YOU GOT...YOU KNOW.
WE'RE AYAKASHI. AND CATS HAVE A NATURAL INSTINCT TO HUNT...
IF HER HEART IS OVERTAKEN BY AN URGE TO KILL, SHE MIGHT NEVER COME BACK... YOU KNOW.
NEVER COME BACK?
IF YOU DON'T LIKE THE SOUND OF IT, JUST TAKE CARE NOT TO LET THAT HAPPEN... YOU KNOW.
TA
TA
TA (TMP)
...NOW WHERE WERE WE?
PACHA (SPLISH)
...THAT WAS LIKE A CHEAP PERFORMANCE. SUCH FUN... HEE.
ZA (ZIP)
ZA
MY WATER WILL SPLIT EVERYTHING AND PIERCE ALL THAT STAND BEFORE ME...
ZA
YOUR CURTAIN HAS BEEN RAISED ON THIS STAGE, BUT... I WILL TEAR IT RIGHT DOWN...YOU KNOW!
ZA
ZA

SFX: GAKU (WOBBLE) GAKU

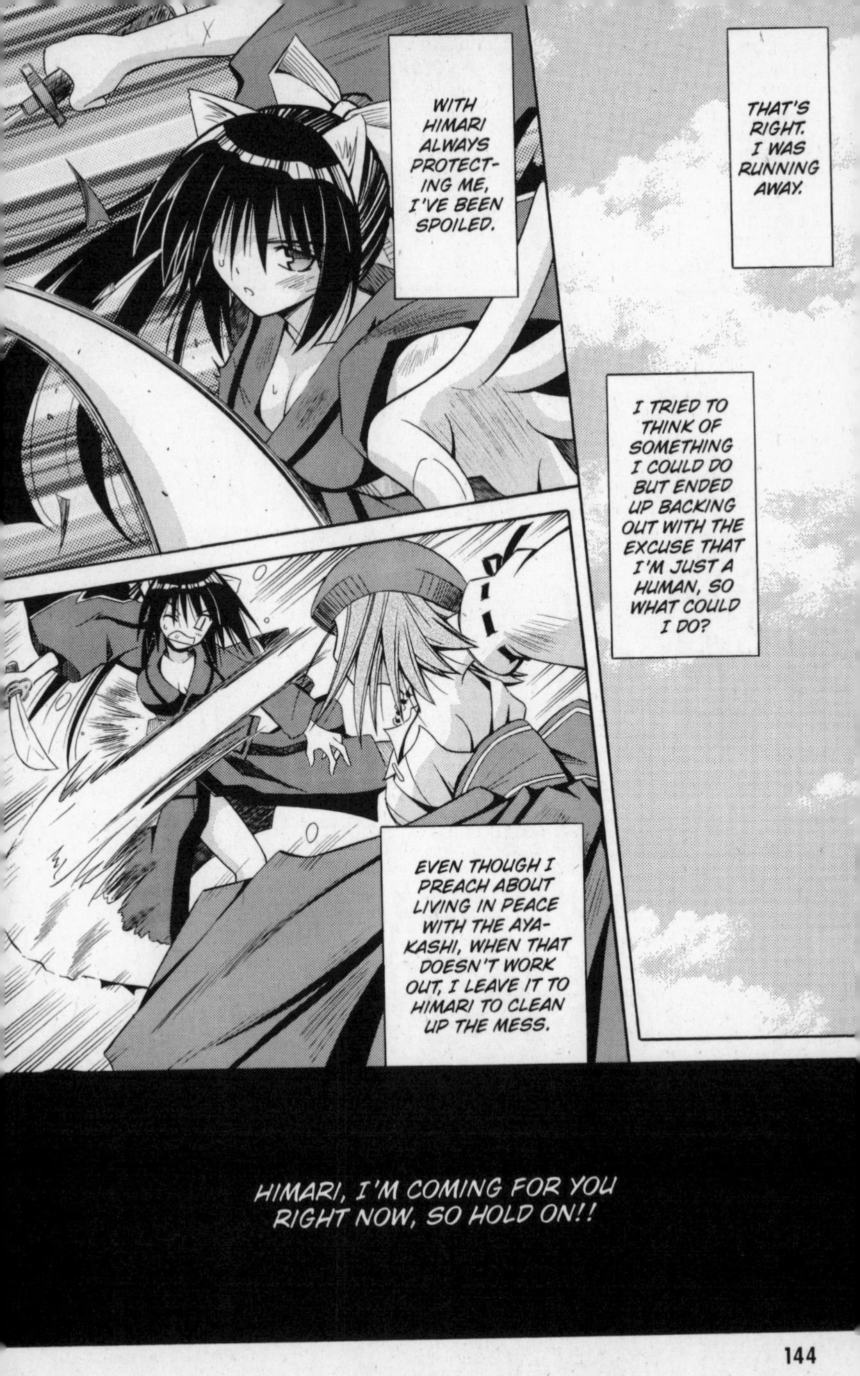
THAT'S RIGHT. I WAS RUNNING AWAY.
I TRIED TO THINK OF SOMETHING I COULD DO BUT ENDED UP BACKING OUT WITH THE EXCUSE THAT I'M JUST A HUMAN, SO WHAT COULD I DO?
WITH HIMARI ALWAYS PROTECTING ME, I'VE BEEN SPOILED.
EVEN THOUGH I PREACH ABOUT LIVING IN PEACE WITH THE AYAKASHI, WHEN THAT DOESN'T WORK OUT, I LEAVE IT TO HIMARI TO CLEAN UP THE MESS.
HIMARI, I'M COMING FOR YOU RIGHT NOW, SO HOLD ON!!

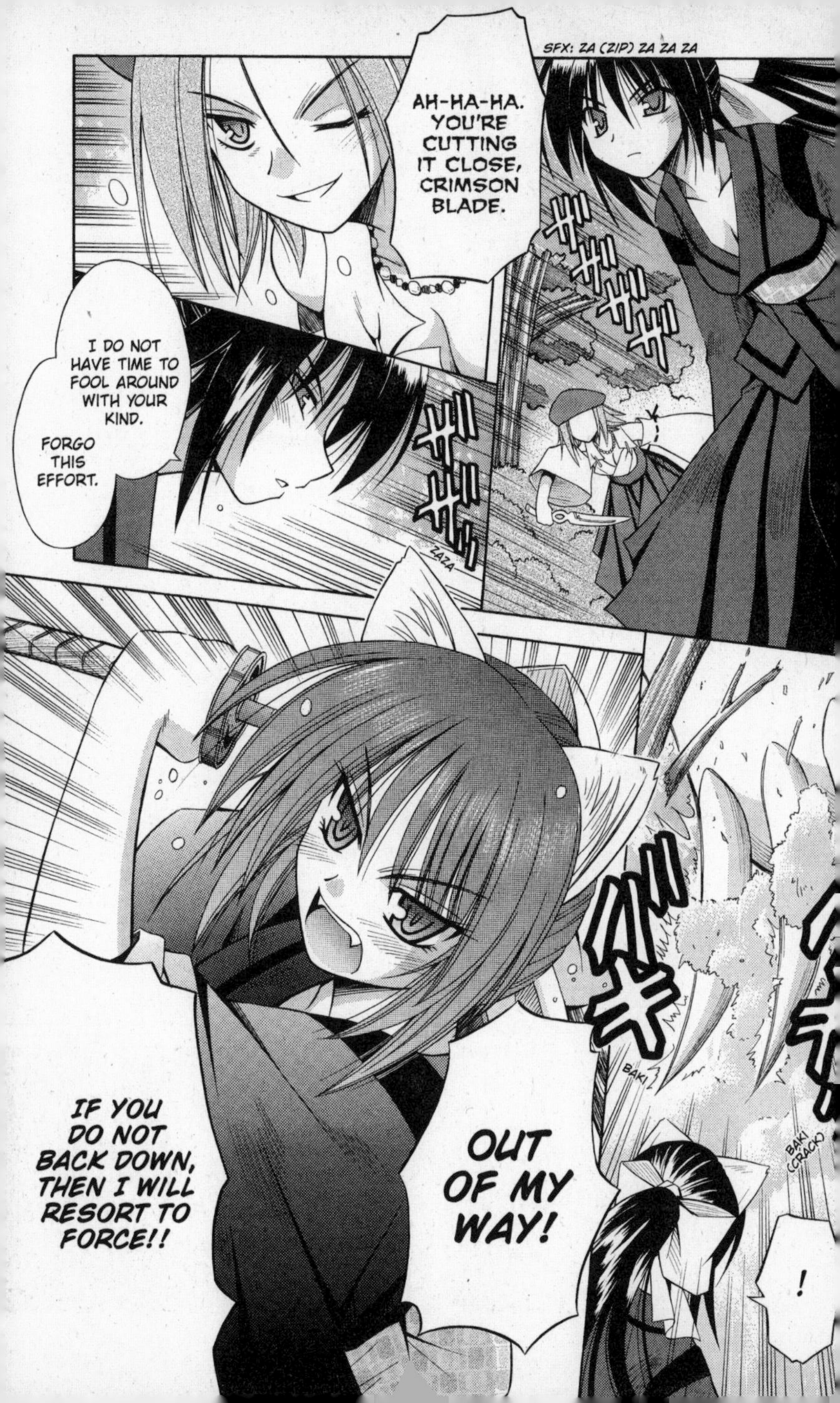
SFX: ZA (ZIP) ZA ZA ZA
ZAZA
AH-HA-HA. YOU'RE CUTTING IT CLOSE, CRIMSON BLADE.
I DO NOT HAVE TIME TO FOOL AROUND WITH YOUR KIND.
FORGO THIS EFFORT.
BAKI (CRACK)
BAKI
!
OUT OF MY WAY!
IF YOU DO NOT BACK DOWN, THEN I WILL RESORT TO FORCE!!

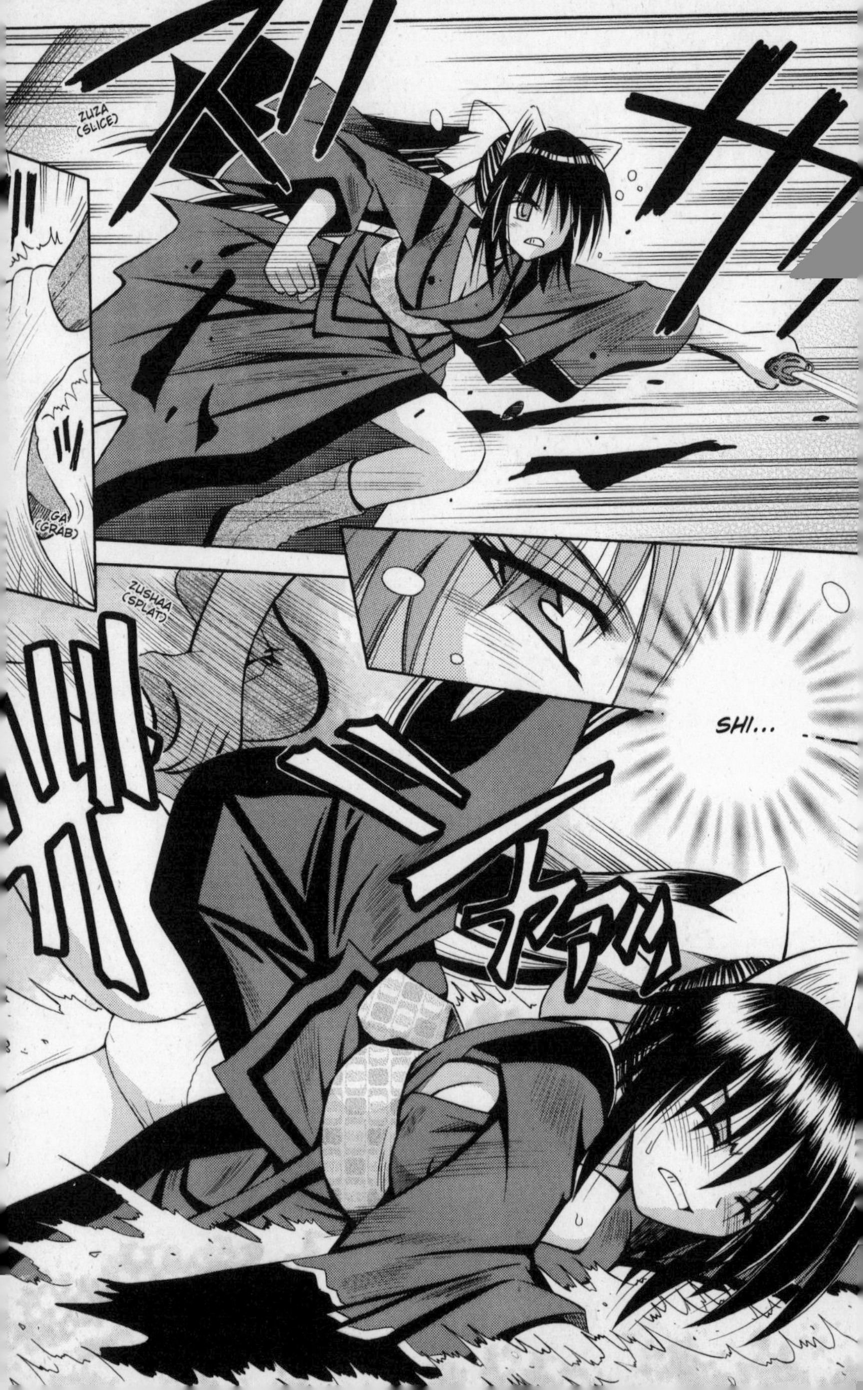
ZUZA (SLICE)
GA (GRAB)
SHI...
ZUSHAA (SPLAT)

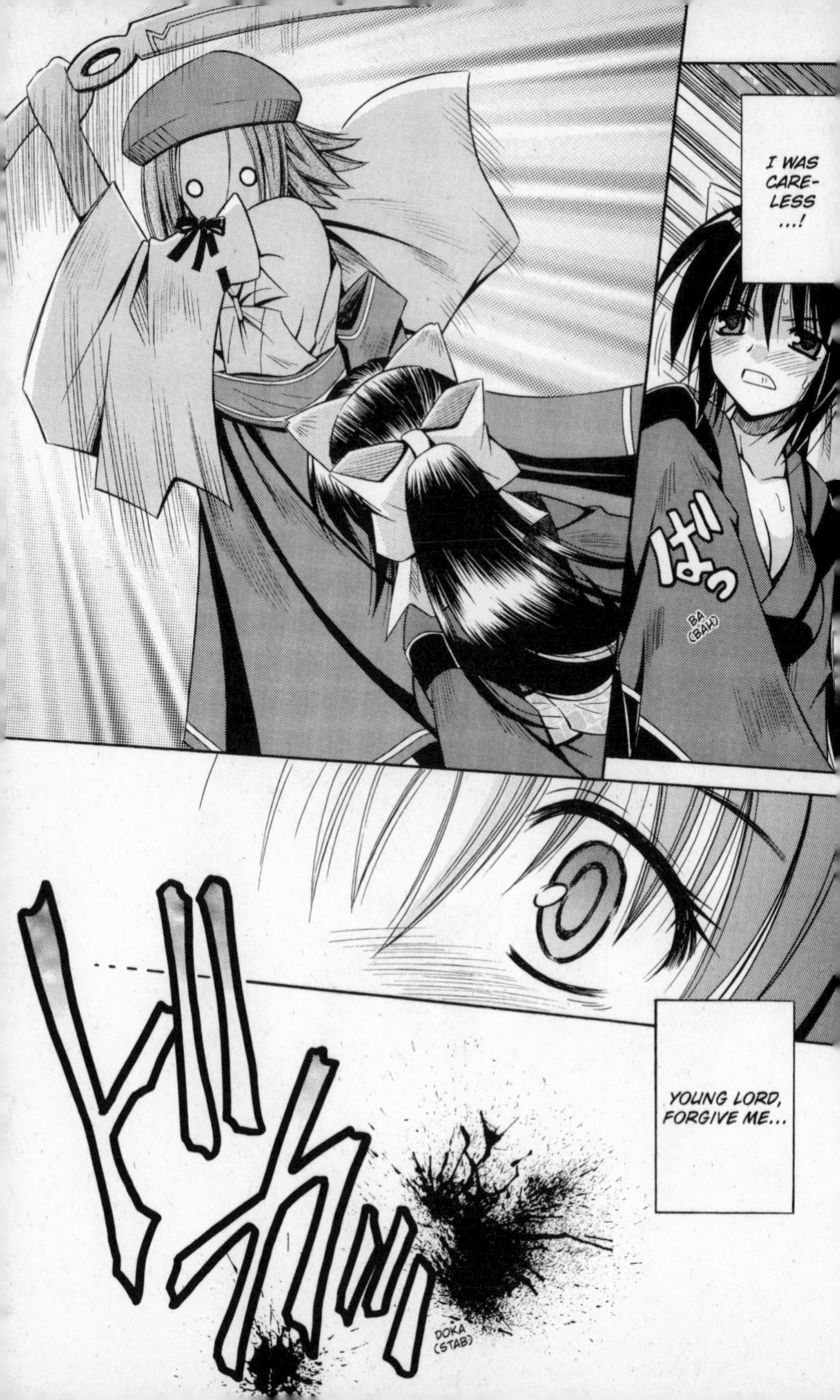
I WAS CARE-LESS ...!
ばっ
BA (BAH)
YOUNG LORD, FORGIVE ME...
ドカッ
DOKA (STAB)

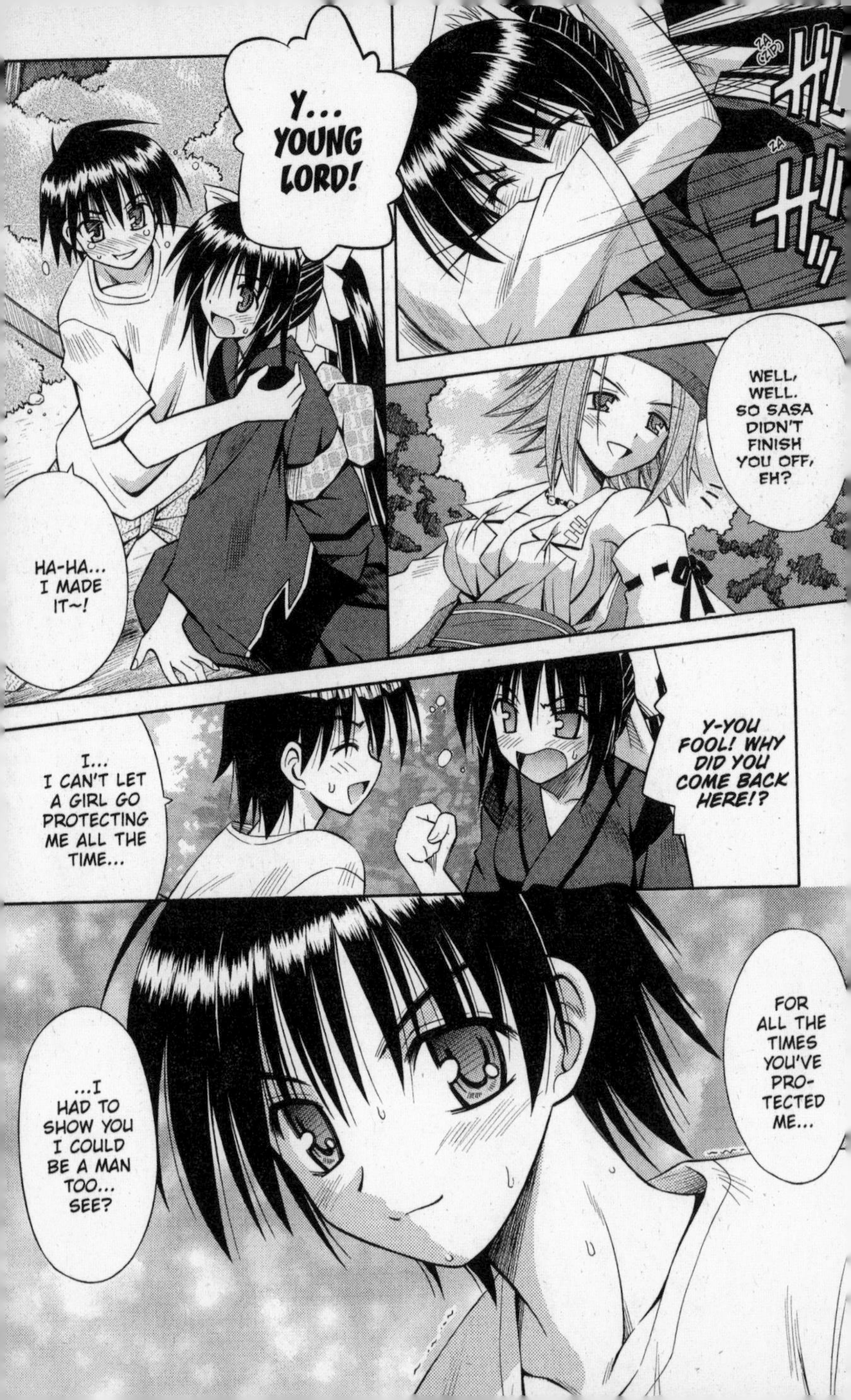

ZA
ZA
Y... YOUNG LORD!
WELL, WELL. SO SASA DIDN'T FINISH YOU OFF, EH?
HA-HA... I MADE IT~!
Y-YOU FOOL! WHY DID YOU COME BACK HERE!?
I... I CAN'T LET A GIRL GO PROTECTING ME ALL THE TIME...
FOR ALL THE TIMES YOU'VE PRO-TECTED ME...
...I HAD TO SHOW YOU I COULD BE A MAN TOO... SEE?

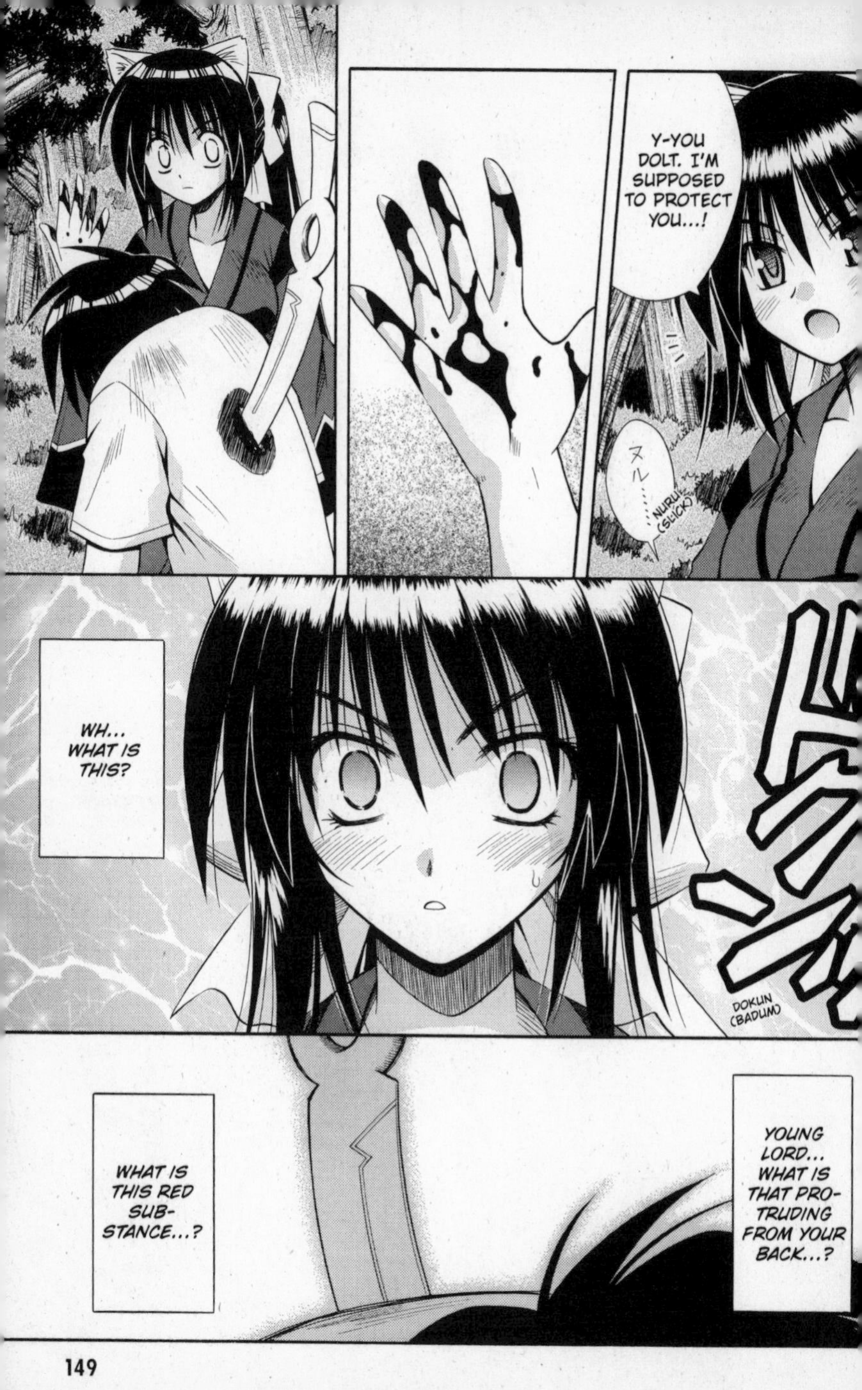
Y-YOU DOLT. I'M SUPPOSED TO PROTECT YOU...!
ヌル……
NURU (SLICK)
DOKUN (BADUM)
WH... WHAT IS THIS?
YOUNG LORD... WHAT IS THAT PRO-TRUDING FROM YOUR BACK...?
WHAT IS THIS RED SUB-STANCE...?

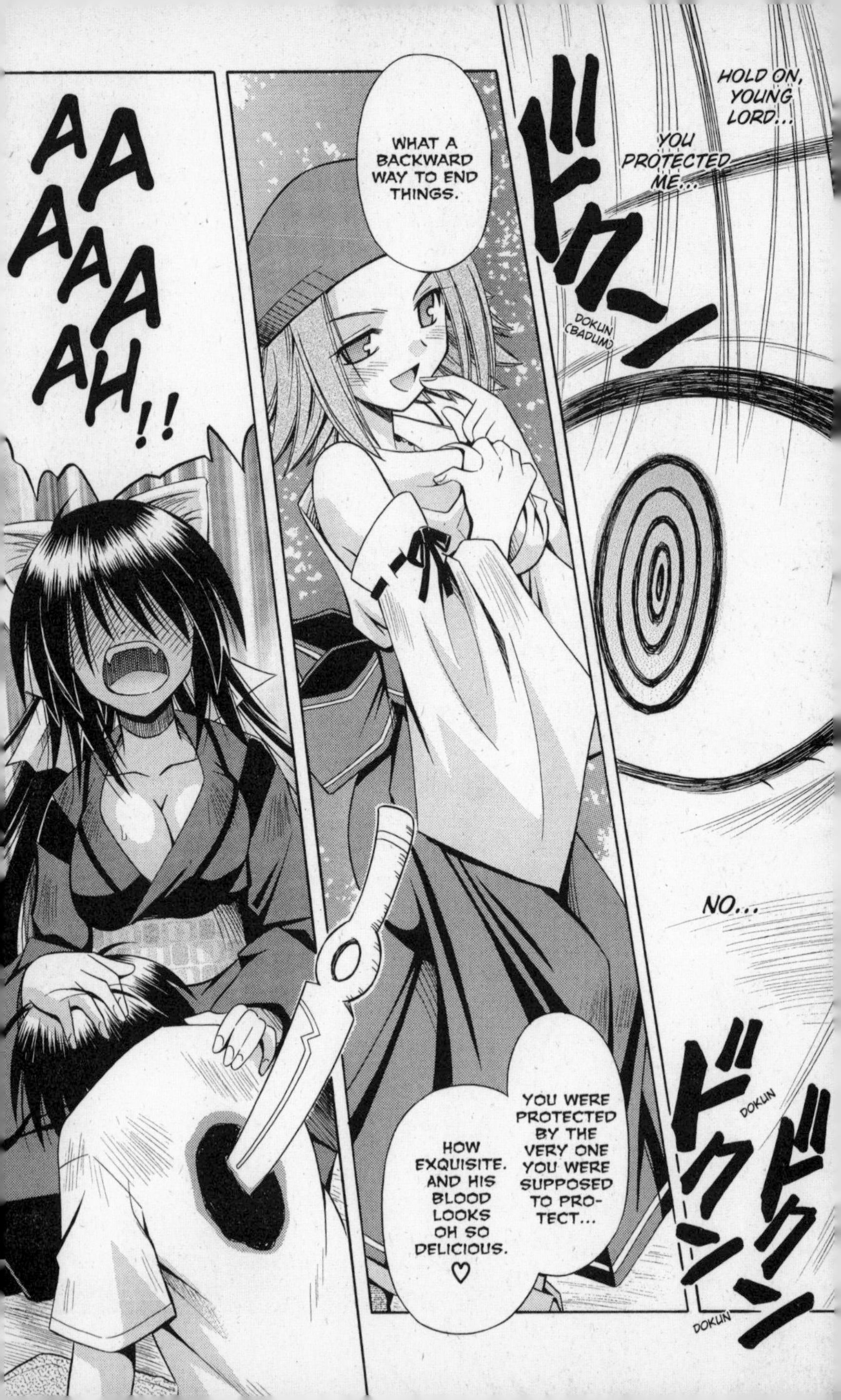
HOLD ON, YOUNG LORD...
YOU PROTECTED ME...
DOKUN (BADUM)
NO...
DOKUN
DOKUN
WHAT A BACKWARD WAY TO END THINGS.
YOU WERE PROTECTED BY THE VERY ONE YOU WERE SUPPOSED TO PRO-TECT...
HOW EXQUISITE. AND HIS BLOOD LOOKS OH SO DELICIOUS. ♡
AAAAAAH!!

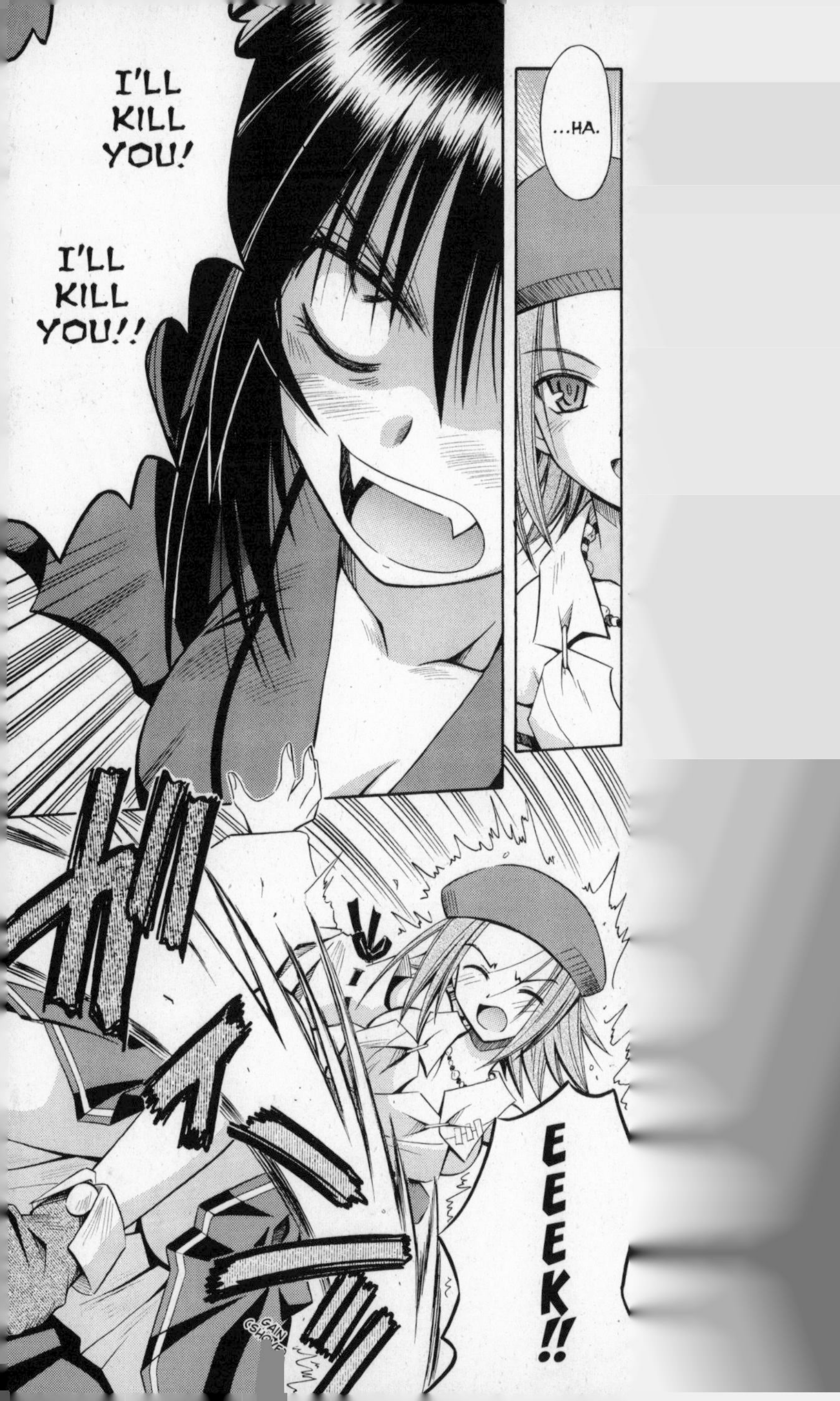
...HA.
I'LL KILL YOU!
I'LL KILL YOU!!
EEEK!!
GAIN

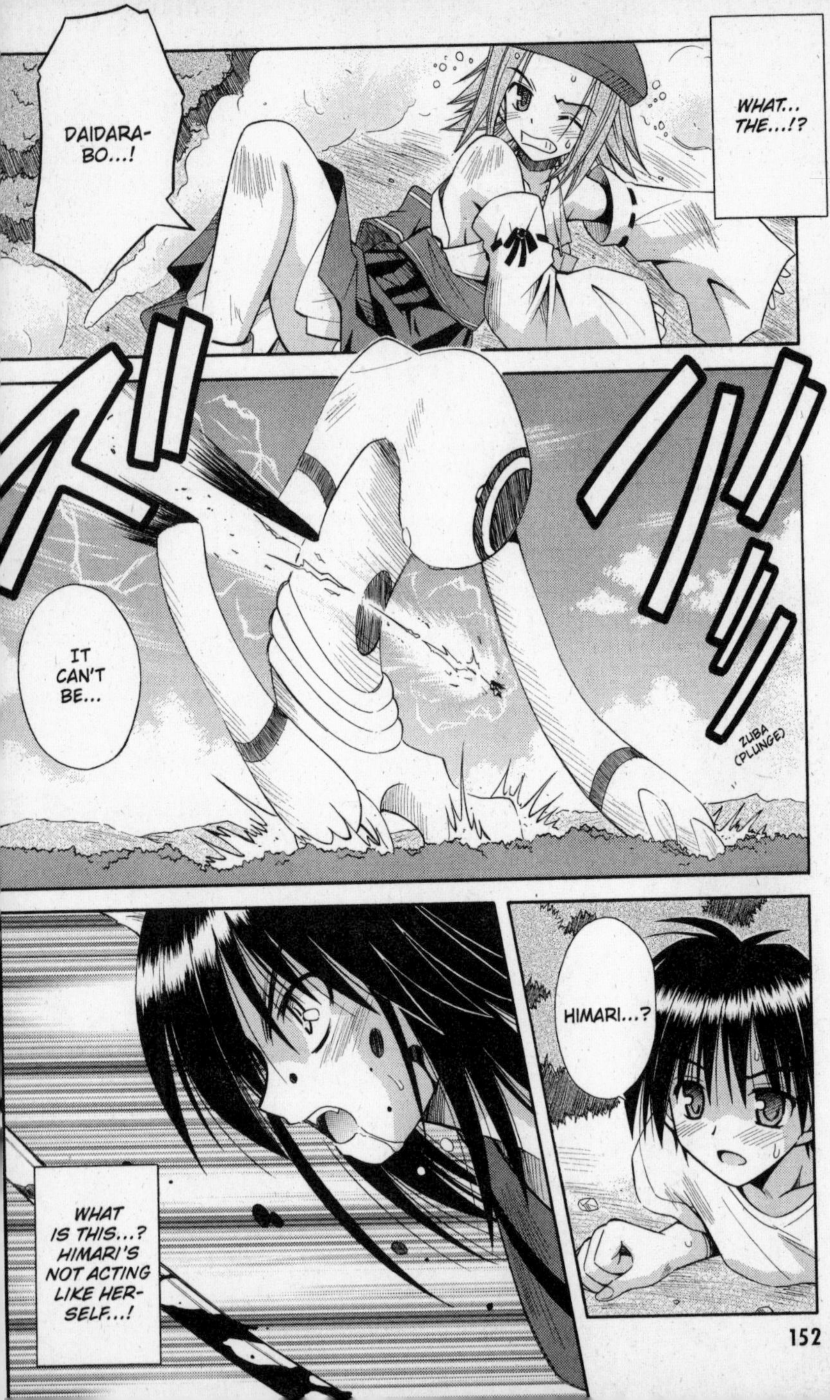
WHAT... THE...!?
DAIDARA-BO...!
ZUBA (PLUNGE)
IT CAN'T BE...
HIMARI...?
WHAT IS THIS...? HIMARI'S NOT ACTING LIKE HER-SELF...!

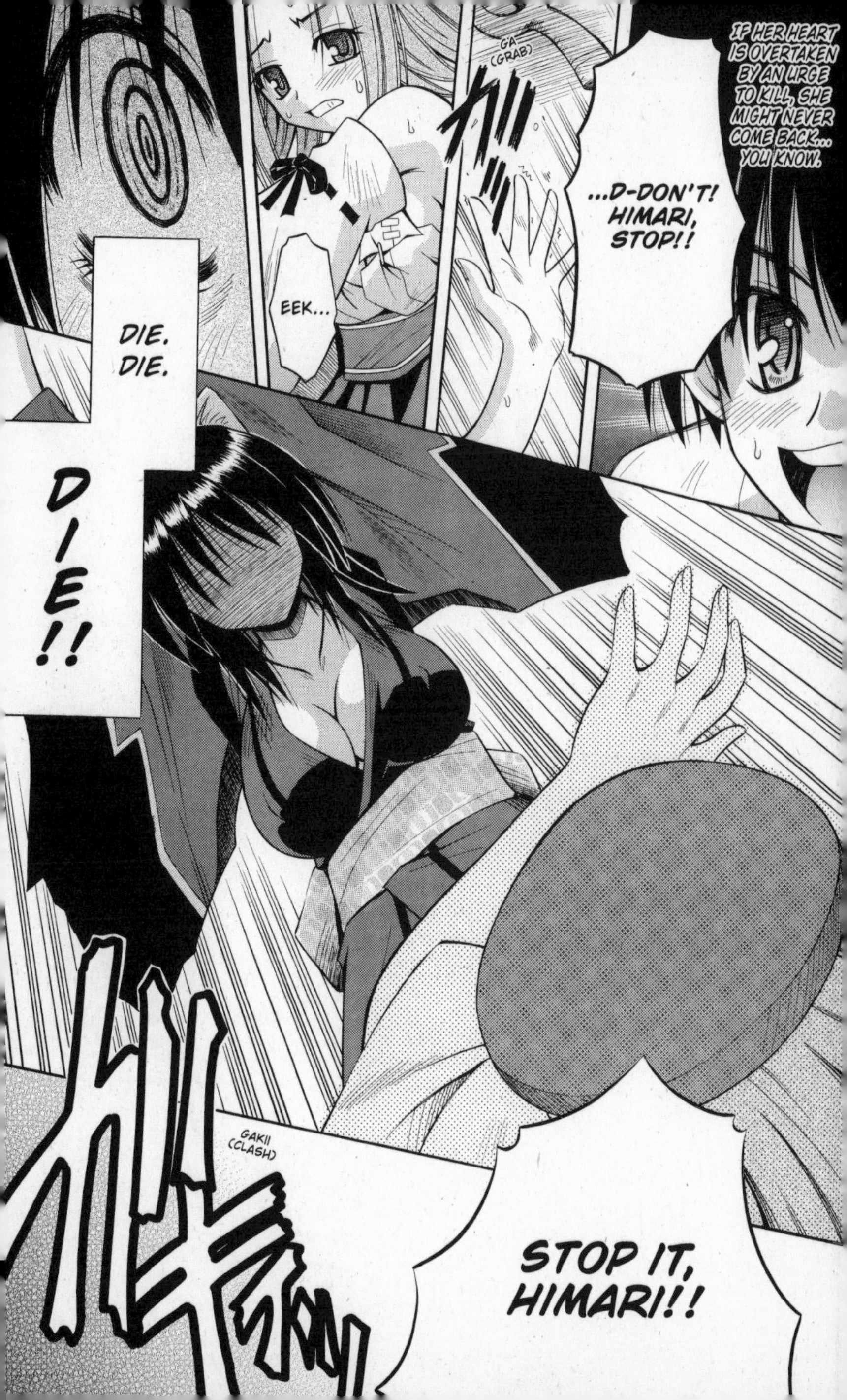
IF HER HEART IS OVERTAKEN BY AN URGE TO KILL, SHE MIGHT NEVER COME BACK... YOU KNOW.
...D-DON'T! HIMARI, STOP!!
GA (GRAB)
EEK...
DIE. DIE.
DIE!!
STOP IT, HIMARI!!
GAKII (CLASH)

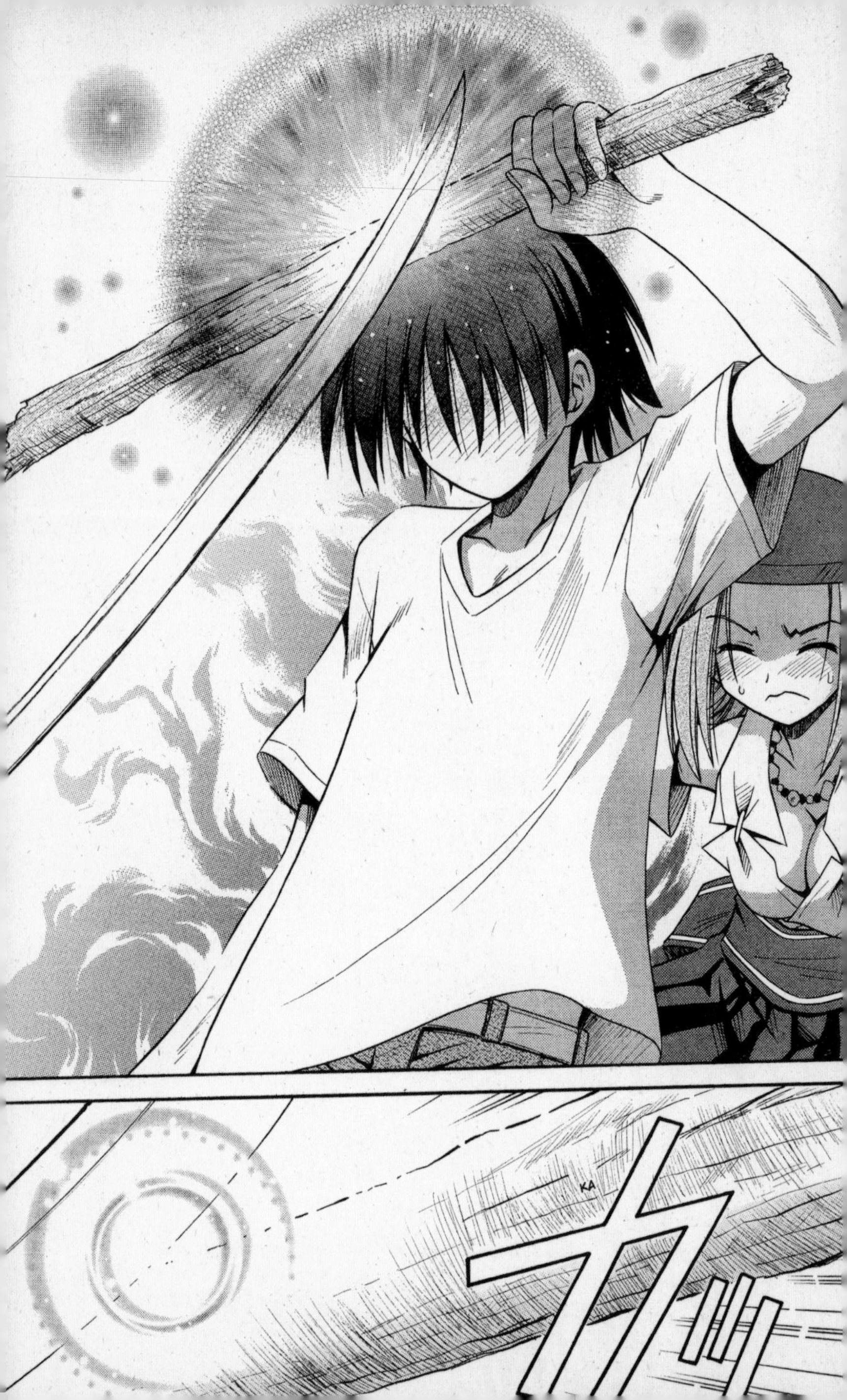
KA
カッ

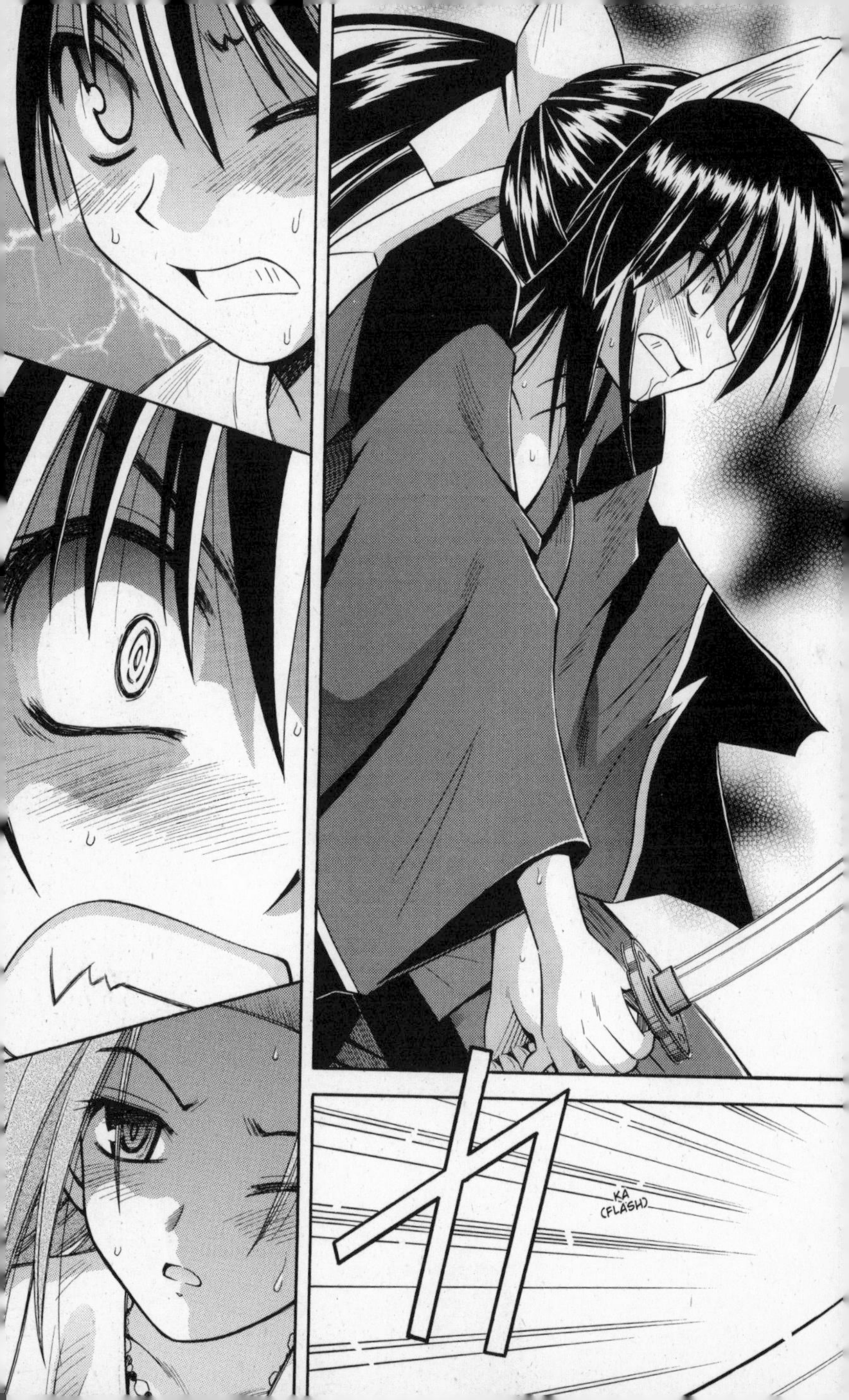
KA
(FLASH)

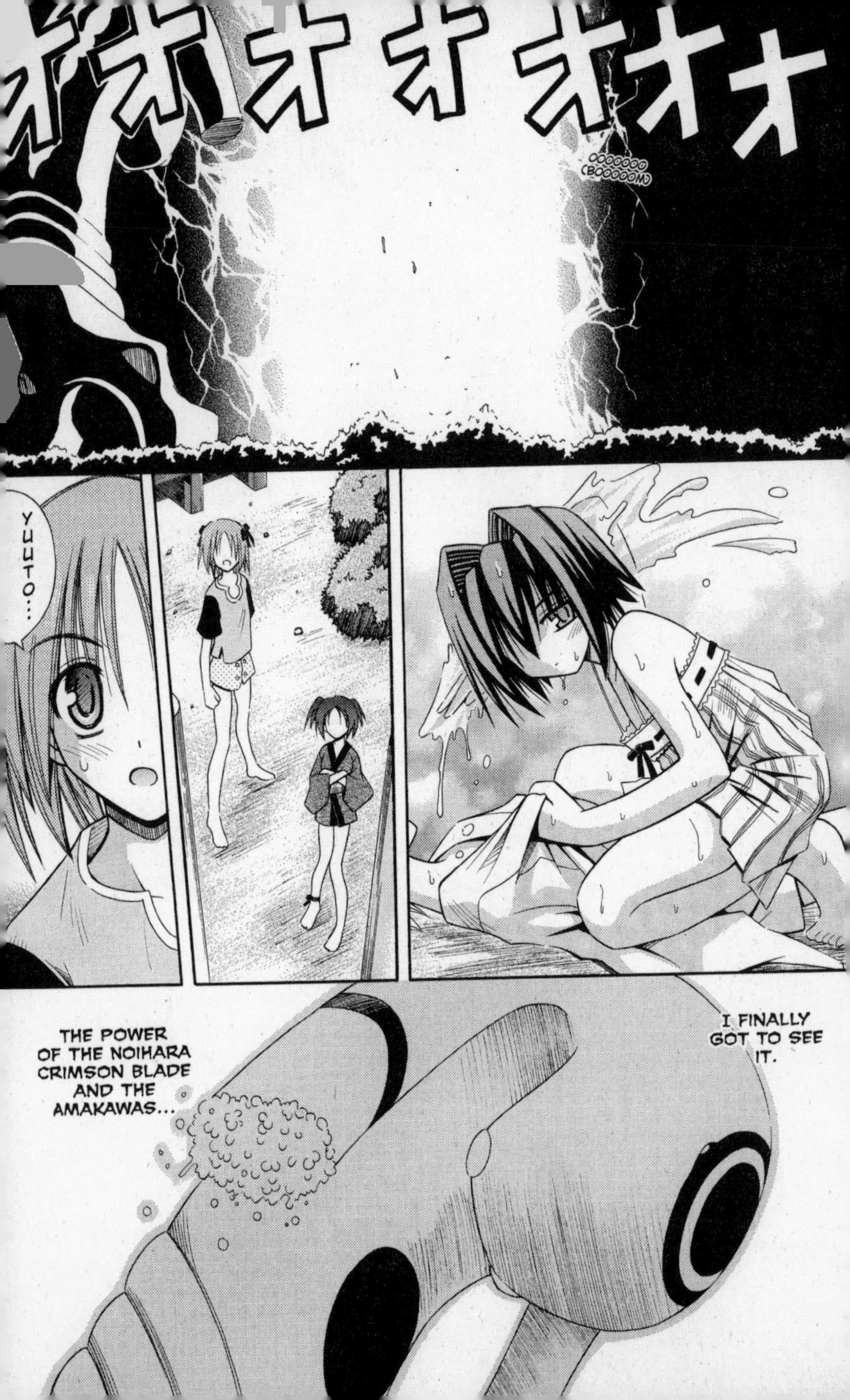
OOOOOOO
(BOOOOOOM)
YUUTO...
I FINALLY GOT TO SEE IT.
THE POWER OF THE NOIHARA CRIMSON BLADE AND THE AMAKAWAS...

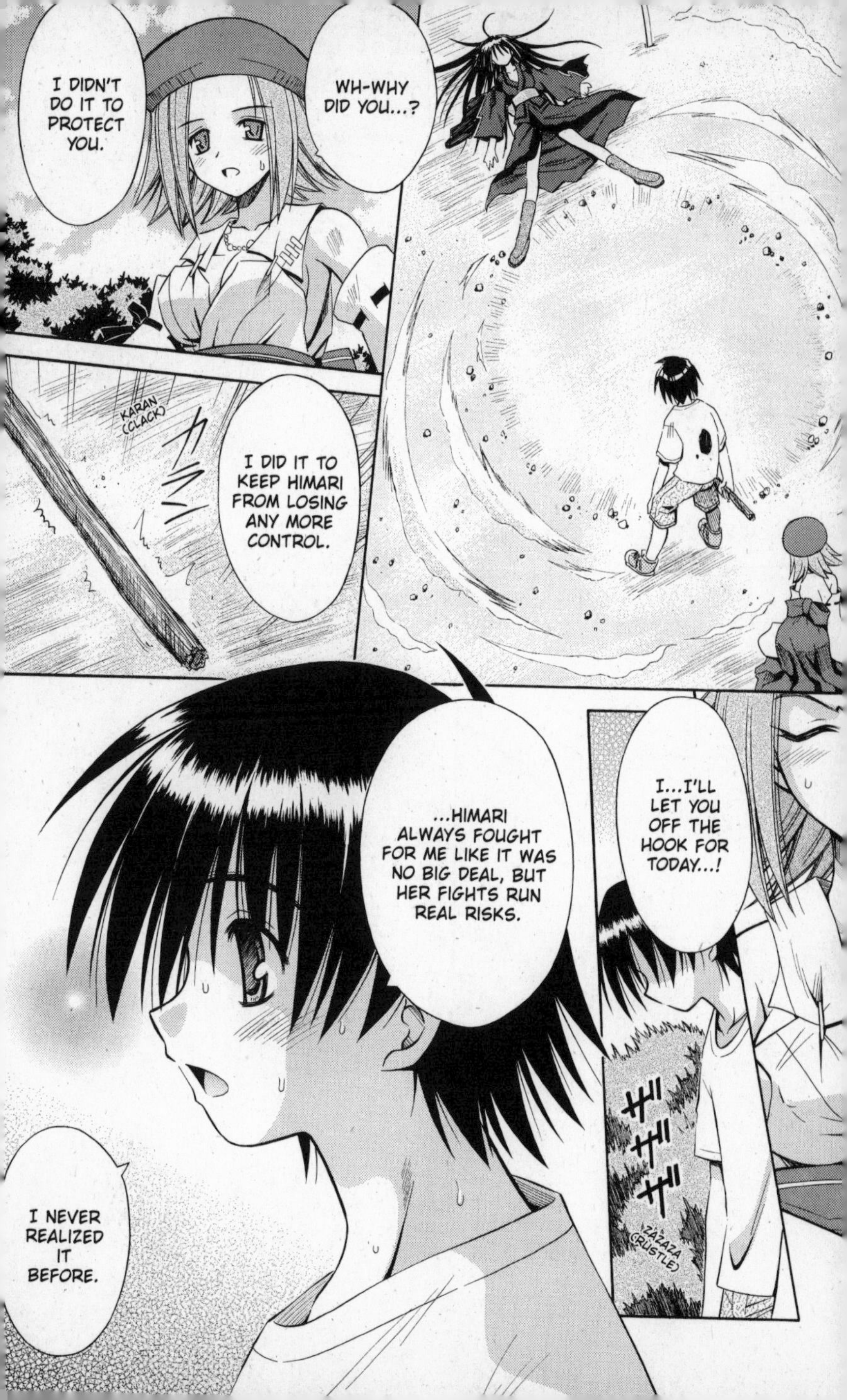
WH-WHY DID YOU...?
I DIDN'T DO IT TO PROTECT YOU.
KARAN (CLACK)
I DID IT TO KEEP HIMARI FROM LOSING ANY MORE CONTROL.
I...I'LL LET YOU OFF THE HOOK FOR TODAY...!
ZAZAZA (RUSTLE)
...HIMARI ALWAYS FOUGHT FOR ME LIKE IT WAS NO BIG DEAL, BUT HER FIGHTS RUN REAL RISKS.
I NEVER REALIZED IT BEFORE.

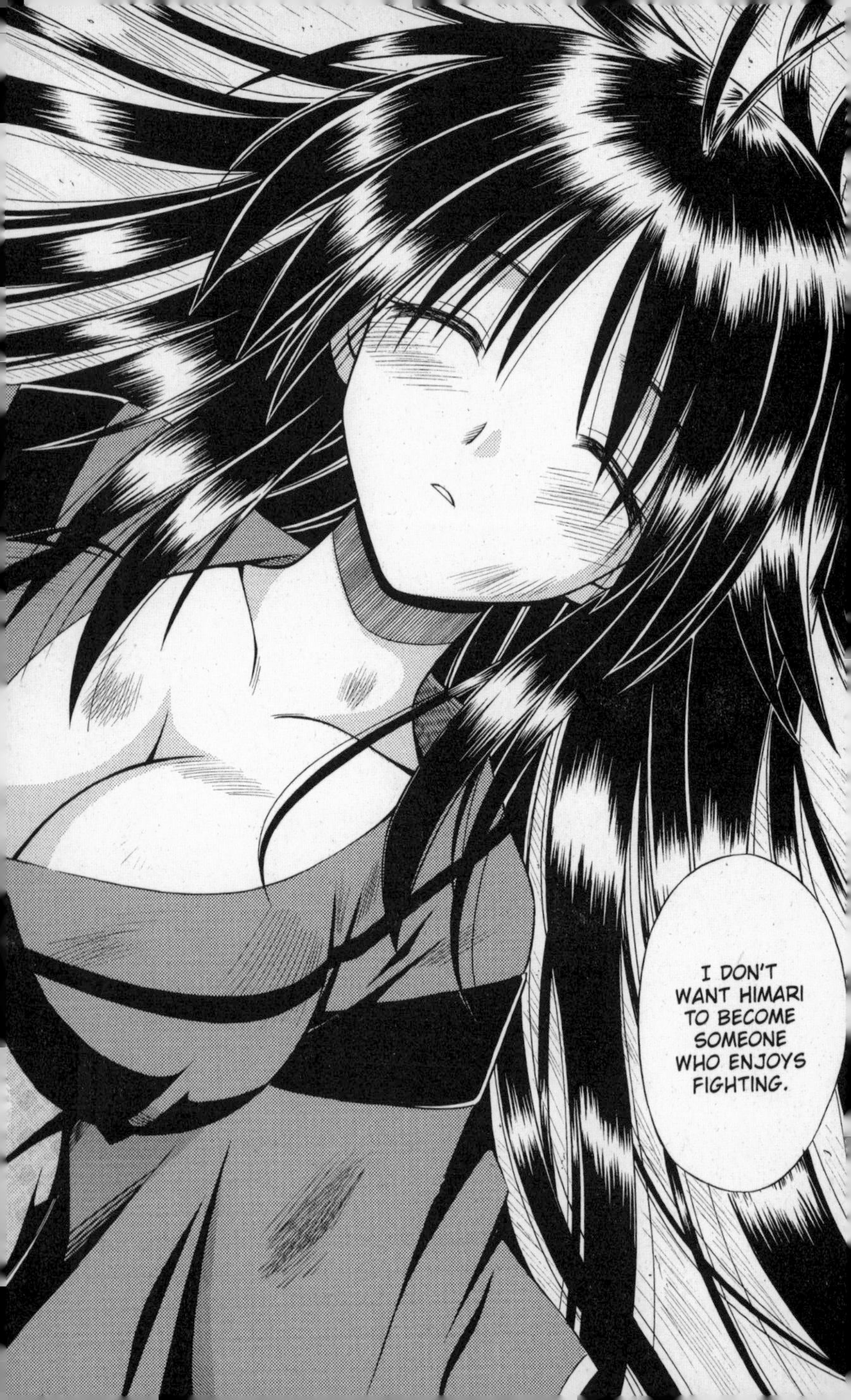
I DON'T WANT HIMARI TO BECOME SOMEONE WHO ENJOYS FIGHTING.

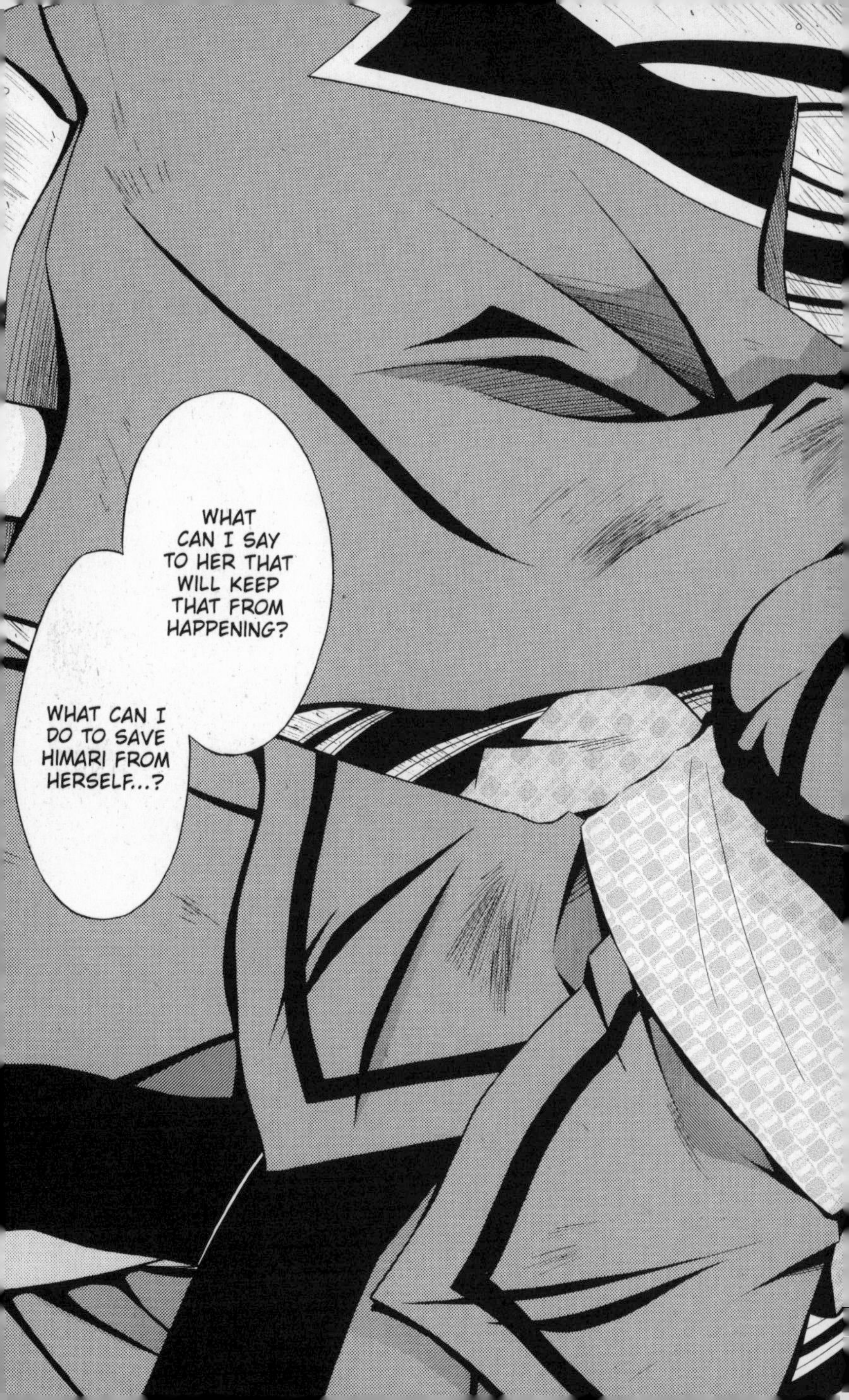
WHAT CAN I SAY TO HER THAT WILL KEEP THAT FROM HAPPENING?
WHAT CAN I DO TO SAVE HIMARI FROM HERSELF...?

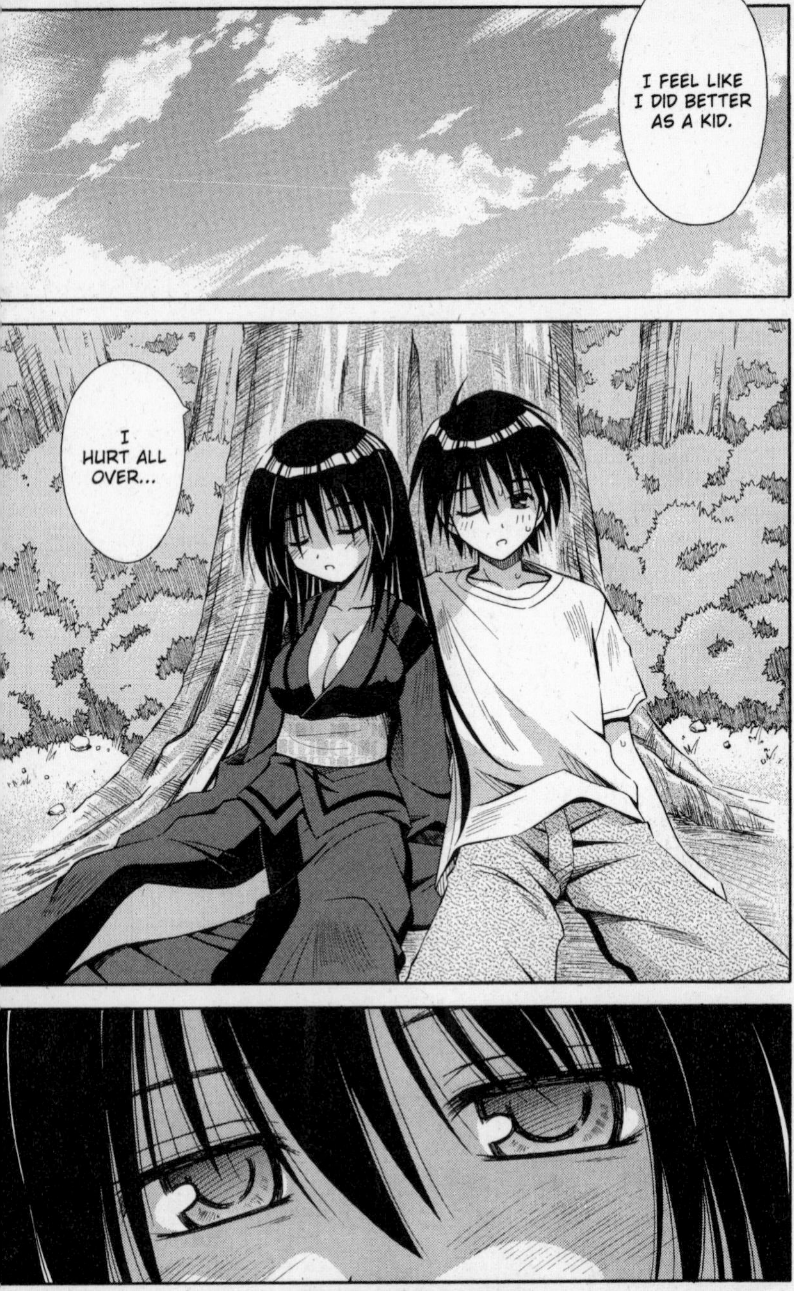
I FEEL LIKE I DID BETTER AS A KID.
I HURT ALL OVER...

TO BE CONTINUED

AFTERWORD

I REALLY LET MYSELF GET CARRIED AWAY IN THIS SECOND VOLUME. THERE WERE SERIOUS SCENES AND COMEDIC SCENES, BOTH OF WHICH WERE STEEPED WITH EROTIC TONES. I CAN ONLY PROMISE THAT YOU CAN EXPECT MORE PROGRESS IN THAT DIRECTION IN GENERAL FROM ME. (HA!)

2007.6 的良みらん

THANKS TO NAGU-SAN & MOGAMI-KUN

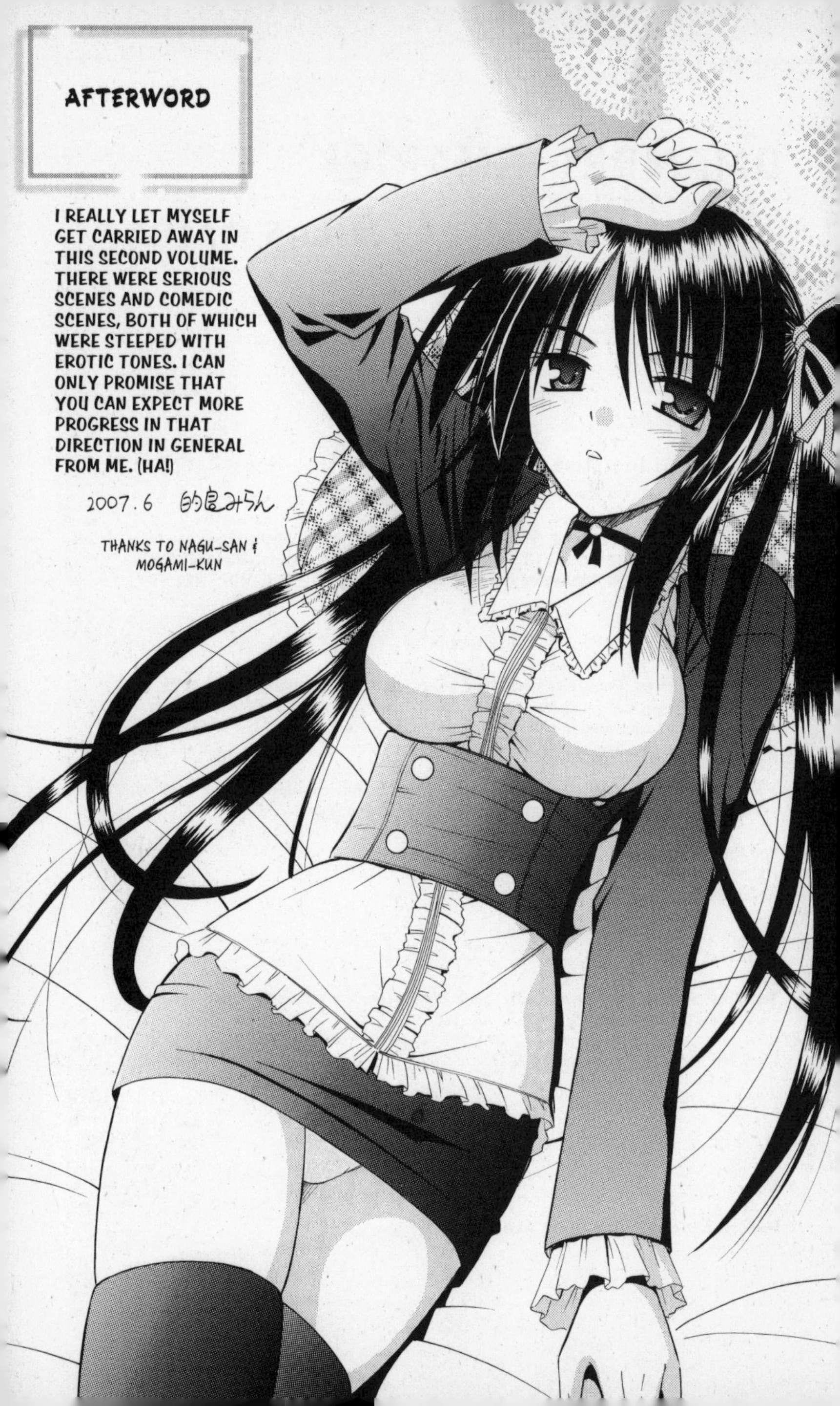

OMAMORI HIMARI ❷
MILAN MATRA

Translation: Christine Schilling • Lettering: Hope Donovan

OMAMORI HIMARI Volume 2 © MATRA MILAN 2007. First published in Japan in 2007 by FUJIMISHOBO CO., LTD., Tokyo. English translation rights arranged with KADOKAWA SHOTEN Publishing Co., Ltd., Tokyo through TUTTLE-MORI AGENCY, INC., Tokyo.

Translation © 2011 by Hachette Book Group, Inc.

Yen Press
Hachette Book Group
237 Park Avenue, New York, NY 10017

www.HachetteBookGroup.com
www.YenPress.com

Yen Press is an imprint of Hachette Book Group, Inc. The Yen Press name and logo are trademarks of Hachette Book Group, Inc.

First Yen Press Edition: January 2011

ISBN: 978-0-7595-3180-2

10 9 8 7 6 5 4 3 2 1

BVG

Printed in the United States of America